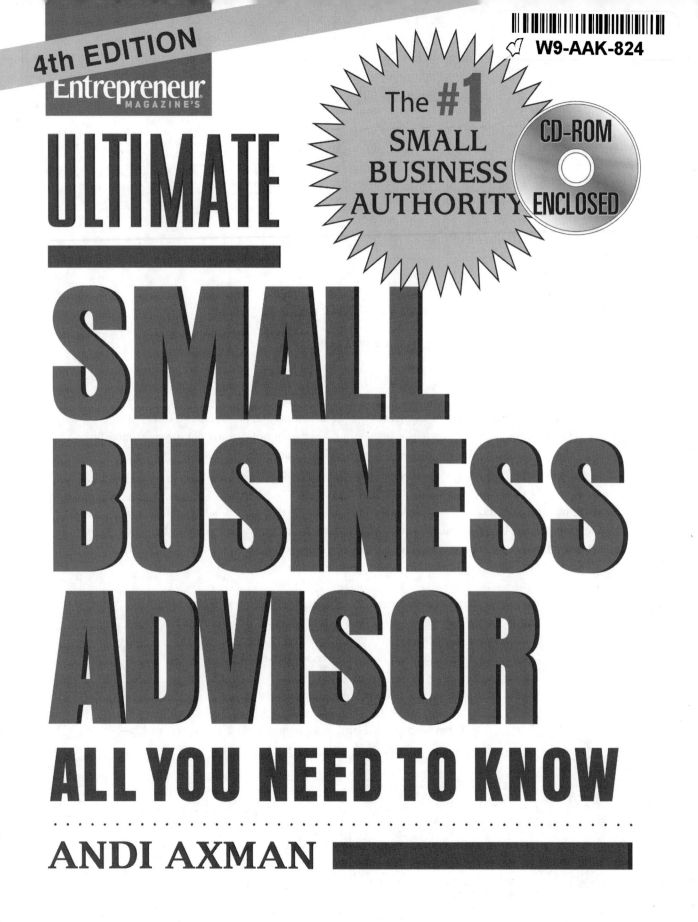

4th EDITION

Entrepreneur MAGAZINE'S

W9-AAK-824

ULTIMATE

The **#1** SMALL BUSINESS AUTHORITY

CD-ROM ENCLOSED

SMALL BUSINESS ADVISOR

ALL YOU NEED TO KNOW

ANDI AXMAN

Managing Editor: Jere Calmes
Cover Design: Beth Hansen-Winter
Composition and Production: MillerWorks

This publication is designed to provide accurate and authoritative information in regard to the subject
matter covered. It is sold with the understanding that the publisher is not engaged in rendering legal,
accounting, or other professional services. If legal advice or other expert assistance is required, the
services of a competent professional person should be sought.

Library of Congress Cataloging-in-Publication Data

Axman, Andi.
    Ultimate small business advisor / by Andi Axman—4th ed.
       p. cm.
    ISBN-13: 978-1-59918-085-4 (alk. paper)
    ISBN-10: 1-59918-085-5 (alk. paper)
      1. Small business--Handbooks, manuals, etc. 2. Entrepreneurship—
Handbooks, manuals, etc. I. Title. II. Title: Small business advisor.

HD62.7.E568 2007
658.02'2--dc22   2007008271

Printed in Canada

Contents

LIST OF FIGURES

LIST OF TABLES

Acknowledgments

I'd like to offer very special thanks to Jere Calmes, editorial director of Entrepreneur Media, for giving me the opportunity to write this fourth edition of *The Ultimate Small Business Advisor*. I've had the pleasure of working with Jere for years and there's no doubt in my mind that he's the most knowledgeable and best editor in the business!

I'm also grateful to:

- The authors of the first and second editions of *The Small Business Advisor* for giving me a terrific launching pad for this book

- Friend, mentor, and fellow author Andy Bangs, who knows everything there is to know about small business

- Karen Billipp, for giving this book a new, much improved look

- Bill Gamber and Bill Johnson of Big Agnes, and Magnus and Carina Thorsson of the Gray Ghost Inn, for generously sharing their business plans in Chapters 9 and 10

- Marci Richardson of the Elegant Ewe for generously sharing her marketing plan

- Brian McLarney, CPA, for his thorough review of tax planning matters covered in this book

- All the wonderful clients and colleagues I've had the pleasure of working with over the years

- My husband Mark Goldstein, for his unbounded support of my homebased business

- My Chesapeake Bay Retriever, Rosie, for always being available for lunch—even at a moment's notice.

Introduction

Unlike the title of the hit 1960s Broadway musical, you can't succeed in business without really trying—really, really hard. Running a profitable and thriving business takes time and effort, expertise in managing people and finances, knowledge of your industry and markets, and the ability to look ahead and plan. You need to know yourself well, capitalize on your strengths, and compensate for those skills you lack by hiring the appropriate partners or key employees when necessary.

While you have to wear many hats when you own and manage a small business, I hope that the *Ultimate Small Business Advisor* can help you figure out which hats feel right on you and which ones are best left for others to wear. When starting a business, many of us "do it all," from bookkeeping to marketing, and strategic planning to managing staff—and on top of all that, whatever it is that we got into business to do in the first place. That strategy can work for a while, but once a business begins to grow, its success depends on how well you, the owner, manage your resources (financial, human, and otherwise). Find your niche in the company and cultivate it, and do the same for your employees. If

everyone enjoys what he or she is doing, your company will profit as a result.

The same principle applies on a larger scale to your business relative to its market. Carve out a place where your company stands apart from your competitors. By differentiating your business in some way (or ways) from other similar businesses in your market, you provide something that no one else can. Do you offer the best price? The highest quality merchandise? The easiest return policy? A convenient location? The quickest turnaround? Unparalleled customer service? Your aim is to convey that what you have to offer customers is truly special. Southwest Airlines gives its customers low fares, friendly (and often entertaining) flight attendants, quick turnarounds at the gates, planes that don't break down, and fewer delayed flights than any other airline. No wonder Southwest is perceived as a threat by its rivals!

The other challenge business owners face is that we have to give our customers a reason to buy from us rather from someone else. Remember that people buy solutions to their problems (such as a wrinkle-free shirt), not features of a product (a cotton-polyester fabric). As Charles Revson, founder of Revlon, said, "In the factory we make cosmetics. In the store we sell hope." Apply the same principle to your marketing efforts.

While what we need to do to succeed in business may seem daunting at times, those things are less so if you break them up into manageable steps, as outlined by the chapters in this book. Follow Henry Ford's advice: "Nothing is particularly hard if you divide it into small jobs."

Your success in business—no matter what type of business you run—also depends upon making the right financial decisions. Be comfortable with the basics, such as cash-flow management, budgeting, and how to use financial statements. If financial management isn't your "thing," then take a course to gain an understanding. Or ask your CPA or local SBA chapter for help. Your grasp of the numbers will help you make sound and appropriate financial decisions.

By wisely and prudently managing your financial resources at all stages of your business' growth, you can help ensure your business' success. Some new business owners—particularly those who cut their teeth during the exhilarating business climate of the late 1990s—are loath to running their venture on a shoestring. But doing so is like having insurance. By being conservative with your funds now, they're more likely to be around later when you need them and your business is more apt to stay on course with its growth.

Bootstrapping, or wise use of resources, is addressed in this book both for start-ups and growing businesses.

Bootstrapping doesn't necessarily mean pinching pennies—although it can when a business is launched and there are no other options than to buy secondhand furniture, recycle paper clips, and lease the company vehicle. But bootstrapping also makes sense when it adds to a growing company's bottom line. It did for the $29 million New Technology Management, a Reston, Virginia, company that saved more than $15,000 a year by using photocopies of its fancy letterhead, which cost 80 cents a page, when it faxed more than 1,000 pages each month.

Each dollar you save by bootstrapping is a dollar you can use for working capital or one that you don't have to borrow, either from your savings, a bank, or an investor or other lender. Regardless of what's going on in the economy, cash is always king. With your focus on the bottom line, your company can concentrate on generating cash and will be well positioned to take advantage of opportunities that it couldn't afford if it were strapped for funds.

To further bolster your chances of success, work with knowledgeable experts who have experience in your industry. Don't cut corners when it comes to finding the best CPA, business attorney, financial manager, banker, retirement planner, insurance agent, and other experts in their fields—ones with whom you're comfortable working. Getting the best advice you can is one of the best investments you can make in your business, one that pays big dividends in the future.

Here's wishing you the best of luck in your venture!

PART 1

Starting Your Business

Businesses are born of dreams. Many first-time entrepreneurs have always longed to be their own boss or build that "better mousetrap." Some aspire to financial independence, while others are more concerned with building a business that complements a certain lifestyle in a particular location. Whatever your dream, making it come true takes planning and hard work. By following the suggestions outlined in the following chapters, you'll be heading in the right direction.

CHAPTER 1

Your Personal Goals

Why do you want to be in business for your-self? For most first-time entrepreneurs, the answer has little to do with money but lots to do with achieving personal goals, such as pursuing a passion, expanding a hobby, capitalizing on years of experience and a vast network of contacts, or wanting to invest in your own future instead of someone else's. I have always loved the independence that comes with having my own consulting business, of working on a variety of projects with different people. Working for a large corporation never appealed to me, and I've always wanted to have my business based at home.

Whatever your reasons, give them careful consideration so you can determine what type of business fits you best. Take the following factors into account:

- Your skills
- Your likes and dislikes
- The amount of effort you're willing to expend
- Your financial goals
- Whether you can initially devote all of, or just part of, your time
- Your business management experience and skills
- Your capacity for meeting new challenges and following through on commitments
- How much capital you have available
- How much credit you have available

KNOW YOUR STRENGTHS AND WEAKNESSES

As you begin thinking about the type of business you'd like to start or buy, keep in mind that businesses don't fail—people do. That's why entrepreneurs need to follow Socrates' advice and "know thyself." Push your ego aside and be honest with yourself, so you can build upon your strengths and shore up on your weaknesses.

You can get a clear picture of your strengths and weaknesses by evaluating the major accomplishments in your personal and professional life, along with the skills required to complete those tasks. To perform this evaluation, do the following.

- *Create a resume.* Start by listing your professional experience. For each job you've held, write a short description of the various duties you were responsible for and the degree of success you achieved. Next, list your educational background and any extracurricular activities that you participated in during your scholastic career. Third, write about your hobbies and involvement in community or volunteer activities. On a separate sheet of paper, make a list of activities you don't like to do.

- *Describe your personality.* Are you self-motivated? A hard worker? Do you have lots of common sense? Are you good with numbers? Do you like people? Do you have effective written and verbal communications skills? Are you well organized? Energetic? Persistent? What are your shortcomings? Are you quick-tempered? Impatient? Judgmental? Be thorough—and honest.

- *Detail your professional attributes.* List the various management roles and tasks you performed within a business, such as sales, marketing, financial planning, accounting, advertising, administration, personnel management, and research. Beside each function, write down your competency level—excellent, good, or needs work.

By putting together a resume, if you don't already have one, and quickly listing your attributes, you will have a fairly good idea of your likes and dislikes as well as your strengths and weaknesses. Once you identify these characteristics, you'll be clearer about the qualities you'll bring to the business and the areas in which you may require training or assistance.

Your areas of expertise and track record, as well as those of your partners, are key to finding the "right fit" in business. These areas also contribute to your success when approaching lenders and investors.

SET OBJECTIVES

Many people go into business to meet personal goals they've established for themselves. For some it's as simple as having the freedom to do what they want, when they want. For others, achieving financial security is a major personal goal. Whatever your goals, consider if you have what it takes to be an entrepreneur. The Entrepreneurial Innovation Checklist (Figure 1.1) will help you identify your entrepreneurial potential.

Goals, whether personal or business-related, are most useful when they're:

- *Specific and detailed.* Whether your goal is to start a

business, raise capital, or lose weight, be specific. What type of business? Located where? How much money will you need? How much weight do you want to lose?

- *Positive and in the present tense.* A financial goal is not to pay bills but rather to be profitable, financially secure. Set your financial goals to a specific dollar amount in a given period.

- *Realistic and attainable.* If your objective is to earn $100,000 a month when you've never earned that in a year, that goal is not very realistic. Begin with a first step: a realistic percentage increase over what you make now. Once you meet your first goal, you can then make adjustments and set a new, reasonable, and achievable goal.

- *Short-term, medium-term, and long-term.* Short-term goals are attainable in a period of weeks, months, or one year. Medium-term goals will be achieved between one and three years. Long-term goals have a horizon of three to five years, but they should still be realistic. You are the only one who can set these parameters. You must decide what is a realistic time frame and what is not.

After establishing parameters, decide exactly what you want to achieve by going into business for yourself. Most people set objectives according to specific areas in their life that are key to self-satisfaction. They usually include the following.

- *Being the boss.* One of the foremost reasons people go into business for themselves is that they have what they think is a great idea and they're tired of working for someone else. Because they've built up certain areas of expertise, they want to be in control and "call the shots." If you're the type of person who likes to have control over the direction of the business, think carefully when determining management responsibilities, especially if you're dealing with partners.

- *Income.* Many entrepreneurs are motivated by financial security for themselves and their families. When setting financial goals, consider what you would like to make during the first year of operation and each year thereafter, up to five years.

- *Lifestyle.* Think about how many hours per week you'd like to work, if you mind traveling on business

| FIGURE 1.1 | Princeton Entrepreneurial Innovation Checklist |

Read each statement carefully, then mark the answer that most accurately describes your behavior, feeling, or attitude as it actually is, not as you would like it to be or think it should be. Try to mark your first reaction.

	Agree	Disagree
1. My parents encouraged me to take an interest in discovering things for myself.		
2. At least one of my close relatives is an entrepreneur.		
3. Throughout my education, I had many part-time jobs.		
4. One or both of my parents had many unorthodox or unconventional ideas.		
5. If I were stranded in an unfamiliar city without friends or money, I would cope quite well.		
6. I am curious about more things than most people are.		
7. I enjoy ventures in which I must constantly keep trying new approaches and possibilities.		
8. I always seek challenging problems to solve.		
9. I am not too painstaking in my work.		
10. I am able to work for extended periods of time, frequently to the point of exhaustion.		
11. When faced with a problem, I usually investigate a wide variety of options.		
12. While working on one project, I often think of the next one I want to tackle.		
13. Before taking on an important project, I learn all I can about it.		
14. When confronted with a difficult problem, I try solutions others would not think of.		
15. Once I undertake a new venture, I'm determined to see it through.		
16. I concentrate harder on projects I'm working on than most people do.		
17. I cannot get excited about ideas that may never lead to anything.		
18. When brainstorming with a group of people, I think up more ideas quicker than others.		
19. I have broader interests and am more widely informed than most people.		
20. When the chips are down, I display more personal strength than most people do.		
21. I need social interaction and am very interested in interpersonal relationships.		
22. I find it easy to identify flaws in others' ideas.		
23. I regard myself as a "specialist," not a "generalist."		
24. When evaluating information, I believe the source is more important than the content.		
25. I am easily frustrated by uncertainty and unpredictability.		
26. I can easily give up immediate gain or comfort to reach long-term goals.		
27. I have great tenacity of purpose.		
28. Things that are obvious to others are not so obvious to me.		

	Always	Often	Sometimes	Rarely	Never
29. I get a kick out of breaking the rules.					
30. I become upset if I cannot immediately come to a decision.					
31. Ideas run through my head at night to the point that I can't sleep.					

FIGURE 1.1	Princeton Entrepreneurial Innovation Checklist, continued

	Always	Often	Sometimes	Rarely	Never
32. I get into trouble because I'm too curious or inquisitive.					
33. I am able to win other people over to my point of view.					
34. I tolerate frustration more than the average person does.					
35. I rely on intuition when trying to solve a problem.					
36. I can stick with difficult problems for extended periods of time.					
37. My problem-solving abilities are stronger than my social abilities.					
38. A logical step-by-step method is best for solving problems.					
39. I can readily allay other people's suspicions.					

40. Below is a list of adjectives and descriptive terms. Indicate with a check mark 12 words that best describe you:

Energetic	❏	Predictable	❏	Open-minded	❏	Persuasive	❏	Self Confident	❏
Tactful	❏	Observant	❏	Informal	❏	Inhibited	❏	Fashionable	❏
Dedicated	❏	Enthusiastic	❏	Formal	❏	Original	❏	Innovative	❏
Persevering	❏	Quick	❏	Poised	❏	Curious	❏	Good Natured	❏
Acquisitive	❏	Cautious	❏	Helpful	❏	Practical	❏	Habit Bound	❏
Perceptive	❏	Alert	❏	Resourceful	❏	Courageous	❏	Forward Looking	❏
Egotistical	❏	Stern	❏	Organized	❏	Independent	❏	Clear Thinking	❏
Unemotional	❏	Efficient	❏	Factual	❏	Thorough	❏	Understanding	❏
Dynamic	❏	Modest	❏	Polished	❏	Realistic	❏	Self Demanding	❏
Involved	❏	Absent-minded	❏	Flexible	❏	Sociable	❏	Well Liked	❏

Scoring Instructions

To score the test, circle and add up the values for your answers.

	Agree	Disagree			Agree	Disagree			Always	Often	Sometimes	Rarely	Never
1.	4	1		19.	4	1		29.	2	3	5	1	0
2.	3	1		20.	4	1		30.	0	2	3	5	1
3.	4	1		21.	1	4		31.	2	4	5	3	0
4.	3	1		22.	3	1		32.	3	4	5	1	0
5.	4	1		23.	1	4		33.	3	4	5	1	0
6.	4	1		24.	1	4		34.	3	4	5	1	0
7.	4	1		25.	1	4		35.	5	4	3	1	0
8.	3	1		26.	4	1		36.	4	5	3	1	0
9.	0	4		27.	4	1		37.	4	5	3	1	0
10.	4	1		28.	4	1		38.	1	2	5	3	0
11.	4	1						39.	3	4	5	1	0
12.	3	1											
13.	4	1											
14.	4	1											
15.	4	1											
16.	4	1											
17.	1	4											
18.	4	1											

| FIGURE 1.1 | **Princeton Entrepreneurial Innovation Checklist,** continued |

40. The following characteristics score 2 points each:

energetic, observant, persevering, resourceful, independent, dedicated, original, perceptive, enthusiastic, innovative, curious, involved, flexible.

The following score 1 point each:

self confident, forward looking, informal, courageous, thorough, open-minded, alert, dynamic, self demanding, absent-minded.

Interpreting Your Score

125–186. If you scored in this range, you are probably a highly innovative person. Ideas come readily to you, and you have a keen awareness of and concern for unsolved problems. On the whole, you take an innovative approach to solving problems. You also discern possibilities and opportunities in areas where others find little potential. You are original and individualistic, and you have no problem resisting pressures to conform. You have the courage to pit yourself against uncertain circumstances, and you have the innovation to come out ahead.

77–124. A score in this range indicates that you are moderately innovative. While you lack some of the autonomy, self-sufficiency, and self-confidence of the highly innovative entrepreneur, you compensate with your predilection for method, precision, and exactness. You also have faith in the successful outcome of your present and future entrepreneurial efforts.

While entrepreneurs with an innovative flair may succeed in a variety of enterprises, they are sometimes surpassed by other less creative entrepreneurs who possess keener abilities in marketing, deal-making, negotiations, finance, and human relations. So although you may need to beef up on innovation, your abilities in other areas will still help you succeed.

27–76. If you scored in this range, you may be more successful operating a franchise or working for someone else than you would be starting your own business. However, remember: innovative abilities can be developed and cultivated, either through on-the-job training or by attending workshops or seminars. So if you're determined to own your own business, don't give up!

or doing physical labor, how much of your personal assets you're comfortable investing (e.g., are you willing to take out a second mortgage on your house?), and how close to the business you'd like live.

- *Type of work.* It's no secret that the more you like your work, the greater satisfaction you'll derive from your efforts and the more successful you'll be. A survey conducted by the National Federation of Independent Businesses asked small business owners what makes them consider their businesses successful. Answers that did not turn up were market dominance and rapid growth. The number-one answer that was given was personal satisfaction, followed by quality product and ethical treatment of employees, customers, and business associates. Think carefully about the type of work you'd like to do in your business—working outdoors, in an office with computers, on the phone, with a great number of people, and so on.

ASSESS AND REDUCE RISK

Every business venture—regardless of economic climate, market conditions, products, personnel, and capitalization—has risks. Once you assess those risks, you can begin taking steps to reduce them. Start by taking these actions.

- *Research similar businesses.* Look at their locations, advertising, staff requirements, hours they're open, and equipment. This preliminary analysis of your competition is a gold mine of important information.

- *Evaluate current market trends.* What seemed like a hot idea over the past few months might have been a fad. Find last year's phone book and call several new businesses. Are they still around? (If you live in a small community or want to expand your research, your local telephone company or local library may have phone books from other cities.)

- *Know your strengths and preferences.* Is this type of business a good fit? Does it capitalize on your strengths? To compensate for areas that you have little or no expertise in, can you fill in the gaps either with staff members, partners, or consultants?
- *Examine your family budget.* How big a financial cushion do you have, in case your financial projections show that you won't be able to draw a paycheck for the first year? What other income can you reasonably expect while you're in the start-up phase? It always helps if your spouse or partner has a full-time job with health-insurance coverage and other benefits through his or her employer. Remember that you're not in this alone and realize that your family is there for you, to share the benefits as well as the risks. To ensure their support, make sure they understand exactly what you're doing and why.
- *Know how changes in the economy will affect your business.* What would happen to a business in your industry if inflation rose by two points? How has your type of business performed in various economic conditions? If the business is a seasonal one, will its patrons travel or spend less?
- *Write a business plan.* Your business plan will help you shape your business, determine your financing needs, evaluate your competition, and figure out marketing strategies. It enables you to foresee problems and make a plan to avoid them—in short, becoming a valuable management tool in running your business. See Chapter 8 for a detailed description of how to write a business plan.

PLAN TO SUCCEED

When you're launching a business or starting out as the new owner of an existing business, proper planning and research are absolutely necessary. There are no shortcuts, and I can vouch for that. When my partner and I bought a run-down old shutter mill in New Hampshire, I spent many, *many* hours researching and writing our business plan. That turned out to be time well-spent. Not only did we get the financing we needed to revive the shutter business and generate our own hydropower—we had also carefully thought out our strategy, found and gotten quotes from appropriate contractors and engineers,

established budgets, and gotten a handle on income and expenses.

If you don't take time to write a business plan and analyze your prospective business concept, you'll probably be confronted by one of the following situations:

- Not having sufficient capital
- Skewed sales projections because of an overly optimistic assessment of market opportunities
- A market saturated by the competition
- Poor access to markets due to a bad location
- Inadequate projections for equipment and personnel needs

Don't let any of these blunders happen to you. Do your homework—the required market research is detailed in Chapter 3—and make writing your business plan your first order of business.

How Much Money Will You Need to Start?

You don't necessarily need piles of money to start a business. Apple Computer was started in a garage by Steve Wozniak and Steven Jobs. UPS (United Parcel Service) was started in 1907 when founder Jim Casey borrowed $100 from a friend. Yahoo! was founded by a pair of Stanford University graduate students, Jerry Yang and David Filo, to help their fellow students locate cool web sites. There's nothing wrong with this approach if you're willing to invest a great amount of time and energy into making the business work. But keep in mind that undercapitalization is the number-one killer of start-up businesses. Don't skimp on getting enough money to start your business right.

To determine how much you'll need for start-up, account for all opening expenses along with your initial operating expenses. Although different businesses have different costs associated with them, the main start-up costs include the following:

- *Rent.* Under many lease agreements, you'll be expected to provide the first month's rent plus a security deposit. Many leasors also require the last month's rent.
- *Phone and utilities.* Some telephone and utility companies require deposits, while others do not. A deposit may not be required if you own real estate or have a previously established payment record with the company. Telephone deposits are determined by

the number of phones and the type of service required. Deposits for gas and electricity (when required) will vary according to your projected usage, so get accurate information and carefully project your numbers.

- *Equipment.* Equipment costs vary from one business to another. At a minimum, most businesses need office equipment, signage, and security systems. To determine your costs, list all the equipment you must have to efficiently operate your business. Next, price those items by obtaining quotes or bids from at least three vendors. Use the quotes you receive to estimate your start-up equipment costs.
- *Fixtures.* This broad category includes partitions, paneling, signage, storage cabinets, lighting, checkout counters and all shelves, tables stands, wall systems, showcases, and related hardware for product display. The cost of fixtures depends on your business location, the size and condition of your facility, the type of business you're in, what kind of image you want it to project and whether you're purchasing new or used fixtures.
- *Inventory.* Like equipment, inventory requirements vary from business to business. Some businesses, such as retail stores, are inventory-intensive, whereas others, such as personal shopping services, don't require any inventory at all except office supplies.
- *Leasehold improvements.* These non-removable installations, either original or the result of remodeling, include carpeting and other floorings, insulation, electrical wiring, plumbing, bathrooms, lighting, wall partitions, windows, ceiling tiles, sprinkler systems, security systems, some elements of interior design, and sometimes heating and/or air-conditioning systems. Because the cost of improvements can vary tremendously, get several estimates from reputable contractors.
- *Licenses and tax deposits.* Most cities and counties require business operators to obtain various licenses or permits to show compliance with local regulations. Licensing costs vary from business to business, depending on the requirements of your particular location. In addition to these fees, you'll also need start-up capital for tax deposits if yours is a retail business. Many states require a deposit against future taxes to be collected.
- *Marketing budgets.* Most companies determine their first year's advertising budget as a percentage of projected gross sales, typically 2–5 percent.
- *Professional services.* Before you officially open your business, get help from a knowledgeable lawyer and accountant who work with small business owners to make sure you meet your legal and tax obligations. Their fees will range according to their expertise, and the location and size of their practices.
- *Pre-opening payroll.* If your business is going to be a full-time venture, then set aside a salary for yourself in addition to a three-month reserve, just to play it safe. This rule of thumb also applies to any employees you might hire during this phase of business start-up.
- *Insurance.* Plan on allocating the first two quarters' cost of insurance to get your business rolling.

A word of caution when estimating these costs: If there's ever a time to be conservative, it's now. Err on the high side when you project expenses, and on the low side when you project revenue. And don't forget to add a "rainy day" or contingency fund to cover the costs of unforeseen expenses—somewhere around 5 percent of your budget is a typical amount to set aside. This financial cushion will help you—and your investors—avoid panic in case you're faced with an expense you hadn't budgeted for.

How Much Income Will You Need?

To determine how much money you have to invest in a business, figure out your net worth by filling out a personal balance sheet (see Figure 1.2). A balance sheet compares what you own to what you owe and gives a snapshot of your personal finances at a given time. Begin by listing all your assets and their value in the top portion of the form: your house, investments, car, jewelry, artwork, and so on. Next list all your debts in the bottom portion: credit cards, mortgage, bank notes, personal debts, auto loans, and so on. By subtracting line B from line A, you arrive at the value of your net worth.

If the value of your assets exceeds that of your liabilities, you'll have a positive net worth, and therefore more options for finding cash to invest in your business. The lower your debts are relative to your assets, the more favorably bankers and other investors will view you as a candidate for a second mortgage, a home-equity line of credit, a business or other type of loan. The greater your liabilities relative to your assets, the more difficult it will be for you to borrow money by tapping your home equity or accumulating more credit card debt, both of which are typical sources of start-up funding for small business owners.

Failure Factors

Every year, thousands of businesses of all sizes fail. According to the Small Business Administration's (SBA)

FIGURE 1.2 **Personal Balance Sheet**

Personal Balance Sheet as of _____, 20_____
month, day

Assets		Totals
Cash, checking, & savings		
Marketable securities		
Real estate owned: home, vacation, or rental property		
Partial interest in real estate equities		
Automobiles		
Personal property (jewelry, artwork, and so on)		
Personal loans outstanding		
Cash value/life insurance		
Other assets/itemize		
Total assets	A	

Liabilities		Totals
Secured loans (car, home improvements, equipment)		
Unsecured loans		
Charge account bills		
Real estate mortgages		
Unpaid income tax		
Other debts/itemize		
Total liabilities	B	
Net worth (A minus B = C)	C	
Total Liabilities & Net Worth (B + C)	D	

Office of Advocacy (www.sba.gov/advo/), one-third of small businesses close after two years, half after four years, and 60 percent after six years.

Why do businesses fail? Most small business surveys show that the primary reason for failure lies in the following areas:

- Running out of money
- Lack of business planning
- Inefficient control of costs and quality of product
- Insufficient inventory control
- Underpricing of goods sold
- Poor customer relations
- Failure to promote and maintain a favorable public image
- Bad relations with suppliers
- Terrible management
- Illness of key personnel
- Reluctance to seek professional assistance
- Failure to minimize taxation through tax planning
- Inadequate insurance
- Loss of key personnel
- Lack of staff training
- Insufficient knowledge of the industry
- Inability to compete
- Failure to anticipate market trends
- Inadequate cash-flow control
- Growth without adequate capitalization
- Ignoring data on the company's financial position
- Incomplete financial records
- Overextending credit
- Overborrowing
- Overdue receivables
- Excessive demands from creditors

The best way to avoid these pitfalls is by planning. Since starting a business is a long process, give yourself enough time—six months to a year is recommended—to do the necessary research for your business plan. Work for someone else to learn more about the type of business you've chosen. Take courses to beef up your management skills. Talk with other business owners. Invest in yourself before you make one of the biggest investments in your life. Doing so will help ensure your success and prevent disasters like running out of money, making the wrong hiring decisions, not taking advantage of market opportunities, choosing the wrong partner or location, and so on.

Inspiration for Your New Business

Successful entrepreneurs are energetic innovators, passionate about their work, and intrepid explorers of new markets. They've done their homework and have a thorough knowledge of their industry. They're farsighted enough to spot a new trend or technology, inspired to think in new ways, motivated to find applications for their idea in the market, and diligent enough to successfully accomplish their goals.

Starting a business from scratch is one of the most exciting and gratifying accomplishments in life. Just ask anyone who's done it. I remember the thrill of reaching certain milestones with the mill restoration, from getting approval of our bank loan, to generating our first kilowatt of electricity, to manufacturing the first shutter using the original equipment that we'd motorized, to being invited to appear on the PBS series, *This Old House.* To say I was elated would be an understatement!

Whether you're improving an existing product or developing something completely new, being an entrepreneur is exhilarating. But the work is hard, the hours are long, the pressures never end, and the costs—both personal and financial—can be high. No business, even a franchise, is failure-proof.

The good news is that you can minimize the risks associated with starting a business. Researching your market (Chapter 3) and writing a business plan (Chapter 8) will help you obtain the necessary financial and human resources to successfully run your business. But before you tackle these projects, make sure your business idea has legs to stand on and that it makes your heart sing.

FIND NEW BUSINESS IDEAS

How do you finally settle on an idea for a new business that's right for you? It can be a daunting task. Organize your search with the Opportunity Evaluation Checklist (Figure 2.1). Make a copy of this checklist for each business idea you come up with. Go down the list and rate the potential of each factor on a scale from zero to three, with a rating of three being the best. Once you've completed the form, total the ratings for both the opportunity and marketability sections. The business idea with the highest rating will be the best match to your goals and lifestyle.

How do you find inspiration for new ideas? Be a voracious reader of business and trade publications, both in print and online. Go to trade shows, become well-acquainted with your industry—both in this country and abroad—and talk to other business owners. Stay on top of what's happening in your industry until you discover a need in the market that beckons you to fill it. Keep investigating sources of new business ideas until you find the one that's right for you.

Look at businesses selling products or services that are similar to the one you're thinking about. Determine whether those products or services have captured a significant share of the available market, or whether a potentially profitable portion of the market is untapped. If a market is far from saturated, that means there's room for you, an opportunity for you to build and run a successful business. If those products or services have already captured a significant share of the market, you'll waste time and money competing head-to-head with an established winner.

FIGURE 2.1 Opportunity Evaluation Checklist

This evaluation form will help you determine how successful you will be if you enter a given business and sell a given product. Fill out the entire form for each business and product you consider. In the columns on the right side of the form, indicate how well a given opportunity or product meets a given requirement for success (3-Excellent, 2-Good, 1-Fair, 0-Poor). The opportunities and products with the highest total points are your strongest candidates for success.

Opportunity	3	2	1	0
Relevance of your previous experience to opportunity				
Familiarity with the daily operations of this type of business				
Compatibility of business with your investment goals				
Compatibility of business with your income goals				
Likely profitability of business				
Likelihood of business to meet your desire for personal fulfillment				
Projected growth for the industry				
Acceptability of risk level				
Acceptability of hours you will need to work				
Marketability of Product	**3**	**2**	**1**	**0**
Probability of use by target market				
Compatibility with image desired				
Competitiveness of price				
Number and strength of promotable features				
Probability that product will enhance sales of current line				
Projected stability of demand				
Ability to overcome seasonal or cyclical resistance				
Uniqueness of product				
Ability of business to obtain needed equipment				
Likely acceptance potential				
Ability of business to afford the development and production of product				
Total				

Inventor and Trade Shows

Trade and inventor shows, as well as conventions and civic groups, can yield a wealth of information in this initial research phase. Trade shows and conventions are sponsored by trade associations for specific industries, and there are thousands of associations running shows every year. To find an appropriate association for the industry you're interested in, look through the *Encyclopedia of Associations* published by Gale Research. You may also want to check magazines and newsletters such as *Tradeshow Week* or go through the *Tradeshow Week Data Book*. These publications should be available at your local library.

To find out when the next trade or inventor show will occur in your area, contact your local convention facility. The space for such shows must be reserved well in advance, and if there's one planned during the next year, the facility manager's office will be able to give you the dates. You can also check with your local Chamber of Commerce for information about trade or inventor shows in your area. And don't forget to search the web for shows outside your area. When I Googled the words "trade show," more than 189,000 links to web sites were brought up. You can refine your search by adding words that indicate your industry, like "publishing," "software," "housewares," "food," and so on.

Looking Abroad

Foreign products can be exotic, attractive, and often of a superior quality compared to their counterparts available in this country. That's one reason that Irish lace, Swiss watches, Colombian coffee, and Limoges china are perennial favorites.

But no matter how old a product might be in its country of origin, in a new market it's a new product. If you find a product that you like, for which an international distribution system does not yet exist, and if you can develop a distribution system for that product, you can be on your way to discovering a potential market niche for your business idea. To help you further investigate this type of business idea, contact the foreign consulate in your area or the Department of Commerce in Washington, D.C. (www.doc.gov). Many foreign countries with products available for export also publish trade magazines, which should be available at either your library or through a specific consulate.

The Media

Four dailies cover the major markets where new business trends and ideas are regularly developed: *The Wall Street Journal*, *The New York Times*, *The Los Angeles Times*, and *The London Times*. Trade magazines relevant to your business idea and small business in general, such as *Entrepreneur* and *Inc.* magazines, are other important resources.

Usually, dailies and trade journals have classified ads in the back pages of the publication. Cull them for ideas. And don't forget TV; there's a wide range of business programming designed to inform and educate the public about new products and new ideas. If time to watch each of these shows is an issue, program your VCR to tape them. You can quickly review the tapes at a later time, scanning them just as you would skim through a textbook for pertinent information.

Manufacturers

Original equipment manufacturers (OEMs) can be fertile ground for research. Just as an established foreign product can become a new product in a new market, a product that a manufacturer has decided to take out of production may be worth investigating. Perhaps production was discontinued because of a distribution or marketing problem. If marketing or distribution is one of your strengths, a market opportunity could be waiting for you.

When you learn that a company has decided to discontinue Product X, make sure to also find out the basis for the decision. Finding out what products will not sell, and why, is marketing information that's extremely valuable.

The Government

The U.S. government publishes a slew of useful information that most of us don't even know exists. Take a look at the U.S. Government's *Directory of Publications*, a centralized directory that provides access to all federal U.S. government web sites and documents, at www.firstgov.gov.

For example, Teflon™ was developed in 1938 and has been used in the space program since its infancy. When Neil Armstrong took his "giant leap for mankind" in 1969,

Teflon™ was used in his space suit, as well as on the heat shields and insulation on his mooncraft. Today, what the *Guinness Book of Records* calls "the world's most slippery substance" is used on nonstick cookware, on stain-resistant carpet, and in fabric to make socks that reduce friction and eliminate blisters for people with sensitive skin.

NASA innovations can also be found in Regional Technology Transfer Centers (RTTC), formed in 1991 to help federal agencies make technology developed in government labs available to American companies. The six technology transfer centers throughout the country will perform searches through federal technology databases, engineering reports, and other sources to find information consistent with what you require. RTTCs can also help put together a feasibility study of the new technology showing how it might best be applied in your business, and they will help you conduct in-depth, value-added studies on different ways to apply a specific technology.

RTTCs can also refer you to university researchers, federal laboratories or private companies that might be interested in working with you. They may even be able to recommend you to venture capital sources interested in funding the commercial application of new technology.

The Official Gazette of the U.S. Patent and Trademark Office, a weekly publication, lists patents that have been granted as opposed to those merely applied for. You can subscribe to the *Gazette* by contacting the Superintendent of Documents at the Government Printing Office at 732 North Capitol Street NW, Washington, D.C. 20401, (202) 512-0000. Or visit the U.S. Patent and Trademark Office's web site at www.uspto.gov read the publication online.

You may also want to obtain a list of public domain patents from the U.S. Patent and Trademark Office. After a 20-year period, patents are no longer valid and can be developed without any licensing requirements or royalties payable to the original patent holder. Remember, however, that just because a patent has expired does not mean the product ceases to exist. An example of this is the single-element typewriter patented by IBM. Once the period of protection ended when the patent expired, many manufacturers produced their versions of this product, most of which sold quite well.

For comprehensive information on all things relevant to small businesses, check out the Small Business Administration or SBA. Its Small Business Investment Company (SBIC) programs offer an alternative to bank financing for small businesses. Licensed and regulated by the SBA, SBICs are privately owned and managed investment firms that make capital available to small businesses through investments or loans. These new companies might welcome inquiries from potential marketers, distributors, wholesalers, or retailers for its products. For a list of currently active SBICs, visit the SBA web site www.sba.gov.

Also worth looking into is the Small Business Technology Transfer (STTR) program. In STTR, small businesses collaborate with nonprofit research institutions, usually universities or national laboratories, in a partnership designed to deliver promising technology to the marketplace. STTR also provides up to $100,000 for the first phase of work, if the companies applying for the funds do at least 40 percent of the work themselves.

The Department of Energy (DOE), which manages the largest collection of federal laboratories in the nation, is one agency that offers the STTR program. Others include the Departments of Agriculture, Commerce, Defense, and Transportation, along with the Environmental Protection Agency, NASA, and the National Science Foundation. More information is available at these agencies' web sites.

Research and Development

Large corporations' research and development (R&D) efforts offer additional opportunities for small businesses. For every product brought to market, there are many others that aren't, for one reason or another. If the market was deemed too small for the corporation to make a profit in, that doesn't necessarily exclude a small company like yours from getting involved. You can begin a direct-mail inquiry campaign to Fortune 500 companies. Many firms may not respond, but a few of these giants may be happy to correspond with you.

New products must be manufactured, marketed, distributed, and sold. At any one of these points, niches become apparent that can mean opportunities for you. With some intelligent investigation, you could become part of the next big product success and build a business around it. All you have to do is ask.

| FIGURE 2.2 | Tracking Small Business Trends Checklist |

To track emerging trends that can affect small businesses in general and your business in particular, stay informed. To do so:

❏ Read a major metropolitan newspaper, as well as one or two papers serving your local community. This way, you can keep abreast of current events on both a local and a global scale.

❏ Read local and national journals and magazines that deal with small business or business in general. Publications such as *The Wall Street Journal* and *Entrepreneur* are valuable sources of trends that are developing on a national scale as well as detailed information on specific business opportunities.

❏ Join associations that serve your industry. These are an excellent source of current news geared specifically to businesses like yours. To find an appropriate association, consult the *Encyclopedia of Associations*, published by Gale Research, Inc. You can find this publication in larger libraries.

❏ Keep track of nonfiction books that sell well. Although these books may not always apply directly to your business, they may indicate trends that you can follow closely.

❏ Contact government agencies or consult government publications for specific questions. The Departments of Commerce and Labor and the Census Bureau, for instance, may have data indicating various trends. You might also consult large libraries, particularly those in large public universities, for information gathered by the government. Such libraries often have sections devoted to government publications.

❏ Contact manufacturers, wholesalers, and distributors serving your industry. They can furnish information not only on the products they provide but also on market research they may have done.

❏ If you have access to an online information service or to electronic bulletin boards, you might be able to find a source of the latest information on your industry.

❏ Subscribe to relevant trade periodicals and newsletters. Many trade associations publish periodicals that report on your industry. These publications are usually filled with valuable management tips, industry trends, buying guides, etc.

❏ Attend industry conventions and inventor trade shows. These venues offer an exciting array of information regarding specific industries as well as new product ideas.

For entrepreneurial inspiration, think of those ubiquitous Bic pens. They were developed in 1945 by Marcel Bich, who purchased a factory outside Paris with his partner to manufacture fountain pen parts and mechanical lead pencils. Bich saw enormous potential in a ballpoint pen that offered both quality and value. Today the company has offices around the world, is traded on the New York Stock Exchange and sells lighters, shavers, and sailboards in addition to pens.

The Licensing Broker

Just as you're searching for products to license, manufacturers who have those products available are searching for you. Many of them use licensing brokers to discover potential licensees. These consultants have many contacts, not to mention years of experience in the manufacturing field. Many of these professionals can also help you finalize the actual licensing agreement you will need to get under way.

How can you find them? Contact the International Licensing Industry Merchandisers' Association (ILIMA, 350 Fifth Avenue, Suite 1408, New York, N.Y. 10118, (212) 244-1944, www.licensing.org). Members include agents and property owners who are involved in licensed properties, along with manufacturers, consultants, lawyers, and accountants. Ask if they can recommend a broker in your area. Your attorney may be another resource for recommending a qualified licensing broker.

EVALUATE YOUR IDEA

How good is your idea? Quite often, entrepreneurs—particularly first-time business owners—don't know how to evaluate their ideas. Many flawed ideas fail unnecessarily in the market place when a detailed and systematic evaluation could have corrected these defects, or at the very least, prevented those business owners from committing capital and efforts to a lost cause. If you plan to enter the marketplace with a new concept, performing a strenuous evaluation of your idea before you commit lots of time and money will significantly improve your chances of success.

Product/Service Life Cycle

Traditional theory suggests that every product, idea, or concept has a five-stage life cycle that can be charted according to the following criteria.

1. *Introduction.* The product debuts in the market; sales are low because prices are relatively high.
2. *Growth.* Sales increase while prices begin to decline.
3. *Maturity.* Sales level off, and competition increases, placing more pressure on pricing.
4. *Saturation.* Competition increases, leading to low profit margins.
5. *Decline.* Sales begin to fall, and profits diminish.

Additional Factors for Consideration

The Princeton Checklist for Evaluating Ideas (Figure 2.3) will help you assess the feasibility of your idea. Your objective in considering these factors is to determine whether any external or internal changes in the status quo will help or hinder your success. To prevent unforeseen elements or circumstances from harming your efforts, consider these elements:

- *Stability.* How durable is the market for your new idea? How much competition is there within the market? (Some competition is healthy, while a complete lack of competition is a red flag—see Chapter 8, Writing a Business Plan, for more on this.) Is it a fad market? Are there nationwide applications for your product or service? Could you develop foreign markets? Do you have a captive market? Is your product easy for other manufacturers to copy? How would the market react to a recession?

- *Growth.* Is your idea unique? Will demand for your product or service grow? Can it survive a major technological surge, or will it become obsolete? How do you envision facilitating growth of your business? If the idea or product involves new technology, will consumers willingly learn the skills necessary to use it, or will you encounter significant consumer resistance?

- *Marketability.* What type of sales structure will your company require to market the product? How well has your competition done in this market? Will you be targeting a market niche that involves selling a large volume to just a few customers?

- *Research and development.* Can you develop your new idea with your current knowledge? If not, what additional help will you need to get your business launched? Will you be able to use existing equipment and facilities? Will you complete your research efforts before your competitors enter the market?

- *Production.* If you're bringing a new product to market, are you familiar with the production techniques? Will they create any maintenance problems? Are there any hazards associated with the production process? Will you have to conduct training prior to beginning full-scale production?

Sound evaluation techniques can mean the difference between profit and loss, between the success and failure of your small business. As your business expands and you gain experience, you'll develop methods individually geared to your ideas. But when you're just starting out, it's wise to have a solid, proven set of parameters with which to gauge your ideas so you'll make fewer mistakes along the way, especially since every mistake is expensive, both in terms of time and money. Make sure you take these steps.

1. Base your business on your past experience, both personally and professionally.

2. Plan on making a profit in your new venture.

3. Protect your product with a patent, trademark, or copyright as soon as possible.

4. Avoid industries that are heavily regulated by the government because lots of regulations usually mean lots of red tape and high costs.

5. Evaluate all channels of distribution, including sales

agents or manufacturer's reps, to help get your product into the marketplace quickly, efficiently, and profitably.

6. Continually refine your ideas concerning pricing, distribution, marketing, and production.

TEST THE MARKET WITH YOUR IDEA

Introducing a new product or service without first testing the market is like jumping off a cliff into the sea, blindfolded—unthinkable, life-threatening, treacherous, and unnecessarily risky. Many new ideas and products are

---

FIGURE 2.3   Princeton Checklist for Evaluating Ideas

Princeton Creative Research developed this checklist, which is particularly well suited to entrepreneurs. Ask yourself the following questions when evaluating an idea for a business or a product.

- ❏ Have you considered all the advantages or benefits of the idea? Is there a real need for it?
- ❏ Have you pinpointed the exact problems or difficulties your idea is expected to solve?
- ❏ Is your idea an original, a new concept, or a new adaptation?
- ❏ What immediate or short-range gains or results can be anticipated? Are the projected returns adequate? Are the risk factors acceptable?
- ❏ What long-range benefits can be anticipated? Will they support the company's objective?
- ❏ Have you checked the operational soundness of the idea? Can it be produced by the company? Are the company's engineering, production, sales, and distributions facilities adequate for implementation?
- ❏ Have you checked the idea for faults or limitations?
- ❏ Are there any problems the idea might create? What are the changes involved?
- ❏ Have you considered the economic factors of its implementation? What development time, capital investment, marketing costs, etc., does it entail? What personnel will be involved? Who else is needed to perform the job? What other divisions or departments of the company will be affected?
- ❏ How simple or complex will execution or implementation be?
- ❏ How well does it fit into the current operation of the organization?
- ❏ Could you work out several variations of the idea? Could you offer alternative ideas?
- ❏ Does it have a natural sales appeal? Is the market ready for it? Can customers afford it? Will they buy it? Is there a timing factor?
- ❏ What, if anything, is your competition doing in this area? Can your company be competitive?
- ❏ Have you considered the possibility of user resistance or difficulties?
- ❏ Does your idea fill a real need, or does the need have to be created through promotional and advertising efforts?
- ❏ Is it compatible with other procedures or products of the company and its overall objectives?
- ❏ Is it a good idea or a good product area for the organization to pursue?
- ❏ Are there any specific circumstances in your organization that might make the acceptance of the idea difficult?
- ❏ How soon could it be put into operation?

As you can see by the preceding examples, there are many methods available for evaluating your idea. Pick and choose the criteria that best suit your needs, depending on the type of company and/or the type of product you seek to evaluate.

successful because their creators identified an unmet need in the market and verified the viability of that concept. Although accurately determining the demand or consumer reaction to a new product in advance may be tough, you need as much information as you can get to guide your entry into the market. Every dollar and every hour you spend researching are time and money well invested in the long term. Through correct and vigorous market research, you'll uncover the following vital information:

- Demand for a product or service in your market
- Sales figures within a market for a particular product or service
- Who your customers are
- What those customers think about your product or service and what they think about your competitors', so you can capitalize on your strengths
- Where and how customers buy your product or service, so you can establish the most effective distribution and marketing channels
- How much customers are willing to pay, so you can figure out a competitive price for them and realistic profits for you
- Who your direct and indirect competition is
- How to position your product or service so that you take advantage of its unique selling proposition
- Which governmental regulations your product or service will be subject to on local, state, and federal levels
- Which sales, advertising, display, and promotion methods are most effective

Begin your research by looking up names of relevant trade publications in the business publications volume of the *Standard Rate and Data Service Directory* (SRDS), or *Bacon's Magazine and Newspaper Directory*. Both are available at your local library. Subscribe to publications relevant to your particular industry.

Trade associations that generate their own publications are another good resource. You can find a listing of the thousands of U.S. trade associations in the *Encyclopedia of Associations*, published by Gale Research. If your research budget is tight, see which publications your library receives. You can gather information from

the library copies at a minimal cost and subscribe to those others you might need to completely cover the field.

You will not become an expert in the field simply by reading trade magazines. Reading is no match for experience. But you will obtain vital information, and finding out as much as you can about your proposed field is the key to entering the market with confidence.

Protecting Your Idea

Before you begin marketing an idea, talk with your attorney about whether you need to protect your interest in it. There are two routes you can go. You can either get a patent, which may cost upwards of $3,000 without an attorney, or as much as $12,000 with one. Or you can file a disclosure statement with the federal government documenting your claim that you were the first person with your idea.

Although disclosure is not a patent, and it does not provide you with complete protection, it will back up your claim to the idea for two years. So if you have a brand-new product that you want to bring to market, it may make sense for you to file a disclosure document. You have one year from the point of first public exposure to actually file the patent. If you do this, you can find out whether the idea is going to work and whether you have a big winner on your hands before you invest all the money needed to get through the patent process. Make sure you enclose a disclosure document with any mailings you do on the product to manufacturers, reps, and the like. You need to be careful because you can easily lose an idea to copiers who may have more capital and distribution channels available to them than you do.

Idea Insurance

While idea protection vehicles such as a copyright, trademark, or patent provide you with some protection, realize that it is not ironclad. In reality, copyrights, trademarks, and patents are frequently abused, and it is up to you to prove any type of infringement of your intellectual property as well as the extent of the damages. This costs time and money. In fact, the American Intellectual Property Law Association (www.aipla.org) reports that the median cost of litigating a patent claim is more than $1.2 million.

So what do inventors in small businesses do to protect themselves beyond the scope of the patent? They can take out patent abatement insurance. While still rare with most insurers, patent abatement insurance provides patent holders with a safety net if they do have to challenge an infringement of their intellectual property. There is an annual premium for the policy, and if a claim is filed, there is a co-payment.

Models and Prototypes

Once you've taken the initial steps to protect your idea, the next step is to determine whether the invention will work. To do this, you'll need to first make a model of the invention and then a prototype.

A model is a representation of the product as it will be manufactured. The model demonstrates what your invention will do, but it is not always an exact replica of the finished product. In building your model, consider these issues: the item's sale price, materials, manufacturing costs, marketing details, safety factors, how it will be sold and distributed, and the profit margin. If you plan to license your invention to a manufacturer, you can often do so with a model.

A prototype is an exact replica of the product as it will be manufactured, including details such as color, graphics, packaging, and instructions. The cost for making a prototype or sample is usually much greater than the actual unit costs once the item is in full production. For example, a prototype might cost $500, though the product itself might retail for only $2 to $10. But it's well worth the investment. You can make drawings or photographs of the sample to use in brochures, mailings, pamphlets, and advertising, and use the prototype to show to prospective buyers.

When you're ready to put together your prototype, obtain bids from several manufacturing companies. Get prices for producing one, one thousand, and five thousand units. Make sure the bid you get includes tooling costs and specifies the terms the manufacturer will provide. At the same time, make sure you know for certain when delivery will occur, so you can speak authoritatively with buyers. This will help you determine your initial pricing structure.

When people hear the word "prototype," they often assume that its purpose is to test the effectiveness of manufacturing or production methods. Although this is one motive for making a prototype, employing it in your market research is just as important to the ultimate success of your product. Nothing can replace the data obtained through the use of a prototype. Whether a product is as complex as a computer or as simple as a welding torch, market testing with a prototype will tell you how prospective buyers will react to your product.

Analyzing the Competition

A quick and easy way to compare your product or service with similar ones on the market is to make a competition grid. Down the left side of a piece of paper, write the names of four or five products or services that compete with yours. To help you generate this list, think of what the consumer would buy if he or she did not buy your product or service.

Across the top of the paper, list the main features and characteristics of each product or service. Include such things as target market, price, size, method of distribution, and extent of customer service for a product. For a service, list prospective buyers, where the service is available, price, web site, toll-free phone number, and other features that are relevant. A glance at the competition grid will help you see where your product fits in the overall market.

Reevaluate Your Idea

If you have a new product to sell, test the water using your prototype, price estimates, and preliminary market data in a couple of stores or whatever other principal channel of distribution you have chosen. Make sure the stores don't give your new product special treatment or attention so that the test of your product against those of your competitors will be a fair one.

Another great way to test your product is to offer it on eBay, the online marketplace (www.ebay.com). With millions of registered users, eBay is one of the most popular shopping sites on the internet. Perhaps the most valuable services eBay can provide to business owners is helping them eliminate the guesswork in pricing by helping them determine what buyers are willing to pay.

Based on the success or failure in your experiments, modify your product to make it better and more attractive to consumers. Don't give up if your product sales aren't as high as you expected, considering that you haven't done any advertising or promotion for it. What you're concerned about at this point is getting valuable feedback from a few prospective customers regarding your product's design and features, and your proposed marketing strategy for it.

CONSULT THE EXPERTS

Don't forget to talk with industry experts about your new product. They will give you feedback about how well the product works, whether it meets their needs, how well they think it will sell, how it's priced, whether it's easy to find in stores, on the web or other markets, and so on.

It's always wise to consult with a marketing expert or firm at this stage. Firms typically charge an hourly rate for writing a marketing plan and a flat or project-based rate for actually implementing that plan. Travel and other expenses are extra. Rates vary, depending on where you're located—firms in major metropolitan markets will charge a higher rate than those doing similar work in a smaller market where overhead costs are lower.

If you don't want to absorb the expense of retaining either a consultant or a market-research firm, think about contacting the marketing department of your local college or university, preferably one with a strong program in small business or entrepreneurship, or one that houses a Small Business Development Center (SBDC). SBDCs are cooperative efforts among the SBA, a college or university, the private sector, and state and local governments; their services include business counseling, training and technical assistance. Visit the dean of the business school and investigate the possibility of having the business school's students do your testing for a reasonable cost, or perhaps even free of charge, in exchange for course credit. This type of real-world experience can be invaluable for students involved in an entrepreneurship program. The students may be able to perform on-site market survey work, and they (or you, with their help) can tabulate the results and perform any analyses necessary.

Another option to consider is a business incubator. Business incubation programs are often sponsored by private companies or municipal entities and public institutions, such as colleges and universities. Their goal is to help create and grow young businesses by providing them with necessary support and financial and technical services. There are approximately 1,100 business incubators nationwide, according to the National Business Incubation Association.

Incubators provide numerous benefits to owners of start-up businesses. Their office and manufacturing space is offered at below-market rates, and their staff supplies advice and much-needed expertise in developing business and marketing plans as well as helping to fund fledgling businesses. Companies typically spend an average of two years in a business incubator, during which time they often share telephone, secretarial, and office and production equipment expenses with other start-up companies, in an effort to reduce everyone's overhead and operational costs.

Be careful. Not all business incubators are alike, so if you have a specialized idea for a business, try to find the incubator that best suits your requirements. For instance, there are two incubators in Cincinnati, one geared toward biomedical firms and another toward low-income entrepreneurs.

If you're interested in finding an incubator in your state, visit the National Business Incubation Association's web site (www.nbia.org) or give them a call at (740) 593-4331. And get in touch with your local economic development agency, located in the phone book under the listing for your state government. Call the information offices of your local colleges and universities to see whether they have any business incubation programs.

If an incubation program seems interesting to you, be prepared to submit a fleshed-out business plan. The plan will be reviewed by a screening committee to determine whether or not you meet the criteria for admission. Incubators carefully screen potential businesses because their space, equipment, and finances are limited, and they want to be sure they're choosing to nurture businesses with the best possible chance for success.

CHAPTER 3

Market Research

Accurate and thorough market research is the foundation of all successful business ventures because it provides a wealth of information about prospective and existing customers, the competition, and the industry in general. It allows a business owner to determine the feasibility of a business before committing substantial resources to that venture.

Market research provides relevant data to help solve marketing challenges that a business will most likely face—an integral part of the business planning process. In fact, strategies such as market segmentation (identifying specific groups within a market) and product differentiation (creating an identity for a product or service that separates it from those of the competitors) are impossible to develop without market research.

I remember one instance where doing this preliminary market research was a gold mine of opportunities. Upon becoming the new owners of an arts-and-entertainment weekly, my business partner and I spoke to countless advertisers, readers, community members, artists, and performers to find out what they wanted from our newspaper. Not all of their ideas were possible to implement, but we did glean some useful information that

enriched our business planning process. Some of the best things to come out of this market research project were the public relations opportunities it afforded us—we were able to personally introduce ourselves as the paper's new owners to the community, initiate new relationships with our various constituents, and set ourselves apart from the previous publishers and their history with the paper.

For more information on how you can use the information discussed in this chapter in your business, see Chapter 25, The Marketing Plan.

GATHER INFORMATION

Market research involves two types of data.

1. *Primary information* is research that you compile yourself or hire someone to gather for you.
2. *Secondary information* is already compiled and organized for you. Examples of secondary information are reports and studies by government agencies, trade associations, or other businesses within your industry. Most of the research you gather will be secondary.

Primary Research

When conducting primary research, you can gather two basic types of information: exploratory or specific. Exploratory research is open-ended, helps you define a specific problem, and usually involves detailed, unstructured interviews in which lengthy answers are solicited from a small group of respondents. Specific research, on the other hand, is precise in scope and is used to solve a problem that exploratory research has identified. Interviews are structured and formal in approach. Of the two, specific research is more expensive. Figure 3.1 shows a sample cost analysis form for different research methods.

When conducting primary research using your own resources, first decide how you'll question your targeted group: by direct mail, telephone, or personal interviews. If you choose a direct-mail questionnaire, the following guidelines will increase your response rate:

- questions that are short and to the point
- a questionnaire that is addressed to specific individuals and is of interest to the respondent
- a questionnaire of no more than two pages
- a professionally prepared cover letter that adequately explains why you're doing this questionnaire
- a postage-paid, self-addressed envelope to return the questionnaire in. Postage-paid envelopes are available from the post office
- an incentive, such as "10 percent off your next purchase," to complete the questionnaire.

Even if you follow these guidelines, keep in mind that mail response is typically low. A return rate of three percent is typical; five percent is considered very good. Phone surveys are generally the most cost-effective. Some telephone survey guidelines include:

- have a script and memorize it—don't read it
- confirm the name of the respondent at the beginning of the conversation
- avoid pauses because respondent interest can quickly drop
- ask if a follow-up call is possible in case you require additional information.

In addition to being cost-effective, speed is another advantage of telephone interviews. A rate of five or six interviews per hour is typical, but experienced interviewers may be able to conduct more. Phone interviews also can cover a wide geographic range relatively inexpensively. Phone costs can be reduced by taking advantage of less expensive rates during certain hours. One of the most effective forms of marketing research is the personal interview. It can be either:

- *A group survey.* Used mostly by big business, group interviews or focus groups are useful brainstorming tools for getting information on product ideas, buying preferences, and purchasing decisions among certain populations.
- *An in-depth interview.* These one-on-one interviews are either focused or non-directed. Focused interviews are based on questions selected ahead of time, while non-directed interviews encourage respondents to address certain topics with minimal questioning.

Secondary Research

Secondary research uses outside information assembled by government agencies, industry and trade associations, labor unions, media sources, chambers of commerce, and so on. It's usually published in pamphlets, newsletters, trade publications, magazines, and newspapers. Secondary sources include:

- *Public sources.* These are usually free, often offer a lot of good information, and include government departments, business departments of public libraries, and so on.
- *Commercial sources.* These are valuable, but usually involve cost factors such as subscription and association fees. Commercial sources include research and trade associations, such as Dun & Bradstreet and Robert Morris & Associates, banks and other financial institutions, and publicly traded corporations.
- *Educational institutions.* These are frequently overlooked as valuable information sources even though more research is conducted in colleges, universities, and technical institutes than virtually any sector of the business community.

Public Information Sources

Government statistics are among the most plentiful and wide-ranging public sources. Helpful government publications include:

- *State and Metropolitan Area Data Book.* This book provides a wide variety of statistical information on

FIGURE 3.1   Cost Analysis of Primary Research Methods

Mail Surveys	Cost	
Preparing questionnaire		
Envelopes		
Postage for mailing questionnaire and returning it		
Incentives for questionnaire response		
Staff time and cost for analysis and presentation of results		
Independent researcher cost, if any		
Other costs/itemize		
Total Mail Survey Costs		

Phone Surveys	Cost	
Preparing questionnaire		
Interviewer's fee		
Phone charges		
Staff time and cost for analysis and presentation of results		
Independent researcher cost, if any		
Other costs/ itemize		
Total Phone Survey Costs		

Personal Interviews	Cost	
Preparing questionnaire		
Printing questionnaire and prompt cards		
Training interviewers		
Incentives for questionnaire response		
Staff time and cost for analysis and presentation of results		
Independent researcher cost, if any		
Other costs/itemize		
Total Personal Interviews Costs		

FIGURE 3.1	Cost Analysis of Primary Research Methods, continued

Group Discussions	Cost	
Interviewer's fee and expenses to recruit and assemble the groups		
Rental fee for conference room or other facility and cost of recording media such as tapes, if used		
Incentives for group participation		
Staff time and cost for analysis and presentation of results		
Independent researcher cost, if any		
Other costs/itemize		
Total Group Discussion Costs		

states and metropolitan areas in the United States. Published in 2006 by the U.S. Census Bureau, it is available online for $47 through the U.S. Government Printing Office (http://bookstore.gpo.gov) and at larger libraries.

- *Statistical Abstract of the United States.* This work provides tables and graphs of statistics on the social, political, and economic conditions in the United States. Published in 2006 by the Census Bureau, the paperbound edition is available online for $35 through the U.S. Government Printing Office (http://bookstore.gpo.gov) and at larger libraries.

The U.S. government online bookstore at the U.S. Government Printing Office (http://bookstore.gpo. gov) has an abundance of publications on topics ranging from agriculture, aviation, and electronics, to insurance, telecommunications, forest management, and workers' compensation. Check it out!

The U.S. Census Bureau web site (www.census. gov) also contains valuable information relevant to marketing. The bureau's business publications cover many topics and trades—such as sales volume at furniture stores and payrolls for toy wholesalers—and are useful for small businesses as well as large corporations in retail, wholesale trade, and service industries. Also available are census maps, reports on company statistics regarding different ethnic groups, and reports on county business patterns.

One of the most important information resources you'll find is the Small Business Administration (SBA, www.sba.gov). The SBA was created by Congress in 1953 to help American entrepreneurs start, run, and grow successful small enterprises. Today there are SBA offices in every state, the District of Columbia, the U.S. Virgin Islands, Puerto Rico, and Guam. Among the services offered by the SBA are financial assistance, counseling services through Small Business Development Centers (SBDCs), management assistance through programs like SCORE (Service Corps of Retired Executives), and low-cost publications. For more information on SBA programs, see Chapter 15.

Call your local SBA field office (look in the white pages of your phone book under the general heading "United States Government" or check www.sba.gov) to find your local SCORE chapter and the nearest SBDC. The counselors at SCORE can provide you with free consultation on what type of research you need to gather and where you can obtain that information. They may also be able to suggest other means of getting that information from primary sources. SBDCs generally have extensive business libraries with lots of secondary sources for you to review.

One of the best public sources is the business section of your local public, college, or university library. The services provided vary from library to library but usually include a wide range of government publications with market statistics, a large collection of directories with information on domestic and foreign businesses, and a wide selection of magazines, newspapers, and newsletters.

Almost every county government publishes population density and distribution figures in accessible census tracts. These show the number of people living in specific areas, such as precincts, water districts, or even ten-block neighborhoods. Some counties publish reports that show the population ten years ago, five years ago, and currently, thus indicating population trends.

Other public information resources include local chambers of commerce and their business development departments, which encourage new businesses to locate in their communities. They will supply you (usually for free) information on population trends, community income characteristics, payrolls, industrial development, and so on.

Don't overlook your bank as a resource. Bankers have a wealth of information at their fingertips and are eager to help their small business customers get ahead. All you have to do is ask.

Commercial Information Sources

Among the best commercial sources of information are research and trade associations. Information gathered by trade associations is usually limited to that particular industry and available only to association members, who have typically paid a membership fee. However, the research gathered by the larger associations is usually thorough, accurate, and worth the cost of membership. Two excellent resources to help you locate a trade association that reports on the business you are researching include the Encyclopedia of Associations, published by Gale Research, and the Encyclopedia of Business Information Sources 15th Edition, by James Woy (editor), published by Gale Group, 2001.

Local newspapers, journals, magazines, and radio and television stations are some of the most useful commercial information outlets. Not only do they maintain demographic profiles of their audiences (their income, age, gender, amount of disposable income, and types of products and services purchased, what they read, and so on), but many also have information about economic trends in their local areas that could be significant to your

business. Contact the sales departments of these businesses and ask them to send you their media kit, since you're working on a marketing plan for a new product and need information about advertising rates and audience demographics. Not only will you learn more about your prospective customers, you'll also learn more about possible advertising outlets for your product or service.

As you do your market planning, make sure to read *The Wall Street Journal*. It offers broad-based information on the domestic economy in areas that may affect your business such as new tax developments, overviews of specific industries, trends in technology, and new marketing strategies. *The Wall Street Journal* also has a section specifically devoted to international trade.

Dun & Bradstreet is another commercial source of market research that offers an abundance of information for making marketing decisions. It operates the world's largest business database and tracks more than 62 million companies around the world, including 11 million in the United States. For more information, see Dun & Bradstreet Small Business Solutions web site at http://smallbusiness.dnb.com.

Educational Institution Information Sources

Finally, there are educational institutions that conduct research in various ways ranging from faculty-based projects often published under professors' bylines, to student projects, theses, and assignments. You may be able to enlist the aid of students involved in business classes, especially if they're enrolled in an entrepreneurship program. This can be an excellent way of generating research at little or no cost, by engaging students who welcome the professional experience either as interns or for special credit. Contact the university administration and the marketing/management studies departments for further information.

KNOW YOUR CUSTOMERS AND THEIR NEEDS

When gathering market research, you must first define your customer base. When you know their characteristics, you'll have a better idea of what they want to buy from you—and why.

A terrific resource is the U.S. Census Bureau (www.census.gov), which provides a wealth of information on our population and its demographics. You can get national and state population profiles; national, state, and county statistics on age; demographic data on any number of countries in the world; and even information on who owns and uses computers.

Segmentation

The first step is defining the market segment(s) you wish to target. There are many ways to do this, but the most common denominators used by professional market planners are demographics (or customer attributes), geographics, and behavioral segmentation.

Customer attributes or demographic factors often include:

- Lifestyle
- Social class
- Gender
- Age
- Income level
- Business organization
- Company size
- Annual sales

You can also use customer attributes to divide the market by factors such as business organization segments, which are more concerned with specific operations, their size and amount of sales. This segmentation strategy is especially useful for companies that primarily target business through their marketing strategies.

Geographic segments would divide the market into regions such as:

- International markets
- National markets
- Regional zones
- Community districts

Behavioral factors, on the other hand, look at consumers' behavior, such as:

- *Product or service usage.* For example, airlines actively target frequent flyers by providing them with incentives such as free trips and discounts on rates, if they log enough air miles or trips.
- *Type of benefits.* The benefits derived from the product or service are the primary factors that motivate a customer to buy. Examples of benefits are the speed

of a specific computer or a diet plan's promise of weight loss.

- *Pricing sensitivity.* Sometimes a product's price is the main purchasing criterion. For instance, economy hotels and motels appeal to a more price-conscious market than do luxury hotels.
- *Utilization.* How the customer uses the product or service can be significant. For example, car buyers can be segmented by usage, such as buyers of commuter vehicles, off-road vehicles, luxury vehicles, sports cars, vans, and so on.
- *Brand loyalty.* Some product users are committed to a particular product. For instance, there are consumers who prefer fleece jackets from L.L. Bean to all others, while other consumers wouldn't think of buying any car but a Mercedes.

When developing a marketing strategy, decide what market segments will define the scope of your market and whether they all work toward a common goal of determining the total potential market of your product or service. For instance, if you decide to use a combination of specific customer attributes and geographic zones to define the market, your segmentation factors might focus on individuals who meet specific age, income level and lifestyle criteria in a particular geographic area (for example, retirees who play golf in the Boca Raton area).

You can continue using additional segmentation factors to further define your marketing strategy. The more specific you are regarding the market you wish to reach, the more targeted your market strategy and message will be.

Customer Requirements

Once you've identified customer segments, the next step in your market research is to determine the customer requirements for a particular product or service. Prepare a questionnaire that you can either mail to consumers or discuss with them over the phone. The questionnaire should deal with the attributes of your product and how they would affect the purchase decision. You can also include tradeoff questions that ask customers if they would give up one benefit to gain another to determine just which factors are more important than others.

Another way to use your questionnaire is to determine which product or service features the customer feels would help his or her purchasing decision. This can be done by conducting a benefit structure analysis questionnaire, in which you ask users to point out the benefits of the product or service and rate them in terms of importance.

LEARN ABOUT YOUR COMPETITION

Researching your competition provides knowledge about their current strategies, weaknesses, and strengths, along with which opportunities and threats your business faces.

The first step in researching your competitors is to identify them. There are two ways: customer groups and strategic groups.

Customer Groups

This method identifies competitors according to how intensely they compete for a share of your customers' dollars. They can be either:

- *Direct competitors.* These have similar assets and skills, and compete most aggressively for their share of your customer's dollar. For example, McDonald's competes directly against other fast-food chains, such as Burger King and Wendy's.
- *Indirect competitors.* These compete for your target market's dollars with different or unrelated products and services. Indirect competitors of your local movie theater include restaurants, bowling alleys, skating rinks, concert halls, theaters and anywhere else consumers spend their disposable income on entertainment.

You can get some valuable information about competition within your industry by sending a questionnaire to prospective customers within a targeted geographic area. How do you get names of people to send your questionnaire to? You can rent a list of prospects from a list broker—look in the business-to-business Yellow Pages under "Mailing Lists."

In the questionnaire, ask a series of brand loyalty questions, such as which brand the consumer currently buys and whether they've tried other brands of products according to their preferences. Make sure to ask what those preferences are. Also ask what the customer likes about the vendor they're currently buying from, to get an idea of what they value about customer service, the vendor's location, hours of operation, and so on.

Strategic Groups

One way to group competitors is by the strategies they use, such as their:

- Advertising and promotion, as well as the size of their budgets
- Sales tactics, such as direct response or personal sales
- Distribution channels
- Pricing strategy.

A second way to group competitors is by uniform characteristics, such as:

- Size of business and number of employees
- Amount of sales
- Amount of market share.

A third way is to group competitors by similar assets and skills, such as:

- Strategic partnerships with key suppliers
- Strong customer-service programs
- Ownership of intellectual property
- Goodwill among customers.

The Information Stage

Many companies communicate extensively with their suppliers, customers, distributors, government legislators and regulators, and security analysts and stockholders if they are selling stock. Some of this information will be on public record, but other data (such as information about suppliers) won't be. While your competitors' suppliers will most likely not reveal contract terms or any other confidential facts, you can find out their pricing structure and the type of equipment or supplies your competitors may use.

Keep files on all your competitors. It's something I do and advise my clients to do. Clip and save all ads and any articles you may see in your newspaper or in any other publication. "Shop" your competition by visiting their places of business or by placing an order with them to see firsthand what kind of customer service they offer. Get copies of their brochures, letterhead, and other printed material. Visit their web site to evaluate how user-friendly it is. Google them to see what, if any, articles have been published on them.

Evaluate your competitors' ads. This will give you a good idea of the market strategy they are pursuing. Visit trade shows to see what your competitors are up to, get samples of their products, and learn more about their market strategy in your industry.

LEARN ABOUT YOUR INDUSTRY

Your research of the industry must be focused and purposeful so that you can determine its attractiveness and profit potential. In addition, industry research will help you get a handle on trends, threats, and opportunities.

The first step is defining your industry's boundaries, which can be determined from your customer and competition research. You can either confine your boundaries to the primary or direct competitors and their products, or extend it to include indirect or secondary competitors. For instance, if you were researching videotape rentals, the boundaries could include stores or services that rent videotapes, or it could be broadened to include indirect competitors such as movie theaters and cable providers.

Actual and Potential Size

The actual and potential size of the industry gives you an overview of the market share of each of your competitors. Actual industry size can be determined by referring to secondary research sources, such as the Census Bureau and the Department of Commerce, as well as trade associations involved in that particular industry. These sources often provide market information, charting sales by product line, growth, geographic markets, and major players in the industry.

To gauge the potential size of the industry, look closely at gaps within the industry. Such gaps may be in the product line, distribution, usage, competitiveness, or any number of areas. By researching your customers, competitors, and the industry, you'll spot opportunities that can become the profitable niches that your business can target for marketing.

Forecasting Growth

To forecast industry growth, set up several models and examine what has to happen for each to occur. As an example, using a historical analysis of industry activity you project that the industry will grow 15 percent during the upcoming year. Using that 15 percent as a benchmark, you come up with two projections for your business; one is a conservative projection of 3 percent, and the other is slightly more aggressive at 6 percent. Based on these projections, you can determine the strategies you'll need to generate this growth. Will you need to increase your advertising budget? Hire additional sales personnel? Offer additional customer services? Implement a larger direct-response marketing effort? Then you can map out strategies to follow in order to accomplish the growth you've projected.

Industry Structure

A study of the industry structure will reveal how attractive the industry is for a return on long-term investment. Your evaluation of the industry structure should include five components:

1. *Competition between current firms.* Determine the number of competitors in the industry, their comparative size, product lines, strategies, fixed costs, and commitment to the industry.

2. *Threat of competition from potential entrants.* Ascertain the size and characteristics of the industry's entry barriers. For instance, if the cost to establish shelf space through retail distribution avenues is too high, that barrier would prevent many small specialty food manufacturers from gaining a foothold in that industry. If the entry barriers are too formidable, many potentially competitive companies may consider investment in the industry undesirable in light of the projected return on their investment.

3. *Threat of competition from alternate products and technology.* Define which products or services affect the sales growth of the industry. This data can usually be gathered by analyzing secondary competitor groups and contacting associations that keep tabs on those products.

4. *The buying power of customers.* Determine the buying power of customers by charting your competitors' prices. If many of them are discounting prices and not producing a sustainable profit, you will

want to think twice about investing in that industry.

5. *The negotiating power of suppliers.* To determine supplier power within the industry, find out who the major suppliers are and the extent of their product line. You can do this by looking through trade periodicals and contacting associations.

Cost Structure

When researching the cost structure of an industry, the first thing to do is identify the stages where value is added to a product or service. In most instances, these will be during:

- Procurement
- Processing
- Fabrication
- Assembly
- Distribution
- Marketing.

Each stage provides additional value to the final product or service. Most trade associations have percentages for the cost of producing and marketing a product based on surveys of their members.

Distribution Systems

Take a careful look at the various distribution channels currently in use and the companies that command them. Don't forget to identify emerging channels that could provide additional opportunities for your company.

Many large industrial companies use their own sales force to sell directly to their customer base. Other smaller firms might sell directly to retailers or reach their customers through wholesale distributors, jobbers, or brokers. Generally, companies that sell directly to the end user have more control over their marketing efforts but experience a greater margin of risk.

There may also be alternate distribution channels in the development of new trends within the industry. For instance, as discount stores, catalog discount houses, convenience food stores, and specialty kiosks open up, they create new distribution opportunities. And then there's the internet to consider! Note and analyze the possible impact such trends will have on your industry.

Industry Trends

Spotting industry trends is a function of asking yourself several questions concerning your customers, competitors, and the industry in general. They include:

- What do customers want?
- What needs are not being met?
- What new strategies are your competitors starting to employ?
- What are the new trends in distribution?

Take a close look at your market analysis up to this point to recognize the most significant trends in the industry that will affect your future strategy.

Key Factors for Success

Key factors for success in any industry include name recognition, distribution channel power, financial resources, customer loyalty, purchasing procedures, and access to raw materials. Whatever the key factors happen to be in your industry, the completed analysis of the industry should define those and provide you with enough information to make an educated guess about factors for future success. This may lie in the development of new technology, new distribution channels, or finding new ways to use the product. Figure 3.2, the Market Planning Checklist, will help you determine whether your research has uncovered adequate information about the business you're considering.

CULTIVATE INFORMATION NETWORKS

Aside from newspapers and magazines, trade literature is probably the most popular source among executives. Trade literature includes information such as personnel changes, background on people in the industry, meetings, new products, and appointments of agents.

Speeches and announcements reveal management philosophies and intentions. In order to help investors make better decisions, the Wall Street Transcript (www.twst.com) contains a compilation of speeches by company officials to security analysts as well as reports on specific industries.

Annual reports reveal priorities, investment strategies, plans for growth, marketing and strategic goals, and even inconsistencies in polices. Footnotes to financial statements

| FIGURE 3.2 | Market Planning Checklist |

Before you launch a marketing campaign, answer the following questions about your business and your product or service.

- ❏ Have you analyzed the market for your product or service? Do you know which features of your product or service will appeal to which market segments?

- ❏ In forming your marketing message, have you described how your product or service will benefit your customers?

- ❏ Have you prepared a pricing schedule? What kinds of discounts do you offer and to whom do you offer them?

- ❏ Have you prepared a sales forecast?

- ❏ Which media will you use in your marketing campaign?

- ❏ Have you planned any sales promotions?

- ❏ Have you planned a publicity campaign?

- ❏ Do your marketing materials mention any optional accessories or added services that consumers might want to purchase?

- ❏ If you offer a product, have you prepared clear operating and assembly instructions, if required? What kind of warranty do you provide? What type of customer service or support do you offer after the sale?

- ❏ Do you have product liability insurance?

- ❏ Is your packaging likely to appeal to your target market?

- ❏ If your product is one you can patent, have you done so?

- ❏ How will you distribute your product?

- ❏ Have you prepared job descriptions for all of the employees needed to carry out your marketing plans?

point to problems for those who know how to read them. The need to appear optimistic in public makes some of the reports less useful, but tracking and comparing reports over several years can reveal trends in management philosophy.

Records of bankruptcies, customer complaints, and disputes with creditors can be quite interesting and may offer useful insights for your market research.

Items that are available for your inspection include testimony, lawsuits, antitrust information, and other information in court records such as transcripts, evidence, and judgments in civil and criminal cases.

For resources in the field, start with customers. Customers can provide information about competitors products, plans to introduce a new product, pricing, service, personnel and personnel changes, planned plant location, and strategic changes. According to several studies,

customers are the primary source for market and competitive intelligence.

Second to customers as resources for competitive and market intelligence are suppliers. In addition to those who provide companies with raw materials, suppliers also include those who provide services, such as banks, advertising agencies, law firms, and public relations firms. Most suppliers will have an incentive to provide data to you if they believe you may be a good prospect for future business. However, while suppliers will generally provide you with a great deal of information about their pricing, product specifications, and delivery terms, a supplier worthy of your business will not divulge confidential information.

Trade associations supply general industry data, while chambers of commerce can provide data about employment, size of the competitor's facility, interest of companies in relocating, consumer complaints against local businesses, and more.

Internal Networks

Almost every business collects and stores important information about its competitors on the following topics. Make sure you do the same in your business.

- *Customer service.* The customer service department, because of its daily contact with the company's clients, is often the first to hear of a competitor's special promotion, price changes, new product features, and new distribution networks.
- *Distribution.* The distribution department often collects information on their own freight charges, warehouse costs, and warehouse availability, as well as those of its competitors' costs.
- *Purchasing.* Many of your company's vendors also sell to your competitors. The purchasing department, which deals with these vendors on a daily basis, may hear these vendors talk about the competition. For example, a vendor's salesperson may complain that he cannot meet your company's delivery date because a competitor has just come through with a big order that backlogged his company. A salesperson may also brag about her sales to a competitor, revealing previously unknown information about that competitor.

Your Business Location

The old saw about real estate certainly applies to many small businesses: The three most important considerations are location, location, and location. Location is especially important for businesses in the retail and hospitality trades because they rely a great deal on visibility and exposure to their target markets. But location is also important for service and manufacturing ventures, which have costs such as advertising, promotion, and distribution that are a direct result of where they're located.

Service businesses may not have the foot traffic and high visibility requirements of retailers, but their location has to be convenient for customers and their employees need adequate parking. Manufacturers are concerned with keeping operating cost down, and that means locating near key suppliers in areas accessible for pick-ups and deliveries.

TARGET THE RIGHT COMMUNITY

Analyze the community you're thinking about by considering the following questions:

- Is the population base large enough to support your business?

- Does the community have a stable economic base that will promote a healthy environment in which your business can grow?
- Does the demographic profile closely match that of the market you wish to serve?
- What are the community attitudes or outlook?

Population Requirements

Each year, the U.S. Census Bureau publishes *Economic Censuses*, which are comprehensive studies on the number of firms in various areas and the populations of the communities where they're located, called Standard Metropolitan Statistical Areas (SMSAs). Once you find the SMSA in which your business is located, you can extrapolate the information you need, such as what the population is for your community. For more information, visit the Census Bureau's web site at www.census.gov.

Economic Base

A community's economic base can have a direct impact upon your opportunities. People move from one community to another for better job prospects, more money, better schools, and a host of other reasons. To evaluate a community's economic base, check census data and other business statistics for the following information:

1. The percentage of people employed full time and the trend in employment

2. The average family income

3. Per capita total annual sales for goods or services similar to yours.

You can also learn a great deal about your prospective community by looking and listening. Some red flags to pay attention to include:

- The necessity for high school and college graduates to leave town to find suitable employment
- The inability of other residents to find local jobs
- Declining retail sales and industrial production
- Apathetic local business owners, educational administrators, and other residents.

Favorable signs are

- The opening of chain- or department-store affiliates
- Branches of large industrial firms locating in the community
- A progressive chamber of commerce and other civic organizations
- Good schools and public services
- Well-maintained business and residential premises
- Good transportation facilities with access to other parts of the country
- Construction activity accompanied by a minimal number of vacant buildings and unoccupied houses for sale.

Demographic Profile

You must know the demographic profile of your potential customers in order to properly evaluate a community for location. Figure 4.1 provides a sample Demographic Comparison form. To see if the community you're considering offers a population with the demographic traits necessary to support your business, look at the community's:

- *Purchasing power.* Find out the degree of disposable income within the community.

- *Residences.* Are homes rented or owned?
- *Means of transportation.* Do prospective customers in the area own vehicles, ride buses or bicycles, and so on?
- *Age ranges.* Does the community consist primarily of young people still approaching their prime earning years, young professionals, empty nesters, or retirees?
- *Family status.* Are there lots of families in the area or mostly singles?
- *Leisure activities.* What type of hobbies and recreational activities do people in the community participate in?

Detailed demographic information is available from the Census Bureau's web site (www.census. gov). Click on State and County Quick Facts for your state, and you can find county-by-county demographic information. You can also get this kind of information from established businesses within your industry or from a trade association. *Gale's Encyclopedia of Associations*, available in most libraries, lists more than 30,000 trade associations' national headquarters. Many associations also have local or regional chapters that serve members in a variety of ways, with everything from newsletters to lobbying actions.

In addition, the Bureau of Labor Statistics publishes the *Consumer Expenditure Survey* (CES), which you can find at the Bureau's web site at www.bls.gov by clicking on "consumer spending." The CES annually samples 5,000 households through its Quarterly Interview Survey and its Diary Survey to learn how families and individuals spend their money. Unlike other surveys that might ask only how much people are spending on household or home appliances, the CES collects data about nearly every category of expenses—from alcoholic beverages and restaurant meals to pensions and life insurance. Bureau of Labor Statistics analysts then sort the information and group consumers by income, household size, race, gender, and other characteristics relevant to a business.

When you're satisfied that the community you plan to serve has the qualities to support your business and is convenient to your customers, then begin looking for a site.

FIGURE 4.1 Demographic Comparison

To see if the community you are considering offers a population with the demographic profile you need for your business, fill out the following form.

Population	Market A	Market B	Market C
Within 1 mile of your business			
Within 5 miles of your business			
Within 25 miles of your business			

Predominant Income	Market A	Market B	Market C
Under $25,000			
$25,000–$35,000			
$35,000–$45,000			
$45,000–$60,000			
$60,000+			

Age	Market A	Market B	Market C
Preteen			
Teenaged			
20–29			
30–39			
40–49			
50–59			
60–69			
70+			

Residences	Market A	Market B	Market C
Homeowners			
Renters			

Community Attitudes

The way the community feels about itself and its future plays an important role in the success or failure of a small business. If the people in a community don't care about the future of the area, then the community's economic vitality could be at risk.

A community where people are actively involved in promoting its attributes will help existing businesses as well as attract new ones. Look for signs of positive community attitudes by checking for any special tax breaks from the local government and low-interest loans for business start-ups or renovation of existing sites.

CHOOSING A SITE

According to SBA studies, poor location is among the chief causes of all business failures. In determining a site for a retail operation, you must be willing to pay for a good location. The cost of the location often reflects the volume and/or quality of the business you will generate. Never select a site merely because the facility is open and available or because the rent is low. Keep in mind that there is a direct correlation between low rent and high advertising expenses. Base your selection of a site on the market information you've obtained and the potential of the area to generate income for your company. Figure 4.2, Location Checklist, will help you choose a location.

The most important consideration for choosing a site for a service business is convenience for customers. Service businesses that deal directly with customers, like nail salons, travel agencies, and dry cleaners, do not need to locate in high-rent districts—they just need to be conveniently located on the beaten path and visible to their customers. Service businesses that are rarely visited by customers, like TV repair shops and pest control opera-

---

FIGURE 4.2   Location Checklist

Answer the following questions by indicating whether it is a strength (S) or weakness (W) of the potential site as it relates to your business. Once you have completed the checklist for each prospective location, compare their relative strengths and weaknesses to determine the value of each to the strategic success of your business.

Site Questionnaire	S	W
Is the facility large enough for your business?		
Does it meet your layout requirements?		
Does the building need any repairs?		
Will you have to make any leasehold improvements?		
Will you have to do any electrical, plumbing, or ventilation work?		
Is the facility easily accessible to your prospective clients or customers?		
Can you find a number of qualified employees in the area in which the facility is located?		
Is the facility consistent with the image you would like to project?		
Is the facility located in a safe neighborhood with a low crime rate?		
Are neighboring businesses likely to attract customers who will also patronize your business?		
Are there any competitors located close to the facility? If so, can you successfully compete with them?		
Can suppliers conveniently make deliveries to this location?		
If your business expands in the future, will the facility be able to accommodate this growth?		
Are the lease terms and rent favorable?		
Is the location zoned for your type of business?		

tors, can be farther afield. But these types of businesses have to make an ongoing effort to let customers know they're there—hence, the value of display advertising in the newspaper or Yellow Pages, for example.

Manufacturers will usually be restricted to industrial areas by the zoning ordinances of most towns and cities. The main criteria for manufacturers is the suitability of shipping and loading facilities, the distance to key suppliers of raw materials and markets, the availability of cheap fuel, and the skill of the support staff in the local area.

Like manufacturers, wholesalers are restricted by zoning laws within most cities. Their main criterion is proximity to local markets, since they don't want delivery to take too much time, especially if the product is perishable or costs too much. If costs in either time or money are eventually passed on to customers in the form of higher prices, customers could wind up looking for other suppliers.

SITE SELECTION FACTORS

You'll want to consider the following factors when searching for a location for your business.

Restrictive Ordinances

You may encounter unusually restrictive ordinances that detract from an otherwise ideal site, such as limitations on the hours of the day when trucks are permitted to load or unload. Cities and towns are composed of areas—from a few blocks to many acres in size—zoned for only commercial, industrial, or residential development. Within each zone are often further restrictions. A commercial zone may permit one type of business but not another, so make sure to check the zoning regulations of any potential location before pursuing a specific site or spending a lot of time and money on a market survey.

History of the Site

Learn about the recent history of each site you're considering before you make a final selection. There are sites—in malls and big shopping centers, as well as in independent locations—that have been occupied by a succession of businesses that failed. Businesses most often fail because of poor management, but sometimes choosing the wrong location is a factor. Find out how the site

you're considering affected the businesses of previous tenants or owners.

How Much Rent Your Business Can Afford to Pay

Your first-year profit-and-loss projections will tell you the amount of sales your business will most likely generate. To judge your rental expenses (leased space plus any add-on costs) relative to your sales, divide the total amount you expect to pay annually by net sales (gross sales minus returns and discounts). Multiply that number by 100 and compare the percentage with those of similar businesses to see how you'll fare.

Terms of the Lease

Occasionally, an otherwise ideal site may have unacceptable leasing terms. The time to negotiate leasing terms is before you sign the lease.

The Rent-Advertising Relationship

Your advertising budget is closely related to your choice of site and the proposed rent. Malls often allocate a lot of money to advertising, in addition to that spent by so-called "Big Box" and department stores. If you locate in a mall with big department "anchor" stores or have Staples as your neighbor, your cash register will likely be ringing up sales the first day you open your doors, with no advertising effort on your part. Of course, your rental expenses will be proportionately higher than those for an independent location.

Proximity to Other Businesses

Your business neighbors can influence your volume of business. Their presence can work for you as well as against you. Make sure your neighbors attract customers with a similar demographic profile as yours. For example, a shop selling upscale housewares isn't going to benefit by being in the same mall as the tattoo parlor and biker bar.

Anticipated Sales Volume

For some types of retailers, exclusivity is key when it comes to small shopping districts or malls—only one company offering a particular type of goods or services can successfully locate in each area without sparking an ongoing "whose-price-is-lowest" battle. Usually, there's not that much business to spread around. But if the foot traffic is high, if there's a strong market demand, and/or if the business sells a broad range of goods or services, there might be enough business to go around for everybody.

Accessibility to Prospective Customers

When determining accessibility, sit in your car and judge traffic patterns (both on foot and in cars) at different times of the day. Try to determine what hours your business needs to keep in order to be most convenient for customers. Revisit the site on different days to observe any changes in the pattern. Do some informal market research by interviewing people passing by the site you are considering. Do they feel a need for your type of business at this location? Would they patronize it? What kinds of goods or services would they be interested in buying? Where do they now shop for these goods and services?

Customer Parking Facilities

Does the site provide easy, adequate parking and access for customers? Is it well-lit? Is there sufficient security? What is the condition of the parking area? Will it need expansion, resurfacing or striping, possibly at additional cost to tenants? Keep in mind that even large shopping centers and business parks sometimes do not have adequate parking for all their customers. If you plan to locate in a mall or business park, evaluate the parking conditions over a period of days at different times and judge whether or not they are acceptable.

Which Side of the Street?

Market research has demonstrated that the "going-home" side of the street is usually preferable to the "going-to-work" side. People are more likely to stop at stores on the way home than when they are in a hurry to get to work on time. Also, the sunny side of the street is generally less desirable for retail operations than the shady side, especially in warm climates. Research shows that rents are higher on the shady side in high-priced shopping areas.

FACILITY CHOICES

The type of facility you choose depends on the kind of business you have. Ever notice how restaurants, clothing stores, and doctors' offices are usually located near other similar businesses or practices? That's no accident—it's smart marketing.

Shopping Centers

Retailers and service businesses that rely on a great deal of walk-in traffic and exposure often select shopping centers. These commercial centers house many different small businesses as well as one or more well-known chain stores that act as anchors and traffic generators. Shopping centers are generally managed by the developer, or a professional organization hired by the developer, and most of them require their business tenants to join the center's merchant association. Since the association is responsible for funding the marketing and maintenance of the center's common area, each tenant is expected to pay an additional fee beyond the rent in the lease. In fact, triple-net leases (see Chapter 7) are very popular among shopping center developers, as are percentage leases.

Of all the shopping centers, malls are probably the most expensive in terms of the rent, but they are also popular destinations for consumers. Malls can be totally enclosed multilevel buildings or open-air facilities.

If you manufacture retail goods, a factory outlet center offers an opportunity for a distribution channel where you deal directly with the end-user of your product(s). The main attraction of a factory outlet center for the end-user is better prices, usually 30 to 40 percent less than those of retailers. Rent can be high, however.

A strip center or mini-mall usually includes a major chain store and a supermarket as its anchor. Compared with malls, strip centers' rents are a bargain.

The main complaints from shopping center tenants relate to the high marketing and maintenance fees stipulated in the leases. For some small businesses, these expenses can gouge net profits. If you're seriously considering leasing space in a shopping center, determine the sales volume your business can reasonably hope to attain and decide what rent you can afford to pay.

Business Parks and Office Buildings

Professional and service businesses often find offices within a business park or office building appealing. Business parks are usually one or more office buildings located on the same lot and managed by the developer or a professional management company hired by the developer. Office space is commonly leased out on a triple-net basis with the tenants sharing the maintenance costs of the building. Many times, this maintenance cost will include service to tenants' offices as well as security.

The advantage of leasing office space in a business park is the professional image it projects. While image is only part of your promotional efforts in building relationships with your client base, it is the part that grabs your clients' attention first. And as the old saying goes, you never get a second chance to make a first impression.

If you'd like more information on business parks throughout the world, check out *Site Selection*, an online 'zine you can find at www.siteselection.com. As the official publication of the International Development Research Council, *Site Selection*'s November 2006 issue provided business climate rankings, while the July 2006 issue looked at military base re-developments.

Executive Suites

Executive suites lease office space and provide secretarial services to a number of very small—often one-person—businesses.

Executive suites provide tenants with short-term leases, generally six months to one year. Suites usually include a telephone, use of common areas (lobby, conference room, kitchen, etc.), a receptionist, and incoming mail receipt. Office utilities are usually included in the tenant's monthly rent, and a professional office manager runs the groups of suites. Tenants are offered a range of support services, including faxing, photocopying, and word processing, which they use and pay for on an as-needed basis. This arrangement helps control and minimize costs, which is especially important for start-up or fledgling businesses.

Freestanding Buildings

Freestanding locations can be beneficial for retailers, service-oriented companies, and restaurants. Typically, they offer a lower fixed rent (usually based on square footage), looser rules and regulations governing the operation of the business, and no extra advertising or common-area fees that must be paid to a merchants'

association. Another advantage is that dealing with an eager lessor may give a tenant more freedom to negotiate favorable leasing terms. However, the downside of locating a business in a freestanding building is that there's no one to share (and thus reduce) expenses for utilities, pest control, security, trash service, maintenance, and advertising.

Leasing Considerations

Occasionally, a site that is otherwise ideal may have to be ruled out because the terms of the lease are not right for your business. Remember that terms are negotiable, and the time to negotiate is before you sign the lease. For more information on leasing, see Chapter 7.

PHYSICAL PLANT REQUIREMENTS

Say you find the perfect location, but the present structure or lack thereof is incompatible with your requirements. Your choices are to either expand or remodel the building, build a new one, or look for another site. Whatever you do, the site and the building must be right for your business (remember what was said earlier about the importance of projecting a favorable image to your clients/customers).

Physical plant requirements will vary from business to business, based on a number of factors:

- Size of staff
- Storage requirements
- Sales floor or production area space
- Office space
- Parking requirements
- Projected growth
- Image

If You're a Retailer

Retailers have one overall goal: to sell merchandise. That's why they focus on sales floor space, adequate parking for customers, and an overall image that draws in customers. Of secondary interest to many retail operations are office space and storage requirements, since most inventory is on the sales floor.

A retail operation's space is usually subdivided among display, office, and storage. As a rule of thumb, office and storage spaces take up 10 to 25 percent of the total floor area. While the storage and office spaces are important parts of any retail operation—to handle shipping and receiving and related chores, to take care of paperwork, and to store extra inventory—you want to get the most out of all space that's not used for display and sales. Here's where good organizational skills come in handy, along with shelves and cabinets and anything else that helps you maximize your space. If you're not an organizer by nature, hire someone who is. Look in the Yellow Pages under "Organizing Services—Household and Business."

If You're Providing a Service

There's really no rule of thumb for service firms except that the physical plant needs to complement the volume and type of business conducted. For example, nail salons need a facility with an attractive waiting area, a sufficient number of workstations, and adequate parking for customers. There also has to be enough room to store products used in the business as well as a display area for products available to customers.

While nail salons require a physical plant built around the nature of their service to customers, other businesses, such as pool cleaning, need only limited office space for sales and clerical work and storage for chemicals and equipment. Since service firms vary depending on the nature of what they do, one thing all owners of service firms need to evaluate is current volume versus projected growth of business. You wouldn't want to locate in a facility so large that it dwarfs your staffing, storage, and service requirements for years to come. On the other hand, you wouldn't want to settle into a facility that you'll outgrow in six months. Taking time to plan and accurately forecast sales before you sign your lease on the dotted line will pay big dividends later, in terms of fewer hassles and headaches once your business is up and running.

If You're a Manufacturer

Each manufacturer has physical plant requirements specific to its product and manufacturing process. However, no matter what a business produces or how that product is made, all manufacturers' goals are to move materials with minimal effort, to have adequate office and storage space, to meet production deadlines, and to work safely.

To make certain your space maximizes efficiency, make sure you take these steps:

- Plan the shortest route from entrance to exit for materials and semi-finished product.
- Minimize handling by having as many operations as possible performed at each stop.
- Eliminate bottlenecks in production caused by the slowdown of processes at strategic locations. Location and condition of the machinery is a vital factor.
- Recognize that the misuse of space is as important as the misuse of machinery and human resources.
- Eliminate backtracking, overlapping of work, and unnecessary inspection by constantly evaluating the production process.

Management consultants can solve the more complicated problems of factory planning, but you can do a lot for yourself. First, prepare a route sheet for each standardized part or product you manufacture and/or for each job order you process, indicating the proper sequence of factory operations. By arranging equipment according to the sequence of operations, you eliminate backtracking, reduce materials handling, and streamline the flow of work.

See the Manufacturer's Site Planning Checklist (Figure 4.3) to assess the effectiveness of your site plan. Make sure to include storage facilities for raw materials and finished products, staffing requirements, office space for employees not on the production line, and any future expansion of operations.

If You're a Wholesaler

When it comes to facility design, wholesalers' biggest concern is being able to fill orders quickly and efficiently. This means paying close attention to space where merchandise is warehoused and orders are filled and offices where orders are received and processed. Typically, more than 60 percent of a wholesaler's operation is devoted to storage.

LEASES AND LEASING

Generally speaking, it's easier to build than remodel in order to meet specific physical plant requirements. But

| FIGURE 4.3 | Manufacturer's Site Planning Checklist |

When planning the layout of your manufacturing site, make sure you can move raw materials into the plant and process them through the manufacturing procedures as efficiently as possible. With this in mind, ask yourself the following questions.

❑ Does your receiving area provide easy access to large trucks?

❑ Is suitable equipment on hand in the receiving area to unload incoming shipments efficiently?

❑ Do you have enough space to adequately warehouse your raw materials inventory?

❑ Are your raw materials properly labeled in the warehouse area for easy retrieval?

❑ Is your warehouse space for raw material near the first station used in the manufacturing process?

❑ Have you planned out the steps in the manufacturing process and accounted for floor space for necessary equipment in appropriate areas so the product can be processed through each step without having to backtrack to other stations on the floor?

❑ Have you analyzed each station in the manufacturing process to assure equipment is arranged in the most efficient manner?

❑ Are you maximizing the potential of each station for performing as many tasks as possible in that area without creating a bottleneck?

❑ Is your finished product warehouse area located near the last station in the manufacturing process?

❑ Are there proper storage materials and equipment such as floor racks, slip sheets, and pallets to handle the finished product?

❑ Is there appropriate materials-handling equipment to move the finished product into storage and out once it is ready to ship?

❑ Is your shipping area in proximity to the warehouse area for the finished product?

❑ Is your shipping area easily accessible to large trucks?

new construction is also the most expensive way to achieve space needs. That's why most small businesses—especially young ones—are better off leasing a facility and altering the interior and exterior to meet their requirements. This reduces start-up costs and frees up cash for other expenses.

When you sign a lease for $2,000 a month for one year, you're agreeing to pay $24,000, regardless of what happens to your business. If your business is a relatively new one, you might be better served signing a shorter-term lease. If you're not sure what's best for your business, check with your CPA before having your lawyer review the lease prior to your signing on the dotted line.

A one- or two-year lease with an option to renew for five years at an agreed-upon rent is desirable for most beginning retailers. The option to renew protects the business owner from losing the lease at a good location and having to build the business from scratch at a new one.

It may not always be possible to rent space on a year-to-year or multiyear basis. But whatever you do, don't feel pressured to accept what's offered to you. There will always be another space somewhere else, one with better leasing terms that may be even better suited to your business.

A good lease, from a business owner's point of view, is one that can easily be assigned to another tenant in case you need to move or shut your doors. Therefore, make certain the lease you sign contains provision for assignment or subletting. Such a clause allows you to close or move your business and get another tenant for the balance of the lease's term. This clause also allows you to sell your business to a new owner who can assume your lease under the same good terms you have.

Leasehold Improvements

Leasehold improvements are non-removable interior installations that are either new construction or the result of remodeling. Depending on the condition of the physical plant and your requirements, leasehold improvements can amount to a substantial capital investment or a few hundred dollars.

The type of facility you have and its location (mall, strip shopping center, freestanding building) will determine how much you spend. Because the cost of improvements can vary tremendously, do your homework and get several estimates from reputable contractors. When established businesses face high leasehold-improvement costs, developers will sometimes finance a portion of them.

PURCHASING A SITE

Purchasing a facility offers a number of advantages over leasing:

- Lessees do not own their property, which reverts back to the owner when the lease is up.
- Both business owner and the business benefit when the land and building(s) appreciate.
- Property can be sold when the need arises. But lessors, on the other hand, sometimes have non-cancelable clauses in their leases or are charged a steep penalty for early termination.

There are also disadvantages of purchasing over leasing a facility:

- Purchasing may represent a higher monthly financial outlay than a lease, absorbing cash that could best be put to other uses.
- A hefty down payment may be required, anywhere from 10 to 30 percent of the purchase price.
- In the event of bankruptcy, creditors can attach owned property as an asset.
- Maintenance is the responsibility of the owner.
- In a depressed or tight real estate market, selling may be difficult or disadvantageous.
- If you've made major alterations to the property that are unique to your business, you may have difficulty selling to merchants in other industries or may have to reduce the selling price to compensate for necessary buyer renovations.

Methods of Purchasing

Whether to lease or buy is a multifaceted decision. But if your business requires a custom-built facility and your bankroll is not exactly the size of that of Bill Gates, there is another option to consider. You could negotiate a triple-net lease with a developer, who either buys the land and leases it back to you or buys the land and bankrolls the construction of the building, leasing the entire property back to you at a prearranged annual interest rate.

This arrangement reduces otherwise hefty front-end costs to a first-and-last-month payment but also reduces your autonomy, since the developer becomes, in effect, your silent partner. To make the triple-net lease work, some business owners negotiate a lease-purchase, with a balloon payment due at a specified time. This arrangement assures eventual ownership for the business owner while reducing his or her front-end costs.

Seller- or bank-financed purchases are more common, requiring up to 30 percent down and in some cases involving balloon payments. A typical bank-financed arrangement is 20 percent down, with the balance paid over a 15-year period. The cost of land and construction varies by type and region.

Among the ways to structure the purchase of property are:

- *Adjustable-rate mortgages (ARMs).* These come in many forms, but all have interest rates that vary according to the prevailing interest rates. Rate adjustments are limited by floor and ceiling caps, which help avoid extreme fluctuations in interest costs. Without ceiling caps, borrowers could run the risk of not being able to pay down the principal. Set up a worst-case scenario, in which interest rates skyrocket the day after you sign the loan. Are the payments still within the realm of your budget? If not, rethink your plan.
- *Fixed-rate mortgages.* These mortgages have payments that remain constant for the term of the loan. With a fixed-rate conventional mortgage, the bank absorbs the risk of a rising or falling prime lending rate.
- *Growing-equity mortgages (GEMs).* These are fixed-rate mortgages whose monthly payments increase

each year by a fixed increment, generally 3 percent. The mortgage is paid off faster, because the additional payments go directly toward reducing the principal.

- *Graduated-payment mortgages (GPMs).* These are one of the more popular flexible loans, from a lender's point of view. They operate on the basis of negative amortization: instead of your principal decreasing, it actually increases during the early years of the loan. The GPM is a fixed-rate loan with lower monthly payments during the first few years, usually five to ten years. Throughout the graduation period, the monthly payments increase slowly from year to year based on a schedule agreed on by the lender and borrower.

In short, if you're expecting to sell the property or business within three to five years and interest rates are trending downward, an adjustable-rate mortgage might be for you. If you're expecting to hold on to the property/business for more than five years and interest rates are hard to predict (they usually are), a fixed rate is probably a better choice. Ask your banker and CPA for their opinions on the type of mortgage that makes the most sense for your business.

SETTING UP YOUR OFFICE

Regardless of whether you rent or buy your space or where it's located, your office deserves special attention. Think about how much space you need now and in the near future and how accessible your office needs to be for clients and deliveries. Give careful consideration to what you want and need in your office.

Where to Locate Your Office

If your office is going to be at home, a spare bedroom, a formal dining room you use infrequently, or a corner of your basement that's well-lit and private could be converted to office space. Make your decision thoughtfully, as taking over any these spaces will affect how you and your family live, and how clients and customers feel about visiting your office.

Other options include redoing an attic or walk-in closet, using dividers or screens to partition a room, or getting a "mobile" office that closes up when you're not using

it. You can also create new space in a garage or on a porch or by building a loft, dormer, or separate building near the house. Work with a reputable, licensed architect and a general contractor who can build your office to code.

Even small spaces can be transformed into comfortable offices. Make the most of a small space by painting walls a light color, using wall-to-wall carpet instead of area rugs, choosing smaller pieces of furniture and keeping the space uncluttered.

Lighting

Lighting is always important in setting up an office. If you can, situate your office to take advantage of natural light. Diffuse northern light has always been artists' favorite, and it works for offices, too, as it minimizes glare on the computer screen.

Keep the light in your office balanced—arrange for overall light to fall evenly on all surfaces and add spot lighting where needed. To avoid casting shadows, place your lamp opposite the hand you write with.

Electrical

Make sure your office has enough power and outlets to run all your equipment. Check with an electrician if you think you might have to add a circuit.

Power surges, such as those caused by lightning strikes, can ruin computer memory circuits even if the computer is off. Plug your computer and fax machine into a surge protector that diverts power surges.

Air Quality

Your office should have an adequate supply of good, clean air with the right moisture content. If the air is too dry, your skin, lips, and nose will feel it. One trick to improve air quality is to have lots of green plants. NASA research determined that common houseplants like Gerbera daisies, pothos, and spider plants absorb toxins and significantly improve air quality.

Office Furniture

Select office furnishings based on your needs. Your goal is to create an environment that is comfortable, conducive to your productivity, and a boost to your business. A bad office design can not only thwart your productivity and creativity, it can also turn off customers and clients, which can ultimately depress your business profits.

Since you spend most of your time sitting at your desk, selecting a chair deserves special consideration. An improperly designed chair can cause leg swelling, muscle strain, and backache. It can also reduce blood circulation, which can not only cause varicose veins but also decreased blood flow to the brain and lethargy.

Choose a chair that's ergonomically designed and test it to see if it's right for you. Don't order one by mail order unless you've sat in it for at least five minutes. Your chair should offer:

- Adjustability from a seated position
- Upholstery that repels moisture and heat
- A seat that adjusts for height
- Padded backrests and support for the spine
- Padded armrests that feel comfortable against your bare skin
- Casters, smooth swiveling, and five wheels at the base.

If you're buying more than one chair, find one that's adjustable enough to fit most people in your office. This means that the chair is capable of supporting different positions, tasks, and body shapes.

You can buy mid- to high-end furniture from dealers, who usually offer a wide variety of designs. If you're on a tighter budget, you can buy direct from National Business Furniture (www.nationalbusinessfurniture. com) or Office Depot (www.officedepot.com). Without the added over-head of a showroom, direct vendors offer prices 20 to 40 percent lower than retail. Deals get even better when you purchase multiple chairs. However, with direct vendors you don't get to try out the chair before you buy. Superstores like Office Max (www. officemax.com) or Staples (www.staples.com) solve that problem, offer low prices, and usually provide immediate and free delivery.

Wherever you buy your chair or other office equipment, ask for a business discount of 10 to 30 percent off the suggested retail price. Don't overlook business liquidation, estate, and moving sales advertised in the classified section of your newspaper. Since furniture quickly depreciates in value, used furniture is often surprisingly affordable.

Equipment

Making choices about computers, printers, scanners, phones, fax machines, answering machines, cell phones, electronic organizers, and so on can be daunting. With new technology constantly generating new products, your best bet is to get informed—and stay that way.

Talk with people who use the equipment you're interested in, read magazines, shop the stores and catalogs, and get recommendations from user groups, friends, business associates, and so on. To find out more about specific equipment, visit www.buyerzone.com, a leading provider of advice on products for small to mid-sized businesses. *The Wall Street Journal's* technology columns are also helpful. Subscribe to the print edition by calling 1-800-JOURNAL. The online edition is available at http://online.wsj.com.

CHAPTER 5

The Legal Form of Your Business

For all start-ups and new business ventures, one of the most important decisions is the legal form of the business. It can operate as a sole proprietorship, general partnership, limited partnership, corporation, subchapter S corporation, and in some states, a limited liability company (LLC). Each type of entity has its advantages and disadvantages. For a general overview, see Table 5.1.

CHOOSE THE FORM THAT'S RIGHT FOR YOU

Whatever entity you choose for your business, pay careful attention to the documents and written agreements to make certain they protect you from any potential problems, including business failure and lawsuits. Your CPA and attorney can help you make the choice that's right for your business.

SOLE PROPRIETORSHIP

The simplest and most common business form is the sole proprietorship. In fact, if you are the sole owner of your business, you automatically end up as a sole proprietor if you do not establish another business structure. In terms of taxes, sole proprietors, unlike other forms of business, do not file

separate income tax returns—they file a Schedule C for their business with their personal tax returns. Also, FICA (Federal Insurance Contributions Act) taxes for sole proprietor are less than those of partnerships and corporations.

To establish a sole proprietorship, you need to secure a business license, if required, from the city or county where your business will be headquartered.

If you open additional locations in different cities, towns, or counties, you may have to get a business license from each jurisdiction that requires one. Even if you don't maintain a physical location in another city or county but do business within that jurisdiction, you may still have to obtain a business license for that area to legally conduct your business. Call the licensing division of each city or town where you plan to conduct business, as well as the county registrar, to determine the licensing requirements relevant to your business.

In addition to a business license, you'll also need a federal and state I.D. number if you plan to hire employees or if the entities you plan to do business with require one. (The federal employer identification number is secured by filing a form

TABLE 5.1 Legal Forms for Businesses

Control	Liability	Tax	Continuity
Sole Proprietorship Owner maintains complete control over the business.	Owner is solely liable. His or her personal assets are liable in any legal case.	Owner reports all income and expenses on personal tax return.	Business terminates upon owner's death or withdrawal. Owner can sell the business but will no longer remain the proprietor.
General Partnership Each partner has the authority to enter into contracts and make other business decisions, unless the partnership agreement stipulates otherwise.	Each partner is liable for all business debts.	Each partner reports partnership income on individual tax return. The business does not pay any taxes as its own entity.	Unless the partnership agreement makes other provisions, a partnership dissolves upon death or withdrawal of a partner.
Limited Partnership General partners control the business.	General partners are personally responsible for partnership liabilities. Limited partners are liable for the amount of their investment.	Partnership files annual taxes. Limited and general partners report their share of partnership income or loss on their individual returns.	Death of limited partner does not dissolve business, but death of general partner might, unless the partnership agreement makes other provisions.
Limited Liability Company (LLC) Owner or partners have authority.	Partners are not liable for business debts.	Partners report income and income tax on their individual tax returns. The LLC can elect to be taxed as a partnership, corporation, subchapter S, or sole proprietorship if the company is a single member LLC.	Different states have different laws regarding the continuity of LLCs. In some states, LLCs dissolve upon death or withdrawal of an owner.
Corporation Shareholders appoint board of directors, which appoints officers, who hold the highest authority.	Shareholders generally are responsible for the amount of their investment in corporate stock.	Corporation pays its own taxes. Shareholders pay tax on their dividends.	The corporation is its own legal entity and can survive the deaths of owners, partners, and shareholders.
Subchapter S Shareholders appoint the board of directors, which appoints officers, who hold the highest authority.	Shareholders generally are responsible for the amount of their investment in corporate stock.	Shareholders report their shares of corporate profit or loss on their individual tax returns.	The corporation is its own legal entity and can survive the death of owners, partners, and shareholders.

SS-5 with the Internal Revenue Service.) If you operate a business that uses a name other than your own, you'll have to file a fictitious business name statement so that the public knows that you're the owner of that business.

To file taxes as a sole proprietor, report all your income and expenses on Schedule C or C-EZ of IRS Form 1050. (Schedule C—the long form for sole proprietors—must be filled out if you have expenses greater than $2,500.) You must also pay self-employment taxes on your tax return, since there's no withholding from your earnings.

As a sole proprietor, all your personal assets are subject to any legal liabilities you might encounter while operating the business. To guard against potential lawsuits from your customers, make sure to get liability insurance coverage. If you manufacture or sell products, you'll need product liability insurance. Even if you're not at fault, you can still be sued, and insurance usually covers attorneys' costs to defend you in a lawsuit. Your insurance agent can help you determine the right kind of coverage you need.

GENERAL PARTNERSHIP

A business owned by you and others is considered a partnership. Choosing a partner (or partners) is like choosing a husband or wife; it is one of the most important decisions you'll ever make. Proceed with caution and consider these factors to ensure a good and harmonious working relationship.

- Explicitly state each partner's responsibilities to prevent any misunderstandings. Never assume everyone knows who will do what.
- Negotiate a buy-sell agreement early on, in case one partner decides to sell out at some later date.
- Have "key person" insurance coverage. In case you or your partner dies, a "key person" insurance policy provides the surviving partner with funds to buy the deceased partner's share of the business from his or her heirs.
- Work with experts—a CPA, lawyer, banker, other business consultants—when necessary.

A written agreement specifying the relationship between and functions of the partners will help minimize conflicts or prevent problems in the event the partners find they cannot work well together. Although you can purchase the software or forms necessary for a partnership contract, it's always wise to consult with your attorney. He or she has the experience and expertise to foresee questions and raise issues that neither you nor your partner had thought of.

A general partnership agreement should cover all the possible business situations that the partners may encounter and provide resolutions for any problems that may arise. Like marriages, more than half of all business partnerships break up after one to three years due to disputes between partners. To avoid conflicts, communicate clearly and make sure your partnership agreement covers the following:

- Capital contributions of the partners
- Profit and loss sharing of the partners
- Voting rights of the partners
- Delegation of management authority to the partners
- Disposition of a partner's share upon the death of that person
- Methods to resolve possible tie votes between partners on crucial partnership decisions
- The addition of new partners
- Signature authority and number of signatures on partnership bank accounts
- Option to purchase a selling partner's interest and a method to determine the value of that interest

A general partnership under most state laws automatically dissolves upon the death of a partner or if more than 50 percent of the partnership interests changes hands. Partnership law is complex. Therefore, work with an attorney who can help you avoid future problems that could cost many times the attorney's legal fees. Figure 5.1 shows a standard partnership agreement.

In a general partnership, any partner may legally bind the partnership to a contract (unless there are restrictions stating otherwise), and each partner is liable for any and all debts the partnership incurs. In any lawsuit or creditor action, each partner will be sued personally, with the property and bank accounts of each attached. If one partner skips town, the others are left responsible. When a person contributes assets to a partnership, he or she no longer owns them outright but rather acquires an ownership share of them based on his or her equity in the firm.

FIGURE 5.1	Partnership Agreement Form

Date _____

Effective from _____

Effective until _____

Location _____

This partnership agreement Is made on this _____ day of _____ 20____ between the individuals listed below:

_____

_____

The partners listed above hereby agree that they shall be considered partners in business upon the commencement date of this partnership agreement for the following purpose:

_____

_____

The terms and conditions of this partnership are as follows:

1. The NAME of the partnership shall be: _____

2. The PRINCIPAL PLACE OF BUSINESS of the partnership shall be: _____

3. The CAPITAL CONTRIBUTION of each partner to the partnership shall consist of the following property, services, or cash to which each partner agrees to contribute:

Name of Partner	Capital Contribution	Agreed upon Cash Value	% Share

Furthermore, the PROFITS AND LOSSES of the partnership shall be divided by the partners according to a mutually agreeable schedule and at the end of each calendar year according to the proportions listed above.

4. Each partner shall have equal rights to MANAGE AND CONTROL the partnership and its business. Should there be differences between the partners concerning ordinary business matters, a decision shall be made by unanimous vote. It is understood that the partners may elect one of the partners to conduct day-to-day business of the partnership; however, no partner shall be able to bind the partnership by act or contract to any liability exceeding $_____ without the prior written consent of each partner.

5. In the event a partner WITHDRAWS from the partnership for any reason, including death, the remaining partners may continue to operate the partnership using the same name. The withdrawing partner shall be obligated to sell his or her interest in the partnership. No partner shall TRANSFER interest in the partnership to any other party without the written consent of each partner.

6. Should the partnership be TERMINATED by unanimous vote, the assets and cash of the partnership shall be used to pay all creditors with the remaining amounts to be distributed to the partners according to their proportionate share.

7. Any DISPUTES arising between the partners as a result of this agreement shall be settled by voluntary mediation. Should mediation fail to resolve the dispute, it shall be settled by binding arbitration.

In the witness whereof, this PARTNERSHIP AGREEMENT has been signed by the partners on the day and year listed above.

_____
Partner

_____
Partner

_____
Partner

_____
Partner

If the partnership operates under a fictitious name, it will have to file a fictitious business name statement. If the partnership has physical locations in more than one jurisdiction, it will need the appropriate business license or licenses and must apply for a federal Employee Identification Number (EIN) from the Internal Revenue Service using Form SS-5.

Generally, all partnerships must operate using a calendar year and file Form 1065 with the IRS to report partnership income and expenses. That includes Form H-1 to report each partner's share of the income or loss; however, the partnership does not pay any taxes with its tax return. Instead, each partner reports his or her share of annual partnership income on Form 1050 using Schedule K-1.

LIMITED PARTNERSHIP

A limited partnership is similar to a general partnership except that it has two classes of partners. The general partner(s) has (have) full control of the partnership business but also accept full personal responsibility for partnership liabilities. Limited partners have no personal liability beyond their investment in the partnership. Limited partners cannot participate in the general management and daily operations of the partnership business without being considered general partners in the eyes of the law.

The general partner can be either an individual or a corporation. One of the more common limited partnership situations involves a silent partner, where one or more limited partners provide financing for the venture and the general partners run the business. A limited partnership in this case protects the assets of silent partners by limiting their exposure and liability, and acts as a conduit to pass current operating profits or losses on to them.

Most jurisdictions require limited partnership agreements to be in writing and, for the most part, contain the same provisions as those in a general partnership agreement—with some complex additions. Legal costs of forming a limited partnership can be even higher than for a corporation because in some states they are governed by securities laws.

Another aspect of limited partnerships is that in some businesses, the limited partner (also called the passive investor) may be subject to special tax liabilities that can offset the tax shelter advantages. The IRS tends to look at these on a case-by-case basis.

Limited partnerships file an IRS Form 1065 once a year. Individual limited and general partners include their allocable share of partnership income or loss on their individual income tax returns and pay taxes on that share based on their tax bracket. Partners cannot deduct losses greater than their basis in the partnership, which includes their investment plus any funds loaned to the partnership (except for real estate limited partnerships that are governed by special rules).

The 1986 Tax Reform Act limited the amount of losses a limited partner can deduct on a personal tax return. If the partnership is expected to generate tax losses in its early years, your CPA can help determine whether those losses will benefit you.

LIMITED LIABILITY COMPANIES

A limited liability company (LLC) is a relatively new business structure—legislation enabling them was enacted in 1993 and 1994—that combines the best of all worlds for its members (owners of an LLC are called "members" rather than partners or shareholders). Like a corporation, LLCs are a separate legal entity whose members are not liable for its debts or actions. Like a partnership, an LLC's profits or losses flow through the company to the individual members, avoiding the double whammy of paying both corporate and individual taxes. And like a sole proprietorship, an LLC is not required by law to hold meetings and keep minutes.

LLCs are now allowed in all fifty states. Setting one up involves a little more work than establishing a sole proprietorship but is a lot less involved than forming a corporation. To start an LLC, work with your CPA and attorney to:

- *File articles of organization* with the Secretary of State and pay the necessary fee.

- *Draft the operating agreement.* Although not every state requires LLCs to have an operating agreement, it will help your LLC define its ownership, management, profit sharing, and other aspects of running the business.

LLCs offer advantages to small business owners in many circumstances, particularly for those involved in real estate or venture capital projects. It's easy to admit new members to an LLC and unlike a Sub S corporation there are no limits on how many an LLC may have.

CORPORATIONS

A corporate structure is perhaps the most advantageous way to start a business because the corporation exists as a separate entity. In general, a corporation has all the legal rights of an individual, except for the right to vote and certain other limitations. Corporations are given the right to exist by the state that issues their charter. If you incorporate in one state to take advantage of liberal corporate laws but do business in another state, you will have to file for "qualification" in the state in which you wish to operate the business. There is usually a fee that must be paid to qualify to do business in a state.

You can incorporate your business by filing articles of incorporation with the appropriate agency in your state. Usually, only one corporation can have any given name in each state. After incorporation, stock is issued to the company's shareholders in exchange for the cash or other assets they transfer to it in return for that stock. Once a year, the shareholders elect the board of directors, who meet to discuss and guide corporate affairs anywhere from once a month to once a year.

Each year, the directors elect officers such as a president, secretary, and treasurer to conduct the day-to-day affairs of the corporate business. There also may be additional officers, such as vice presidents, if the directors so decide. Along with the articles of incorporation, the directors and shareholders usually adopt corporate bylaws that govern the powers and authority of the directors, officers, and shareholders.

Even small, private, professional corporations, such as a legal or dental practice, need to adhere to the principles that govern a corporation. For instance, upon incorporation, common stock needs to be distributed to the shareholders and a board of directors elected. If there is only one person forming the corporation, that person is the sole shareholder of stock in the corporation and can elect him- or herself to the board of directors as well as any other individuals he or she deems appropriate.

Corporations, if properly formed, capitalized, and operated (including appropriate annual meetings of

shareholders and directors) limit the liability of their shareholders. Even if the corporation is not successful or is held liable for damages in a lawsuit, the most a shareholder can lose is his or her investment in the stock. The shareholder's personal assets are not on the line for corporate liabilities.

Corporations file Form 1120 with the IRS and pay their own taxes. Salaries paid to shareholders who are employees of the corporation are deductible. But dividends paid to shareholders are not deductible and therefore do not reduce the corporation's tax liability. A corporation must end its tax year on December 31 if it derives its income primarily from personal services (such as dental care, legal counseling, business consulting, etc.) provided by its shareholders.

If the corporation is small, the shareholders should prepare and sign a shareholders buy-sell agreement. This contract provides that if a shareholder dies or wants to sell his or her stock, it must first be offered to the surviving shareholders. It also may provide for a method to determine the fair price that should be paid for those shares. Such agreements are usually funded with life insurance to purchase the stock of deceased shareholders.

If a corporation is large and sells its shares to many individuals, it may have to register with the Securities and Exchange Commission (SEC) or state regulatory bodies. More common is the corporation with only a few shareholders, which can issue its shares without any such registration under private offering exemptions. For a small corporation, responsibilities of the shareholders can be defined in the corporate minutes, and a shareholder who wants to leave can be accommodated without many legal hassles. Also, until a small corporation has operated successfully for many years, the business owner will most likely still have to accept personal liability for any loans made by banks or other lenders to the corporation.

While some people feel that a corporation enhances the image of a small business, one disadvantage is the potential double taxation: The corporation must pay taxes on its net income, and shareholders must also pay taxes on any dividends received from the corporation.

Business owners often increase their own salaries to reduce or wipe out corporate profits and thereby lower the possibility of having those profits taxed twice—once to the corporation and again to the shareholders upon receipt of dividends from the corporation.

SUBCHAPTER S CORPORATIONS

A Subchapter S corporate structure makes sense for many closely held businesses. Instead of profits being taxed twice as they are with regular C corporations (once at the corporate level and again as dividends when they're distributed to shareholders), profits flow through the S corporations and are taxed once, at the personal tax rate. Subchapter S corporations offer advantages to new business owners with income from other sources, which can be offset by business deductions to reduce the individual's overall federal tax liability. Take note, however, that some states do not recognize a Subchapter S election for state tax purposes and will tax Subchapter S earnings at the regular corporate rate.

To qualify under Subchapter S, the corporation must:

- Be incorporated within the United States;
- Not be part of an affiliated group that can file a consolidated tax return;
- Have fewer than 100 shareholders;
- Have shareholders who are individuals, estates, or certain types of trusts; and
- Have only one class of outstanding stock.

For more information on the rules that apply to a Subchapter S corporation, ask your CPA.

Forming a Corporation

A corporation's structure consists of the following three components:

1. *Shareholders.* These individuals hold stock in the company. The shareholders generally are not involved in the corporation's day-to-day operation but are responsible for electing the board of directors and removing them from office. In smaller corporations, the shareholders can give themselves more operational powers by including provisions in the articles and bylaws of the corporation.
2. *Directors.* These people are responsible for management of the corporation. The board of directors' legal authority over the corporation extends to all decisions concerning policy, personnel, compensa-

tion, delegation of authority, declaration of dividends and the general supervision over all corporate activities.
3. *Officers.* Selected by the board of directors to carry out the day-to-day operations of the business, officers can be directors as well, as is the case in small corporations. Officers—typically with the titles president, vice-president, secretary, and treasurer—are frequently the most powerful group in the corporation.

Before actually filing with the state in which you wish to incorporate your business, make sure you've thought carefully about corporate structure. Who are the best people to serve on your board and who would make the best officers? A good tactic for smaller companies is to name trusted advisors who are willing to volunteer their services as officers and board members.

Pre-Incorporation Decisions

Once you've made your decisions regarding your board, think about entering into a pre-incorporation agreement so all participants know the roles they'll play in the corporation. A sample Pre-Incorporation Agreement Form is shown in Figure 5.2, but make sure to consult with your attorney before executing such an agreement. These pre-incorporation agreements generally cover

- Who will serve on the board of directors
- Who will purchase the different types of stock in the corporation, in what amounts, and for how much
- Documents that have already been drafted prior to incorporation, such as lease agreements, equipment rental, inventory purchases, and so on. Any documents already drafted by the individuals organizing the corporation will be adopted once the first board of directors is formed.

Pre-incorporation agreements with third parties are usually made between the organizers of the business and the third party. As a result, the organizers of the business are usually liable for provisions in the contract, unless otherwise stipulated through a written contract signed on behalf of the prospective corporation. A contract of this nature usually addresses the:

FIGURE 5.2	Pre-Incorporation Agreement Form

Agreement made this _____ day of _____ 20_____ between _____, _____, _____.

WHEREAS the parties hereto wish to organize a corporation upon the terms and conditions hereinafter set forth; and

WHEREAS the parties wish to establish their mutual rights and responsibilities in relation to their organizational activities;

Now, THEREFORE, in consideration of the premises and mutual covenants contained herein, it is agreed by and between the parties as follow:

FIRST: The parties will forthwith cause a corporation to be formed and organized under the laws of _____.

SECOND: The proposed Articles of Incorporation shall be attached hereto as Exhibit A.

THIRD: Within seven days after the issuance of the corporation's certificate of incorporation, the parties agree that the corporation's authorized stock shall be distributed, and consideration paid, as follows:

1. _____ shares of _____ (insert common or preferred) stock shall be issued to _____ in consideration of his/her payment to the corporation of $_____ cash.

2. _____ shares of stock shall be issued to _____ in consideration of his/her transfer to the corporation of _____ (list property, real or personal, to be transferred).

3. _____ shares of stock shall be issued to _____ in consideration of his transfer to the corporation of _____ .

4. ...etc...

FOURTH: The corporation shall employ _____ as its manager for a term of _____ years and at a salary of $_____ per annum, such employment not to be terminated without cause and such salary not to be increased or decreased without the approval of _____% of the directors.

FIFTH: The parties agree not to transfer, sell, assign, pledge, or otherwise dispose of their shares until they have first offered them for sale to the corporation, and then should the corporation refuse such offer, to the other shareholders on a pro rata basis. The shares shall be offered at their book value to the corporation, and in the event the corporation refuses, the other shareholders shall have thirty (30) days to purchase the shares. If the corporation or other shareholders do not purchase all the offered shares, the remaining shares may be freely transferred by their owner without price restrictions.

SIXTH: The parties to this agreement promise to use their best efforts to incorporate the organization and to commence its business.

_____

_____

_____

- scope of the potential liability,
- rights and obligations under the contract for both organizers of the corporation and the corporation once it is formed,
- provisions should the corporation never be formed,
- provisions for declining the contract once the corporation is formed, and
- a disclaimer of any implied agreements.

When forming such a contract, you must work with your lawyer.

Other Things to Consider Before Incorporation

The defining characteristics of a corporation are that it:

- files a charter or articles of incorporation in a state,
- prepares bylaws,
- has its business affairs overseen by a board of directors, and
- issues stock.

When incorporating your business, choose your name carefully. It cannot resemble the name of an existing corporation in your state, nor can it inaccurately describe what the corporation does. Choosing a name for your corporation is also one of the most important marketing decisions you'll make. It should say what your business does and speak to customers' needs. Avoid names that are vague or misleading, forgettable, or hard to pronounce.

In addition, the name of the corporation must include one of the following words:

- Corporation
- Company
- Incorporated
- Limited

Having one of these terms in the corporate name is required. It signals that the business is a legal entity and therefore the firm, not the officers managing it, is responsible for all its debts and actions.

If you've chosen a name for your corporation and want to reserve it, or if you want to check on the validity of the name, file an application for reservation of corporate name with the state where you wish to incorporate.

The state will then notify you as to whether the name is available. If it is, it will be held for 120 days.

Once you're ready to incorporate, file the articles of incorporation with the secretary of state. The articles need to be signed by one of the individuals forming the corporation and sent in duplicate along with the filing fee to the secretary of state.

To determine the filing fee for the articles of incorporation, check your state's statute or call the secretary of state. In addition to the filing fee, most states also impose a fee for each authorized share of stock that is issued.

Once the state receives the articles of incorporation, processing them generally takes several weeks. When the articles of incorporation have been accepted, the state will issue a certificate of incorporation.

FICTITIOUS NAME

Sole proprietorships and partnerships have the option of choosing distinct names for their businesses. If you want to operate your business under a name different from your personal name (e.g., John Doe doing business as [d/b/a] "The Butler's Pantry"), you may be required by the county, city, or state to register your fictitious name.

Procedures for this vary. In many states, you need only go to the county offices, fill out a fictitious business name statement, and pay a registration fee to the county clerk. Other states require placing a fictitious name ad in a local newspaper. In some cases, the newspaper that prints the legal notice for your business name will file the necessary papers with the county for a small fee.

The easiest way to determine the procedure for your area is to call your bank and ask if it requires a fictitious name registry or certificate to open a business account. If so, ask where to go to get one.

Fictitious name filings do not apply to corporations in most states unless the corporation is doing business under a name other than its own. Documents of incorporation have the same effect for the corporate business as fictitious name filings have for sole proprietorships and partnerships.

CHAPTER 6

Licensing

Although some business owners think that licensing and permit fees are ways for the government to wring even more money from the business sector, most of these programs are intended to protect the general public. In big cities, license bureaus are set up to control business locations—to keep people from operating an auto-repair business next door to a home, or to keep people from running certain types of businesses from their homes. For example, most states forbid certain things from being manufactured in the home, such as fireworks, drugs, poisons, explosives, and medical products.

Failure to comply with the licensing and permit requirements for the type of business you plan to start in your jurisdiction could result in additional fees, penalty payments, or operational restrictions until conditions specified by the regulating authority have been met. So no matter what you think of the licensing process, don't neglect it!

LICENSES YOUR BUSINESS NEEDS

Most small business owners require only a local business license, which allows the business to operate within the city and county where it is located. This business license is either a municipal license, if your business is located within a city, or a county license, if you're located in an unincorporated area of the county. If you intend to open multiple locations or conduct business in different cities or counties, you'll need to apply for a license in each of those jurisdictions.

Operating some types of businesses may require state as well as federal licensing. For example, if your business is food-related, you'll have to deal with local health officials and state regulations. If your state has a "commercial kitchen" law, it may be extremely difficult to set up a food-related business in your home. If your business releases materials into the air and water, you'll have to get approval from your local environmental protection agency. Certain professionals, like accountants and cosmetologists, need occupational licenses from the state agency that administers consumer affairs. If you plan to work with flammable or dangerous materials, you'll need approval from your fire department.

The Business License

Some cities and counties don't require a business to obtain a license, while others collect a business-licensing fee on an annual basis. In addition to the license fee, some cities receive a percentage of a business' gross sales as well as sales taxes if the business is required to collect them.

Before visiting city hall or the county administrative building, call the licensing bureau of the city you plan to operate in or the county registrar's or recorder's office to find out about their licensing requirements and application procedure. This will save you time because you can have all the necessary materials ready prior to applying for your license.

Your application will be checked by the planning or zoning department to make sure that the zone covering your property allows the use you're proposing and that there are enough parking places to meet the code. You should not encounter many problems if you're opening your business in an existing structure that previously housed a similar business. You will not be allowed to operate in an area that is not zoned for your business unless you first have a variance or conditional-use permit (explained under "Zoning Ordinances" later in this chapter).

County Licenses

If you locate in an unincorporated area of the county, you'll need a county business license instead of a municipal license. In addition to county business licenses, sole proprietors and partnerships that choose to operate under a fictitious name will usually be required to file a fictitious business name statement (see Chapter 5 for more information on fictitious business name statements).

State Licenses

Many states require a license or occupational permit for people engaged in certain occupations. Often, these people must pass state examinations before they can conduct business. Licensing is commonly required for auto mechanics, plumbers, electricians, building contractors, collection agents, insurance agents, real-estate brokers, and workers providing services to the human body (barbers, cosmetologists, doctors, nurses, funeral directors, etc.) Some states have licensing requirements based on the product sold, such as liquor, lottery tickets, gasoline, or firearms. Your state government can provide a com-

plete list of occupations for which licensing is required in its jurisdiction.

If the state you operate your business in has a state income tax, you'll have to register and obtain an employer identification number from your state Department of Revenue or Treasury Department. If your business sells retail, you'll need a sales tax license.

Finally, if you have employees, you're responsible for withholding income and Social Security taxes, and complying with minimum wage and employee health and safety laws. Contact your State Department of Employment Security for information on employment law and state unemployment tax requirements. You'll also need information on workers' compensation insurance, which you purchase from your local insurance agent.

Federal Licenses

For information on federal government requirements and services for businesses, see U.S. Business Advisor (www.business.gov), an internet service for entrepreneurs run by the Small Business Administration (SBA). Through its Business Law Center, you can get information on both federal and state requirements for licenses and permits, as well as guides and forms for applying for government-backed loans and other federal assistance. You can also call up economic reports and journals, and get information about starting a company and recent news from dozens of federal agencies.

Although most businesses don't require a federal license or permit, these do:

- Investment advising
- Drug manufacturing
- Preparation of meat products
- Broadcasting
- Ground transportation
- Selling alcohol, tobacco, or firearms

Federal regulations also pertain to the registration of intellectual property, including patents, trademarks, trade names, and copyright. This is to provide the business owner with exclusive use of that intellectual property in the U.S., as well as a large number of foreign countries.

Finally, if your company is not a sole proprietorship and you have employees, you'll have to apply for a federal

Employer Identification Number (EIN) from the IRS. You can visit the IRS web site (www.irs.gov) and download the application form and instructions from there.

BUSINESS PERMITS

Along with licenses mentioned above, you may need to obtain some of the following permits, depending upon your business, to show compliance with local and state laws regulating structural appearances and safety as well as the sale of products.

The Seller's Permit

If you'll be buying merchandise for resale in a state that collects sales tax, you'll need a resale tax number, also called a seller's permit. Suppliers you buy from will want your number for their files; if you sell to dealers, get their numbers for your files. That way you have a record on why you haven't collected tax on a sale, which is only collected on sales to the final user in your state. If you sell to someone in another state, you're not required to collect taxes for that state—only the ones in which you maintain offices or stores. If you sell to dealers who don't have a tax number, you'll have to charge them sales tax on their purchases.

Where and how do you get such a permit? Agencies issuing permits vary from state to state; generally the State Sales Tax Commission or the Franchise Tax Board has this responsibility. Contact the entity that governs taxes in your state and apply for your resale tax or wholesale permit. You'll have to provide documentation that proves you're a retailer—make sure to ask what's acceptable.

Health Department Permit

If you sell food, you'll need a county health department permit. The health department will want to inspect your facilities before issuing the permit. The fee for such a permit depends on the size of your operation and how much equipment you have.

Liquor, Wine, and Beer Licenses

In most states, one type of license is required to serve wine and beer and another, which is more difficult to obtain, to serve hard liquor. In some areas, no new liquor licenses are being issued at all—you can obtain one only by buying it from the present license holder. Although the original license may have cost less than $100, competition has sometimes forced the going price to anywhere from $2,000 to $10,000 or more, depending on the location.

An advantage of buying a restaurant that has served liquor is the possibility of acquiring the existing license as part of the deal. Typically, the rules will require filing an application with the state beverage control board, then posting notice on the premises of your intent to dispense liquor.

In some states, the beverage control board requires holders of liquor licenses to keep all purchase records for a specified number of years, during which time they are subject to inspection by the control board and/or the Internal Revenue Service.

Under most circumstances, a license to serve wine and beer with meals is much easier to obtain than a hard-liquor license. Beer-and-wine licenses are usually issued for periods of one year and are easily renewable if you haven't committed any offenses, such as selling to minors. The white pages of your phone directory will have the number for the nearest beverage-control agency, which can supply you with the information you need.

Fire Department Permits

Many fire departments require businesses to obtain a permit if they use any flammable materials or if customers or the public occupy the premises at large. In some cities, you must secure a permit before you open for business. Other jurisdictions do not require a permit; instead, they conduct periodic inspections of the premises for compliance. If you are not in compliance, the fire department will issue a citation. Theaters, restaurants, clubs, bars, retirement homes, day-care centers, and schools are businesses subject to especially close and frequent scrutiny by the fire department.

Air and Water Pollution Control Permits

Many cities now have departments that supervise the control of air and water pollution. If you burn any material, discharge anything into the sewers or waterways, or use gas-producing products (such as paint sprayers), you may be required to obtain a special permit from this department of your city or county.

Environmental-protection regulations may require you to obtain approval before construction or operation. Check with your state agency regarding federal or state regulations that may apply to your business.

Sign Permits

Many cities and suburbs have sign ordinances that restrict the size, location, and sometimes the lighting and type of sign used. Landlords may also impose their own restrictions; these are likely to be most stringent in a mall. To avoid costly mistakes, be sure to check regulations and secure the written approval of your landlord before you invest in a sign.

ZONING ORDINANCES

If you want to legitimately run your business from home, find out what the zoning ordinances are for your area. Go to your city or town hall and ask for a copy of its zoning regulations. You don't have to explain why you want to see them—it's your right to have access. Look for the section on home-based businesses and carefully read it. If your business operates in violation of zoning regulations, you could be fined or closed down. Certain products cannot be produced in the home. Make sure you're in compliance.

Once you know how your area is zoned, you can get a good idea of whether your planned business is permitted or prohibited. Whatever your conclusion is, consult an attorney who'll be able to interpret the fine points of the ordinance. There is often a substantial difference between what an ordinance says and the way it is enforced.

If you locate your business in a structure previously used for commercial purposes, zoning regulations in most cases will not be a problem. If you're constructing a new facility, acquiring an existing building for a different purpose than its original use, or undertaking an expensive remodeling, carefully check the local building and zoning codes. If zoning regulations do not allow operation of the type of business you wish to open, you may file for a zoning variance, a conditional-use permit, or a zone change.

A variance or conditional-use permit grants you the privilege (conditionally) of operating a business on land not zoned for that purpose. The filing fee varies greatly from a few hundred to several thousand dollars, depending on the municipality or jurisdiction, and it may take several weeks before you get a decision. A zone change, on the other hand, amounts to a permanent difference in the way a particular area is zoned, and therefore in the way it will be used long into the future. It involves a lengthy procedure—it usually takes several months—of filing a petition with the city planning commission, issuing notice, presenting your case at public hearings, and finally getting the city council or other governing body to make a decision.

In some cases, any change in land use, whether permanent (by zone change) or temporary (by variance or conditional-use permit) requires environmental clearance. Local planning or zoning departments can tell you whether your project is exempt from the law or whether you should seek a negative declaration from its regulations. If your project will displace residents, generate a lot of traffic, or affect natural habitat, some municipalities will require you to prepare an environmental-impact report. This can be a costly and time-consuming procedure for which you'll need expert help.

If your request for a zoning variance or change is approved, many restrictions still apply. In addition to meeting local building codes, you will probably be required to observe minimum setbacks at the front, side, and rear of the structure; maximum floor space in relation to land area; maximum heights; minimum provisions for parking; and other factors. You need to get detailed, specific information from your city or town government, since policies vary from place to place.

Essentially, zoning ensures that the community's land uses are properly located in relation to one another; that adequate space is available for each type of development; that the density of development in each area is in proper proportion to the development of streets, schools, recreational areas and utility systems; and that the development is sufficiently open to permit light, air, and privacy for persons living and working within the area.

OTHER REGULATIONS

In addition to licenses and permits, other regulations may apply to your business. Federal and state laws designed to encourage competition forbid practices such as contracts, combinations, and conspiracies that restrain trade. These laws prohibit discrimination in price between different purchasers of commodities similar in grade and quality that may injure competition, and they forbid "unfair" methods of competition and "unfair or deceptive practices."

The term "deceptive practices" refers to false advertising, misrepresentation, imitation of competitive products, and bad-mouthing competitors. Even with violations by a manufacturer or distributor, a retailer may be considered equally guilty if he or she knowingly accepts an illegal concession offered by the vendor.

Any firm conducting business across state lines is subject to Federal Trade Commission (FTC) regulations, as is any business that advertises in more than one state. Even the smallest mail-order business comes under FTC jurisdiction.

A fairly common statute forbids the sale of any article at less than the seller's cost if the intent is to injure competitors. Other laws deal with bait-and-switch selling, withholding appropriate refunds on deposits made by customers, misrepresenting warranties and guarantees, and quality requirements for certain products. For more information, see the FTC web site at www.ftc.gov.

CHAPTER 7

Leasing

A new or growing small business needs the right amount of operating capital—and the know-how to use those funds most efficiently. Investing a big chunk of cash in equipment, vehicles, or a building can drain capital from product or service development, marketing, personnel, or other operational necessities. What's more, a large debt on the balance sheet can inhibit other financing options.

Leasing is one way to get the equipment, facility, furniture, or even staff you need without a large capital outlay. Sometimes leasing makes the most financial sense for a company; sometimes purchasing does. Carefully evaluate the options to see what's best for you.

Where can you find those things (or people!) you need to lease? Leasing companies lease everything from computers to farm machinery, sometimes with the option to purchase the item at the end of the lease term. Auto dealers lease cars and trucks, while manufacturers may offer leasing plans for longer terms and lower monthly payments than if you purchased the item and made loan payments to a bank.

A lease is a contract between an owner and a user of property. The difference between renting and leasing usually depends on the length of the contract. Whereas renting constitutes a short-term contract (a day, month, or year), leasing normally implies a longer-term contract, generally three to five years.

Unlike loans for purchasing equipment or property, which require substantial down payments, leasing offers 100 percent financing. This is where a company can get the most mileage from its cash, at least initially. In the long run, leasing costs more if you decide to purchase the item when the term of the lease ends. This higher cost accounts for the lessor's (the owner of the property) overhead and profit.

The lessor benefits by covering the cost of the leased equipment or property and receiving tax benefits, while making a profit. The lessee, or business owner, benefits by making smaller payments, retaining the ability to walk away from the equipment or property at the end of the lease's term, and possibly by having the lessor pay for the costs of maintenance.

THE PROS AND CONS OF LEASING

When making a decision between leasing and purchasing, you need to know the advantages and disadvantages of leasing. The advantages are:

- Minimum cash outlay. Through leasing you don't finance the entire cost of whatever it is you're leasing—you only pay for what you use and always without a large initial capital outlay. In fact, leases are often 100 percent financed.
- *Less stringent financial requirements.* Lessees usually find it easier to obtain financing to lease an asset than to obtain credit to purchase.
- *The latest equipment.* You can ensure that your equipment is always up-to-date by negotiating a short-term lease and exchanging the equipment when the lease runs out.
- *Built-in maintenance.* Depending on the terms of the lease, maintenance can be included in the lease, thereby reducing your working capital expenses.
- *Tax advantages.* Lease payments show up as expenses, not as debt on the balance sheet.
- *Greater payment flexibility.* Not only can leases be spread over a longer period than a loan, thus reducing monthly payments—they can also be structured to account for variations in cash flow, especially for companies that experience seasonal fluctuations in sales.
- *Expert advice available from the lessor.* This is especially true if the lessor is the manufacturer.

The disadvantage of leasing include:

- *No ownership.* Since lessees do not own their property, they do not accrue tax benefits associated with ownership, like depreciation and the investment tax credit. In addition, lessees don't build equity in the property, unless a lease-to-purchase option agreement is added to the lease.
- *Higher long-term cost.* While leases generally offer lower monthly payments, they do not offer significant tax benefits and provide no equity in the leased property. Therefore, the ultimate cost at the end of the lease is often higher than if you purchased the item or property.
- *Non-cancelable lease contract.* Some leases have non-cancelable clauses in the contract or else charge a severe penalty for early termination of the lease.

REAL ESTATE LEASES

Real estate leases are typically broken down into the following categories, though occasionally you may see a creative combination of more than one type.

The Flat Lease

This lease, which is the oldest and simplest, is becoming harder to find but is the best deal for the lessee because it's based on a set price for a set period of time. The danger here is not to be tempted if the term is too short because a series of short-term leases could cost more in the long run. If your rental term is short but you love your location, you could wind up paying the landlord's high rent increases over and over again.

The Step Lease

The step lease attempts to second-guess what the landlord's expenses (for taxes, insurance and maintenance) will be in the future and compensates for them by increasing rent each year. Therefore, the lease rate may make stepped increases like these over the term of the agreement: first year, $900/month; second year, $960/month; third year, $1,010/month; fourth year, $1,080/month; fifth year, $1,140/month.

The Net Lease

This lease takes the guesswork out of the step lease problem. You pay the base rent and when the taxes go up, you pay the dollar increase or your share if more than one tenant is housed within the same facility. Where proportionate sharing occurs, your share is based on the square footage you occupy as a proportion of the total size of the facility. If store A has 1,450 square feet, store B has 2,400 square feet, and store C has 850 square feet, then the building has a total of 4,700 square feet. Let's say taxes on the building property are $1,760, or 37.4 cents per square foot. So store A's share of the tax is $1,450 x 37.4 cents or $542.30 per year. Store B's share is $2,400 x 37.4 cents or $897.60 per year, and store C's tax increase is $850 x 37.4 cents or $317.90 per year. This method ensures that everyone pays his or her fair share.

The Double-Net Lease

This is a version of the net lease that picks up added insurance premiums as well as tax increases, singularly or on a proportionate basis. However, if you do something in your business that raises insurance premiums, you alone will pick up the tab.

The Triple-Net Lease

This most popular version of the net lease includes similar sharing by tenants of costs for repairs to the building or parking area as well as taxes and insurance.

Cost of Living Lease

Specific expenses are not included in this lease; instead, it takes inflation into account by referring to the government's Cost of Living Index. If, at the end of the year, inflation has been, say, 4.5 percent, your rent will increase by that amount.

Percentage Lease

Landlords favor this kind of lease because it allows them to "share the wealth" of a tenant's prospering business. It sets a minimum or base rent to be paid and/or a percentage of the business' gross, whichever is the largest number. Such percentages commonly run from 3 to 12 percent, depending on the area, type of business, and desirability of the location. These percentages are usually paid on a quarterly, semi-annual, or annual basis, and are adjusted backward, though many shopping centers require a monthly accounting and payment.

The percentage lease is most common for properties in prime retail areas. Within those prime areas, specific locations (e.g., corner locations) may be subject to a higher percentage rate. If you have a percentage lease, the lessor will probably require you to periodically furnish proof of gross sales. This is done by examining your books, sales tax records or, in some cases, by sending a copy of the appropriate attachment to your IRS Form 1040.

Other Leases

A real estate lease usually covers other important matters, such as any remodeling to be done, who pays for it, liabilities and duties assumed by each party, and permission for the tenant to put up signs, engage in additional lines of business, or make future alterations, if needed. Since a lease is a binding legal document, you must seek competent legal counsel before signing one.

Remember that leases are not engraved in stone and can usually be negotiated. If you accept the terms without discussion, you have given up the opportunity to negotiate better terms. If you ask and the lessor's answer is no, you've lost nothing. You can always look elsewhere and come back if you don't find a better offer.

Real estate leases are a major financial commitment. Consider not only the present price per square foot, but also the price at the end of the leasing term. Refer to your financial projections to see if the lease will continue being affordable in the future.

Leasehold Improvements

A lease usually covers any remodeling to the physical structure that needs to be done and specifies who will pay for it. Some of this remodeling is considered leasehold improvements. These can include carpeting and other flooring, insulation, electrical wiring, plumbing, bathroom installations, lighting, wall partitions, windows, ceiling tiles, painting, a sprinkler system, security systems, some elements of interior design, and sometimes heating and/or air conditioning systems.

Leasehold improvements in new shopping centers or malls are by far the most extensive. Prospective operators often discover, to their dismay, that the shopping center provides only concrete walls and flooring. Although the cost of finish work often comes out of the retailer's pocket, a construction allowance can sometimes be negotiated with the lessor to help offset the cost of some leasehold improvements.

Helpful Hints

If you're concerned about the length of your lease and want to protect your location indefinitely, make sure you include a right-of-refusal clause in your agreement. Lessors usually won't object because they aren't giving up anything.

Simply stated, a right-of-refusal clause provides that before selling the real estate, the lessor must first offer you the chance to buy it at the same price as the offer that he or she has received. If you really have your heart set on the property but need some time to arrange financing, nail the price down with an option. If you ultimately decide not to buy the property, you'll forfeit your option money.

Something else to keep in mind is that the time to ask for that new coat of paint—outside or inside—is before you sign the lease. Get it in writing, if not in the lease itself then by a letter of addendum that automatically becomes part of the lease. Make sure the lease specifies that the landlord is responsible for damages such as roof leaks, faulty plumbing or old wiring. You'll have enough to think about running your business without worrying about your building falling apart on you!

Don't hassle your landlord with petty maintenance problems. You should be covered if your lease is written correctly, and your attorney can tell you whether or not you are. Save your negotiations for the big problems.

If you need to modify the premises, don't be shy about asking the landlord to cut appreciably or to forgo the first month's rent. You might not get it, but on the other hand, you might be pleasantly surprised. Always point out that your business will increase the value of the property with the improvements you'll make to the facility from time to time.

Some leases include charges for common-area expenses such as maintenance of walkways, landscaping, parking lots, and security. Though charging for these services is acceptable, some lessors try to turn common-area charges into profit centers, adding on charges such as administration expenses.

Be wary of leases that give landlords the right to remodel at the tenants' expense without their prior approval (see Figure 7.1: Real Estate Lease Checklist).

If your location is in a shopping area, are there added costs for maintenance of common areas? What are these costs? Are they fixed or variable? What kind and how much insurance does the landlord require you to have? Are you paying for coverage that should be the landlord's responsibility? If you're in a small complex, are you being charged for more than your share? Are there municipal or town merchant assessments for common customer parking?

STANDARD LEASE CLAUSES

There are many standard clauses common to all commercial real estate leases. A standard opening clause identifying the names of the parties to the lease might be written this way:

This indenture made the _____ day of _____, between _____ party of the first part, hereinafter called the "lessor" and the _____ Company, a duly organized and existing corporation, having an office and place of business at City of _____ State of _____, party of the second part, hereinafter called the "lessee"....

Subjects covered using standard clauses range from "insurance hazard" to "destruction of premises" and "entry by owner." Carefully examine standard clauses and make sure that there's a clear understanding between you and the lessor. One such clause is the "repairs and maintenance" section. The interior of the building is yours to repair and maintain in "good and sanitary" condition. If you fail to maintain the property as required by the lease, the landlord may make the repairs and charge labor and parts to you.

The section usually titled "Acceptance of Premises as Is" can be tricky. Remember the up-front paint job you may have requested? This section does not relieve the owner of normal maintenance responsibilities, but it can be used as a loophole to override verbal agreements.

Alterations Clause

Alterations usually can be made only after receiving the landlord's consent. If the alterations constitute an addition to the structure, this becomes the property of the landlord. At the end of the lease term, the landlord may require the removal of any modifications and the restoration of the property to its original condition. "Broom clean" is a common term used in a lease to describe the condition the landlord expects the property to be in.

Liability Insurance Key Clause

This clause spells out the amount and kind of insurance the lessee must carry to relieve the lessor of liability and/or expenses for damages. A lessor is most often con-

FIGURE 7.1	Real Estate Lease Checklist

After you have chosen a particular site, check the following before you sign the lease:

- ❑ Is there sufficient electrical power? Enough electrical outlets?
- ❑ Is there enough parking space for customers and employees?
- ❑ Is there sufficient lighting? Heating? Air conditioning?
- ❑ Do you know how large and what type a sign you can erect at your facility?
- ❑ Will your city's building and zoning departments allow your business to operate in the facility?
- ❑ Will the landlord allow the alterations that you deem necessary for your business?
- ❑ Must you pay for returning the building to its original condition when you move?
- ❑ Is there any indication of roof leaks?
- ❑ Is the cost of burglary insurance high in the area?
- ❑ Can you secure the building at a low cost against the threat of burglary?
- ❑ Will the health department approve your business at this location?
- ❑ Will the fire department approve the operation of your business at this location?
- ❑ Have you included a written description of the real property?
- ❑ Have you attached drawings of the property to the lease document?
- ❑ Do you have written guidelines for renewal terms?
- ❑ Do you know when your lease payment begins?
- ❑ Have you bargained for one to three months of free rent?
- ❑ Do you know your date of possession?
- ❑ Have you listed the owner's responsibility for improvements?
- ❑ Do you pay the taxes?
- ❑ Do you pay the insurance?
- ❑ Do you pay the maintenance fee?
- ❑ Do you pay the utilities?
- ❑ Do you pay the sewer fees?
- ❑ Have you asked your landlord for a cap of 5 percent on your rent increases?
- ❑ Have you included penalty clauses in case the project is late and you're denied occupancy?
- ❑ Have you retained the right to obtain your own bids for signage?
- ❑ Can you get out of the lease if the building is never more than 70 percent occupied?
- ❑ Has a real estate attorney reviewed your contract?

cerned about personal liability in case someone gets hurt.

Whatever the type of business, insurers will have an acceptable package deal for you and the owner. Make sure to shop for the best price among several insurance companies. Ideally, you should work with an agent who handles insurance coverage from a variety of carriers.

You'll usually need in the upper limits of $300,000 on personal liability, product liability, and "un-owned auto" or similar coverage (for example, an employee in a company car, or in his or her own vehicle, takes a business-related trip during which he or she is involved in an accident). Two patrons who collide in your parking area may also blame you for their problem.

The lessor must carry fire insurance but may require you to carry "fire legal," which protects the lessor if you start the fire. Also plan to carry contents damage insurance with a minimum $5,000 of protection. Loss coverage of a minimum of $1,000 for valuable papers (e.g., accounts receivable) is a good idea as well.

Many insurance packages contain provisions for loss-of-income protection in the event of fire, disaster, and so on. Set a percentage of, say, 40 percent of your normal income for a period of 90 days. And make sure a clause in your lease states that you're released from the obligation of rent if the landlord can't repair the premises in that time.

Assignment or Sublet Clause

From your point of view, a good lease is one that can easily be transferred to another tenant if you want to sell or relocate your business. Therefore, be certain the lease contains a provision for assigning the lease or subletting. Such a clause will allow you to close or move your business while permitting you to get another tenant to pay your rental obligation for the balance of the lease term. It also allows you to sell your business to a new owner who can assume your lease under the same good terms you have. Make sure the lease contains words to the effect that "the lessor cannot withhold such permission providing sub-lessee meets the original requirements of the lease."

If you sell your business, you may want to sublease rather than transfer the lease outright to the new owner. You're still responsible for the rent if the sub-lessee doesn't pay it. But if for any reason the new owner fails and you want to take the business back, you still have a facility to keep it in.

Bailout Clause

A bailout clause could save you in the event of circumstances that hinder your business' performance. Usually, this clause makes the lease void in cases such as war, riots, labor strikes, and acts of God, when it may become impossible to continue in business.

Another clause to be aware of is the "right of successors" clause. It gives heirs the right to continue the lease under all present terms and conditions in the event of your death.

Recapture Clause

If you enter into a percentage lease agreement, the landlord might include a recapture or cancellation clause. This clause, which could be potentially dangerous to you and your business, states that if your company is not doing the business necessary for the landlord to receive the minimum rent set for the premises, such an occurrence will be considered a breach of contract and you could be evicted.

In this situation, your only recourse would be to pay more than the percentage actually produced by the business to bring the amount up to the minimum required by the landlord (predetermined in the lease). Then you would do one of two things: either build up your business volume to the amount necessary to meet the percentage requirement or give up the lease and vacate.

Co-Tenancy Clause

A co-tenancy clause allows you to break the lease if an anchor store closes or moves. If, for example, you signed your lease knowing Office Max would generate a lot of foot traffic, you can break the lease if Office Max closes or moves.

EQUIPMENT LEASES

Equipment leases differ from real estate leases because they usually offer an option to buy. In addition, these leases address depreciation, selling price, residual value, equipment maintenance, and tax benefits.

Conditional Sales Contract

The conditional sales agreement specifies that the purchaser does not receive title to the equipment until it is paid for in full, and the lessee is bound to purchase the equipment at the end of the lease term. However, a conditional sales agreement can be structured differently for different situations. One lease option specifies a minimum and maximum purchase price that can be put on the equipment at the end of the lease term. This protects the interests of both the lessee and the lessor, and leaves room for negotiations on a fair price. The lessee is protected from paying a price for the equipment that's higher than the market price, while the lessor is protected from coming out on the wrong end of the deal because of the equipment's rapid depreciation.

Another lease structure in the conditional sales contract recognizes the lessee as the owner of the equipment from the beginning of the lease term. This structure grants the tax benefits to the lessee. At the end of the term, the lessee is bound to buy the equipment at a predetermined price that is documented in the contract. This price has been agreed on beforehand by both parties and takes into consideration the lessee's monthly payments and the residual value of the equipment. The residual value is the estimated selling price of the equipment at the end of the lease. It is usually expressed as a percentage of the original selling price.

Net Lease and Gross Lease

The net lease and gross lease both recognize that ownership of the equipment will return to the lessor at the end of the term. The lessee must make all payments for the entire term, as these contracts are irrevocable. The difference between the two leases is that in the net lease contract the lessee is responsible for all maintenance, taxes and insurance during the term, and in the gross lease the lessor is liable.

True Lease

A true lease states that the lessor is the owner during the entire term and leases out the equipment during a specified period of time for periodic payments by the lessee. This lease is similar to renting equipment, as no equity is built up by the lessee, and if he/she wishes to purchase the equipment at the end of the term, the selling price will not take into account any previous payments.

Other Equipment Leases

In addition to the preceding types of equipment leases, other common ones include:

- *The non-payout lease.* This works for equipment with a good resale value history. The lessor might choose to offer a non-payout lease where the equipment is leased for less and the costs aren't completely recovered. At the end of the term, the lessor will either sell the equipment or lease it out again.
- *The payout lease.* This lease simply distinguishes that the lessor will charge a payment schedule that will recover the cost of the equipment.
- *The sale and leaseback lease.* This plan offers an option for the business owner to free up some capital in the assets he or she already owns. In this case, he or she sells the asset and leases it back for a specific term. The business owner is bound to a long-term contract, usually with renewal options, at an annual fee computed as a percentage of the selling price. This annual return for the purchaser will fully amortize his or her investment over the original term of the lease.
- *The operating lease.* Under the terms of this lease, the lessor is responsible for maintaining the equipment, and the lessee can usually be released from the contract before the term is over. This clause must be documented in the contract.

Deciding on an Equipment Lease

You can answer the question of which type of lease is right for you only after carefully evaluating your finances. The first question to ask yourself is whether you'd like the option to buy the equipment when the lease is up. To decide, estimate the residual value of the equipment. Will the equipment have depreciated so rapidly that it will no longer be a valuable asset for your business? If you decide you'd like to purchase the equipment, your best bet might be to go with the conditional sales contract. A lessor who knows there is a guaranteed buyer at the end of the term is likely to give you a better leasing contract.

You must also decide whether or not you want to take advantage of the tax benefits available to you as the owner. If not and the lessor remains the owner and retains all benefits, will he or she be willing to give you reduced payment charges?

DECIDE WHETHER TO LEASE OR BUY

Now that you've taken a look at the advantages and disadvantages of leasing, you may next want to compare leasing to purchasing. To decide which method is best for you, consider your cash flow, the state of the economy, your projections for growth, whether the equipment will be needed for a long or short time, and whether the equipment will become obsolete. The Leasing versus Purchasing Equipment Checklist (Figure 7.2) will help you with the cash-flow part of your decision.

Another factor worth considering is the depreciation rate of equipment. Depreciation is an expense that can be claimed on your tax return. It is generally a recapture expense calculated over a specific period that represents the equipment's useful life. Depreciation can be calculated using a straight-line method or a decline-balance method. (See Chapter 20 for more information on depreciation.)

Also take into account maintenance costs if paid by the lessor. These costs can be can be considered as a cash savings, since you won't be liable for them as operating expenses.

Then there are tax laws to consider. For owners-lessors, the net income from the operation of real estate or equipment is taxable. (Net income is the total income less allowable expenses.) The rate of taxation depends on the type of ownership, such as personal or corporate. Allowable expenses include depreciation, mortgage interest, real estate taxes (if paid by the owner), cost of operation and maintenance (if paid by the owner).

Lessees may deduct the following as business expenses: monthly lease payments, real estate taxes (if paid by lessee), cost of operation and maintenance (if paid by lessee), and depreciation on leasehold improvements (if improvements are paid for by the lessee).

Choosing a Leasing Company

As you look for lessors, be careful not to put all your eggs in one basket. Instead, negotiate two or three proposals—this gives you bargaining power in the final negotiations and increases your chances of obtaining a good, fair lease.

Carefully evaluate what each company has to offer in terms of the lease rate and the lessor's reputation. Check with both the Better Business Bureau and the company's present and former customers to get feedback. If you're working with a lease broker, he or she should research this information for you. If you're considering leasing a car, visit the National Vehicle Leasing Association's Web site at www.nvla.org.

The lease rate is probably where you'll find the greatest variance in lease companies. Their rate will be based on several factors, including:

- the party who receives the tax credit—lessors might give a better rate if they retain this benefit,
- the length of the lease term,
- what kind of equipment the lessee wants to lease, and
- the lessee's credit history.

Ask questions and never assume anything. Look at the leasing language. Are there some terms you don't understand? When leasing different kinds of equipment or property, lessors might use a different term to describe something you're not familiar with. Automobile lessors, for example, distinguish their loans as either "open" or "closed." Most open leases bind the lessee to either provide a buyer or pay for at least some predetermined amount of the car's residual value. While closed leases give the lessee an option to buy the car, the lessee is not obligated to provide a buyer or pay part of the residual value.

In addition, a car company lessor might lease directly or indirectly. "Directly" implies that the company carries its own financing. "Indirectly" means that the company uses another source for its financing, such as a bank or other lending institution. Most companies that finance indirectly work with several lending institutions. Ask to see the comparative rates and make sure you get the best one.

The interest charged on a lease isn't called "interest," and no part of it is tax deductible; however, there is a comparable amount you should be aware of. This amount will be included in your monthly payment and might be called a "money factor" or "cost of money," and is expressed as a range. Ask for the money factor in terms of an annual percentage rate, which is more useful in your comparison-shopping and decision-making process.

FIGURE 7.2   Leasing Versus Purchasing Equipment Checklist

Answer the following questions to help determine whether it is better to lease or purchase equipment for your business in terms of cost, cash availability, tax benefits, and obsolescence. Make a check mark in the column that's most appropriate.

Cost	Lease	Purchase
What down payment is required for the lease or loan?		
What is the length of the lease or loan?		
What is the monthly payment of the lease or loan?		
Are there balloon payments associated with the lease or loan?		
What is the amount of the balloon payments?		
What is the cost of an extended warranty, if purchasing one?		
What is the total cost of the lease or loan (including maintenance and warranties) over its lifetime?		

Cash Availability	Lease	Purchase
Is there sufficient cash flow to handle the monthly lease or loan payments (answer yes or no)?		
Are maintenance costs included in the lease or loan (answer yes or no)?		
What maintenance costs are associated with the item?		
What insurance costs are included in the lease or loan, if any?		
What are the estimated insurance costs associated with the item?		
If business is seasonal, does the lease or loan fit periods of sufficient cash flow better?		

Tax Benefits	Lease	Purchase
Can the item be depreciated for tax purposes in a lease or loan?		
What is the depreciable life of the item?		
What is the estimated depreciable expense of the item over its depreciable life?		
What is the amount of other tax benefits associated with this item?		

Obsolescence	Lease	Purchase
What is the operable lifetime of the item?		
What is the total cost of the item spread over this lifetime (divide cost by lifetime)?		
What is the technological lifetime of the item?		
Will the item need to be replaced due to technological advancement?		
What is the total cost of the item spread over the technological lifetime (divide cost by lifetime)?		

NEGOTIATING A LEASE

Negotiating a lease usually begins with an informal discussion between the lessee and lessor. If all goes well, a verbal agreement follows. The next step requires the lessor to draw up written documentation of the proposal and send it to the lessee for approval.

Further negotiations might occur at this point and assuming the lessee's credit has been approved, both parties will come to a final agreement. Again, the lessor (or the lessor's lawyer) will prepare a final proposal and submit it to the lessee for signing. If you can avoid it, wait until this time to consult with an attorney. Lawyers can be costly, but at this final stage of the contract agreement, they're invaluable as they look for terms that might not be in your best interest. Once your lawyer has reviewed the lease and you're comfortable with its terms, sign it, make a copy for your records and return the original to the lessor.

CHAPTER 8

Writing a Business Plan

A business plan has several uses besides being a financing proposal for bankers or investors. It's also a road map that provides directions for the future, so a business can plan and avoid bumps in the road. The time you spend making your business plan thorough and accurate, and keeping it up-to-date, is an investment that pays big dividends in the long term.

FOLLOW ESTABLISHED GUIDELINES

Your business plan should conform to generally accepted guidelines regarding form and content. Each section should include specific elements and address relevant questions that the people who read your plan will most likely ask. Generally, a business plan has the following components:

- Title page and contents
- Executive summary
- Description of the business
- Explanation of the product or service
- Market strategies
- Analysis of the competition
- Operations and management
- Financial data
- Supporting documents

The following chapters include successful business plans from two actual businesses. Chapter 9's business plan is from Big Agnes, a start-up sleeping bag manufacturer in Steamboat Springs, Colorado. The owners wrote the plan in 2006 in order to obtain a bank line of credit and funds from outside investors. Chapter 10's business plan for The Gray Ghost Inn in West Dover, Vermont, was written by the new owners so they could obtain bank financing for their purchase.

TITLE PAGE AND CONTENTS

A business plan should be presented in a binder with a cover listing the name of the business, the name(s) of the principal(s), address, phone number, e-mail, and web site addresses, and the date. You don't have to spend a lot of money on a fancy binder or cover. Your readers want a plan that looks professional, is easy to read, and is a well-put-together document.

Include the same information on the title page. If you have a logo, you can use it, too.

A table of contents follows the executive summary or statement of purpose, so that readers can quickly find the information or financial data they need.

EXECUTIVE SUMMARY

The executive summary, or statement of purpose, succinctly encapsulates your raison d'être for writing the business plan. It tells the reader what you want and why, right up front. Are you looking for a $10,000 loan to remodel and refurbish your factory? A loan of $25,000 to expand your product line or buy new equipment? How will you repay your loan, and over what term? Would you like to find a partner to whom you'd sell 25 percent of the business? What's in it for him or her? The questions pertaining to your situation should be addressed here clearly and succinctly.

The executive summary or statement of purpose should be no more than half a page in length and touch on the following key elements:

- *Business concept* describes the business, its product, the market it serves, and the business' competitive advantage.
- *Financial features* include financial highlights, such as sales and profits.
- *Financial requirements* state how much capital is needed for start-up or expansion, how it will be used, and what collateral is available.
- *Current business position* furnishes relevant information about the company, its legal form of operation, when it was founded, the principal owners, and key personnel.
- *Major achievements* point out anything noteworthy, such as patents, prototypes, important contracts regarding product development, or results from test marketing that have been conducted.

THE BUSINESS DESCRIPTION

The business description usually begins with a short explanation of the industry. When describing the industry, discuss what's going on now as well as the outlook for the future. Do the necessary research so you can provide information on all the various markets within the industry, including references to new products or developments that could benefit or hinder your business. Base your observations on reliable data and be sure to footnote and cite your sources of information when necessary. Remember that bankers and investors want to know hard facts—they won't risk money on assumptions or conjecture.

When describing your business, say which sector it falls into (wholesale, retail, food service, manufacturing, hospitality, and so on), and whether the business is new or established. Then say whether the business is a sole proprietorship, partnership, or a C or Sub S corporation. Next, list the business' principals and state what they bring to the company. Continue with information on who the business' customers are, how big the market is, and how the product or service is distributed and marketed.

THE PRODUCT OR SERVICE DESCRIPTION

When you describe your product or service, make sure your reader has a clear idea of what you're talking about. Explain how people use your product or service and talk about what makes your product or service different from others available in the market. In marketing, this is called the "Unique Selling Proposition" or USP. Every business has one. It can be a patented product like Post-It Notes®, a trade secret like Kentucky Fried Chicken's recipe, fresh coffee that's available on a 24/7 basis like that of Dunkin' Donuts, the quick turnaround time offered by Kinko's, or the ability to write human resource materials for large corporations. Be specific about what sets your business apart from those of your competitors.

Then explain how your business will gain a competitive edge. For example, will your business be better because you'll supply a full line of products while your competitors don't? Are you going to provide after-sale service while your competitors don't? Will you sell the best dinners in town? Are you the only hardware store within a twenty-mile range of a growing community?

Next explain why your business will be profitable. Describe the factors that you think will make it successful (for example, it's a well-organized business, it has state-of-the-art equipment, its location is exceptional, it's a product in demand at a fair price, the customer service is extraordinary, you have a captive market, and so on).

If your business plan will be used as a financing proposal, explain why the additional equity or debt will make your business more profitable. Give hard facts, such as "new equipment will create an income stream of $10,000 per year" and briefly describe how.

Other information to address here is a description of the experience of the other key people in the business. Whoever reads your business plan will want to know what suppliers or experts you've spoken to about your business and their response to your idea. They may even ask you to clarify your choice of location or reasons for selling this particular product.

The business description can be a few paragraphs to a few pages in length, depending on the complexity of your plan. If your plan is not too complicated, keep your business description short, describing the industry in one paragraph, the product in another, and the business and its success factors in two or three more paragraphs. Regardless of how long your business description section is, make sure the information you convey is relevant, succinct and well-written.

The key is to grab your reader's attention and hold it. If your business plan is long or poorly written, you stand to lose more than just your reader's interest—you risk losing the opportunity to grow your business. If writing isn't your forte, hire someone to write your business plan for you.

MARKET STRATEGIES

Market strategies are the result of a thorough market analysis (see Chapter 3: Market Research) that focuses in on a business' target market. After you've done your market research and know who your prospects are, you can begin crafting strategies to establish and solidify your position in that market. A market analysis will also help you establish pricing, distribution, and promotional strategies that will allow your company to be successful vis-à-vis your competition, both in the short and long term.

Defining the Market

Begin your market analysis by defining the market in terms of size, demographics, structure, growth prospects, trends and sales potential.

Your competitors' total aggregate sales will provide you with a fairly accurate estimate of the total potential market. Your target market is a piece of that pie, whose boundaries are defined by geographic, demographic, and/or product-oriented factors. For example, if you

owned an independent bookstore, your target market would be book lovers within, say, a twenty-mile radius. You could further segment your market by the types of readers you serve: mystery lovers, book group members, kids, investors, gardeners, and so on.

Determining Market Share

Your business plan needs to estimate market share, an important piece of information for bankers and investors.

The first step is figuring out the number of prospects in your target market. If, for example, your target market is defined as households with incomes greater than $100,000, then a trip to your library or a visit to the U.S. Census Bureau's web site at www.census.gov is all you need to take in order to get the necessary data. You can also ask your librarian for other resources to help your research.

Next, determine how often your product or service will be purchased by your target market. Then figure out the potential annual purchase. Say that 10,000 families buy something every month at local bookstores, averaging $25 a purchase. Doing the math gives you 10,000 x 12 x $25, or a total of $3,000,000 in sales.

Then figure out what percentage of this annual sum you either have or can attain. If you can get 25 percent of this market, your sales could reach $750,000 a year. Keep in mind that no one gets 100 percent market share and that a 25 percent share is considered dominant. Your market share will be a benchmark that tells you how well you're doing in light of your market-planning projections.

Positioning Strategy

How you differentiate your product or service from those of your competitors and then determine which market niche to fill is called "positioning." Positioning helps establish your product or service's identity within the eyes of the purchaser. A company's positioning strategy is affected by a number of variables related to customers' motivations and requirements, as well as by competitors' actions.

Before you position your product or service, answer the following strategic questions:

- *What's your customer really buying from you?* Remember that McDonald's isn't just selling burgers and fries. It sells fast food that tastes the same, no matter when or where it's ordered, in an environment that's clean and friendly to families.
- *How's your product or service different from those of your competitors?* A cheeseburger is a cheeseburger, you may think. But look how McDonald's, Burger King, and Wendy's differentiate their fast food. They offer different side dishes (onion rings at Burger King, French-fried potatoes at McDonald's), different toys with kids' meals (a big incentive for the under age-ten set!), and different ways of cooking their burgers (Burger King's are broiled, McDonald's, grilled).
- *What makes your product or service unique?* In New England, McDonald's is the only fast-food chain to offer lobster rolls (a lobster salad sandwich served in a grilled hot-dog roll) in the summer.

Once you've answered these strategic questions based on your market research, you can then begin to develop a positioning strategy for your business plan. A positioning statement for a business plan doesn't have to be long or elaborate, but it does need to point out who your target market is, how you'll reach them, what they're really buying from you, who your competitors are and what your USP (unique selling proposition) is.

Pricing Strategy

How you price your product or service is perhaps your most important marketing decision. It's also one of the most difficult to make for most small business owners, because there are no instant formulas. To determine the right price for your products in your market, you need to do some homework.

First determine what your customers perceive to be of value in your kind of business. Service? Convenience? Expertise? High-quality products? Second, take a look at your costs for overhead, production, storage, financing, and distribution. Third, consider your profit objectives. Keep in mind that you're not in business just to break even—making a profit should be the goal of all business owners! And finally, consider how your competitors price their products or services.

Many methods of establishing prices are available to you, but these are among the most common:

- *Cost-plus pricing* is used mainly by manufacturers to assure that all costs, both fixed and variable, are covered and the desired profit percentage is attained.
- *Demand pricing* is used by companies that sell their products through a variety of sources at differing prices based on demand.
- *Competitive pricing* is used by companies that are entering a market where there's already an established price and it's difficult to differentiate one product from another.
- *Markup pricing* is used mainly by retailers and is calculated by adding your desired profit to the cost of the product.

Each method has its strengths and weaknesses, which are discussed in greater detail in Chapter 21: Pricing.

Distribution Strategy

Distribution includes the entire process of moving the product from the factory to the end user. Make sure to analyze your competitors' distribution channels before deciding whether to use the same type of channel or an alternative that may provide you with a strategic advantage.

Some of the more common distribution channels are shown below.

- *Direct sales* are the most effective distribution channel if the basic plan is to sell directly to the end user.
- *Original Equipment Manufacturer (OEM) sales* are incorporated into the manufacturer's finished product and distributed to the end user.
- *Manufacturer's representatives* are sales people who operate out of agencies that handle an assortment of complementary products and divide their selling time between them. This is one of the best ways to distribute a product.
- *Wholesaler distributors* sell to a retailer or other agent for further distribution through the channel until it reaches the end user.
- *Brokers* are third-party distributors who often buy directly from the distributor or wholesaler and sell to retailers or end users.
- *Retail distributors* sell directly to consumers.

- *Direct mail* includes catalogs, letters, e-mail, and other direct appeals to buy that are used in a targeted campaign to consumers.

Promotion Strategy

Your promotion strategy includes all the ways you communicate with your markets to make them aware of your products or services. To be successful, your promotion strategy should address:

- *Advertising*, including the advertising budget, positioning message(s), and the first year's media schedule.
- *Packaging*, providing a description of the packaging strategy. If available, mock-ups of any labels, trademarks, or service marks should be included.
- *Public relations*, detailing the publicity strategy, including a list of media that will be approached as well as a schedule of special events.
- *Sales promotions*, establishing the strategies used to support the sales message, including a description of collateral marketing material as well as a schedule of planned promotional activities such as special sales, coupons, contests, premium awards, and so on.
- *Personal sales,* outlining the sales strategy, including pricing procedures, returns and adjustment rules, sales presentation methods, lead generation, customer service policies, salesperson compensation, and salesperson responsibilities.

The sales projections in your business plan are determined by how you define the market, position and promote your product or service, and price and distribute it. Most business plans will project revenue for up to three years—anything over that is conjecture.

COMPETITIVE ANALYSIS

The purpose of the competitive analysis is to determine:

- The strengths and weaknesses of the competitors within your market.
- Strategies that will provide you with a distinct advantage.
- Barriers that can be developed to prevent competition from entering your market.
- Any weaknesses that can be exploited in the product development cycle.

The first step in a competitor analysis is to identify both direct and indirect competition for your business, both now and in the future. Direct competitors will have a product or service similar to yours and will go after the same target market as you. For example, ExxonMobil and Shell both compete for your business to keep your car filled with gasoline. But Southwest Airlines must be considered their indirect competitor in the transportation industry, because drivers can be enticed by the low cost and other advantages of flying.

Once you've grouped your competitors, start analyzing their marketing strategies and identifying their vulnerable areas by examining their strengths and weaknesses. These strengths and weaknesses will give you insight into which market niches are worth your efforts and are based on the competitors having or not having key assets and skills.

For instance, in the personal computer operating system software market, Microsoft reigns supreme with Windows. It has established dominance in this industry because of superior marketing and research as well as having formed strategic partnerships with a majority of hardware producers. This has allowed Windows to become the operating environment of necessity for the majority of computers on the market.

One of Microsoft's competitors, Apple, has an excellent operating system but has suffered from weaknesses that Microsoft has been able to exploit. Apple's Macintosh operating system, while superior in many ways to Windows, has been limited to the Macintosh platform and (up until recently) did not run many of the popular business applications readily available to Windows.

Through your competitor analysis, you'll be able to create a marketing strategy that will generate an asset or skill competitors do not have, which will provide you with a distinct competitive advantage, or "edge." Since competitive advantages are developed from key assets and skills, put together a competitive strength grid. This scale lists all your major competitors based on their applicable assets and skills, and shows where your company fits on this scale.

To make your competitive strength grid, take a piece of paper and list all the key assets and skills down the left margin. Along the top, write two column headers:

"Weakness" and "Strength." In each asset or skill category, place all the competitors that have weaknesses in that particular category under the Weakness column and all those that have strengths in that specific category in the Strength column. After you've finished, you'll be able to determine where you stand in relation to the other firms competing in your industry.

Once you've established the key assets and skills necessary for success in your business and have defined your distinct competitive advantage, communicate this information in a strategic form that will attract market share as well as defend it. Competitive strategies usually fall into five areas:

1. Product

2. Distribution

3. Pricing

4. Promotion

5. Advertising

Whoever reads your business plan should be very clear on who your target market is, what your market niche is, exactly how you'll stand apart from your competitors, and why you'll be successful doing so.

OPERATIONS AND MANAGEMENT

The operations and management component of your plan is designed to describe how the business functions on a continuing basis. The operations plan highlights the logistics of the organization, such as the responsibilities of the management team, the tasks assigned to each division within the company, and capital and expense requirements related to the operations of the business.

Organizational Structure and Operating Expenses

The organizational structure of the company is an essential element of the business plan because it provides a basis from which to project operating expenses. This projection is critical in formulating financial statements, which are heavily scrutinized by investors; therefore, the organizational structure as described in your business plan has to be well thought-out, well defined, and realistic.

Although every company's organizational structure is different, most can be divided into several broad areas:

- Marketing and sales (includes customer relations and service)
- Production (including quality assurance)
- Research and development
- Administration
- Human resources

These are broad classifications, and every business will be structured according to its own particular requirements and goals.

Once you get a handle on your business' operations and the labor expenses you'll incur, you can project the expenses associated with the operation of the business—its overhead. "Overhead" refers to all non-labor expenses required to operate the business. Expenses can be divided into fixed—those expenses that must be paid, usually at the same rate, regardless of the volume of business—and variable, which are those that change according to the amount of business.

Overhead usually includes the following expenses:

- Rent
- Advertising and promotion
- Supplies
- Utilities
- Packaging and shipping
- Maintenance and repair
- Equipment leases
- Payroll
- Payroll taxes and benefits
- Uncollectible receivables
- Professional services
- Insurance
- Loan payments
- Depreciation
- Travel

Capital Requirements

In addition to your operating expenses, you'll also need to draw up a capital equipment list to show how much money is needed to purchase equipment for operations. Service businesses don't have nearly the demands as, say, a manufacturer has. A graphic design business would need computer equipment, printers, a fax machine, scanner, copier, and office furniture, while a restaurant owner would need stoves, fridges, pots and pans, dishes, tables and chairs, cutlery, linens, and so on.

Depreciation is an expense that shows the decrease in value of the equipment throughout its effective lifetime. For many businesses, depreciation is based on schedules tied to the lifetime of the equipment. Make sure you and your CPA choose the schedule that is most fitting for your business, as depreciation is a tax deduction as well as a concern for investors.

Cost of Goods

The third list that you need to generate in the operations and management section of your business plan shows the cost of goods. This list is used only by businesses with inventories. For a retail or wholesale business, cost of goods sold, or cost of sales, refers to the purchase of products for resale—the inventory. The manufacturing costs of the products that are sold are logged into cost of goods as an expense of the sale, while those that aren't sold remain in inventory.

For manufacturing firms, cost of goods refers to what the company pays to manufacture its product. Three elements are usually included:

1. Material
2. Labor
3. Overhead

Like retail, the merchandise that is sold is expensed as a cost of goods, while merchandise that isn't sold is placed in inventory.

Cost of goods is an important yardstick for measuring a company's profitability for the cash flow and income statements. It shows the flow of inventory through your operations, the placement of assets within the company, and the rate at which your inventory turns.

FINANCIAL COMPONENTS OF YOUR BUSINESS PLAN

After defining the product, market, and operations, the next area to turn your attention to are the three financial statements that form the backbone of your business plan: the income statement, the cash flow statement, and the balance sheet.

The Income Statement

The income statement is a simple and straightforward report on the business' cash-generating ability. It is a scorecard on the financial performance of your business that reflects when sales are made and when expenses are incurred. It draws information from the various financial models developed earlier such as revenue, expenses, capital (in the form of depreciation), and cost of goods. By combining these elements, the income statement illustrates just how much your company makes or loses during the year by subtracting cost of goods and expenses from revenue to arrive at a net result, which is either a profit or loss. It differs from a cash flow statement because the income statement doesn't show when revenue is collected or when expenses are paid. It does, however show the projected profitability of the business over the time frame covered by the plan. For a business plan, the income statement should be generated on a monthly basis during the first year, quarterly for the second, and annually for the third.

Your income statement lists your financial projections in the following manner.

- *Income* includes all the income generated by the business.
- *Cost of goods* includes all the costs related to the sale of products in inventory.
- *Gross profit margin* is the difference between revenue and cost of goods. Gross profit margin can be expressed in dollars, as a percentage or both. As a percentage, the GP margin is always stated as a percentage of revenue.
- *Operating expenses* include all overhead and labor expenses associated with the operations of the business.
- *Total expenses* are the sum of cost of goods and operating expenses.
- *Net profit* is the difference between gross profit margin and total expenses. The net income depicts the business' debt and capital capabilities.
- *Depreciation* reflects the decrease in value of capital assets used to generate income. It's also used as the basis for a tax deduction and an indicator of the flow of money into new capital.

- *Earnings before interest and taxes* shows the capacity of a business to repay its obligations.
- *Interest* includes all interest payable for debts, both short-term and long-term.
- *Taxes* includes all taxes on the business.
- *Net profit* after taxes shows the company's real bottom line.

In addition to the income statements, include a note analyzing the results. The analysis should be very short, emphasizing the key points of the income statement. Your CPA can help you craft this.

The Cash Flow Statement

The cash flow statement is one of the most critical information tools for your business, since it shows how much cash you'll need to meet obligations, when you'll require it, and where it will come from. The result is the profit or loss at the end of each month and year. The cash flow statement carries both profits and losses over to the next month to also show the cumulative amount. Running a loss on your cash flow statement is a major red flag that indicates not having enough cash to meet expenses—something that demands immediate attention and action.

Unlike the income statement, the cash flow statement doesn't show whether the business will be profitable, but it does show the cash position of the business at any given point in time by measuring revenue against outlays.

The cash flow statement should be prepared on a monthly basis during the first year, on a quarterly basis for the second year and annually for the third year. The following seventeen items are listed in the order they need to appear on your cash flow statement:

1. *Cash* refers to cash on hand in the business.
2. *Cash sales* are income from sales paid for by cash.
3. *Receivables* are income from the collection of money owed to the business resulting from sales.
4. *Other income* is income from investments, interest on loans that have been extended and the liquidation of any assets.
5. *Total income* is the sum of total cash, cash sales, receivables and other income.
6. *Material/merchandise* is the raw material used in the manufacture of a product (for manufacturing opera-

tions only), the cash outlay for merchandise inventory (for merchandisers such as wholesalers and retailers) or the supplies used in the performance of a service.

7. *Direct labor* is the labor required to manufacture a product (for manufacturing operations only) or perform a service.
8. *Overhead* is all fixed and variable expenses required for the operations of the business.
9. *Marketing/sales* is all salaries, commissions, and other direct costs associated with the marketing and sales departments.
10. *R&D* is labor expenses required to support the research and development operations of the business.
11. *G&A* is labor expenses required to support the general and administrative functions of the business.
12. *Taxes* are all taxes, except payroll, paid to the appropriate government institutions.
13. *Capital* represents the capital requirements to obtain any equipment needed to generate income.
14. *Loan payments* are the total of all payments made to reduce any long-term debts.
15. *Total expenses* are the sum of material, direct labor, overhead expenses, marketing, sales, R&D, G&A, taxes, capital and loan payments.
16. *Cash flow* is the difference between total income and total expenses. This amount is carried over to the next period as beginning cash.
17. *Cumulative cash flow* is the difference between current cash flow and cash flow from the previous period.

As with the income statement, you'll need to analyze the cash flow statement in a short summary in the business plan. Once again, the analysis doesn't have to be long and should cover highlights only. Ask your CPA for help.

The Balance Sheet

The last financial statement you'll need is a balance sheet. Unlike the previous financial statements, the balance sheet is generated annually for the business plan and is, more or less, a summary of all the preceding financial information broken down into three areas:

1. Assets

FIGURE 8.1   Personal Balance Sheet

Balance Sheet

Name of Your Business
Date

ASSETS	LIABILITIES
Current assets	Current liabilities
Cash	Accounts payable
Accounts receivable	Accrued liabilities
Inventory	Taxes
Total current assets	Total current liabilities
Fixed assets	Long-term liabilities
Capital/plant	Bonds payable
Investment	Notes payable
Miscellaneous assets	Total long-term liabilities
Total fixed assets	
TOTAL ASSETS	TOTAL LIABILITIES
	OWNER'S EQUITY/NET WORTH (total assets minus total liabilities)

2. Liabilities

3. Equity

Balance sheets are used to calculate the net worth of a business or individual by measuring assets against liabilities. If your business plan is for an existing business, the balance sheet from your last reporting period should be included. If the business plan is for a new business, try to project what your assets and liabilities will be over the course of the business plan to determine what equity you may accumulate in the business. To obtain financing for a new business, you'll need to include a personal financial statement or balance sheet. A personal balance sheet is generated in the same manner as one for a business and follows the format of Figure 8.1.

The top portion of the balance sheet lists your company's assets in order of liquidity, from most liquid to least liquid. Current assets are cash or its equivalent or those that will be used by the business in a year or less. They include the following.

- *Cash* is the cash on hand at the time books are closed at the end of the fiscal year. This refers to all cash in checking, savings, and short-term investment accounts.

- *Accounts* receivable are the income derived from credit accounts. For the balance sheet, it is the total amount of income to be received that is logged into the books at the close of the fiscal year.

- *Inventory* is derived from the cost of goods table. It is the inventory of material used to manufacture a product not yet sold.

- *Total current assets* are the sum of cash, accounts receivable, inventory, and supplies.

Other assets that appear in the balance sheet are called long-term or fixed assets because they are durable and will last more than one year. Examples of long-term assets include the following.

- *Capital and plant* is the book value of all capital equipment and property (if you own the land and building), less depreciation.
- *Investment* includes all investments owned by the company that cannot be converted to cash in less than one year. For the most part, companies just starting out have not accumulated long-term investments.
- *Miscellaneous assets* are all other long-term assets that are not "capital and plant" or "investment."
- *Total long-term assets* are the sum of capital and plant, investments, and miscellaneous assets.
- *Total assets* is the sum of total current assets and total long-term assets.

After listing the assets, you then account for the liabilities of your business. Like assets, liabilities are classified as current or long-term. Debts that are due in one year or less are classified as current liabilities. If they are due in more than one year, they are long-term liabilities. Examples of current liabilities follow:

- *Accounts payable* are all expenses incurred by the business that are purchased from regular creditors on an open account and are due and payable.
- *Accrued liabilities* are all expenses incurred by the business that are required for operation but have not yet been paid at the time the books are closed. These expenses are usually the company's overhead and salaries.
- *Taxes* are those still due and payable at the time the books are closed.
- *Total current liabilities* is the sum of accounts payable, accrued liabilities, and taxes.

Long-term liabilities include the following:

- *Bonds payable* are the total of all bonds at the end of the year that are due and payable over a period exceeding one year.
- *Mortgage payable* is loans taken out for the purchase of real estate that are repaid over a long-term period. The mortgage payable is that amount still due at the close of the fiscal year.
- *Notes payable* are the amount still owed on any long-term debts that will not be repaid during the current fiscal year.
- *Total long-term liabilities* are the sum of bonds payable, mortgages payable, and notes payable.
- *Total liabilities* are the sum of total current and long-term liabilities.

Once the liabilities have been listed, owner's equity can then be calculated. The amount attributed to owner's equity is the difference between total assets and total liabilities. The amount of equity the owner has in the business is an important yardstick used by investors to evaluate the company. Many times, it determines the amount of capital they feel they can safely invest in the business.

In the business plan, you'll need to create an analysis for the balance sheet just as you need to do for the income and cash flow statements. The analysis of the balance sheet should be kept short and cover key points. Again, ask your CPA for help.

SUPPORTING DOCUMENTS

In this section, include any other documents that are of interest to your reader, such as: your résumé; contracts with suppliers, customers, or clients; letters of reference; letters of intent; a copy of your lease, and any other legal documents; tax returns for the previous three years and anything else relevant to your business plan.

Big Agnes's Business Plan

AN EXAMPLE FOR A START-UP BUSINESS

THE MOTHER OF COMFORT!

Bill Gamber and Brad Johnson

Big Agnes, Inc.

P.O. Box 773072

735 Oak Street

Steamboat Springs, Colorado 80477

July 2006

INTRODUCTION

In the summer of 1875, Big Bob McIntosh worked his way up into the mountains high above his homestead in Northwest Colorado in search of his fortune. He, his dog, and his horse followed the old Ute trail up the Elk River valley. He turned north and followed a raging creek that took him to a lake surrounded by a high mountain cirque. We imagine the higher he got, the higher he got. He set up camp for the night and the next morning searched for a spot to dig. Dig? You might ask. Yes, dig. He was looking for gold, but instead found mica—and a low-grade mica at that. Poor guy. His efforts weren't worth a can of beans.

McIntosh spent the summer panning for gold and silver in the local lakes, streams, and rivers. He bagged some of the surrounding peaks and named a few along the way. One of his favorites was Big Agnes Mountain. (We wonder what she would have looked like as a person!) McIntosh could see far and beyond from her summit. To the north, he could see the headwaters of the Encampment River and into Wyoming; to the south, Lost Ranger Peak and Mt. Ethel. To the west, he could see over Little Agnes Mountain and far into the Yampa and Green River valleys, and on a good day he may have even seen Cross Mountain. When the snow started to fly, McIntosh left for lower ground. We bet that if he'd had the Big Agnes Sleeping System, he probably would have stayed.

One hundred and twenty-five years later, we decided to do a little digging ourselves. We both have been working in the outdoor industry in design and manufacturing for a good while—more than 40 years, if you add them up. Brad has had this sleeping bag idea brewing for a long time. We decided it was time to bring it to life. It needed a name, and we wanted it to be fun, new, and genuine. After some good names and some not-so-good names, we kept coming back to Big Agnes. Thanks, Bob—we couldn't have come up with a better name. Big Agnes products are functional, backcountry tools—just like the ones that McIntosh needed!

If you ever want to talk shop—or, better yet, get an up-to-date snow report—give us a call at (970) 871-1480.

We look forward to working with you,

Bill and Brad

TABLE OF CONTENTS

THE BUSINESS

FINANCIAL STATEMENTS

1

BIG AGNES EXECUTIVE SUMMARY

Big Agnes, Inc. was founded in November 2003 to produce and distribute integrated sleeping systems for the outdoor camper and backcountry traveler. Integrated sleeping systems include sleeping bags, sleeping pads, and shelters (tents and bivys). These sleeping system components fall under the equipment category of the outdoor industry—the second-largest segment of the industry, accounting for $412 million in annual sales. Under the equipment category are numerous subcategories. Sleeping bags are the third-largest subcategory, accounting for 14 percent of all equipment sales. Tents represent the fifth-largest subcategory at 7 percent of equipment sales. Sleeping pads are part of the accessory subcategory (the largest subcategory at 34 percent of sales) and represent 10 percent of accessory sales.

The products being sold under sleeping systems have seen relatively few changes during the last 15 years. Currently, the sleeping bag segment of the market has the greatest opportunity for development and growth. Today's sleeping bags offer limited comfort and are heavy and bulky. Big Agnes has developed a sleeping bag system that is different than anything else on the market—our sleeping pad is attached to the bottom of the bag and is an integral part of the bag's insulation. This design provides for much greater sleeping comfort and is one-third the weight and bulk of comparably rated sleeping bags.

In addition, Big Agnes has developed a self-inflating sleeping pad that is more comfortable and provides more insulation than the industry's standard pad. In 2003, we will integrate our sleeping bags and pads into shelters to provide complete sleeping comfort and protection all in one. This complete integrated system will be the lightest, most packable sleeping system available. At this time, no other company offers such an integrated system.

Big Agnes is distributing our products via the outdoor wholesale market in a limited and exclusive distribution to the best outdoor retailers world wide. In February 2005, Big Agnes began selling direct—via the internet, catalog, and through the Big Agnes section of the BAP store.

MISSION STATEMENT

Big Agnes aspires to be the one-stop source for the most comfortable, lightest, and least bulky sleeping systems available for all outdoor camping needs.

2

PRODUCTS

Sleeping Bags

Big Agnes is offering two three-season sleeping bags that are rated to 15 degrees and one summer bag rated to 40 degrees. The Encampment is a 15-degree bag insulated with Polarguard 3D, the best synthetic fill currently available. Synthetic fill bags are popular because they're less expensive and they insulate even when wet. The Lost Ranger is a 15-degree bag insulated with 600-fill goose down. Down is very durable and won't lose its insulating value with age. It's also lighter and more packable than synthetic fills. Both bags are built to achieve a 15-degree rating, the ideal rating for three-season use.

The Cross Mountain summer bag is filled with Polarguard 3D synthetic insulation and is warm to 40 degrees. In addition, the summer bag works as an overbag. The user can place either of our two 15-degree bags or any other three-season bag inside to get a warmth rating of a winter camping bag good to -100 to -200 degrees. The Big Agnes two-bag system provides greater sleeping comfort and a quarter of the weight and bulk of any other comparably rated sleeping bag.

Pads

Big Agnes's seven self-inflating sleeping pads vary in length, width, thickness, and shape. We're working with a manufacturer in China and have developed a pad that is a better product than what is currently being offered. Our pads use a high-density foam that is thicker inside the air chamber. This provides more protection and comfort from uneven and bumpy ground, even for a bigger person. In addition, the denser and thicker foam layer has twice the insulation value as that used by our competitors. Our pad demos we've recently sent out have all tested better than industry standard pads. The main reason, we hear, is that the Big Agnes pads provide more support and sleeping comfort. The testers also feel that our pads are more solidly constructed.

In our market research, we've found that the retailers were only getting about a 40 percent markup on their pad and bag sales. They're not happy with these margins when compared to a 50 percent markup that they get for clothing, which is the largest sales category in the outdoor market. One of our goals is to improve the retailers' markups in these categories while still maintaining a Big Agnes company-wide markup of more than 50 percent. To date, we're on track to accomplish this goal. We've been able to give the retailers a 48 percent markup on the pads and a 45 percent markup on the bags.

We believe that the pads will initially be our best-selling products. They are considered an accessory and more of a commodity than the sleeping bags. The sleeping bags are more innovative in design, which will generate media and consumer interest.

To keep ahead of our competition and secure Big Agnes's position as a company setting the standards for new and better products, we will continue to develop new, cutting-edge products each year. Our initial offering of three sleeping bags and seven pads for spring and summer of 2005 was a significant beginning. We are now working on an ultra-light, blow-up sleeping pad that will be the lightest high-performance pad available. This pad is so light and packable it will stay inside any of our bags when stuffed for travel—a first in the industry. Our ultra light pad and any Big Agnes bag will be as light and packable as any comparable bag without a pad. The new pad will be available for sale this spring.

We've also started developing a series of lighter, more streamlined, yet comfy sleeping bags for the minimalist and extreme outdoorsman. Also in the development stages is our first shelter. The new bag series and shelter was available for delivery in spring

3

of 2006. For 2007, we are in the conceptual stages of developing our car camping bags. These bags will be more moderately priced and will be more appealing to the general sporting goods market.

All Big Agnes products come with an unconditional guarantee. Big Agnes will provide maintenance service on all products that have been damaged by misuse or aging for minimal cost. These services will be done out of the sewing facility that we share with BAP.

THE CUSTOMER

Anyone who sleeps in a tent is a prospective Big Agnes customer. The range of users' ages is quite diverse. There's a large group of first-time bag purchasers between the ages of 18 and 26. Our goal is to grow up with this market segment.

Another important segment ranges from age 25 to 55. These users already have one or two bags and are knowledgeable outdoor enthusiasts. They have the disposable income and interest to buy whatever they feel will significantly enhance their comfort and technically outperform their current products.

Our market efforts will target the younger segment but will tell a story that traditionalists will appreciate. We will advertise in publications that reach both segments at national and regional levels.

THE MARKET

The need for outdoor sleeping comfort is as old as man. While today's sleeping systems have come a long way, the majority of outdoor enthusiasts consider their comfort level to be less than acceptable when camping out and sleeping on the ground. That's because today's sleeping bags are cut in a mummy shape. Mummy bags are narrow and limit the user's ability to move and roll freely. After several hours of natural sleep movement, the user often gets entangled and wakes up. It's also easy to roll off the sleeping pad and onto the hard and usually cold

ground, again interrupting sleep. The widely used self-inflating pads lack good support, allowing most ground irregularities to be felt. They're narrow, to minimize bulk and weight, and easy to roll off of. After one or two nights of poor sleep, camping starts losing its appeal.

Big Agnes believes that many people's negative sleeping experiences have limited tent camping and negatively affected the market. Those of us willing to do anything just to get outside have accepted these shortcomings and have grown accustomed to the experience. We have also accepted the sleeping discomfort of mummy-shaped bags and the current pads, because they're lighter and more packable. These products are the current industry standard.

THE COMPETITION

As a new company, it's important that our products are immediately positioned as superior to those of our competitors. Retailers have told us that the market for existing performance sleeping bags is saturated and stale. They feel that the market is ripe for something new and improved. Better, in this case, means more comfortable, lighter, and more packable. Big Agnes products address these market needs.

Our competition regarding sleeping bags comes from many of the largest companies in the outdoor industry, including Mountain Hardwear, Marmot, Sierra Design, REI, EMS, and The North Face. These companies control about 80 percent of sales in the sleeping bag market. Several smaller companies, such as Feathered Friends and Western Mountaineering, have niches in the high-end sleeping bag market. None of these companies offer bags like Big Agnes's. They have many years and financial resources invested in promoting the traditional mummy bag design as the best.

Several years ago, Marmot introduced a bag somewhat like ours that didn't have the success that they were hoping for. We feel that Marmot's concept was a

4

good one but that their failure came from poor positioning in the market. We think that their merchandising failure was due to not knowing how to position this sleeping bag with their more traditional bags. They were concerned with hurting their existing business and thus manipulated the new product to fit into that business. We believe that the other leading companies have had similar ideas and haven't ventured from the norm for similar reasons. We know that with the acceptance of our design as the new "standard" for comfort and performance, the competition will make the switch to duplicate our efforts.

Regarding sleeping pads, there are basically two styles in today's outdoor market: the self-inflating pad and closed-cell foam pad. The difference between the two is night and day. The self-inflating pads are constructed with an airtight outer shell that encapsulates an open-cell foam. This construction provides greater comfort in addition to being lighter and more packable than the closed-cell foam pads. The self-inflating pads cost approximately $65 and sell two to one over the closed cell-foam pads, which retail for around $15.

The technology and manufacturing of self-inflating pads is extremely limited due to the difficulty in making such a product. Currently there is only one manufacturer of self-inflating pads in the U.S. outdoor specialty market. Their product is very good, and they've had free reign to market and develop their position in this product. They've also done a good job in servicing the industry and building strong relationships with all of their retailers. We feel that even with such strong competition, there is always a need for two options in any market, as long as the offerings have a notable difference in terms of performance and/or value.

As long as Big Agnes stays on the offensive with new innovations that provide greater comfort and performance, we'll secure our position as the market leader in sleeping comfort.

MARKETING OBJECTIVES

Our current short-term goal is to quickly build brand and name recognition for Big Agnes products among North American outdoor consumers. Then our direct sales division will kick in and propel Big Agnes into a stronger financial position. We feel that within five years Big Agnes will be positioned for significant expansion or profitable acquisition. To accomplish our initial objective, we've developed a comprehensive plan to implement and manage our marketing and sales activities, our product development, and our administrative and operational expansion.

Big Agnes's long-term growth and success will come from our direct sales division. To achieve our short-term goal, we've implemented several programs. The first, more conventional marketing program was to develop a wholesale division that sells Big Agnes products to a select group of North American retailers. The wholesale division provides Big Agnes an affordable and quick avenue to get our product in front of consumers nationwide. In addition, it will generate immediate preseason sales. The wholesale division's sales and production numbers will serve as the foundation for growing the initially slower direct sales division.

The second program, directed at achieving our early goals, is a focused public relations and advertising campaign. Our public relations agency, Backbone Media, is getting Big Agnes products highlighted in all the outdoor consumer and industry publications via product reviews and feature articles. Additionally, we will promote Big Agnes by advertising in several select consumer outdoor publications. In a two-year period, Big Agnes brand recognition among consumers should begin to drive our direct sales division.

MANAGEMENT

The management team includes founders and owners Bill Gamber and Brad Johnson. Bill and Brad together have 40 years of experience directly related

5

to the outdoor market, and both have spent years climbing, kayaking, fly fishing, biking, skiing, and snowboarding.

Bill owns and operates BAP, Inc., which has manufactured outdoor clothing since 1986. Products are sold both wholesale and direct through the BAP store and the company's web site. As president of Big Agnes, Inc., Bill manages operations including administration, fulfillment, customer service, sales, and public relations. Bill has a degree in business administration and owns the building the store is in, which also houses Big Agnes's office space and R&D facilities.

Bill has been married to Lisa for five years, and they have a son. Bill's hobbies include training and racing in triathlons (he's competed in 12 Ironman Triathlons, four of them the Hawaiian Ironman Triathlon), fly fishing, climbing, and telemark skiing.

As vice president of Big Agnes, Inc., Brad manages product development and merchandising, manufacturing, and marketing. Brad founded and operated the Alpine Trails outdoor education center for eight years. This program was run out of the Whiteman School in Steamboat Springs, Colorado, and offered high school students the opportunity to backpack, raft, bike, and sail while earning credits and traveling internationally. He also cofounded and was partner of First Light, a manufacturer and wholesaler of outdoor clothing, where he was responsible for marketing, sales, and product merchandising, design, and development.

Before coming to Colorado, Brad worked for Lands' End as a product manager for both the sweater and outerwear divisions. For these $20 million and $35 million divisions, respectively, Brad managed the budgets, product merchandising and development, international sourcing, quality assurance, and marketing. For the last eight years, Brad has worked as a consultant to fabric and clothing manufacturers in the outdoor market on merchandising, design, and manufacturing.

Brad has been married to Janet for 29 years and they have three children. His hobbies include snowboarding, minimalist camping, kayaking, and woodworking.

Outside management advisors include bookkeeper Rich Hagar and accountant Jim Nowak. Both have offices in Steamboat Springs. Rich takes care of all entries and payables at the Big Agnes office, while Jim prepares quarterly and year-end state and federal reports. Our corporate attorney is John Grassby. Big Agnes has hired Backbone Media to handle promotion and public relations. Backbone's current accounts in the outdoor industry include Malden Mills, the manufacturers of Polartec fleece; Black Diamond, the leading climbing equipment manufacturer in the outdoor market; Eagle Creek travel luggage; and Pur Water Filters. Big Agnes's ads are prepared in-house by a graphic designer.

PRODUCTION

Instead of working with foreign product agents, we work directly with our manufacturers in China. We've hired a quality assurance agent with offices in China who will oversee our production and quality requirements. This structure has allowed us to get the best possible pricing and helped to establish an excellent relationship with our two manufacturers. Bill went to China to meet with the owners of each company and to see their facilities. We've also met with both manufacturers here in the United States.

By buying a finished product, we don't have to purchase any fabrics and trim in advance. This limits up-front cash needs and minimizes some administrative responsibilities. We've also made arrangements so we don't have to supply letters of credit—instead, we transfer money upon our manufacturers' shipping of our products. This allows our inspection team to give final approval before we have to make any payments.

6

Our pads are made by the Goodway Corporation, which specializes in sleeping pads and waterproof luggage. Goodway is the largest private label pad manufacturer to the European market, and they have been manufacturing these products for over 20 years. Goodway is a family-owned business run by the father, mother, and two sons, who were educated in the United States and graduated from the University of Southern California and the University of Colorado. The two sons and father speak fluent English. We've established a relationship with this family, which allows us to pay upon shipment of finished goods—an unusual arrangement that helps our peace of mind and cash flow.

The sleeping bag manufacturer is Tung Sang Sleeping Bag Factory. Tung Sang is family owned and managed by the father and son, who graduated from The University of Vancouver. Tung Sang has been manufacturing sleeping bags for more than 20 years and has a worldwide reputation for being one of the best—if not the best—sleeping bag manufacturer. They currently make bags for EMS, REI, L.L. Bean, Cabelas, Marmot, and Moonstone. We have also been able to set up payment upon shipment of final goods with Tung Sang.

Our products are manufactured in early December and ship from Hong Kong in late December. Each year, we anticipate receiving all products in Steamboat Springs by the end of January. We use a freight forwarder out of Denver, where our products clear Customs.

In addition to the sleeping bags and pads, Big Agnes manufactures and sells stuff sacks and compression straps. These are support products for the bags and pads and are also manufactured in China.

DISTRIBUTION

Big Agnes's wholesale division was developed to help speed up brand awareness. Additionally, working the wholesale market will bring in immediate and predictable preseason sales and help us with manufacturing minimums for our direct sales.

By selling our products to the top 150 retailers in the outdoor specialty market, Big Agnes products will be identified with, promoted by, and sold by the most successful outdoor retailers. We will entice the top retailers by giving them a product to sell that is new and better, provides better margins than similar products, and gives them large exclusive territories to support growth and specialty recognition. We will continue to attend industry trade shows, where we meet with retailers and distributors from around the world to show and sell Big Agnes products. These shows are held every January and August.

Direct sales will come when the consumer starts seeing products in their favorite store, reading product reviews, seeing Big Agnes ads, and hearing from friends about the value of our products. In all of our literature, workbooks, ads, product reviews, etc., we list our web site and toll-free number so consumers can easily get more information.

Fulfillment for wholesale and direct sales is handled out of our shop. While we maintain some inventory there, the bulk of our goods is stored at a local warehouse.

SUMMARY

The testing of and feedback about our integrated sleeping bags and pads has been overwhelmingly positive. The standard comment is, "It's hard to imagine that no one has thought of this before." Our most notable testimony came from Will Steger, a famed Arctic explorer who took our –10/60 system to the North Pole last winter. He said, "It was like sleeping in my bed. I was warm, never rolled off my pad and the system was far more compact." We know that after people get into a Big Agnes bag and experience the room and mobility, they're sold on its comfort and design.

7

The Big Agnes founders have years of specific outdoor-related business experience needed to build the company. The day-to-day challenges of operating a business are not new to the management team. We know what to plan for and have prepared our business plan with that experience in mind. No business is without crises; we've experienced many and know to be prepared for the worst. We know the success of persistence, hard work, and some good luck.

Our product line is limited to select styles and colors, which has allowed us to contract our manufacturing with two factories that specialize in sleeping bags and pads. These factories are within a short distance of one another and within a two-hour drive of Hong Kong, which allows our quality assurance team to easily oversee production from their Hong Kong office.

With an emphasis on marketing and public relations, we are certain that Big Agnes products will be quickly recognized as the most comfortable and best sleeping bag value on the market. Consumer awareness will fuel sales and fast growth and propel us toward our short- and long-term goals

8

FINANCIAL STATEMENTS

2006 Balance Sheet

2005 Profit and Loss

2006 Profit and Loss

Three-Year Cash Flow Projection

9

Big Agnes, Inc., 2006 Balance Sheet
March 31, 2006

		March 31, 2006
ASSETS		
Current Assets		
Checking/Savings		
1000 - 1st National Bank		$8,388.47
1450 - Prepaid Shipping & Duty		13,319.66
Total Checking/Savings		$21,708.13
Accounts Receivable		
1200 - Accounts Receivable		105,823.40
Total Accounts Receivable		$105,823.40
Other Current Assets		
1010 - Petty Cash		$40.00
1020 - A/R Trade		203.00
1120 - Inventory Asset		166,082.53
1499 - Undeposited Funds		8,955.22
1500 - Inventory Materials		5,506.60
Total Other Current Assets		$180,787.35
Total Current Assets		$308,318.88
Fixed Assets		
1300 - Machines & Equipment		$5,106.22
1325 - Product Design		
1325-10 - Bag Hang Tags	450.00	
1325-12 - Dealer Handbook	2,150.00	
1325-15 - Logo	500.00	
1325-30 - Stuff Sack Packaging	250.00	
1325-40 - Header Cards	1,500.00	
1325-50 - Design Miscellaneous	300.00	
1325-60 - POP Design	250.00	
Total 1325 - Product Design		5,400.00
1350 - Marketing Development		13,035.87
1375 - Product Development		
1375-05 - Fabric & sample bags	10,330.68	
1375-10 - F/W Patterns & Samples	3,417.60	
1375-20 - S/S Patterns & Samples	4,346.33	
1375 - Other	−141.45	
Total 1375 · Product Development		17,953.16
1380 · Web Design		1,979.95
1399 · Organizational Costs/Start Up		1,064.00
Total Fixed Assets		$44,539.20
TOTAL ASSETS		**$352,858.08**

10

Big Agnes, Inc., 2006 Balance Sheet, continued
March 31, 2006

		March 31, 2006
LIABILITIES & EQUITY		
Liabilities		
Current Liabilities		
Accounts Payable		
2000 - Accounts Payable		10,839.13
Total Accounts Payable		$10,839.13
Other Current Liabilities		
Gift Certificates		100.00
2200 - Sales Tax Payable		23.52
2300 - Loan Brad & Bill		195,000.00
2400 - Bill Gamber Loan		120,136.96
2500 - Loan—Bill Gamber		15,000.00
2510 - Brad Johnson		15,000.00
Total Other Current Liabilities		$345,260.48
Total Current Liabilities		$356,099.61
Total Liabilities		$356,099.61
Equity		
1110 - Retained Earnings		−66,387.53
3000 - Opening Bal Equity		
3100 - Gamber	18,100.00	
3200 - Johnson	18,100.00	
3300 - First Light Sales	15,000.00	
3000 - Opening Bal Equity – Other	3,316.12	
Total 3000 - Opening Bal Equity		54,516.12
Net Income		$8,630.00
Total Equity		$3,241.53
TOTAL LIABILITIES & EQUITY		**$352,858.08**

11

Big Agnes, Inc., 2005 Profit and Loss
January through December 2005

	January–December 2005	
Ordinary Income/Expense		
Income		
4300 - Direct		
4325 - REM Pads	7,107.65	
4350 - Sleeping Bags	33,560.10	
4375 - Accessories	2,322.25	
4300 - Other	49.00	
Total 4300 - Direct		$41,039.00
4500 - Wholesale		
4525 - REM Pads	48,640.38	
4550 - Sleeping Bags	94,134.40	
4560 - POP Displays	2,240.00	
4575 - Accessories	4,245.00	
4500 - Wholesale–Other	750.00	
Total 4500 - Wholesale		$150,009.78
4600 - Rental /Demo Sales		
4100 - Retail-BAP	3,976.64	
4625 - REM Pads	60.00	
4650 - Sleeping Bags	317.50	
4680 - Rental/Sample Sales	2,881.56	
Total 4600 - Rental /Demo Sales		$7,235.70
4800 - Other Income		
4900 - Sales Discounts	−4,682.27	
5550 - Finance Charges	223.18	
5600 - Shipping & Handling	5,722.11	
5700 - Over & Short	0.00	
Total 4800 - Other Income		$1,263.02
Total Income	$199,547.50	
Cost of Goods Sold		
5100 - Sleeping Bags	53,696.69	
5300 - Mattress Pads	27,208.96	
5500 - Accessories	5,998.20	
5900 - Warehouse	2,659.38	
5905 - Import Shipping	15,406.22	
5910 - Shipping	15,239.71	
Total COGS	$120,209.16	
Gross Profit		79,338.34
Expense		
6125 - Bad Debts		1,446.11
6135 - Contract labor		6,477.06
6143 - Commissions - Reps		6,550.83
6147 - Credit Card Fees		1,039.03
6175 - General & Administrative		
6120 - Bank Service Charges	413.00	
6145 - Computers & Office Equipment	528.17	

12

Big Agnes, Inc., 2005 Profit and Loss, continued
January through December 2005

		January–December 2005
6180 - Insurance		
6185 - Liability Insurance	1,160.75	
Total 6180 - Insurance		1,160.75
6195 - Internet Service		239.40
6200 - Interest Expense		9,143.33
6230 - Licenses and Permits		76.00
6240 - Miscellaneous		16.22
6245 - Office Equipment		542.00
6247 - Office Supplies		1,895.15
6249 - Personal & Training		33.50
6250 - Postage and Delivery		4,025.19
6270 - Professional Fees		
6650 - Accounting	225.00	
Total 6270 - Professional Fees		225.00
6290 - Rent		3,837.09
6325 - Computer Lease		1,026.47
6340 - Telephone		2,217.78
6350 - Travel & Entertainment		1,007.14
6175 - General & Administrative - Other		126.65
Total 6175 - General & Administrative		$26,317.84
6255 - Printing		
6255-20 - Hang Tags		690.97
6255-40 - Product Info Sheets		303.00
Total 6255 - Printing		993.97
6255-50 - POP		809.86
6400-10 - Samples		$5,380.28
6500 - Marketing		
6500-10 - OR Show		
6500-12 - Summer	11,557.53	
6500-13 - Winter	1,757.60	
6500-10 - OR Show—Other	11.35	
Total 6500-10 - OR Show		$13,326.48
6500-15 - Catalog		14,538.30
6500-20 - Advertising		8,999.22
6500-30 - PR Firm		17,897.59
6500-35 - Promotional Giveaways		5,931.65
6500-40 - Miscellaneous		889.13
Total 6500 - Marketing		$61,582.37
6500-37 - Cash Rebates		90.00
6950 - Web Page		
6950-10 - Web Page Design		7,627.77
6950-40 - Rental		890.00
6950-50 - Web Page Maintenance		950.00
Total 6950 - Web Page		9,467.77
Total Expense		$120,350.12
Net Ordinary Income		$-41,011.78
Net Income		$-45,011.78

13

Big Agnes, Inc., 2006 Profit and Loss Projections
January through July 2006

		January 1–July 8, 2006
Ordinary Income/Expense		
Income		
4300 - Direct		
4325 - REM Pads	20,294.24	
4350 - Sleeping Bags	48,766.25	
4375 - Accessories	2,213.25	
Total 4300 - Direct		$71,273.74
4500 - Wholesale		
4525 - REM Pads	71,759.27	
4550 - Sleeping Bags	183,024.85	
4560 - POP Displays	3,080.00	
4575 - Accessories	5,905.05	
Total 4500 - Wholesale		$263,769.17
4600 - Rental /Demo Sales		
4625 - REM Pads	129.50	
4650 - Sleeping Bags	120.15	
Total 4600 - Rental /Demo Sales		$249.65
4800 - Other Income		
4900 - Sales Discounts	−7,675.79	
5600 - Shipping & Handling	9,845.05	
Total 4800 - Other Income		$2,169.26
Total Income		$337,461.82
Cost of Goods Sold		
5100 - Sleeping Bags		100,790.89
5300 - Mattress Pads		51,008.39
5500 - Accessories		7,808.72
5900 - Warehouse		1,812.60
5910 - Shipping		11,244.02
Total COGS		$172,664.62
Gross Profit		$164,797.20
Expense		
6125 - Bad Debts		451.15
6135 - Contract labor		7,430.69
6143 - Commissions - Reps		7,609.97
6147 - Credit Card Fees		1,239.20
6175 - General & Administrative		
6120 - Bank Service Charges	400.00	
6180 - Insurance	1,341.30	
6195 - Internet Service	263.40	
6200 - Interest Expense		
6220 - Loan Interest	5,004.01	
6200 - Other	6,749.21	
Total 6200 - Interest Expense		$11,753.22

14

Big Agnes, Inc., 2006 Profit and Loss Projections, continued
January through July 2006

	January 1—July 8, 2006	
6230 - Licenses and Permits	25.00	
6247 - Office Supplies	656.42	
6250 - Postage and Delivery	2,677.97	
6270 - Professional Fees		
6280 - Legal Fees	2,098.48	
Total 6270 - Professional Fees	$2,098.48	
6290 - Rent	2,100.00	
6300 - Repairs		
6320 - Computer Repairs	50.00	
Total 6300 - Repairs	$50.00	
6325 - Computer Lease	737.48	
6340 - Telephone	1,306.75	
6350 - Travel & Ent	144.95	
Total 6175 - General & Administrative		$23,554.97
6255-50 - POP		832.01
6400-10 - Samples		2,769.87
6500 - Marketing		
6500-10 - OR Show		
6500-12 - Summer	4,452.40	
6500-13 - Winter	250.00	
Total 6500-10 - OR Show	$4,702.40	
6500-15 - Catalog	13,062.61	
6500-20 - Advertising	8,668.37	
6500-30 - PR Firm	9,589.95	
6500-35 - Promotional Giveaways	3,944.66	
6500-40 - Miscellaneous	148.37	
Total 6500 - Marketing		$40,116.36
6950 - Web Page		
6950-10 - Web Page Design	1,750.00	
6950-40 - Rental	72.80	
Total 6950 - Web Page		$1,822.80
Total Expenses		$85,827.02
Net Ordinary Income		$78,970.18
Net Income		$78,970.18

15

Big Agnes, Inc., Three-Year Cash Flow Projection
2005–2007

2005					TOTAL
	Jan - Mar 01	Apr - Jun 01	Jul - Sep 01	Oct - Dec 01	2005
Ordinary Income/Expense					
Income					
4300 - Direct					
4325 - REM Pads	614.00	1,403.00	2,993.97	2,000.00	7,010.97
4350 - Sleeping Bags	2,584.00	5,697.00	14,331.00	9,500.00	32,112.00
4360 - Tents					0.00
4375 - Accessories	129.00	890.00	833.00	500.00	2,352.00
4300 - Direct - Other	49.00	0.00	0.00	0.00	49.00
Total 4300 - Direct	3,376.00	7,990.00	18,157.97	12,000.00	41,523.97
4500 - Wholesale					0.00
4525 - REM Pads	18,774.00	15,976.35	9,893.85	3,000.00	47,644.20
4550 - Sleeping Bags	28,291.75	30,926.70	21,342.00	10,000.00	90,560.45
Tents					0.00
4560 - POP Displays	0.00	840.00	1,120.00		1,960.00
4575 - Accessories	1,458.50	1,479.50	958.50	1,400.00	5,296.50
Total 4500 - Wholesale	48,524.25	49,222.55	33,314.35	14,400.00	145,461.15
4600 - Rental /Demo					0.00
4625 - REM Pads	0.00	60.00	0.00	0.00	60.00
4650 - Sleeping Bags	0.00	317.50	0.00	0.00	317.50
4680 - Rental/Sample Sales	581.60	2,299.96	8,000.00	4,000.00	14,881.56
Total 4600 - Rental /Demo	581.60	2,677.46	8,000.00	4,000.00	15,259.06
4800 - Other Income					0.00
4900 - Sales Discounts	−2,609.49	−713.58	418.30	−418.00	−3,322.77
5550 - Finance Charges	0.00	0.00	60.00	250.00	310.00
5600 - Shipping & Handling	1,108.05	1,766.21	1,937.62	900.00	5,711.88
5700 - Over & Short	0.00	0.00	0.00	0.00	0.00
Total 4800 - Other Income	−1,501.44	1,052.63	2,415.92	732.00	2,699.11
Total Income	50,980.41	60,942.64	61,888.24	31,132.00	204,943.29
Cost of Goods Sold					0.00
5100 - Sleeping Bags	14,525.60	16,611.40	13,897.44	7,000.00	52,034.44
5300 - Mattress Pads	9,898.20	9,195.20	5,718.04	1,800.00	26,611.44
Tents					0.00
5500 - Accessories	886.62	2,250.94	2,156.82	750.00	6,044.38
5900 - Warehouse	698.38	984.00	425.00	450.00	2,557.38
5905 - Import Shipping	2,970.35	4,021.29	4,180.65	3,200.00	14,372.29
5910 - Shipping	3,250.42	3,566.59	4,139.05	4,000.00	14,956.06
Total COGS	32,229.57	36,629.42	30,517.00	17,200.00	116,575.99
Gross Profit	18,750.84	24,313.22	31,371.24	13,932.00	88,367.30
Expense					0.00
Bad Debt					
Management Salaries					0.00
Workers Comp					0.00
Unemployment Taxes					0.00
Management Life Ins.					0.00
6135 - Contract Labor	1,029.47	2,501.28	1,638.06	1,700.00	6,868.81
6143 - Commissions - Reps	0.00	2,658.77	2,618.47	700.00	5,977.24
6147 - Credit Card Fees	12.19	260.23	479.56	150.00	901.98
6175 - General & Administrative					0.00
6120 - Bank Service Charges	72.00	-40.00	144.00	50.00	226.00
6145 - Computers & Office Equipment	434.42	0.00	0.00	0.00	434.42
6180 - Insurance					0.00
6185 - Liability Insurance	1,160.75	0.00	0.00	0.00	1,160.75
Total 6180 - Insurance	1,160.75	0.00	0.00	0.00	1,160.75

16

Big Agnes, Inc., Three-Year Cash Flow Projection, continued
2005–2007

2005	Jan - Mar 01	Apr - Jun 01	Jul - Sep 01	Oct - Dec 01	TOTAL 2005
6195 - Internet Service	59.85	59.85	59.85	59.85	239.40
6230 - Licenses and Permits	76.00	0.00	0.00	0.00	76.00
6240 - Miscellaneous	0.00	0.00	0.00	0.00	0.00
6245 - Office Equipment	542.00	0.00	0.00	0.00	542.00
6247 - Office Supplies	285.62	881.05	637.31	20.00	1,823.98
6249 - Personal & Training	8.41	25.09	0.00	0.00	33.50
6250 - Postage and Delivery	380.04	1,316.94	763.50	500.00	2,960.48
6270 - Professional Fees					0.00
6650 - Accounting	225.00	0.00	0.00	0.00	225.00
Legal				500.00	500.00
Total 6270 - Professional Fees	225.00	0.00	0.00	500.00	725.00
6290 - Rent	900.00	900.00	900.00	900.00	3,600.00
6325 - Computer Lease	195.98	292.71	294.83	293.00	1,076.52
6340 - Telephone	379.27	684.67	636.09	600.00	2,300.03
6350 - Travel & Entertainment	100.49	847.30	59.35	100.00	1,107.14
6175 - General & Administrative - Other	0.00	0.00	126.65	0.00	126.65
Total 6175 - General & Administrative	5,861.49	10,387.89	8,357.67	5,572.85	30,179.90
6255-50 - POP	15.16	550.73	0.00	243.97	809.86
6400-10 - Sample	906.00	1,027.48	1,280.10	1,600.00	4,813.58
6500 - Marketing					0.00
6500-10 - OR Show					0.00
6500-12 - Summer	2,392.50	0.00	4,922.46	3,400.00	10,714.96
6500-13 - Winter	1,757.60	0.00	0.00	0.00	1,757.60
6500-10 - Other Show	0.00	0.00	11.35	0.00	11.35
Total 6500-10 - OR Show	4,150.10	0.00	4,933.81	3,400.00	12,483.91
6500-15 - Catalog	7,463.34	3,810.35			11,273.69
Dealer Insert	2,809.61				2,809.61
6500-20 - Advertising	2,798.75	2,598.25	1,732.59	1,000.00	8,129.59
6500-30 - PR Firm	3,393.39	4,850.48	4,998.83	4,700.00	17,942.70
6500-35 - Promotional Giveaways	1,611.74	1,162.16	1,843.05	1,400.00	6,016.95
6500-40 - Miscellaneous	63.21	799.59	−26.11	25.00	861.69
Total 6500 - Marketing	19,480.53	13,220.83	16,291.78	10,525.00	59,518.14
6500-37 - Cash Rebates	0.00	0.00	90.00	0.00	90.00
6950 - Web Page					0.00
6950-10 - Web Page Design	2,400.77		0.00	0.00	2,400.77
Web Writing	4,000.00	1,220.00			5,220.00
6950-40 - Rental	620.00	120.00	30.00	30.00	800.00
6950-50 - Web Page Maintenance	0.00	480.00	0.00	300.00	780.00
Web Miscellaneous					0.00
Total 6950 - Web Page	7,020.77	1,820.00	30.00	330.00	9,200.77
Total Expense	33,283.95	27,006.93	26,049.55	18,271.82	104,612.25
Net Ordinary Income	−14,533.11	−2,693.71	5,321.69	−4,339.82	−16,244.95
Net Income BIT	−14,533.11	−2,693.71	5,321.69	−4,339.82	−16,24.95
Balance Sheet Items					
Loans Principal & Interest					
Interest					
6200 - Interest Vectra Note	2,046.67	2,527.77	1,586.67	2,500.00	8,661.11
Interest BG					
Taxes					
Net Income					

17

Big Agnes, Inc., Three-Year Cash Flow Projection, continued
2005–2007

2006	Jan - Mar 02	Apr - Jun 02	Jul - Sep 02	Oct - Dec 02	TOTAL 2006
Ordinary Income/Expense					
Income					
4300 - Direct	4,390.00	7,050.00	6,950.00	4,200.00	22,590.00
4325 - REM Pads	15,900.00	18,500.00	25,200.00	17,555.00	77,155.00
4350 - Sleeping Bags					0.00
4360 - Tents	973.00	945.00	1,325.00	973.00	4,216.00
4375 - Accessories	0.00	0.00	0.00	0.00	0.00
4300 - Direct — Other	21,263.00	26,495.00	33,475.00	22,728.00	103,961.00
Total 4300 - Direct					
4500 - Wholesale	22,597.00	39,200.00	26,500.00	7,000.00	95,297.00
4525 - REM Pads	65,419.00	85,500.00	71,500.00	45,849.00	268,268.00
4550 - Sleeping Bags					0.00
Tents	2,240.00	2,100.00	0.00	0.00	4,340.00
4560 - POP Displays	2,745.00	2,800.00	1,200.00	400.00	7,145.00
4575 - Accessories	93,001.00	129,600.00	99,200.00	53,249.00	375,050.00
Total 4500 - Wholesale					
4600 - Rental /Demo	85.00	600.00	200.00		885.00
4625 - REM Pads	0.00	3,000.00	200.00		3,200.00
4650 - Sleeping Bags	0.00	2,000.00	3,000.00	1,500.00	6,500.00
4680 - Rental/Sample Sales	85.00	5,600.00	3,400.00	1,500.00	10,585.00
Total 4600 - Rental/Demo					
4800 - Other Income	−2,954.00	−2,800.00	−1,000.00	−300.00	−7,054.00
4900 - Sales Discounts	0.00	0.00	75.00	418.00	493.00
5550 - Finance Charges	3,617.00	4,210.00	3,500.00	1,500.00	12,827.00
5600 - Shipping & Handling	0.00	0.00	0.00	0.00	0.00
5700 - Over & Short	663.00	1,410.00	2,575.00	1,618.00	6,266.00
Total Other Income	0	0	0	0	0
Total Income	115,012.00	163,105.00	138,650.00	79,095.00	495,862.00
Cost of Goods Sold	105,000.00	73,000.00			178,000.00
5100 - Sleeping Bags	53,000.00	0.00			53,000.00
5300 - Mattress Pads					0.00
Tents	0	0	0	0	0
5500 - Accessories	4,000.00				4,000.00
5900 - Warehouse	750.00	950.00	950.00	450.00	3,100.00
5905 - Import Shipping	16,000.00	10,000.00			26,000.00
5910 - Shipping	3,208.00	3,500.00	3,000.00	1,500.00	11,208.00
Total COGS	181,958.00	87,450.00	3,950.00	1,950.00	275,308.00
Gross Profit	−66,946.00	75,655.00	134,700.00	77,145.00	220,554.00
Expenses					
Bad Debt	451.00				451.00
Management Salaries	0	0	22,500.00	22,500.00	45,000.00
Workers Compensation	0.00				0.00
Unemployment taxes	0	0	684.00	684.00	1,368.00
Management Life Ins.		1,000.00			1,000.00
6135 - Contract Labor	1,952.00	6,000.00	6,000.00	5,000.00	18,952.00
6143 - Commissions - Reps	1,670.00	9,000.00	11,400.00	6,100.00	28,170.00
6147 - Credit Card Fees	254.00	700.00	845.00	500.00	2,299.00
6175 - General & Administrative					0.00
6120 - Bank Service Charges	36.00	75.00	0.00	0.00	111.00
6145 - Computers & Office Equipment	0.00	125.00	125.00	125.00	375.00
6180 - Insurance					
6185 - Liability Insurance	1,341.00	0.00	0.00	0.00	1,341.00
Total 6180 - Insurance	1,341.00	0.00	0.00	0.00	1,341.00

18

Big Agnes, Inc., Three-Year Cash Flow Projection, continued
2005–2007

2006					TOTAL
	Jan - Mar 02	Apr - Jun 02	Jul - Sep 02	Oct - Dec 02	2006
6195 - Internet Service	60.00	60.00	60.00	60.00	240.00
6230 - Licenses and Permits	0.00	0.00	0.00	0.00	0.00
6240 - Miscellaneous	0.00	250.00	250.00	250.00	750.00
6245 - Office Equipment	0.00				0.00
6247 - Office Supplies	259.00	625.00	625.00	625.00	2,134.00
6249 - Personal & Training	0.00	50.00	50.00	50.00	150.00
6250 - Postage and Delivery	1,657.00	1,500.00	500.00	1,000.00	4,657.00
6270 - Professional Fees					
6650 - Accounting	0.00	125.00	125.00	125.00	375.00
Legal	2,098.00	1,000.00			3,098.00
Total 6270 - Professional Fees	2,098.00	1,125.00	125.00	125.00	3,473.00
6290 - Rent	900.00	900.00	900.00	900.00	3,600.00
6325 - Computer Lease	388.00	300.00	300.00	300.00	1,288.00
6340 - Telephone	514.00	1,200.00	1,200.00	1,200.00	4,114.00
6350 - Travel & Ent	145.00	750.00	1,000.00		1,895.00
Total 6175 - General & Administrative	11,725.00	23,660.00	46,564.00	39,419.00	121,368.00
6255-50 - POP	0.00				0.00
6400-10 - Samples	1,303.00	1,000.00	500.00		2,803.00
6500 - Marketing					
6500-10 - OR Show	0	0	0	0	0.00
6500-12 - Summer	3,200.00	6,000.00	3,200.00		12,400.00
6500-13 - Winter	250.00		2,400.00	2,400.00	5,050.00
6500-10 - Other Show	0	0	0	0	0.00
Total 6500-10 - OR Show	250.00	3,200.00	8,400.00	5,600.00	17,450.00
6500-15 - Catalog	13,012.00				13,012.00
Dealer Insert		3,500.00			3,500.00
6500-20 - Advertising	5,236.00	3,500.00	2,500.00	1,000.00	12,236.00
6500-30 - PR Firm	4,832.00	4,500.00	4,500.00	4,500.00	18,332.00
6500-35 - Promotional Giveaways	2,046.00	300.00	1,500.00	900.00	4,746.00
6500-40 - Miscellaneous	12.00	350.00	350.00	250.00	962.00
Total 6500 - Marketing	25,388.00	11,850.00	20,750.00	12,250.00	70,238.00
6500-37 - Cash Rebates	0.00	45.00	45.00	45.00	135.00
6950 - Web Page					
6950-10 - Web Page Design	1,750.00				1,750.00
Web Writing	0	0	0	0	0.00
6950-40 - Rental	25.00	120.00			145.00
6950-50 - Web Page Maintenance		100.00	100.00	100.00	300.00
Web Miscellaneous	250.00	250.00	250.00	250.00	1,000.00
Total 6950 - Web Page	1,775.00	100.00	220.00	100.00	2,195.00
Total Expense	40,191.00	42,655.00	54,579.00	38,314.00	175,739.00
Net Ordinary Income	−107,137.00	33,000.00	80,121.00	38,831.00	44,815.00
Net Income BIT	−107,137.00	33,000.00	80,121.00	38,831.00	44,815.00
Balance Sheet Items					
Loans Principal & Interest					
Interest	1302	5000	5000	4000	15,302.00
6200 - Interest Vectra note	0	0	0	0	0.00
Net Income					8,513.00

Big Agnes, Inc., Three-Year Cash Flow Projection, continued
2005–2007

2007	Jan - Mar 03	Apr - Jun 03	Jul - Sep 03	Oct - Dec 03	TOTAL 2007
Ordinary Income/Expense					
Income					
4300 - Direct					
4325 - REM Pads	4,500.00	10,500.00	9,000.00	6,000.00	30,000.00
4350 - Sleeping Bags	15,500.00	30,500.00	42,000.00	26,300.00	114,300.00
4360 - Tents	500.00	1,500.00	2,500.00	912.00	5,412.00
4375 - Accessories	550.00	1,560.00	2,460.00	2,035.00	6,605.00
4300 - Direct - Other	0.00	0.00	0.00	0.00	0.00
Total 4300 - Direct	21,050.00	44,060.00	55,960.00	35,247.00	156,317.00
4500 - Wholesale					
4525 - REM Pads	51,000.00	59,900.00	32,698.00	7,722.00	151,320.00
4550 - Sleeping Bags	105,000.00	130,300.00	95,903.00	66,100.00	397,303.00
Tents	13,450.00	23,300.00	10,967.00	8,210.00	55,927.00
4560 - POP Displays	1,200.00	1,000.00			2,200.00
4575 - Accessories	5,544.00	4,312.00	1,848.00	618.00	12,322.00
Total 4500 - Wholesale	176,194.00	218,812.00	141,416.00	82,650.00	619,072.00
4600 - Rental/Demo					
4625 - REM Pads	200.00	600.00	200.00		1,000.00
4650 - Sleeping Bags	400.00	3,000.00	200.00		3,600.00
4680 - Rental/Sample Sales	1,000.00	3,000.00	2,500.00	1,000.00	7,500.00
Total 4600 - Rental/Demo	1,600.00	6,600.00	2,900.00	1,000.00	12,100.00
4800 - Other Income					
4900 - Sales Discounts	−2,500.00	−2,000.00	−500.00	−200.00	−5,200.00
5550 - Finance Charges			200.00	400.00	600.00
5600 - Shipping & Handling	6,000.00	6,820.00	5,500.00	4,000.00	22,320.00
5700 - Over & Short					0.00
Total 4800 - Other Income	3,500.00	4,820.00	5,200.00	4,200.00	17,720.00
Total Income	202,344.00	274,292.00	205,476.00	123,097.00	805,209.00
Cost of Goods Sold					
5100 - Sleeping Bags	80,000.00	80,000.00			160,000.00
5300 - Mattress Pads	75,000.00				75,000.00
Tents	35,000.00				35,000.00
5500 - Accessories	7,000.00				7,000.00
5900 - Warehouse	1,350.00	1,350.00	1,350.00	900.00	4,950.00
5905 - Import Shipping	16,000.00	10,000.00			26,000.00
5910 - Shipping	4,500.00	5,500.00	3,000.00	2,000.00	15,000.00
Total COGS	218,850.00	96,850.00	4,350.00	2,900.00	322,950.00
Gross Profit	−16,506.00	177,442.00	201,126.00	120,197.00	482,259.00
Expense					
Bad debt					
Management Salaries	25,000.00	25,000.00	25,000.00	25,000.00	100,000.00
Workers Comp					0.00
Unemployment Taxes	1,500.00	1,500.00	1,500.00	1,500.00	6,000.00
Management Life Ins.				1,000.00	1,000.00
6135 - Contract Labor	7,500.00	7,500.00	7,500.00	7,500.00	30,000.00
6143 - Commissions - Reps	10,000.00	23,200.00	10,600.00	5,549.00	49,349.00
6147 - Credit Card Fees	404.61	875.67	1,632.00	1,147.00	4,059.28
6175 - General & Administrative					0.00
6120 - Bank Service Charges	100.00	100.00	100.00	100.00	400.00
6145 - Computers & Office Equipment	250.00	250.00	250.00	250.00	1,000.00
6180 - Insurance					0.00
6185 - Liability Insurance	1,500.00				1,500.00
Total 6180 - Insurance	0.00	1,500.00	0.00	0.00	1,500.00

20

Big Agnes, Inc., Three-Year Cash Flow Projection, continued
2005–2007

2007					TOTAL
	Jan - Mar 03	Apr - Jun 03	Jul - Sep 03	Oct - Dec 03	2007
6195 - Internet Service	60.00	60.00	60.00	60.00	240.00
6230 - Licenses and Permits					0.00
6240 - Miscellaneous	250.00	250.00	250.00	250.00	1,000.00
6245 - Office Equipment					0.00
6247 - Office Supplies	700.00	700.00	700.00	700.00	2,800.00
6249 - Personal & Training	50.00	50.00	50.00	50.00	200.00
6250 - Postage and Delivery	3,500.00	2,500.00	500.00	1,500.00	8,000.00
6270 - Professional Fees					0.00
6650 - Accounting	125.00	125.00	125.00	125.00	500.00
Legal	250.00	250.00	250.00	250.00	1,000.00
Total 6270 - Professional Fees	375.00	375.00	375.00	375.00	1,500.00
6290 - Rent	1,500.00	1,500.00	1,500.00	1,500.00	6,000.00
6325 - Computer Lease	300.00	300.00	300.00	300.00	1,200.00
6340 - Telephone	1,000.00	2,000.00	2,000.00	1,500.00	6,500.00
6350 - Travel & Entertainment	2,000.00			2,000.00	4,000.00
6175 - General & Administrative - Other					0.00
Total 6175 - General & Administrative	54,489.61	68,660.67	54,317.00	47,281.00	224,748.28
6255-50 - POP	400.00				400.00
6400-10 - Samples	1,000.00	1,000.00	1,000.00		3,000.00
6500 - Marketing					0.00
6500-10 - OR Show					0.00
6500-12 - Summer		3,200.00	2,000.00	3,200.00	8,400.00
6500-13 - Winter	1,500.00		3,200.00	3,200.00	7,900.00
6500-10 - Other Show		2,000.00	1,500.00	2,000.00	5,500.00
Total 6500-10 - OR Show	1,500.00	8,400.00	3,500.00	8,400.00	21,800.00
6500-15 - Catalog	14,500.00				14,500.00
Dealer Insert				3,500.00	3,500.00
6500-20 - Advertising	6,000.00	7,000.00	4,000.00	3,000.00	20,000.00
6500-30 - PR Firm	4,500.00	4,500.00	4,500.00	4,500.00	18,000.00
6500-35 - Promotional Giveaways	1,000.00	500.00	1,000.00	500.00	3,000.00
6500-40 - Miscellaneous	250.00	250.00	250.00	250.00	1,000.00
Total 6500 - Marketing	27,750.00	20,650.00	16,750.00	16,650.00	81,800.00
6500-37 - Cash Rebates	50.00	100.00	75.00	25.00	250.00
6950 - Web Page					0.00
6950-10 - Web Page Design	6,000.00				6,000.00
Web Writing	3,500.00				3,500.00
6950-40 - Rental	120.00		120.00		240.00
6950-50 - Web Page Maintenance		250.00		250.00	500.00
Web Miscellaneous	250.00	250.00	250.00	250.00	1,000.00
Total 6950 - Web Page	9,870.00	250.00	620.00	500.00	11,240.00
Total Expense	93,559.61	90,660.67	72,762.00	64,456.00	321,438.28
Net Ordinary Income	−110,065.61	86,781.33	128,364.00	55,741.00	160,820.72
Net Income BIT	−110,065.61	86,781.33	128,364.00	55,741.00	160,820.72
Balance Sheet Item					
Loans Principal & Interest		8,000	10,000	15,000	33,000
Interest					
6200 - Interest Vectra note	9,000	7,000	5,000	3,000	24,000
Interest BG					
Taxes				35,000	35,000
Net Income					$68,820.72

21

The Gray Ghost Inn Business Plan

AN EXAMPLE FOR PURCHASING A BUSINESS

Business Plan for
The Gray Ghost Inn
at Mount Snow, Route 100
West Dover, Vermont 05356

Submitted by
Magnus and Carina Thorsson

December 15, 2003

STATEMENT OF PURPOSE

Magnus and Carina Thorsson seek a bank loan for $500,000 to purchase the personal property, assets, and business known as The Gray Ghost Inn in West Dover, Vermont. The loan, together with our equity investment of $244,000, will be sufficient to acquire the inn and provide the working capital necessary to ensure the ongoing success of the inn.

BUSINESS DESCRIPTION

The Gray Ghost Inn is a successful, year-round hospitality facility. Magnus and Carina Thorsson are proposing to purchase the real estate personally and operate the business either as a C or Sub-S corporation. The Inn will offer limited food service, breakfast, and lodging to customers seeking comfortable accommodations when staying in the Mount Snow area.

The Gray Ghost Inn operates as a bed-and-breakfast facility during much of the year and offers clean and comfortable rooms at a modest rate. Customers perceive the inn as a great value. An important segment of the business is providing all meals to summer and fall bus-tour groups. The innkeepers' gracious hospitality combined with an "at-home" feel creates a memorable experience and results in repeat business.

The Inn is located within a mile of Mount Snow, making it a destination for skiers in winter. In the summer, people are attracted to the area by activities including the Mount Snow Golf School, organized mountain biking tours and trails, and antique shopping. During the summer and in the fall, The Gray Ghost Inn has a well-established business of servicing and guiding bus tours. The current owners will assist in booking business for the coming year (12 tours are already booked), attending applicable shows, and helping guide the tours in the first year of our ownership.

The Inn has 26 rooms with rates ranging from $48 per person per night in the off season to $130 during the busy ski season. There are four additional rooms used as owners' quarters located on the lower level of the property, which will provide comfortable accommodations for our family. The Inn has a large dining room/sitting room with great opportunities for food and beverage service. Amenities include a sauna and large game room on the lower level, as well as three viewing areas with cable TV.

Operating The Gray Ghost Inn as a country inn will continue to be very profitable. The opportunities that we will capitalize on will make the business even stronger in the future. Mount Snow will continue to draw crowds from Boston, New York, and Washington, and 100-percent snow-making capabilities extend the ski season for as long as possible.

We will apply our extensive experience in the hotel and restaurant business to tap into other food and beverage revenue opportunities, as well as using Carina's years of experience in sales to increase room occupancy as well as food sales.

The Gray Ghost Inn will continue to be operated on a year-round basis. The focus of the business will be to service the current clientele and to devote sales and marketing efforts to attracting business during the slower seasons.

Both of us have extensive experience in the hospitality industry, having spent the majority of our careers working in hotels and restaurants in various capacities. We feel that our combination of education and hands-on experience, along with hard work, will make us successful innkeepers.

THE COMPETITION

The Mount Snow area has numerous hospitality facilities, and visitors seeking accommodations have many options. There are nine lodges, including The Gray Ghost Inn, within one mile of Mount Snow. Weekend rates during the ski season range from $204 with breakfast to $480 with no meals. The Gray Ghost Inn competes well as a moderately priced,

2

clean and comfortable lodge with a strong price/value image.

There are many establishments within a one-mile radius of The Gray Ghost Inn that offer food service. The selection and quality is good. We intend to review the demand for food service and focus on the current promise of quality breakfast and pre-arranged meals for groups.

The Gray Ghost Inn will continue to benefit from the aggressive marketing efforts of the Mount Snow area and American Skiing Company. The Gray Ghost Inn is well positioned for growth, considering its location—seven-tenths of a mile from the base of Mount Snow, and within minutes of two golf courses and many other attractions.

THE MARKETING PLAN

We have two marketing objectives. First, we will continue to market to and service the customer base that the current owners have developed. Second, we will simultaneously expand our market to better utilize the capacity that The Gray Ghost Inn offers. The Inn currently operates at a 35 percent occupancy rate on a year-round basis and can increase business with a more aggressive approach to marketing. By extending the seasons and adding revenue-generating services and amenities, we will realize increased occupancy, revenue, and ultimately profits. Our approach to achieving this is to implement our plan in two distinct seasons.

Winter Season

During the winter season, the Inn derives business from individual travelers and families seeking to ski the Mount Snow area and engage in related winter activities. The area has been greatly improved and modernized by its new owner, American Skiing Company, which will ensure Mount Snow's continued popularity. Being located less than a mile from the slopes, The Gray Ghost Inn is very desirable for skiers. We will review the existing marketing media to reach current clients as well as implement new methods. We plan to upgrade and improve the web site with interactive links, an online reservation system, and availability chart. The web site will get more exposure through online booking services and lodging listings, which will have to be reviewed based on effectiveness and exposure.

Summer/Bus Tour Season

Bus tours represent about 40 to 50 percent of the Inn's annual business. It's important to maintain the current contacts with the coach and tour leaders, both to sustain the current base of group business and to solicit new groups. We will do this by word-of-mouth advertising, video, and print advertising material. Carina will use her years of experience in catering sales to solicit business for the Inn. We will look at the feasibility of traveling to the market areas in person to make presentations at senior centers and to bus-tour organizers. Upgrading the food service and offering interesting foods, such as southern-style barbecue, grilled steak dinner, or blue crab dinner served outdoors, will generate additional business. Golf and mountain biking are growing in the area, which in turn have increased the demand for lodging. Promoting our service to those groups during the early summer months will enable us to increase occupancy rates. Working with local fly-fishing and bird-hunting guides will also generate additional room sales in the early spring and late fall.

Food Service

During the ski season, the Mount Snow area population can swell to 30,000 people, many looking for a place to eat. Although there are many restaurants in the area competing for dinner guests, we believe that by offering a fixed-price, all-inclusive, simple menu during busy periods, we can generate additional revenue. Offering an inclusive dinner to overnight

3

guests on weekends would further increase our revenue (and profit) per occupied room.

Overseas Tours

Using contacts in Iceland both with Iceland Air and in tour sales, we will create a package with arrival in Boston with a weekend stay in Boston at an Iceland Air selected hotel and then a three-night, four-day package of skiing at Mount Snow and Killington. (Skiing in Iceland is limited). During the spring and early summer, golf tours will be offered with a similar combination of one or two nights in Boston and three nights at The Gray Ghost Inn. We are fluent in four languages, thus better able to target and service foreign tours. We expect the first groups to arrive next November.

THE MANAGEMENT PLAN

We plan to manage the Inn as a couple. Although all decisions will not be cooperatively handled, some will be. We will divide the responsibility of running the business according to our past experience and training. Specifically assigned responsibilities for the operation will be as follows:

MAGNUS	CARINA
Overall operation	**Front services**
Housekeeping	Reservation
Maintenance	Sales/billing
Kitchen/cooking	Dining room
Administration	Greeting guests
Cost control	Record keeping
Procurement	Correspondence
Daily and periodical	Tour director and
accounting	guide
Business plan	
monitor/update	

JOINT RESPONSIBILITIES
Business analysis
Capital expenditures
Personnel responsibilities
Marketing

FINANCIAL ANALYSIS

Income Statement

The historic income statements demonstrate a strong base of sales, an excellent level of operating income, and tight cost controls, with the exception of excess compensation paid to family members.

Gross Revenue

Gross revenue ranges from $223,068 to $272,358 over the period from 1995 through 1998. Please note that 1998 figures are below normal because the ski season ended earlier than usual, there was little skiing over Christmas, and buses canceled tours in October (there were only 11 bus tours). Revenue through October 2003 has surpassed year-end sales in 2002, and assuming a normal December, revenue in the $270,000 to $280,000 range is expected.

Gross Profit Margin

Gross profit margins are in the range of 90.7 percent to 91.3 percent, which is considered good. Cost of goods sold has been consistent with a range of 9.3 percent to 8.7 percent. The profitability of rooms appears to be above industry standards for full-service hotels. We can maintain or reduce labor costs further. Additional business can be generated in April through July as well as in November. There are segments of the leisure industry we feel can be promoted and catered to during these periods, which have not been considered in the past, such as bird hunters and fly fishermen, along with golfers.

Labor Costs

Labor costs are currently below industry averages of 20 percent to 25 percent for full-service hotels. We can maintain or lower labor costs further. The current owners have overcompensated their daughter and her husband (who works part-time on full-time pay). These people are paid even during the slower

4

seasons when the business can be operated with no outside help. The labor percentage of overhead has been 17.7% to 22.4% for the past four years. We believe we can successfully run the Inn with one full-time employee, with varied workload, and two part-time employees, which will give us a lower labor percentage.

Expenses

The current owners have run their business very effectively. We feel that maintaining the tight control in the first year of operation is imperative to continued financial success. As we get familiar with the operation, we will scrutinize each line item for any adjustment that could enhance profitability. We expect operating expenses to be higher in the first year.

PRO FORMA FINANCIAL ANALYSIS

Critical Success Factors

The total income to the owners can be substantially improved by increasing current levels of occupancy and sales per occupied room by offering meals to weekend skiers. Furthermore, seeking new markets such as overseas travelers, fly fishermen, and bird hunters will improve occupancy during the slow periods. Factors facilitating this improvement are:

1. Lodging levels must be sustained if not increased to ensure continued market share.

2. Cost control must be diligently monitored to ensure maximum utilization of resources.

3. The business must have a strong marketing program supported by financial resources and management time to sustain current volume and build a solid foundation for future growth.

ASSUMPTIONS

1. The historic occupancy levels can be sustained and even increased by marketing and attracting business during the low-level occupancy periods. The biggest opportunity to improve occupancy exists during midweek. By aggressively marketing attractive packages for midweek stays offering inclusive amenities such as admission to attractions or food and beverages, we can improve occupancy during slower times.

2. Currently the Inn only serves breakfast. Offering limited food and beverage service both to overnight guests and to the public will increase traffic and overall revenue. This can be done with minimal additional cost other than cost of goods. We intend to draw upon our education and experience to run the food and beverage operation ourselves with little added variable labor cost.

3. Computerizing the business will increase the efficiency of routine accounting functions and help with the cost-control and analytical functions of running the business. Computerizing will further enable us to create a continually updated database of customers to perform concise marketing. The current owners have not done any direct mailings in the last few years.

4. Working with local fly fishing and hunting guides, we intend to bring in business during the otherwise slow months of May, June and November. Furthermore, midweek during the months of November and December, we hope to bring Icelandic tourists in for inexpensive shopping in southern Vermont and Boston, as well as the excellent skiing not found in Iceland. We will do this in cooperation with Iceland Air, which offers inexpensive fares to Boston during these two months.

5. Total debt service coverage is 1.96 times given an average historical discretionary income of $115,000.00. Total debt service coverage will be 2.13 based upon our projected first-year income from operations.

5

FINANCIALS

MAGNUS AND CARINA THORSSON
PERSONAL BALANCE SHEET
NOVEMBER 30, 2003

Current Assets		Liabilities	
Cash and savings	$44,000	Mortgage	$132,000
Deposit with Country Business, Inc.	$10,000		
Stocks	$2,000		
CD	$12,000		
Retirement Fund			
401(k)	$7,100		
Fixed Assets			
Real estate*	$195,000		
Personal property	$15,000		
Automobiles	$8,000		
Total Assets**	$293,100	**Total Liability**	$132,000
Net Worth	**$161,100**		

*Our home is under contract for $195,000 and scheduled to close on December 28. Net proceeds from the sale of our home will be $49,000.

**In addition to the above net worth, an additional cash investment of $122,000 will be made from Magnus's parents.

SOURCES AND APPLICATION OF FUNDING

Sources

Buyers' equity	$122,000
Magnus's parents	122,000
Bank financing	500,000
Total	**$744,000**

Applications

Purchase business	$695,000
Inventory	1,500
Closing cost	13,000
Utility deposits	3,000
Working capital	31,500
Total	**$744,000**

6

THE GRAY GHOST INN PROJECTED INCOME STATEMENTS

	YEAR 1	YEAR 2	YEAR 3
REVENUE			
Lodging	275,000	295,000	300,000
Food & beverage	15,000	16,000	20,000
Total Revenue	**290,000**	**311,000**	**320,000**
Cost of goods sold			
Beginning inventory	2,000	2,000	2,500
Food & beverage	29,500	31,725	32,150
Ending inventory	−2,000	−2,500	−2,500
Total cost of goods sold	**29,500**	**31,225**	**32,150**
Gross profit	**260,500**	**279,775**	**287,850**
EXPENSES			
Advertising	12,000	10,000	10,000
Auto expense	4,500	4,500	4,500
Insurance	8,000	12,000	12,000
Legal & professional services	1,200	1,000	1,000
Office supplies	324	350	400
Repairs & maintenance	8,565	10,500	11,500
Supplies	1,200	1,200	1,200
Taxes & licenses	6,500	7,500	8,000
Meals & entertainment	1,500	1,500	1,500
Utilities	16,599	17,500	18,000
Wages & related taxes	44,500	45,000	46,000
Bank charges	1,887	2,177	2,300
Cleaning and laundry	8,582	9,330	9,500
Dues & subscriptions	1,200	1,200	1,300
Licenses	760	810	850
Miscellaneous	800	800	800
Owners' salary	0	0	0
Postage	1,500	1,500	1,700
Tour/guest entertainment	15,000	18,000	18,000
TOTAL EXPENSES	**134,617**	**144,867**	**148,550**
Owners' discretionary income	125,883	134,908	139,300
Debt service (P&I)	55,920	55,920	55,920
Owners' income after debt service	69,963	78,988	83,380
Owners' salary	14,400	24,000	24,000
Depreciation	15,000	15,000	15,000
Amortization	7,000	7,000	7,000
Net Income	**33,563**	**32,988**	**37,380**

7

THE GRAY GHOST INN MONTHLY CASH FLOW STATEMENT

	Pre-start-up	Feb	Mar	Apr	May	Jun	Jul	Aug	Sep	Oct	Nov	Dec	Jan
Cash beg. of period	47,500	26,340	39,442	48,933	39,741	33,729	27,886	30,604	36,484	46,125	85,205	79,322	90,888
Revenue													
Cash	0	30,250	19,250	0	5,500	5,500	19,250	30,250	29,700	66,000	11,000	28,600	29,700
Advance deposits	0												
Total revenue	**0**	**30,250**	**19,250**	**0**	**5,500**	**5,500**	**19,250**	**30,250**	**29,700**	**66,000**	**11,000**	**28,600**	**29,700**
Subtotal	47,500	56,590	58,692	48,933	45,241	39,229	47,126	60,854	66,184	112,125	96,205	107,922	120,588
Expenses													
Advertising			1,500	1,000	1,000	2,000	2,000	1,000	540	2,960			12,000
Auto expense		375	375	375	375	375	375	375	375	375	375	375	375
Insurance	2,000	2,000			2,000			2,000			2,000		
Legal, prof, closing	13,000	360		480				180				180	
Office supplies		27	27	27	27	27	27	27	27	27	27	27	27
Repairs & maintenance				1,500	1,000	1,000	1,000	1,500			2,565		
Supplies		144	120	0	24	24	84	152	156	162	48	142	144
Taxes & licenses		780	650	0	130	130	455	826	845	878	260	767	780
Meals & entertainment		180	150	0	30	30	105	191	195	203	60	177	180
Utilities	3,000	600	750	200	200	581	1,162	1,245	1,411	2,075	1,411	1,925	1,975
Wages & related taxes		5,340	4,450	0	890	890	3,115	5,652	5,785	6,008	1,780	5,251	5,340
Bank charges		226	189	0	38	38	132	240	245	255	75	223	226
Cleaning and laundry		1,030	858	0	172	172	601	1,090	1,116	1,159	343	1,013	1,030
Dues & subscription		100	100	100	100	100	100	100	100	100	100	100	100
Licenses	500	380						380					
Miscellaneous		96	80	0	16	16	56	102	104	108	32	94	96
Owners' salary		800	800	800	800	800	800	1,600	1,600	1,600	1,600	1,600	1,600
Postage		50	50	50	50	500	50	50	50	50	500	50	50
Tour/guest entertainment							1,800	3,000	2,850	6,300	1,050		
Subtotal	16,500	12,488	10,099	4,532	6,852	6,683	11,862	19,710	15,399	22,260	12,223	12,374	23,923
Debt services		4,660	4,660	4,660	4,660	4,660	4,660	4,660	4,660	4,660	4,660	4,660	
Total cash expenditures	16,500	17,148	14,759	9,192	11,512	11,343	16,522	24,370	20,059	26,920	16,883	17,034	23,923
Cash at end of period	26,340	39,442	48,933	39,741	33,729	27,886	30,604	36,484	46,125	85,205	79,322	90,888	96,665

Note: prepayment of oil will reduce fuel cost during the first few months

8

THE GRAY GHOST INN HISTORIC OCCUPANCY FIGURES

2003	JAN	FEB	MAR	APR	MAY	JUN	JUL	AUG	SEP	OCT	NOV	DEC	TOTAL
Nights Open	31	28	31	0	11	30	31	31	30	31	30	31	315
Avail. Rm Nights	806	728	806	0	286	780	806	806	780	806	780	806	8,190
Nights Sold	305	381	250	0	14	95	111	312	334	466	32	320	2,300
Average Occ.	37.9%	52.4%	31.0%	0.0%	5.0%	12.1%	13.8%	38.7%	42.8%	57.8%	4.1%	40%	24.6%

PROJECTED OCCUPANCY FIGURES

2004	JAN	FEB	MAR	APR	MAY	JUN	JUL	AUG	SEP	OCT	NOV	DEC	TOTAL
Nights Open	31	29	31	30	31	30	31	31	30	31	30	31	366
Avalbl. Rm Nights	806	754	806	780	806	780	806	806	780	806	780	806	9,516
Nights Sold	400	474	250	0	78	120	250	390	340	500	33	320	3,155
Average Occ.	50%	63%	31%	0%	10%	15%	31%	48%	44%	62%	4%	40%	33%

9

SUPPORTING DOCUMENTS

Resumes of Magnus and Carina Thorsson

Magnus Thorsson

Store Manager

Experience 11/98–Present   *Sutton Place Gourmet; McLean, VA*

- Special project involving revenue and profit enhancement. Revenue up 20 percent YTD on budget increased by 13 percent.
- Increased profit margin in a focus department above budget.
- Effectively controlling costs resulting in favorable operating contribution YTD.
- Trained department managers on control of profit margins and variable costs as well as monitored their progress month to month.
- Developed pricing structure for department-specific, value-added program for entire chain.
- Set merchandising plan for special monthly sales drives.

Store Manager

10/96–11/98   *Sutton Place Gourmet; Reston, VA*

- Opened two stores, installed systems and started operation.
- Managed retail food operation with 90 employees.
- Interviewed, selected, trained, rewarded and terminated employees.
- Acting general manager for four months.
- Annual gross revenue of $7 million.
- Directly accountable for financial performance of assigned departments.
- Initiated new programs, now standard for entire company.
- Developed store budgets for second year of operation.

Room Service Manager

6/95–10/96   *Washington Hilton; Washington, DC*

- Accountable for day-to-day operations for room service for 1,100 rooms.
- Developed menus and oversaw installation.
- Controlled costs and managed personnel.
- Managed service for catering and special events.
- Clients included President of the U.S.

Executive Steward

8/94–6/95   *New York Hilton; New York, NY*

- Directly accountable for annual budget of $3 million.
- Managed four assistants and a staff of 120.
- Negotiated service contracts and oversaw equipment purchases for food and beverage operation.

10

Magnus Thorsson, continued

Assistant Executive Steward

11/93–8/94   *New York Hilton; New York, NY*

- Accountable for specific areas of the operation.
- Responsible for managing shifts.
- Monitored and maintained installed programs.
- Designed a new process layout saving the hotel $40,000 per year, which has been implemented and is working successfully.
- Designed a practical work-layout installed to decrease work-related accidents.

Tutor

10/92–8/94   *Johnson and Wales University; Providence, RI*

- Main fields of concentration were micro and macro economics, statistics, and financial management.
- Assisted students with comprehension of class material.
- Instructed according to text and materials covered in classes.

Food and Beverage Consultant/Manager

1992 and 1993 Summers   *Hotel Ork; Hveragerdi, Iceland*

- Advised with planning procedures realizing 30-percent cost improvement.
- Managed kitchen operations.
- Launched new menus, developed standardized recipes.
- Enhanced existing controlling systems.

Chef/Kitchen Manager

1989–1991 Summers   *Hotel Isafjördur; Isafjördur, Iceland*

- Created menus for both a la carte and banquets.
- Ordered, received, and handled food.
- Cooked for 120-seat restaurant.
- Main focus on seafood and game.

Education

1991–1993   *Johnson and Wales University, Providence, RI*

    BS, Hotel-Restaurant Institutional Management.
    GPA 3.77, graduated Magna Cum Laude.
    A.S., Hotel-Restaurant Management.

1987–1991   *Hotel and Catering School of Iceland, Iceland.*

    Journeyman certificate in culinary arts.
    Four years hands-on program, including three years in a kitchen.

Interests: Fly-fishing, clay shooting, bird hunting, food, wine, wildlife habitat preservation.

Other: Vice President of the Icelandic Association of Washington, DC.
Culinary advisor to the Embassy of Iceland.

11

Carina Thorsson

Employment

SENIOR CATERING SALES MANAGER   8/99–PRESENT

The Grand Hyatt Washington; Washington, DC

OFF-PREMISE CATERING SALES MANAGER   11/97–8/99

Bittersweet Catering; Alexandria, VA

- Team production of booking a company total revenue of $1,740,000.
- Market segment: primarily weddings as well as office parties, open-house receptions.
- Exceeded goals by 100%.

CATERING SALES MANAGER   11/95–10/97

The Hyatt Regency Washington on Capitol Hill; Washington, DC

- Market segment: catering for local groups of more than 100 guests, i.e. fund raising, political and corporate events, conventions
- Beverage revenue of $3,240,000 for the local market.
- Responsible for booking 30 percent of the total catering department's annual food budget. Solicited and coordinated off-property catering events for the off-site catering division, Regency Caterers by Hyatt.
- Responsible for soliciting local accounts and maintaining relationships with existing accounts.
- Developed competitive menu proposals.
- Coordinated client outings and chef tables.

CATERING SALES MANAGER   08/93–11/95

The Waldorf-Astoria Hotel; New York, NY

- Booked $3 million in combined food and beverage annual revenue out of a departmental total of $28 million for 1995.
- Booked events ranging from smaller corporate breakfasts and luncheons to weddings and fund-raising dinners for 1,000 guests.
- Coordinated catering for conventions.
- Conducted site inspections, promoted facilities and services.
- Developed client menus, wrote contracts and letters, and organized all other arrangements as they related to social and corporate events.
- Coordinated the overall set-up and implementation of events and meetings.
- Communicated with relevant departments to ensure proper servicing of accounts.

CATERING SALES ADMINISTRATOR   11/92–8/93

The Waldorf-Astoria Hotel; New York, NY

- Forecasted, monitored, and evaluated catering sales, and food and beverage revenue.
- Communicated information throughout the hotel.
- Evaluated inquiries.
- Managed automated function book (diary) system and space.
- Processed contracts and proposals.
- Administered catering sales department staff.

12

Employment (continued)

DIARY MANAGER
01/92–11/92

The Waldorf-Astoria Hotel; New York, NY

- Transferred manual diary system to automated function book.
- Maintained control of meeting room space as bookings were generated by the sales and catering departments.
- Entered, revised and cancelled bookings as defined by the department to ensure proper availability.

NEW YEAR'S EVE RESERVATIONS MANAGER
11/91–01/92

The Waldorf-Astoria Hotel; New York, NY

- Supervised all aspects of sales and coordination for the operation of three annual New Year's Eve gala parties in the hotel, total sales of $250,000.

ASSISTANT RESTAURANT MANAGER
04/91–11/91

Oscar's Restaurant, The Waldorf-Astoria Hotel; New York, NY

- Scheduled and coordinated the daily activities of 40 employees.
- Managed high volume casual restaurant with $4.2 million annual revenue and served 800 to 1,300 breakfast, lunch and dinner covers daily.
- Set financial goals, met revenue and payroll forecast.
- Engineered menus, food and beverage service, quality, consistency and productivity standards.
- Developed and implemented procedural training manual, supervision, coaching and disciplinary action.
- Maintained total guest satisfaction by following through with Oscar's standards.
- Maintained a positive working atmosphere in a union environment by balancing the company's goals and objectives with union rules and regulations.

MANAGEMENT TRAINEE
03/90–04/91

The Waldorf-Astoria Hotel; New York, NY

- Rotated one to three weeks throughout the hotel's departments. Gained valuable knowledge of the entire operation.
- Food and beverage office—area of specialization.
- Chef's department—area of specialization.

Education

BS SERVICE ECONOMICS AND MANAGEMENT
1990

The University of Gothenburg, School of Economics, Gothenburg, Sweden

LANGUAGES: Swedish: mother tongue; English: fluent; French: working knowledge

COMPUTER SKILLS: Windows application, Excel, Word Perfect, Microsoft Publisher

TRAINING: Hyatt Professional Selling Skills and Professional Negotiations Skills
Hilton Costume Focused Catering
Front Line Leadership and Facilitating for Results

TRAVELS: United States, Canada, Mexico, Sweden, Iceland, Norway, Denmark, Finland, Germany, France, Switzerland, Austria, England, Netherlands, Cyprus, Saudi Arabia, Kenya, Uganda, Tanzania, Zambia, Zimbabwe, South Africa, Indonesia, Thailand and Singapore

13

LETTER OF INTENT TO PURCHASE THE BUSINESS

November 17, 2003

Philip H. Steckler, III
Country Business, Inc.
PO Box 940
Brattleboro, VT 05301

RE: Acquisition of The Gray Ghost Inn

Dear Phil:

On the basis of financial statements and other information made available to us through the owners, we hereby express our intention to acquire the business known as The Gray Ghost Inn located in West Dover, Vermont (hereinafter sometimes referred to as the "Business").

It is our intention to enter into a contract for the purchase of the Business to include at minimum the following basic terms:

A. *Description.* The property and business assets used in the operation of the Business, to include the following: the real estate, all furnishings, fixtures, and equipment (except for some select personal items for which a list will be provided and become a part of this agreement), contracts and contract rights, leasehold rights and improvements, goodwill, the name of the Business, know-how, trade secrets, customer list, supplier list, vendor arrangements, publicity materials, and business records all free and clear of liens, restrictions or encumbrances. Cash, accounts receivable, prepaid assets, vehicles and all liabilities are not included in the purchase.

B. *Purchase Price.* The purchase price will be $675,000 plus inventory at cost.

C. *Terms.* The purchase price will be paid as follows:
   (1) $10,000 evidence of good faith received and held by Country Business, Inc. on the date of execution of this Letter of Intent by the Buyer.
   (2) $20,000 additional earnest money deposit paid upon execution of the final Purchase and Sale Agreement by Buyer and Seller.
   (3) An additional $645,000 plus the cost value of inventory, cash or certified check, on date of closing (note: this to be comprised of an additional equity investment of $165,000 from purchaser) and $480,000 plus the value of inventory from a financial institution.
   (4) It may be necessary to obtain bridge financing of up to $20,000 from either the seller or a bank until June.

D. *Closing.* This letter of intent anticipates a closing on or about January 15, 2004. Additionally, we agree to have our attorney develop the draft of a Purchase and Sale Agreement, embodying the contingencies that follow, with specific details, to be ready for the Seller's attorney within four weeks of the execution of this Letter of Intent.

14

E. *Non-competition.* The present owner of the Business will be expected to agree not to compete with the Business for a period of five years within a 100 mile radius of West Dover.

F. This Letter of Intent is contingent upon Buyers obtaining satisfactory financing within 45 days of this letter. Buyer agrees to begin preparing a business plan immediately for the purpose of bank financing.

Our intentions, of course, presuppose the accuracy of financial statements and other data provided to and to be provided to us. In the absence of any material or adverse change in the Business prior to the closing date, we are ready to negotiate the terms of a definitive contract for the purchase of the Business.

Before a contract of purchase is finalized, we will want to be satisfied to at least the following matters:

1. We will want to become familiar with and be satisfied with the terms and assignability of all contracts, licenses, and permits materially affecting the Business and its prospects.
2. We will want our accountant to become familiar with the method of accounting used by the Business, including the review of all financial data to ensure that the business has been represented accurately.
3. We will want a list of all equipment and fixtures included and excluded in the sale, with any changes therein to be subsequently reported to us prior to the execution of the Purchase and Sale Agreement subject to our approval.
4. We will want to be aware of any actions, expressed, or implied, that would limit our ability to run the Business in an effective manner.
5. We will expect the Seller to comply with any applicable bulk sale or similar law, or to provide mutually acceptable measures in substitution thereof.
6. We will want to be assured that the Business is operating in compliance with all legal and environmental codes and standards, in a manner consistent with good business practices.
7. Seller warrants that the facility, systems, and equipment will be in good working order at time of closing.
8. We will want to be aware of any warranty or liability considerations that have or could be made. This would include possible legal action.
9. Included in the purchase price shall be the Buyers' right to use the name The Gray Ghost Inn.
10. Allocation of the purchase price as to furnishings, equipment, goodwill and Covenant not to Compete to be agreed upon between Buyer and Seller prior to the Purchase and Sales Agreement.
11. This letter is contingent upon Buyer obtaining all federal, state, and local licenses needed to operate The Gray Ghost Inn.
12. Seller agrees to deliver The Gray Ghost Inn free and clear of any and all business debts and will execute an affidavit in lieu of compliance, and meet required UCC filings.
13. Seller agrees to familiarize Buyer with all aspects of the operation of the Business. As part of this transaction, Seller agrees to work with Buyer on a full-time basis for one week after the closing, and on an as-needed basis for an additional week. Thereafter, Seller agrees to answer all questions by phone for up to one year after closing. It is understood that bus tour groups are important to the business, and that the Seller will need to assist Buyer in a way that extends beyond the specific "hands-on" time specified above. Seller will work with Buyer in instructing Buyer as to the selling tours, planning itineraries, taking purchasers to sites being visited, and make appropriate introductions.

15

At Buyers' expense, Seller will assist at applicable shows within one year of sale. As part of this transaction, Seller will act as tour guide for the two bus tour groups that are booked in June and July of 2004. In addition, Seller is willing to be the tour guide, if the Buyer wishes, for the remainder of the year and will be paid at the rate of $60/day.

Seller is expected to put forth his best effort to maintain the reputation and earnings of The Gray Ghost during the transition period from Seller to Buyer, and continue to book future business.

14. Seller will make available all existing town and state land use permits and zoning permits that may be in Seller's possession. If any environmental assessments have been done, such reports shall also be made available.

15. If we are unable to obtain satisfactory financing, or a satisfactory Purchase and Sales Agreement is not reached, or should any of the contingencies set forth in this letter not be satisfied at the time of closing, the Earnest Money Deposit is to be returned in full to the Buyer and this offer to purchase shall be null and void.

Please present this proposal to the Seller and if it is acceptable, ask Seller to so indicate by signing the enclosed copy of this letter. It is understood by both parties that it is our mutual intention to exercise due diligence in completing this transaction as outlined or subsequently agreed to in a Purchase and Sales agreement.

Please let John and Kay know that we look forward to working closely with them in making this a smooth transition.

Yours sincerely,

_____   _____
      Magnus Thorsson   Carina Thorsson

SS # _____-_____-_____   SS # _____-_____-_____

Acknowledged and concurred in this _____ day of _____, 20 ____ .

_____   _____

16

CHAPTER 11

Buying a Business

While building a business from scratch sounds exciting, it's risky because it's the most difficult way to get into business. A better option for many entrepreneurs is buying a going concern—it shortens the learning curve, reduces the costs of "on-the-job training," and helps avoid many of the errors that you might make in developing your business from the ground up. In an already existing business, everything is in place, from customers to a credit line at the bank. Other advantages include:

- *History*. The business already has a proven track record, which you can carry on if your management skills and experience are a good match for the business. The better you are at successfully running the business, the sooner you'll realize a return on your investment.
- *Established base*. You're buying a proven concept with an established customer/ client base, supplier network, and trained employees.
- *Fewer or no purchases*. You don't have to buy new equipment or inventory.
- *Simpler financing*. Financing is easier because an existing business has established credit, and growth can be financed through tradi-

tional sources like banks. Financing is always available to help the right person buy a profitable business.

- *Advice from the previous owner*. The previous owner is often available for consultation, and existing records can help you formulate a strategic business plan.

The disadvantages of buying a business include:

- *Inherited problems*. If the business had problems (a poor image, equipment obsolescence, inferior marketing materials, a bad location, or weak customer relations), you will inherit them.
- *A difference in management style*. Culture clashes with employees can occur as you make changes in the business.
- *Profit pressures*. Any loans incurred from the purchase of the business, as well as inadequate financial controls and credit management policies of the previous owner, will place pressure on a new owner's cash flow and reduce profitability.
- *An inflated business valuation*. An overvalued appraisal will result in a too-high purchase price for the business.

- *Market or industry challenges.* A changing marketplace or industry may be the real reason why the owner is selling. Find out why he or she is "retiring."

In some businesses, the new owner will have to compete with the reputation already established by the old owner. Frequently you'll see signs on buildings that say, "Under New Management." These announcements bring in customers who might have been dissatisfied with the previous management but are willing to give the business another chance. Sometimes in these circumstances, it pays to change the name of the business and begin an aggressive public relations campaign. In cases where previous management was strong and had a good rapport with the public, however, it's not a good idea to change the name or put up an "Under New Management" sign.

Keep in mind that all businesses are for sale for a reason. And it's up to you to discover what that reason is, whether it's financial or personal. Do your homework

BUSINESS FAILURES

One of the primary reasons for selling a business is that it has failed or is about to fail. The symptoms of failure are important to recognize so you can isolate the problems and either solve them if you buy the business, or not buy the business.

Some businesses try to expand without proper capitalization and in doing so they ruin their credit. Suddenly they're on a COD or cash-only basis and have limited cash flow. The business might be very productive and profitable if it could be expanded to the next level, where it would operate economically and with sufficient cash flow. Sellers who are undercapitalized usually aren't going to admit it to you, so be wary. However, there is always the chance you could get a good buy if the seller is up front with you.

A healthy business shouldn't have financial problems if it were properly capitalized. Usually you can determine if over-expansion is the case by looking at the aging of payables and observing whether the company has been slow to pay its bills or has any suits, judgments, or liens against it.

To determine the aging of payables, look at the invoice dates and see when the bills are paid. If bills in the industry are typically paid in thirty to sixty days and these invoices were paid in ninety days, you have an indication that the seller was short of capital.

Another way to determine whether the business is properly capitalized is to look at its bank statements. You can also run a credit check on the company through the local credit bureau; if you are not a member of the credit bureau in your area, you may be able to have your lawyer or banker do this for you.

Sometimes businesses have a poor collection procedure with their receivables, which creates a cash flow problem. Or they can be careless about the way they grant credit. A bad cash flow alone need not deter you from buying a business—many financial problems can be remedied through implementing proper credit procedures and strong financial controls.

After undercapitalization, poor management is the next most common reason businesses fail. A business may have everything going for it, but the owners don't know how, or are reluctant, to delegate.

People often go into business with optimistic, even grandiose, ideas of what they're going to do and what kind of money they're going to make. They are not very realistic. While optimism is useful for a business owner, it's also important to be realistic. Unless businesses expand to include a sufficient number of employees to take care of it, the business may show low profits and require a lot of the owner's time. These businesses may fail because owners do not know how to manage their workload.

and investigate thoroughly before you even consider investing.

INVESTIGATE BEFORE INVESTING

Your investigation should be in-depth and meticulous. During this process, you may feel pressured for a variety of reasons:

- Another buyer is in the wings
- Interest rates are rising
- Time is running out
- You're feeling anxious to get started
- The opportunity seems ideal to you.

Buying a business is a complex and highly emotional transaction. To make the best decision and achieve the most favorable terms, be aware of your feelings at all times, as they reveal why you're passionate about a particular business. And don't forget to bounce your thoughts off your attorney, CPA, and other advisors.

Preliminary Evaluation

Use the Business Evaluation Checklist (Figure 11.1) to conduct your own evaluations of prospective businesses. Make several copies of the form so you can use one for each business you assess.

To conduct your preliminary investigation, make an outline of items to research that don't have to involve the seller. They include.

- *Location.* How important is location to this particular business? Is the location ideal? Is the area undergoing any major changes, such as construction of high-rise office buildings, shopping centers, and apartment complexes? Are there any other changes in the neighborhood that could eventually alter the location's present status either positively or negatively? How dependent is the company on walk-in business? How long has the business been in that location?
- *Management.* Does the owner or management have good relationships with the customers and employees? How will a change in ownership affect the clientele and staff?
- *Goodwill.* Has the management supported local or industry events either through membership, dona-

tions of goods or services, or participation? If so, to what extent? What's the procedure for handling customer complaints? Check the written and stated policies.
- *Equipment.* How well is the physical location maintained? Is it clean and well-organized?
- *First impressions.* What's your first reaction to the business?

Establish a Relationship with the Seller

If, after your preliminary investigation, you decide to continue investigating the purchase of a business, begin to establish a relationship with the owner. Be careful, however, with what you say to staff, vendors, suppliers, customers, and the public at large, as they may not yet know that the business is for sale. At this stage, confidentiality is a key concern.

Make arrangements to meet the seller at a neutral location, like a restaurant or coffee shop. You may want to start out by providing the seller with your résumé and talking about your experience in the industry. Also include a financial statement, so the seller can verify your ability to deal in good faith. A CPA can prepare an audited financial statement, or you can have a bank prepare an unaudited one. Don't forget to provide the seller with some references. Once you establish yourself as a qualified buyer, you're in a position to get more information on the business for sale.

Here are some questions to ask the seller, possibly at the first meeting but no later than the second meeting. Feel free to take notes while asking:

- What do you like best about this business?
- Would you be available for consultation for a period of time?
- How did you get started in this business?
- If you were the new owner, knowing what you do about this business, where would you make additional investments?
- Do the employees know that the business is being sold? How do they feel about it? (If confidentiality is not an issue, ask permission to chat with staff and management.)
- Why are you selling and how quickly do you want to sell?

FIGURE 11.1	Business Evaluation Checklist

If you find a business that you would like to buy, consider the following points before you decide whether to purchase it. Take a good look at the business and answer the following questions. They will help you determine whether it is a sound investment.

❑ Why does the current owner want to sell the business?

❑ Does the business have a high potential for future growth, or will its sales decline?

❑ If the business is in decline, will you be able to save it and make it successful?

❑ Is the business in sound financial condition? Have you seen audited year-end financial statements for the business? Have you reviewed the most recent statements? Have you reviewed the business' tax returns for the past five years?

❑ Have you seen copies of all of the business' current contracts?

❑ Is the business now, or has it ever been, under investigation by any government agency? If so, what is the status of any current investigation? What were the results of any past investigations?

❑ Is the business currently involved in a lawsuit, or has it ever been involved in one? If so, what is the status or result?

❑ Does the business have any debts or liens against it? If so, what are they for and in what amounts?

❑ What percentage of the business' accounts are past due? How much does the business write off each year for bad debts?

❑ How many customers does the business serve on a regular basis?

❑ Who makes up the market for this business? Where are the customers located? (Do they all come from your company or from across the state, or are they spread across the globe?)

❑ Do sales fluctuate with the season?

❑ Does any single customer account for a large portion of the sales volume? If so, would the business be able to survive without this customer? (The larger your customer base is, the more easily you will be able to survive the loss of any customers. If, on the other hand, you exist mainly to serve a single client, the loss of that client could finish your business.)

❑ How does the business market its products or services? Does its competition use the same methods? If not, what methods does the competition use? How successful are they?

❑ Does the business have exclusive rights to market any particular products or services? If so, how has it obtained this exclusivity? Is it making the best possible use of this exclusivity? Do you have written proof that the current business owner can transfer this exclusivity to you?

❑ Does the business hold patents for any of its products? Which ones? What percentage of gross sales do they represent? Would the sale of the business include the sale of any patents?

❑ Are the business' supplies, merchandise, and other materials available from several suppliers, or are there only a handful who can meet the business' needs? If you lost the business' current supplier, what impact would that loss have on your business? Would you be able to find substitute goods of the appropriate quality and price?

❑ Are any of the business' products in danger of becoming obsolete or of going out of style? Is this a "fad" business?

❑ What is the business' market share?

❑ What competition does the business face? How can the business compete successfully? Have the business' competitors changed recently? Have any of them gone out of business, for instance?

❑ Does the business have all of the equipment you think is necessary? Will you need to add or update any equipment?

| FIGURE 11.1 | **Business Evaluation Checklist,** continued |

❑ What is the business' current inventory worth? Will you be able to use any of this inventory, or is it inconsistent with your intended product line?

❑ How many employees does the business have? What positions do they hold?

❑ Does the business pay its employees high wages, or are the wages average or low?

❑ Does the business experience high employee turnover? If so, why?

❑ What benefits does the business offer its employees?

❑ How long have the company's top managers been with the company?

❑ Will the change of ownership cause any changes in personnel?

❑ What employees are the most important to the company?

❑ Do any of the business' employees belong to any unions? If so, have they ever held any strikes? How long did the strikes last?

DOING DUE DILIGENCE

After you've met with the seller and received answers to your questions, it's time to conduct an in-depth investigation. Some sellers of small businesses may complain about providing the data you're requesting, if only because they may not have analyzed their business that thoroughly. Your response should be that without this kind of information you cannot consider buying the business. If the business is being sold through a broker, or you decide to enlist the services of one, he or she will get this financial data for you.

Most likely you'll have to sign a confidentiality agreement with the seller and assure him or her that you will not contact anyone for additional information about the business without his or her prior approval. The last thing a seller wants to do is disrupt or threaten important relationships with staff or suppliers by prematurely announcing the sale of the business.

As you begin evaluating businesses for sale, verify the values and examine the status of the following 25 items.

Inventory

Inventory refers to all products and materials on hand for resale to or use by a client. You or a qualified representative should be present at any inventory valuation proceeding and determine what's on hand at present, how long it's been there, and what was on hand at the end of the last fiscal year and the one preceding that. What condition is the inventory in? Is it salable? Are you interested in selling it? Inventory valuation is usually subject to negotiation.

Furniture, Fixtures, Equipment, and Building

Get a list from the seller that includes the name and model number for each piece of equipment. Then determine its present condition, market value when purchased, present market value, and whether the equipment was purchased or leased. Find out how much the seller has invested in leasehold improvements and maintenance to keep the facility in good condition. Determine what modifications you'll have to make to the space to suit your needs.

Copies of All Contracts and Legal Documents

These include leases, purchase agreements, distribution agreements, subcontractor agreements, sales contracts, union contracts, business employee agreements, and any other legal documents concerning the business such as fictitious business name statements, articles of incorporation, registered trademarks, copyrights, and patents. For any leases (equipment, office space, etc.), find out whether they're transferable and whether the lessor's permission is necessary to assign the lease. If the business you're considering has valuable intellectual property such as a trade name, patent, or trade secret, make sure to consult with an attorney who specializes in intellectual property law.

Incorporation

If the company is a corporation, check to see what state it's registered in.

Tax Return

Make sure you have access to the previous five years' returns. Many small business owners make use of the business for personal needs. They may buy products they

personally use and charge them to the business, or take vacations through the company, go to trade shows with their spouses, and so on. You and your CPA may have to read between the lines to determine the actual net worth of the company.

Financial Statement

You want to evaluate the books and financial statements for the past five years to determine the earning power of the business. Examine the sales and operating ratios with a CPA familiar with this type of business. The operating

WHERE TO LOOK FOR A BUSINESS

Where do you find businesses for sale? First, check the classified sections in newspapers and trade magazines. Editions of newspapers usually have numerous listings in the classified section, especially in large metropolitan newspapers like *The New York Times*. *The Wall Street Journal* also lists businesses for sale under "Business Opportunities." In addition, trade magazines usually have classified sections that list businesses for sale.

Realtors are another good source. Many brokers not only deal in residential and commercial properties but also offer a number of other services. One of them is selling businesses.

You may want to inform people you see frequently (friends, neighbors, business associates) that you're in the market for a business. This could lead you to a company with an immediate reference that can be advantageous in your initial dealings with the seller.

Business brokers will be one of your best routes for finding an existing company. Be careful when dealing with brokers, however, because some will list businesses on an exclusive basis, thereby limiting your exposure to other firms that may be for sale in your area.

Your local chamber of commerce can also be an invaluable resource. Many maintain files of businesses for sale within the area as well as interested buyers. Most chambers of commerce will not only be able to bring together a buyer and a seller but will also supply information about business conditions within the area.

Additional avenues to find existing businesses for sale might require more research on your part but could end up paying off with the right business for you. These sources include suppliers, distributors, manufacturers, and trade associations that deal in the type of business you're interested in starting. They may be able to tell you whether such a business is for sale in your area.

Also, check with attorneys, accountants, and bankers who deal with small businesses. They usually know what is happening in the business community or can guide you in the right direction.

As a last resort, you might question business owners within the area. You'll find that most people with small businesses are very helpful with one another. They also are knowledgeable about business conditions within their market areas and can tell you whether or not a business is for sale. You might even get lucky and run into an owner who is getting ready to sell a business.

ratios should also be compared to industry ratios, which can be found in annual reports produced by Robert Morris & Associates as well as those by Dun & Bradstreet.

Sales Records

Although sales will be logged in the financial statements, take a careful look at the monthly sales records for at least the past 36 months. Break down sales by product lines, if several products are involved, as well as by cash and credit sales. This provides you with some understanding of cycles that the business may go through, and you can compare the industry norms of seasonal patterns with what you see in the business. Also, obtain the sales figures of the ten largest accounts for the past twelve months. If the seller doesn't want to release his or her largest accounts by name, it's acceptable for the seller to code them. What you're interested in is the pattern of sales.

Complete List of Liabilities

Consult an independent attorney and CPA to examine the list of liabilities and determine the potential costs and legal ramifications. These may be items like lawsuits, liens by creditors against assets, or the use of assets such as capital equipment or receivables as collateral to secure short-term loans. Your CPA should also be on the lookout for unrecorded liabilities, such as employee benefit claims and out-of-court settlements.

All Accounts Receivable

Break these down by 30, 60, 90, and more than 90 days. Checking the age of receivables is important because the longer they're outstanding, the lower the value of the account. You should also make a list of the top 10 accounts and check their creditworthiness. If the clientele is creditworthy and the majority of the accounts are outstanding beyond sixty days, a stricter credit collection policy may speed up collection of receivables.

All Accounts Payable

Like accounts receivable, accounts payable should be broken down by thirty, sixty, ninety, and more than ninety days to determine how well cash flows through the company. For payables older than ninety days, check to see if any creditors have placed liens on the company's assets.

Debt Disclosure

This includes all outstanding notes, loans, and any other debt to which the business has agreed. Are any business investments on the books that may have taken place outside of the normal area? Were any loans made to customers?

Merchandise Returns

Does the business have a high rate of returns? Has it gone up in the past year? If so, can you isolate the reasons for returns and will you be able to correct the problem(s)?

Customer Patterns

If this business can track customers, define the current customers: How many are first-time buyers? Were any customers lost over the past year? When are the peak buying seasons? When does consumer demand slacken? What type of merchandise is the most popular, and at what price?

Marketing Strategies

How does the business solicit customers? Are discounts offered? What public-relations campaigns are carried out? Is there aggressive advertising? Get copies of all sales literature and assess the type of image being projected. Pretend you're a customer being solicited by the company to get a feeling for how the company is perceived by its market.

Advertising Costs

Analyze costs to see if they came in as budgeted and scrutinize the results of the advertising. Did sales go up? Did foot traffic increase? If not, find out why.

Prices

Evaluate current price lists and discount schedules of all products, the date of the last price increases, and the percentage of increase. Determine when you're likely to be able to raise prices again. Compare what you see in this business to standards in the industry.

Industry and Market History

Analyze the industry as well as the specific market segments the business targets to evaluate the business' profit potential—see Chapter 3. Determine whether sales in the industry, as well as those in the business' market, are growing, declining, or remaining stagnant.

Location and Market Area

Look back at Chapter 4 and conduct a thorough analysis of the business' location, taking into account the surrounding trading areas' demographics, the general economic outlook, and the business' nearby competition. See if there are any difficulties with receiving products from vendors or delivering products to markets.

The Business' Reputation

How is the business perceived by customers as well as suppliers? Image is extremely important and can be an asset or a liability. Interview customers, suppliers, bankers, and owners of other businesses in the area to gather information about the reputation of the business.

Seller-Customer Ties

Are any customers related or connected in a special way to the present owner? How long has such an account been with the company? What percentage of the company's business is accounted for by this particular customer or set of customers? Will this customer continue to purchase from the company if ownership changes?

Salaries

Make sure salaries are realistic and consistent with industry and market standards.

List of Current Employees and Organizational Chart

Learn who's who in the business, who reports to whom and who's been earning what for how long. Key personnel are an especially valuable asset. Get an understanding of the management practices of the company. Examine any management-employee contracts that exist aside from a union agreement, as well as details of employee benefit plans; profit-sharing; health, life, and accident insurance; vacation policies; personnel policies; and any employee-related lawsuits against the company.

Occupational Safety and Health Administration (OSHA) Requirements

If a manufacturing plant is involved, find out whether the plant has been inspected and meets all occupational safety and health requirements. If you feel the seller is hedging and that some things on the premises may be unsafe, you may, as a prospective buyer of a business that may come under OSHA scrutiny, ask the agency to help you with a check. Some sellers may be less than thrilled with this idea, but you need to protect your interests.

Insurance

Find out what type of insurance coverage the company has, who the underwriter and local company representative are, and how much premiums cost. Some businesses are underinsured and operating under potentially disastrous situations in case of fire or other catastrophe. Make sure the business is adequately protected.

Product Liability

Product liability insurance is important for manufacturing companies. Certain insurance coverages dramatically change from year to year, which can have a big effect on the company's cash flow.

FINANCIAL DOCUMENTS AND REVIEW

One of the most common reasons for new-owner failures is incomplete due diligence. All financial documents need close scrutiny, starting with the income statement. Concentrate on those items that affect the profitability of the business, with an eye toward eliminating unnecessary expenses. Get a handle on which costs are fixed and which are variable. Other areas to focus on include:

- *Monthly gross sales.* In addition to checking sales data in the income statement, check sales tax reports and IRS statements. Be sure to cross-check any single source against a second source to verify the validity of these numbers. If you're dealing with a service business for which no sales tax is collected, the federal income tax statement will provide sufficient information.

- *Cost of sales.* Review invoices from suppliers and compare those figures with national averages. Retailers, wholesalers and manufacturers often keep a cost-of-goods statement as well. Ask to look at this statement as its information helps determine an accurate profit margin for the business.
- *Rent.* Check terms and conditions of the lease and make sure the lessee's numbers agree with those of the lessor.
- *Salaries.* See how the company's payroll records and 1099 statements jibe with the numbers on the income statement.
- *Advertising and sales expenses.* Sometimes these figures are inflated or padded with other expenses. Review the business records for sales commissions, advertising, and media schedules and costs, as well as any sponsorships the company may have offered. Compare this information to 1099 statements issued to salespeople and invoices from designers, copywriters, and ad agency reps.
- *Profitability.* Subtract the cost of goods from monthly gross sales to arrive at a gross profit. Next, add together all the operating expenses and then subtract those from the gross profit, and your result will be the net profitability of the firm. For sole proprietorships and partnerships, "net profit" usually translates into "owner's income," which isn't listed in the income statement. To determine profitability in these instances, check the figure for owner's income. If he or she is serious about selling the business, there shouldn't be a problem disclosing this information.

To illustrate how to evaluate an income statement, refer to Example 1 in Figure 11.2, Sample Income Statements, which is the sample income statement of a restaurant with $100,000 annual sales. After deducting food costs, operating costs and debt service, the restaurant's net profit is $6,300. If the asking price is $30,000, and you make a down payment of $15,000 discharging the remaining debt (10% note amortized over three years) out of business earnings, $6,300 profit is actually a 21 percent return on an investment of $30,000. Not bad. That's five times what you could get in most banks.

But hold on. You only put $15,000 as a down payment. A $6,300 return on $15,000 is really 42 percent! A good deal? You bet! And if you had put up an even lower down payment through the techniques of leveraged buyout, you could have had an even better return.

In the income statement, however, you are evaluating the current operating figures. What about potential? Suppose you're really enthusiastic about the restaurant and decide to stay open an additional day each week and serve breakfast, in addition to lunch and dinner. You might be able to increase business by 25 or 30 percent. Your fixed and variable costs will increase a little, but so will your profit margin.

Now suppose you can persuade the seller to take a five-year note instead of a three-year note. At a minimum rate of 10 percent interest, that reduces your debt payment from $5,500 to $3,300. While this means the ultimate cost of money will be higher, it also means that short-term cash flow is markedly strengthened.

Example 2 of Figure 11.2 reviews the same restaurant with these revised conditions. Your return has just increased from $6,300 to $19,100. That's an increase of more than 200 percent, improving your return on investment to 64 percent.

DETERMINING THE RIGHT PRICE

Determining the value of a business is part art, part science. Buyers and sellers have different points of view, since each party has different objectives and different needs. This is all the more reason to work with a qualified business broker or a CPA.

Placing a value on a business is tricky. Several factors influence price, among them economic conditions. Businesses typically sell for higher prices when the economy is expanding, while prices drop during recessions. The owner's motivation in selling also plays a role. Is he or she retiring? Getting divorced? Having personal financial problems? In some circumstances, a quicker turnaround time can translate into a lower price for the buyer.

There are several ways to determine the value of a business, including using multipliers, book values, return on investment (ROI), capitalized earnings, and intangible values.

FIGURE 11.2   Sample Income Statements

Example 1	Totals	
Gross annual sales	$100,000	
Food cost (40%)	$40,000	
Gross Profit		$60,000
Rent	$7,200	
Salaries	$16,000	
Utilities, insurance, overhead	$5,000	
Owner salary	$20,000	
Operating costs		$48,200
(10% note amortized 3 years)	$5,500	
Total		$53,700
Net Profit		$6,300

Example 2	Totals	
Gross annual sales	$125,000	
Food cost (40%)	$45,000	
Gross Profit		$80,000
Rent	$7,200	
Salaries	$23,000	
Utilities, insurance, overhead	$7,400	
Owner salary	$20,000	
Operating Costs		$57,600
(10% note amortized 5 years)	$3,300	
Total		$60,900
Net Profit		$19,100

Multipliers

One way to gauge the value of a business is to use a multiplier of either the monthly gross sales, monthly gross sales plus inventory, or after-tax profits.

While the result obtained by using the multiplier formula may seem accurate to begin with, getting the right value for a business depends on using the right multiplier. For example, individuals within a specific industry may claim that certain businesses sell at three times their annual gross sales, or two times their annual gross sales plus inventory. Depending on which formula the owner uses, the gross sales are multiplied by the appropriate number, and voila! A price is generated.

For instance, if a business had sales of $100,000 a year and the seller was using a formula where the multiple of gross sales was 300 percent based on industry averages, then the price would be generated using the following equation:

$$\$100,000 \times 3 \quad = \quad \$300,000$$

You can check the sales figures by looking at the income statement, but the big question is whether the multiplier is accurate.

Don't place too much faith in multipliers. If you run across a seller using the multiplier method, use that figure as an estimate, not a final price.

Book Values

To arrive at a price of a business based on its book value, subtract the liabilities from the assets and you arrive at that business' net worth, a figure you'll find on the business' balance sheet. The net worth is then multiplied by one, two or some other figure based on industry standards to arrive at the book value.

Book values are tricky because on the balance sheet, fixed assets are usually listed by their depreciated value, not replacement or market value. If the assets have been depreciated over the years to a level of zero, the book value will not give an accurate value of the business.

Return on Investment (ROI)

The most common means of placing a value on a business is by evaluating its ROI, or the amount of money the buyer realizes from the business in profit, after debt service and taxes, based on how much he or she has put into the business. However, ROI and profit are not the same thing. ROI is the amount of money the buyer puts into the business measured against the performance of the business. Profit is a yardstick by which the performance of business is measured.

For example, say a business is selling for $80,000. The buyer plans to offer $40,000 down and finance the rest through a five-year note at 12 percent interest. Gross sales for the business are $200,000 annually with a net profit after taxes of $20,000, which results in a return on investment of 25 percent. Typically, a small business should return anywhere between 15 and 30 percent on investment. This is the average net in after-tax dollars.

Depreciation, a tax-planning and cash-flow tool, should not be counted in the net because it should be set aside to replace equipment.

The wisdom of buying a business lies in its potential to earn money on the money you put into it. You determine the value of that business by evaluating how much money you are going to earn on your investment. The business should have the ability to pay for itself. If it can do this and give you a return on your cash investment of 15 percent or more, then you have a good business. This is what determines the price. If the seller is financing the purchase of the business, your operating statement should include a payment schedule.

Does a 15-percent net for a business seem high? Everybody wants to know if a business makes two, three, or ten times profit. They hear the words "price-earnings ratios" but forget that they commonly refer to large, publicly traded corporations. In small businesses, such ratios have limited value. A big business can earn 10 percent on its investment and be extremely healthy. Big supermarkets net two or three percent on their sales, but this small percentage represents enormous volume.

Capitalized Earnings

Placing a value on a business based on capitalized earnings is similar to the ROI method of assessment, except normal earnings are used to estimate projected earnings. This figure is then divided by a standard capitalization rate.

The capitalization rate is determined by learning what the risk of investment in the business would be compared with other investments, such as government bonds or stock in other companies. For instance, if the rate of return on investment in government bonds is 6 percent, then the business should return 6 percent or better on the investment into it. To determine the value of a business based on capitalized earnings, use the following formula:

$$\frac{\text{Projected earnings}}{\text{Capitalization rate}} \quad = \quad \text{Price}$$

After analyzing the market, the competition, the demand for the product, and the organization of the business, say you determine that projected earnings could increase to $25,000 per year for the next three years. If your capitalization rate is 6 percent, then the value of the business would be:

$$\frac{\$25,000}{.06} = \$416,667$$

If the seller is asking much more than what you've determined the capitalized earnings to be, then you will have to try to negotiate a lower price.

Intangible Value

Some business owners try to include goodwill in the value of a business. While there is no doubt that goodwill has value, particularly if the business has built up a regular trade and a strong clientele, it is the financial value of the accounts that need to be placed on financial statements. You as a buyer should assess the business based on the return on the investment.

NEGOTIATE THE TRANSACTION

The process of buying a business is no different from the maneuvering involved in buying a home or a car. Very seldom will you pay the first price advertised. Selling a business is an emotional process, particularly when the owner has put a lot of hard work into building a successful company. For this reason, the initial price of the business may be too high. This is why you need to find out how long the business has been on the market.

What is your position in all of this? When negotiating any kind of sale, the smartest approach is to be friendly, well-informed and a good listener. An aggressive, stubborn buyer who's rough on people isn't going to be able to negotiate anything. If the initial price set by the seller is on the high side, voice your objections in a positive way. Point out that the asking price will not allow you to make a decent return and that consequently the business is of no value to you.

When negotiating alone with the seller, you must confirm in writing all the terms upon which you've agreed. This is not necessarily a formal contract but rather a letter of agreement. Mail it right away, requesting immediate corrections of anything that may have been misquoted or misunderstood.

Remember that in negotiation, no one gets everything he or she wants. Every transaction involves compromises on the part of both parties. If you establish proper criteria for buying a business and this conflicts with the seller's perception of its value, then don't buy the business. Stick to your guns and make sound financial decisions.

Red Flags to Watch for When Dealing with Sellers

No business, particularly one someone has put his or her heart and soul into, is easy to let go of. The business may have been part of the owner's life for many years, and the seller often has emotional and psychological attachments to the business. Unless the right owner with the right finances comes along at the right time, an owner may not be prepared to sell. If an owner isn't quite ready to sell, you may see one or more of the following red flags.

Price Is Too High

The owner may decide not to sell unless a specific price can be attained or may demand too high a down payment—often the case where the business is bleeding cash. The seller thinks the business is going to fail, so he or she tries to get as much money up front as possible.

Failure or Refusal to Provide Records

A seller who doesn't provide crucial documents may be afraid you'll find the problem that will kill the sale and tries to get around that danger by refusing to give you information. But you need this data to properly place a value on a business. If you encounter a secretive seller, your best bet is to look elsewhere for a business.

Sellers Who Want Too Much Collateral

If you run across a seller who wants collateral in addition to the business, you could be dealing with a naïve or anxious person regarding negotiation. After all, a good business is its own security. The seller may argue that you may not be as fine a manager as he or she is and that you might ruin the business. Don't accept that argument—stand behind your integrity and expertise in business. In a worst-case scenario, the seller can always recoup the business. Don't put up any other collateral to buy a business apart from the business itself.

Seller Claims Additional Income

If a seller says, "The income shown is for tax purposes. I actually take a little more out," you need to look carefully at the financial statements. Not reporting income for tax purposes is a felony. But has the seller really committed a felony? Or is he or she just trying to make you believe there is more money in the business than the financial records indicate? Do due diligence to verify the volume of the business. Make sure the profits are real and that the business revenue is strong.

Business Relationship Cover-ups

Suppose a business has one primary customer whose trade accounts for 30 to 40 percent of sales. After doing your homework, you discover that this major account is the seller's brother-in-law. Is he loyal to the business or to his family? Find out.

"Round-Robin" Invoices

A round-robin invoice is one that shows money coming in, but the money on the invoice never goes into the bank. The invoice may be for material or services that were never rendered. They are stamped "PAID" and indicate that the account is up-to-date. Yet the company never really purchased what the invoice indicates. In extreme cases, the customer's company never existed! If your CPA conducts an audit, he or she will be able to detect any discrepancies between what the statements show and the actual financial condition of the business.

Cash-Float Accounts

A seller with a lot of money aside from that generated by the business may float this money through the operation to make it look like sales. This increases the apparent value of the business and, with it, the purchase price. Cash floating is easy to conceal if a seller has two different businesses. Money will be floated from one business (so there are no taxes paid on the operation of that business) to the one being sold so that taxes are paid on that operation only. This is done in several ways.

Floating cash through bank accounts makes it appear as if the second business is taking in money. It can have great impact on the sale price of certain retail businesses, such as those where a lot of cash changes hands. This is particularly true if the retail business is one with relatively low-priced items.

Invoices will come in for one company but be paid by the other, or sellers will funnel receivables from the more profitable business into the less profitable one that might be for sale, thus making a business that doesn't do much volume look good on paper.

In labor-intensive businesses, a seller will take a low salary from one business or put some of the employees from one company on the payroll of the other; therefore, the payroll expense implicit in the business for sale is not reflected in the profit and loss statement (P&L). The seemingly low labor costs in a labor-intensive business can make it extremely attractive to an unwary buyer. Yet high labor costs may be the very reason that the business is being sold. Remember the adage, "*Caveat emptor?*" Buyer beware! Find out whether the seller of the business you want to buy owns any other businesses, and if so, what kind of businesses they are. Investigate the financial records with a critical eye to make sure no cash is being floated.

Updating Receivables

Instead of showing a nine-month-old invoice, an owner can re-date the invoice and show it in the books as current. The new date on the invoice doesn't offend the company that owes the money. On the contrary, they are only too happy that their aging receivables are given a new lease on life. Suddenly they are not behind in their payments.

Inflating Inventory Value

If you're not wise to standards and practices in the industry you are about to enter (how various products sell, what doesn't sell), you may be buying old or outdated material. An apparel or gift retailer may have too much inventory that's going out of style.

Inflating Equipment Value

In recent years, computers have decreased in cost while increasing in capability. Suppose the seller has a computer system on the books for $20,000, less depreciation for several years' use. You might be able to buy better equipment for a fraction of the cost. Your best bet, if you're interested in the business, is to get a valuation from an independent equipment appraiser to figure out just what the equipment is worth.

Hidden Maintenance Costs

To increase the value of equipment included in the purchase price, the owner may try to bury the maintenance costs or fail to provide you with information. This is most likely if the equipment is old and reaching the end of its serviceable life. Accordingly, it is a good idea to find out the life expectancy of the equipment and how long it can operate effectively between maintenance calls.

Common Mistakes That Buyers Make

Don't be too anxious when you're looking to buy a business. Take your time and recognize that businesses typically don't sell overnight. And make sure to avoid these practices:

- *Buying on price.* Buyers don't take into account ROI. If you're going to invest $20,000 in a business that returns only a 3-percent net, you're better off putting your money in a CD or municipal bond.

- *Running out of cash.* Some buyers use most of their cash for the down payment on the business and don't reserve enough for working capital. This is folly of the worst kind—putting the business' future on the line. Cash is king and needs to be managed thoughtfully. As a rule of thumb, at least 10 percent of your cash should be considered contingency funds and at least three-months' worth of operating expenses should be set aside as working capital.

- *Buying all the receivables.* It generally makes good sense to buy the receivables, except when they are ninety days old or older. The older the account, the more difficult it will be to collect. You can protect yourself by having the seller warrant the receivables—what is not collected can be charged back against the purchase price of the business. Receivables beyond ninety days belong to the seller for collection.

- *Failure to verify all data.* Most business buyers accept all the information the seller gives them without doing due diligence (preferably by a CPA who can audit financial statements).

- *Heavy payment schedules.* During the first year or so, it makes sense to have smaller payments, graduating to larger payments as the business grows and becomes successful. This can easily be negotiated with a seller.

Working with Business Brokers

People who buy and sell properties know the value of a professional broker. These veteran negotiators are valuable to both buyer and seller for a number of reasons. According to Brian Knight, president of the Manchester, Vermont-based business brokerage firm Country Business, Inc. (802 362-4710), a business broker can help a buyer in several ways:

- *Make sure that funds for purchase and operation are sufficient.* An experienced business broker knows that undercapitalization is the number-one reason that businesses fail. Consequently, he or she will make sure that the acquisition is properly capitalized, that there is enough working capital for the business' first year's operations, and that the business' longer-term growth can be funded.

- *Match a buyer to the business.* A good broker first learns about your needs and abilities, then helps you choose the type of business that's right for you.

- *Orchestrate the negotiation process.* This is where brokers really earn their money, by keeping emotions in check and all parties focused on the goal—a win-win situation for both sides.

- *Weed out "tire kickers."* Experienced business brokers have a network of qualified buyers and can distinguish buyers who are serious from those who are not.

- *Take care of all administrative tasks and file the appropriate paperwork.* From licenses and permits, to financing and escrow, good brokers know what needs to be done by whom—and when.

Not all business brokers are the same. Some are chiefly real estate brokers who happen to have a business brokerage license and occasionally sell a business. Selling a business is very different than selling real estate, even though selling a business might involve the sale of real estate. Make sure the broker you're dealing with has expertise in selling businesses.

The principal value of a broker is to act as a buffer between buyer and seller. A broker can say certain things to a buyer and certain things to a seller, and wind up with a productive discussion. The broker can tell the owner the price is too high, relay what has to be done to make a deal—very openly and candidly—and discuss how the differences in viewpoint can be ironed out effectively.

Brokers' fees range anywhere from 5 to 10 percent, depending on negotiations with the broker, state laws, and other factors. This is oftentimes money well spent. Although the seller pays the broker's fee, the broker can usually get more money for the business, make negotiations run smoothly, handle a lot of clerical and other details, and make a sale possible, whereas an individual business seller might not be able to accomplish all these things.

If the seller has not retained a broker, you as the buyer can always hire one to represent your interest. You can hire a broker on a consulting basis and negotiate the fee, or you might be able to work with the seller and both of you share the fee. Make sure your lawyer and CPA are also part of this process.

HOW TO FINANCE THE PURCHASE OF A BUSINESS

There are many ways to finance the purchase of a business. You can get loans from banks, friends, family, the SBA, venture capitalists, and a host of others by putting up real estate, accounts receivable, inventory, or equipment as collateral. There are also the following techniques.

Real Estate Leveraging

It's possible to use real property that is already providing you with a little money to gain ownership of a business that is in debt and not producing enough profit to manage the payments properly. The first step is to analyze the profit-making potential of the business in question on a realistic basis. Insufficient capitalization, overbuying on inventory and poor management policies are among the most frequent causes of business failure. The wise application of capital and/or management might save the business. If you can save this business and at the same time become it's new owner, you're ready to proceed.

Find out to whom the business owner owes money and tell the lending institution that you'd like to buy the loan on the business by offering your income-producing real estate as collateral. One portion of this loan should be used to buy the debt of the present owner. The other portion should be cash for working capital.

Doing this, you put yourself in a good financial position (providing you can get the business going) for two reasons:

1. You retain the rental income from your real estate. You've only used it to secure a loan, not sold it outright to the bank.

2. You've bought the profit-making potential of the business.

The lending institution also realizes substantial benefits from this method:

1. The potential bad debt on a nonproductive and mismanaged business is eliminated.

2. The real-estate collateral you offer on the new loan is worth twice the business itself.

Moreover, if you're successful, the new loan will be paid off, probably ahead of schedule. Talk about a win-win situation: the seller avoids bankruptcy, the bank continues receiving interest payments on the loan, and you become the new owner of a business you believe can be profitable. However, this all hinges on your having carefully analyzed the market and the business, and your having the necessary skills and resources to make the business perform.

Using the Seller's Assets

You can often finance the purchase of a business by using its assets. Tangible assets you can use to raise capital include real estate, equipment, accounts receivable, purchase orders, and inventory.

In businesses that are equipment intensive, you can use equipment to help you finance the purchase of the business. The first step is to find out the amount of money the business owner could get by selling the business to another party or piece-by-piece—in this case the major pieces of equipment needed for a viable business operation—whether on consignment or at a business-equipment auction. Sometimes, the building and the real estate are also considered by the party needing to sell.

Get realistic projections on the amount of money the business owner can receive for the equipment on the open market. If you can come up with a figure that meets the realities of the owner's needs versus the market value of the equipment, nine times out of ten you'll be able complete a deal.

After you've determined that you want to buy and the seller wants to sell the business equipment, the next step is to determine how title will pass from party to party. Some sellers prefer to keep the title themselves until the equipment is paid for. If you encounter such a situation, simply tell the seller that you need ownership of the equipment to complete the sale. If you don't own the equipment you're buying, you won't be able to use it as collateral for a bank loan. No collateral means no loan. If you have no loan, you can't very well buy the owner's equipment in the first place.

When you go to the bank, bring an itemized list of the equipment. If you have technical specifications that explain the equipment's capabilities in lay terms, all the better. If the bank determines that there is sufficient value in the equipment, it will most likely grant you a loan. If you can get enough cash for a down payment on the equipment to the seller, plus some working capital, then you're in a great position to assume control of the business.

If you're buying land along with the equipment, then you can obtain cash by assuming a mortgage and refinancing it. This second mortgage money allows you to pay the seller and get the business going again.

Purchase orders can also be used to raise money to buy the business. Some investors and commercial banks will lend money on purchase orders. To obtain this type of financing, get copies of the actual purchase orders from the seller to present either to an investor or a finance company.

Accounts receivable offer another financing avenue. Most finance companies and banks will only finance 80 percent of your receivables but will raise that to 100 percent if you include the inventory as collateral. A spin-off of receivables financing is to ask the seller to keep the receivables. A seller who does this in effect is accepting the receivable as part of the payment for the business, thereby reducing the amount of cash you have to pay for it.

Employee Stock Ownership Plans (ESOPs)

ESOPs represent a new trend in financing the purchase of a small business. With this method, you raise sufficient capital to purchase the business by selling stock in the company to its employees. To structure an effective ESOP for the purchase of the business, divide stock into voting and nonvoting shares. You then sell only the nonvoting shares to the employees so that you retain control of the company even though the employees own a percentage of it.

Leasing the Business

If you don't have enough money to buy, some sellers will allow you to lease their businesses with an option to buy. All you need to do is come up with the down payment. If you have the down payment, approach the seller and let him or her know that you are extremely interested in buying the business but don't have enough money at the time. Offer the seller the down payment on the purchase price so that you become a minority stockholder. Then operate the business as if it were your own, eventually paying off the seller by getting another partner or by using your profits from the business.

Debt Consolidation Loans

Sometimes it's possible to take over a business and consolidate its debts. With a debt-consolidation loan, you can work with a bank and perhaps arrange for the creditors to accept 40 to 50 cents on the dollar. In extreme cases, you may want to acquire a Chapter 11 bankruptcy filing, which allows you to obtain protection for the company from its creditors. Again, the creditors may eventually be induced to accept 40 cents on the dollar.

However, the improper use of the Bankruptcy Code's Chapter 11 provisions by larger corporations has put companies in similar situations under strict scrutiny. This method of obtaining some gain from a business that you've bought requires the advice of a competent bankruptcy attorney. Additionally, plan on taking from two to four years to complete the judicial cycle of Chapter 11 proceedings.

CHAPTER 12

Buying a Franchise

Franchising accounts for more than 40 percent of all U.S. retail sales, according to the International Franchise Association (IFA, www.franchise.org), an organization in Washington, DC. IFA says that more than 760,000 businesses in more than 75 industries in the United States, such as McDonald's, Holiday Inn, Mail Boxes Etc., Dunkin' Donuts, and H&R Block, are operated under franchise agreements. These business generate more than $1.5 trillion in annual retail sales and employ more than eighteen million people. That's a lot of business from franchises!

But just what is a franchise? Essentially, a franchise is a written agreement that allows a business owner to sell certain products or services for a particular period at a specific location. The franchisee typically pays a fee to a franchiser to obtain the franchise, along with a percentage of the firm's sales, to the franchiser. In return, the franchiser provides the franchisee with personnel training, financial assistance, and advertising, and allows the franchisee to use a well-known trade name.

FRANCHISE TYPES

There are several different types of franchises.

- *Product and trade-name franchises* are primarily used to set up distribution networks for franchisers through dealer companies. By franchising out the distribution of its products, the franchiser is able to control the way the dealer company operates by restricting the sale of competitive products or the type of marketing that can be done. In turn, the dealer, or franchisee, receives the recognition that accompanies a well-known firm such as ExxonMobil or Firestone. They may also receive financial, marketing, and managerial support from the franchiser.

- *Business-format franchises* grant the franchisee the use of the name, products, marketing techniques, operating system, internal controls, and operations procedures. The franchisee winds up managing an established business that in some cases is a turnkey operation.

- *Affiliate or conversion franchises* are primarily used by a group of independent entrepreneurs in a fragmented industry to produce more visibility by combining their resources. They do this by having each business affiliate with all the others under one name to create a franchise network. As a result, the companies are able to pool their purchasing power, advertising clout, and marketing abilities to capture a greater share of the market. The affiliate companies are not legally bound to use the banner name of the franchise, which doesn't have to be a trademark or brand name. Many affiliates will, in fact, use the franchise name as well as their own, as is the case with Century 21 Realtors.

The scope of franchising today is such that anyone planning to open a business dominated by franchising or characterized by aggressive franchiser advertising would do well to consider joining them rather than beating them. Unless you bring a good deal of knowledge, expertise, and marketing judgment to the table, you could shoot yourself in the foot by trying to compete with the big guys.

PROS AND CONS OF BUYING INTO A FRANCHISE

A franchise offers the following advantages to the buyer.

- *Reduced risk of failure.* You're buying a tried-and-true business concept where most of the problems have already been worked out by someone else.
- *Turnkey operation.* In many cases, franchises offer a trademark that's been registered, patents that have been filed, and certain design concepts. These are all part of the total package, which includes many other things, such as a proven system of operation and identity (people will recognize the name of your business because they've seen it somewhere else before). The turnkey business is a big advantage for people who don't know what equipment to buy, how much of it to buy, how much space they need to get started in the business, how much inventory they should have, and what kind of items sell in a given area.
- *Standardized products and systems.* There is already an established product line and operating system that, for the most part, take the guesswork out of purchasing and administrative procedures.
- *Financial and accounting systems.* Since you're using a standardized system, franchisers can monitor what you're doing from thousands of miles away. Your system includes inventory control forms, hourly cash register readings, and profit and loss statement formats. In addition, there are monthly reviews of financial and accounting statements.
- *Collective buying power.* A small-business owner who purchases in small quantities can't compete with the buying power of national chains and other large franchises. When you become a franchisee, you have the collective buying power of the entire franchise system.
- *Supervision and consulting.* Most franchisers offer ongoing advice, provide updated training, and in many cases are available for emergency problem solving. From the day you open the doors, there's someone to help hire your employees, train them, and consult with you on a regular basis if problems develop.
- *National and local advertising programs.* You've seen what the big franchisers, like McDonald's, Kentucky Fried Chicken, and the large automotive companies, have been able to accomplish through their advertising. They've built nationally recognized brands that have legions of loyal customers.
- *Point-of-sale advertising.* Things such as mobiles hanging from the ceiling, posters, and so on are expensive to develop but helpful in encouraging that extra point-of-sale impetus for buyers. Sophisticated advertising materials, provided for you by the franchiser, give you a proven image and identity.
- *Uniform packaging.* The franchiser has done the necessary research and worked out the best size and type of packaging for the product. As a franchisee, you don't have to reinvent the wheel—a big advantage and cost saver.
- *Ongoing research and development.* Most franchisers are constantly working on new products, new variations of current products, and new systems. Their research and development has a budget that's normally out of the ballpark for small business owners. As a franchisee, you get to share the rewards of their hard work.
- *Financial assistance.* In some cases, the franchiser will actually finance part of your initial purchase, whether it's equipment, leasehold improvements, or land.

- *Site selection.* What makes a good site for a service station may not make a good site for a restaurant or retail store. Certain kinds of businesses belong in shopping centers, but it can be tricky getting into an established shopping mall unless you have the credibility of a successful franchise behind you. The franchiser has already addressed issues that have to do with location, and they know what sites are most appropriate (and will increase the likelihood for success) for that particular type of business.
- *Operations manual.* Since one of the biggest challenges in business is hiring and training people, this operating manual is a very handy tool, indeed.
- *Sales and marketing assistance.* The franchiser will share with you the techniques that have made the business successful, which you then use in developing your own business.
- *Planning and forecasting.* Franchisees know what to expect in terms of sales, business activity, stock, personnel, and training, which makes it easier to plan ahead.
- *Less capital.* There's no guesswork about the equipment you need, and franchisees often get better prices on equipment because of the franchiser's buying power. Franchiser financing may enable you to buy equipment by amortizing it on a long-term basis rather than by using your initial capital.

Even with all these advantages, there are drawbacks to buying a franchise:

- *Loss of control.* It isn't your name or concept that you'll be promoting through your business. You're subject to guidelines set forth by the franchiser and, in some ways, are more of a manager than your own boss.
- *High cost.* Franchises are expensive to purchase, and usually you must pay the franchiser ongoing royalty fees, often 2 to 6 percent a month. Generally, while it costs less in upfront capital to start a franchise, in the long run the total purchase price is usually higher than that for an independent operation. The royalty fee, combined with debt service on any financing, puts pressure on a business' cash flow.
- *A binding contract.* You must sign an agreement with the franchiser that binds you to detailed guidelines on how the franchise will be operated, what types of fees you'll pay, and so on. These agreements tend to be quite restrictive, and if you encounter any problems with the franchiser, remember that you are legally bound by your contract to adhere to its guidelines.
- *The franchiser's problems are also your problems.* If the franchiser hits hard times, you'll most likely feel them as well. You are inevitably tied to the franchiser, not only by contract, but by concept, name, and product or services sold.

FRANCHISEE OBLIGATIONS

In terms of capital investment, your franchise fee will be determined by the profitability of the business. Most companies have a scale of franchise fees ranging anywhere from $1,000 to $300,000. In addition to this front-end franchise fee, the one-time charge that a franchiser assesses you for the privilege of using the business concept, attending the training program, and learning the business, there is also a royalty fee.

Some of the other costs associated with a franchise include:

- *Facility/location.* In some cases, you may also have to buy or rent land or a building. If you lease a building, you'll be responsible for not only the monthly rent but also the security deposit and any leasehold improvements. In some cases, the owner of the building will factor their costs into your rent, and the franchiser might provide you with an allowance for leasehold improvements.
- *Equipment.* Equipment costs are generally long-term obligations, and some types of businesses require more equipment than others.
- *Signs.* Outside signs can be very expensive, and most franchisers have developed a sign package that the franchisee is obligated to purchase.
- *Opening inventory.* Most franchisers have an opening inventory requirement of at least a two-week supply, unless the business requires a more complicated inventory to start.
- *Working capital.* For rent, you may be required to deposit funds to cover the first and last month's rent,

as well as a security deposit. You'll also have to pay a deposit to the electric, gas, and telephone companies prior to receiving service and will need funds to operate until your cash flow gets going, money in the cash drawer to make change, and cash to make payroll.

- *Advertising fees.* There's usually a fee for advertising on either a regional or national basis. Most larger franchisers require their franchisees to pay a certain amount into a national fund used to advance the concept. The benefits are substantial in terms of the visibility that you get with this type of advertising.

Usually, you can't negotiate the franchise agreement, which imposes certain conditions, restrictions, and standards that you have to follow. You may not agree with its standards, but under the franchise agreement you will have to operate in the specified way. In most cases, a franchise agreement describes step-by-step operations procedures and gives the franchiser the option to make changes as desired.

If you have a lot of initiative and like to do things on your own, you may find that the franchise agreement restricts you. The key is to "know thyself," and to think long and hard before you sign on the dotted line.

Franchising Laws

While the vast majority of franchisers are legitimate, there are some unscrupulous people willing and ready to exploit the gullibility of buyers who lack business experience and are therefore easy targets. Just as in buying a business, the same two words come to mind when discussing franchising: Caveat emptor (buyer beware).

Federal and state authorities have passed numerous disclosure regulations and laws to protect prospective franchisees from financial disaster and provide them with recourse in the legal system. The Federal Trade Commission's (FTC) Franchising and Business Opportunity Ventures Trade Regulation Rules and Subsequent Guidelines apply nationally. In 1993 the FTC voted unanimously to approve new Uniform Franchise Offering Circular (UFOC) guidelines proposed by the North American Securities Administrators Association (NASAA). Currently, eight states (California, Maryland, Minnesota, New York, North Dakota, Rhode Island, South Dakota, and Washington) require franchisers to file

offerings with a state agency. These states have disclosure regulations like those of the FTC.

For more information, see *A Consumer's Guide to Buying a Franchise.* Copies are available by calling the FTC at 202-326-2222 or online at www.ftc.gov/bcp/online/pubs/invest/buyfran.htm.

Federal Franchising Laws

Prospective franchisees are protected by the FTC's franchise rule, put into effect October 12, 1979. This rule requires franchisers to fully disclose the information a prospective franchisee needs in order to make an informed decision about whether or not to buy the franchise. This disclosure must take place at the first personal contact where the subject of buying the franchise is discussed. This means a franchiser, franchise broker, or anyone else representing franchises for sale must present an accurate and clearly written disclosure document, similar to a prospectus for stock offerings.

The disclosure material must be provided at least ten business days prior to signing any contract with the franchiser, which gives prospective franchisees and their attorneys time to carefully review the materials and make an informed decision about what they're doing. Furthermore, franchisees must be given completed contracts covering all material points at least five days prior to the actual date of execution of the documents.

If a franchiser does not provide a disclosure document containing accurate information, or if a salesperson makes outlandish claims that are inconsistent with that document, the franchiser could be liable for a fine per violation, plus damages, if any. The same applies if a franchiser does not provide contracts at the proper time or fails to refund deposits, such as a down payment that is defined as refundable in the disclosure document.

State Franchising Laws

The FTC does not require franchisers to register with it or any other government agency. However, the eight states mentioned above have registration rules requiring franchise sellers to register in a manner similar to registering a security offering as an investment.

Some of these state laws, which are not overridden by the new FTC rules, are tougher than others, but most have adopted the UFOC guidelines for their disclosure requirements. Under UFOC guidelines, the franchiser will have to disclose more information regarding the history of the parent company and any affiliates. The guidelines also specify that a franchiser disclose more information regarding markups on products supplied to franchisees as well as any legal settlements involving displeased franchisees.

It would be a mistake, however, to assume that simply because a franchise is registered with a state or is required to provide some type of full disclosure document that you as a consumer are completely protected from the possibility of failure or fraud. The only thing that a state reviewing agency can do is assure that the franchiser has responded and filed the necessary documents and let franchisees know whether any complaints have been received. But state and federal authorities don't have the time or personnel to check information included in the documents. It's up to you to do the necessary homework.

If Something Smells Fishy

The bottom line with franchising is to thoroughly investigate before you invest. But what happens if you believe a franchiser has committed acts of misrepresentation or fraud has taken place? Help is available from the FTC, consumer protection agencies, your district attorney, or state attorney general— if only to prevent the same thing from happening to another person somewhere else in the country.

There's no substitute for checking franchisers' track records and talking to at least ten prior purchasers in person. That's why the FTC Franchise Rule requires companies to include in the disclosures a list of names, addresses, and phone numbers of at least ten prior purchasers who are geographically closest to you. It's your job to follow up.

To get information about consumer complaints, write to Freedom of Information Act Request, Federal Trade Commission, Washington, DC 20580.

Identify your letter as an "FOIA Request," and include your name, address, and daytime phone number, along with the name and address of the company you're requesting information on.

If you've had a problem with a franchiser or business opportunity seller and want to file a complaint, send a short (one- to two-page) letter describing what you thought was misleading or deceptive to Franchise and Business Opportunity Complaint, Federal Trade Commission, Room 238, Washington, DC 20580.

If you want your request kept confidential, write "Confidential" at the top of each page. Send copies, not originals, of any documents you think are relevant to your complaint.

SELECTING A FRANCHISE

Where do you begin to search for a franchise that's right for you? Selecting one that interests you and meets your criteria will take time. The first step is revisiting your personal goals. Refer to Chapter 1 to identify your strengths and weaknesses, both personally and professionally, so you can determine what type of business you'd be happy owning. From your list of objectives, begin taking a closer look at your options. Ask yourself: What type of franchise will help me fulfill those objectives? What type of business appeals to me? Which franchise concepts and categories are currently growing at a healthy rate?

To determine what's hot and what's not in the franchising industry, keep an eye on the economy and subscribe to magazines and trade journals that can help you narrow down your search. Every January, *Entrepreneur* magazine publishes its annual Franchise 500 issue, which ranks more than 500 franchises and provides contact addresses, capitalization requirements, franchise fees, experience requirements, strength of the franchise in number of units, and any royalties. *Entrepreneur's Franchise and Business Opportunities Buyer's Guide* is published in the fall and also lists contact names and addresses, unit strength, capitalization requirements, franchise fees, experience requirements, and any royalties. *Entrepreneur* is available at newsstands or by subscription by visiting www.entrepreneurmag.com.

Another resource is the International Franchise Association. The IFA's *Franchise Opportunities Guide* gives a comprehensive list of franchise companies in more than 75 kinds of businesses and is available for $20 ($12 for members), plus shipping and handling, by calling 1-800-543-1038. You may also order online (www.franchise.org) by clicking on "Books and Publications."

Analyzing the Franchise

Once you've found a franchise you're interested in, the next step is to determine whether it's really worth buying. You can gather information to help your decision-making process by:

- Interviewing the franchiser
- Interviewing current franchisees
- Examining the Uniform Franchise Offering Circular (UFOC)
- Examining the franchise agreement
- Examining the audited financial statement, an earnings-claim statement, a balance sheet, and a sample unit income (profit and loss) statement
- Reviewing trade-area surveys, the organizational chart, and the list of current franchisees
- Reading newspaper or magazine articles about the franchise

From this research, get answers to the following questions.

- *Are both the franchiser and the current franchisees making money?* After all, if the franchiser isn't making a profit, or if franchisees are having trouble staying afloat, you will, too.
- *How well-organized is the franchise?* You don't have to know anything specific about the business to know whether or not a franchise is well organized. If you visit a franchise's retail outlets and see that they're not well-stocked or well-run or that personnel don't seem to know what they're doing, then the franchise is not worth investing in.
- *Is the franchise perceived favorably by the general public?* While it's good to be unique, you don't want your business to be so far ahead of the curve that people are just not ready to accept it. Make sure the concepts that the franchise are built on are tried, true, and proven.
- *What is the franchise's unique selling proposition?* What makes this franchise stand out from the others in similar industries? Take a close look at the franchise's target market, its product or service, its packaging, its price, and its promotion. What are the competitive advantages that you foresee could be capitalized on over time with your management?

- *How good are the franchiser's financial controls?* Your franchise needs to be backed by a franchiser with strong financial management ability, which lets you evaluate the financial health of the organization at both the corporate and unit level.
- *Does the franchise have a good track record?* The franchise should have enough of an operating history to show that it's a viable concept. This includes a solid credit rating, which indicates financial well-being.
- *What kind of publicity has the franchise received, and how has the public reacted?* Search for articles about the franchise in newspapers, magazines, and trade journals. Were opinions overwhelmingly positive? If not, what criticisms were levied at the franchise?
- *Are the cash requirements reasonable?* If the franchise you're interested in promises a $20,000-a-year return, you shouldn't have to make a $200,000 investment. Make sure to get your CPA's help to determine what numbers work for you.
- *Does the franchiser show integrity and commitment?* If the franchiser is willing to take your money without first checking you out, that's a red flag. The more particular a franchiser is, the more confident you can be that the other people in the organization have passed inspection and are as capable as you.
- *Does the franchiser have a monitoring system?* This provides valuable feedback and allows you to know how you're doing and how to deal with problems most effectively.
- *Which goods are proprietary and must be purchased from the franchiser?* Keep in mind that the franchiser generates profit by the sale of proprietary stock at a markup from the wholesale or manufactured cost. Determine which items are proprietary and must be purchased through the franchiser and which ones aren't and can be acquired through outside vendors at a lower cost.
- *What is the success rate for the industry?* If eight out of every ten businesses started in this industry fail, that's not very promising for you. Although franchises typically have a low failure rate, they're not immune to bankruptcy.

Don't be shy about asking for the required materials from the franchiser. After all, the company will be checking you out just as completely as you're investigating them. If they aren't, then that's a cause for concern.

Another warning sign is a request by the franchiser for you to sign a disclaimer stating that you haven't relied on any representations not contained in the written agreement. Such a requirement could indicate that the franchiser doesn't want to be held responsible for claims made by the company's sales representatives. The franchiser could also be in financial hot water and willing to sell a franchise to anyone who comes along to produce a better cash flow. Either way, a thorough analysis will reveal potential problems.

THE UNIFORM FRANCHISE OFFERING CIRCULAR (UFOC)

After you've contacted the franchiser and filled out their questionnaires to determine whether you fit the profile of "their kind" of franchisee, you'll receive two documents in the mail. One will be the UFOC, which contains information about the franchise, and the other will be the franchise agreement. State and federal laws require that the franchiser give you these documents at least ten days before taking your deposit and signing you on as a franchisee.

Carefully examine the information in these documents before getting the advice of your CPA and attorney, and do not sign anything without their approval. Just because these documents appear to comply with the FTC rules and/or various state filing requirements, doesn't mean they do or that the terms are in your favor. Most of those regulations only require the franchiser to make complete and full disclosure of various categories of information the law requires in the document. So long as the disclosure is made in the proper manner, the franchiser can draft the terms and conditions of its franchise and its obligations to you as a franchisee in almost any manner it wishes.

The first section in the UFOC is a brief history of the franchise. The history should document who founded the company, when it began doing business, incorporation dates, if any, and when it first started franchising. This data lets you know what kind of expertise and experience the franchiser has to offer. A franchiser that has only been in business for a few years and began franchising a year after

start-up doesn't have a lot of experience in the business.

The next section discusses franchise fees and royalties. The front-end franchise fee and royalties are fully disclosed. The continual royalty (usually monthly) may run up to 15 percent, and an additional advertising royalty may be 5 percent or more. The front-end franchise fee may be $1,000 to $300,000 or more. It usually does not include the costs involved in actually starting the business, such as inventory, equipment, facility, and leases. Make sure to include these fees in your financial projections, so you can accurately gauge the business' ability to generate profits in the future.

Next is a section that contains a brief summary of the officers, directors, and other executives. Read carefully to determine their level of experience and expertise. See if any have ties with suppliers or vendors from whom you'll purchase supplies or inventory and whether such ties present conflicts of interest.

The UFOC will also include a brief description of any major civil, criminal, or bankruptcy actions that the officers and executives have been involved in or that the franchise company is a party to. Lawsuits are common today, and the fact that someone has been sued or has filed suit is not necessarily a red flag. However, if the lawsuits involve problems with franchisees or vendors, or if they are numerous, investigate further to determine the stability and integrity of the franchiser.

The terms of the franchise agreement are one of the most crucial parts of the UFOC, and one that you need to review carefully. Many franchisers offer initial terms of five to ten years with options to renew for additional periods. However, it is not uncommon to encounter agreements for five-to-ten year terms with no option for renewal. This means that when the initial term expires, the franchiser may terminate the franchise and open his own company store, or charge the franchisee a large fee to continue. If the franchise agreement does not give you an option to renew, you have no protection and could lose all the goodwill you built up during the period you operated the business.

Franchisers are required to list an approximation of the initial costs of starting the franchise in addition to the franchise fees. Those costs usually include equipment, inventory, operating capital, and insurance. Keep in mind that these costs are estimates and are not inclusive. In fact, many franchise litigation specialists point out that franchisers show zero working capital or an unrealistically low figure. If there is a working capital figure located in Item Seven of the UFOC, ask if it includes operating expenses for the business until it is fully self-supporting, including an owner's salary. When interviewing other franchisees, ask them what they consider sufficient working capital for the first year of operation. Most important, have your CPA help you put together your own estimates.

Although some franchisers will supply you with projections of the sales and expenses of a new franchise location, most won't. This area is heavily regulated by the FTC to prevent franchisers from making unfounded claims. Now, however, more franchisers are beginning to provide projections. This shift in philosophy is due to regulatory changes in the late 1980s, which provided guidelines for franchisers on how to present earnings information.

Because financial projections for a new franchise location are generally not provided, ask existing franchisees about the financial performance of their business. This is an essential step addressed further on in this chapter. You may want to consider purchasing an existing franchise. Although the price may be higher, you have the security of knowing the historical sales and expenses of that business.

A large section of the UFOC lists the many reasons a franchiser may terminate before the contract expires. They include poor condition of the location, failure on the part of the franchisee to pay royalties in a timely manner, failure to supply an account, and excessive customer complaints.

If you're deemed a "good," i.e. "profitable," franchisee, the franchiser will not use these clauses to end its relationship with you. However, if the franchiser thinks it can operate the location better than you can, or has a more desirable applicant for the location, it may use one of those reasons to attempt to terminate you. Therefore, if you sign on, you must be careful to comply with all conditions that, if not met, permit termination.

Regardless of the UFOC provisions permitting termination, some states have strong laws that can make it difficult for the franchiser to terminate a franchise early. Much of the litigation between franchisers and fran-

chisees involves attempts on the part of franchisers to terminate franchisees' licenses prematurely.

Never assume that purchasing a franchise will give you an exclusive, protected territory. Many UFOCs state that you do not receive an exclusive territory but that it is the "policy of the franchiser" not to locate another franchise within three miles. However, "policies" can and do change. The UFOC may also say that if the franchiser decides to open another location in your area, you have the right of first refusal to purchase the new location. Another common provision allows you exclusivity in an area only if your sales are maintained at a certain predetermined level.

If you're purchasing a retail-product or food franchise, often the agreement will provide that you must purchase your goods from approved suppliers and that you can only carry goods that are previously approved by the franchiser. One clothing store franchiser requires that all goods sold by franchisees contain the label of the franchiser. Such a policy greatly restricts the lines franchisees can carry and the sources from which they can purchase inventory, reducing the effectiveness of controlling costs through competitive sourcing.

Read carefully the sections outlining the franchiser's responsibilities to you. Usually those obligations include providing you with a training manual, picking a suitable location, training you and/or an employee, helping plan or attending a grand opening, and offering some sort of continuing assistance with advertising and managing the store. In addition, you usually have the right to use certain trademarked symbols and names for the term of the franchise.

The UFOC usually includes only a general description of the duties the franchiser has to the franchisee. Therefore, before signing on, ask to see the manual, learn more about the training, and meet the franchiser's personnel who are going to assist you. And, if you're still interested, make sure to get your lawyer's and CPA's blessings before you sign on the dotted line.

The Franchise's Financial Statements

One of the UFOC's strengths is that it delivers three years of audited financial information about the franchiser. In Item 21 of the offering circular, it states that the franchiser should include the balance sheet for the most recent fiscal year and an income statement (as well as changes in financial position for the most recent three years). These financial statements are audited reports prepared by a CPA. Subsidiaries are allowed to use a parent's financial information, but only if the parent corporation will guarantee the obligations of the subsidiary franchiser.

The sample pro forma operating statement provides a forecast of projected sales and expenses that might be incurred by a franchisee in the geographic zone where the unit might be located. Very few franchisers provide this information or make any earnings claim. This is in part because, according to the FTC, such claims must be substantiated.

Any earnings claimed by the franchiser must satisfy rigid FTC criteria. They must be based on fact, not hype, and the franchiser must have substantiating material on file. The claim must also be geographically relevant to your area. "Geographically relevant" means that data from nearby franchisees—or data from franchisees in an area similar to yours from a demographic, socioeconomic, or market standpoint—can be used.

Earnings claims must represent what the average franchisee can achieve, not what one unit made in the program. They can never guarantee that any franchise will achieve a stated level of performance.

The sample pro forma will be accompanied by the following words of caution required by the FTC:

These figures are only estimates of what we think you may earn. There is no assurance you'll do as well. If you rely on our figures, you must accept the risk of not doing as well.

Although many franchisers are reluctant to provide earnings projections, insist on seeing one because you'll need a realistic forecast that states what your income and expenses might be. But don't rely on these figures alone for an accurate projection of income and expenses. Do your homework and ask other franchisees what their income and expenses are. In addition, talk to industry associations and independent business owners involved in the type of business you'll be purchasing.

The Franchisee List

Along with the UFOC and financial statements, you'll also receive a list of current franchise operations—an invaluable resource. Plan to contact as many operators as possible. Some will not want to tell you much, but others will. Visit as many stores as you can to get a clear picture of how successful and well received they have been.

THE FRANCHISE AGREEMENT

The franchise agreement gives both parties a clear understanding of the basis upon which they'll operate. It should ensure uniformity to protect all franchisees as well as the franchiser. Remember, your Burger King is only as good as the one across town. If people have a bad experience with your franchise somewhere else, chances are they're not going to want to do business with you either.

Uniformity, which is ensured by the franchise agreement, is one of the standards of operation. If your business lacks uniformity, you'll be a detriment to the entire system. Consider uniformity one of the assets you're acquiring. It establishes standards of operation, including the quality of products you'll use and services you provide. A lot of problems can be avoided by knowing that a certain activity is a violation of the franchise agreement.

The franchise agreement provides for remedies in the event of defaults. It outlines what will happen if you do something wrong, including the steps the franchiser will take, how much time you'll have after the notice is given and what recourse you have.

What else does the franchise agreement include? It states that you're paying a certain fee to be part of the franchise, specifies location provisions, and makes sure that your equipment conforms to company specifications. That's because the franchiser has a vested interest in your success; if you succeed, so do they.

The agreement covers the use of the proprietary market and the use of the franchise name and requests that you notify the franchiser if somebody else is using the franchise name in your area. The franchiser also asks that you conform to the operating manual and use the products, systems, and supplies specified by the company.

This can be a tricky area. For example, it's a violation of antitrust laws for a company to require that you buy a product that is available at a better price somewhere else. Some franchisers have gone out of business because of violating antitrust laws or have been sued by franchisees through the FTC regulations. The bottom line is that a franchiser can require you to use certain secret formulas that it feels are the essence of its product or concept and can specify certain standards of quality, but it cannot force you to pay a higher price for something or charge more than it is worth in the marketplace.

Franchisers can specify a certain product if they don't make a profit on it. For example, they can specify that you use a certain ingredient in the formulation of your product. If they require you to buy breading from them, for example, it must have a secret and legitimate ingredient to comply with the antitrust laws.

Generally, franchisers will want to approve all advertising copy, materials, packaging, promotional materials, and signage that you use to ensure that they're consistent with the concept. Companies may establish a national advertising fund to which you contribute and of which you will be a beneficiary during any national advertising campaign. They may require you to spend a certain amount of your gross income on local advertising.

Franchisers want you to follow the operating manual, to keep it confidential, and adopt any and all revisions to it. The manual includes sections on maintenance and repairs, and specifies how you'll need to maintain the interior and exterior of the location. In some cases, franchiser provisions require the franchisee to construct additional buildings if the franchiser feels they are necessary to accommodate the business. Generally, these provisions have not been accepted very well by most states.

In the agreement are provisions that require you to keep certain records, such as weekly sales reports, semimonthly sales reports, and monthly profit and loss sales reports. Franchisers will want to inspect your records through their area supervisors or representatives to ascertain that you're not understating your sales and thereby cheating them out of royalties. You'll be asked to provide annual, audited statements by a CPA.

The more labor-intensive your operation, the more franchisers will insist on certain procedures. If you're handling a franchise that simply dispenses a pre-made product, there isn't as great a concern on the part of the franchiser, but in cases where a product is made on the premises, whether it's food or a manufactured item, the quality control provisions will generally be substantial.

This is as much for your benefit as a franchisee as it is for the franchiser.

The franchise agreement establishes what royalty you'll pay—an ongoing fee that's a percentage of sales or a fixed monthly or annual amount that will be remunerated to the franchiser for the continued use of the franchised concept. The franchiser determines what kind of program is necessary, what kind of support will be provided on an ongoing basis, and how the fees are assessed and collected.

Insurance provisions establish the amount necessary for workers' compensation, general liability, product liability, bodily injury, and property damage in accordance with established limits set by the franchiser.

A section outlining terms establishes how long your franchise agreement will be in effect, and what are the options beyond that period of time. The term clauses are generally coordinated with the lease so that if you have a lease for fifteen years, you'll have a fifteen-year agreement. A long-term agreement assures the royalty to the franchiser for a longer period of time, and it gives the franchisee more security. The shorter term gives the franchiser the ability to adjust the royalty upward more quickly, and it eliminates undesirable franchisees. When their term expires, they simply are not renewed.

For a franchisee, the short term can also be an advantage because it's a way to get out of the agreement and not pay a royalty. On the other hand, you may want to hold the franchiser to the agreement for a longer period. This is something that you'll have to assess according to your interest in working for the particular franchiser.

There are generally covenant sections restricting a franchisee from copying or diverting business, hiring employees, or divulging secrets. These restrictive covenants are subject to state or antitrust laws. Some states will not allow restrictive covenant sections, while others will. Some antitrust laws prohibit certain restrictions of a person's ability to earn a living. Franchisers will indicate that you as a franchisee cannot simply open an identical business, using all the franchiser's operating systems, know-how, marketing tools and so on, without using the franchise name and paying a royalty.

A section in the franchise agreement deals with what constitutes the right of the franchiser to terminate you or to say that you're in default. If you become bankrupt, for example, that is usually a condition for terminating the franchise agreement. If the franchiser gives you notice to cure a certain defect, you will have a limited amount of time in which to comply.

The length of the notice will vary from state to state. In some states it's ten days, in others, it's thirty days. The company must notify you that you're doing something wrong and that unless you alleviate the deficiency, it will terminate your franchise. You could be terminated for the following reasons:

- You don't pay the royalties or the fees to the company.
- You don't submit the reports or the financial data called for in the franchise agreement.
- You vacate your premises or abandon your business.
- You fail to comply with the franchise agreement in general.

Both parties have certain rights and duties on expiration or termination, and they are spelled out in your franchise agreement. There is often a provision that deals with the operation of the franchise if you are disabled or die. The franchiser then has the right to operate the business.

Another section addresses your requirements to pay any tax assessments or liens, fully comply with all federal, state, and local laws, and obtain all permits, certificates, and licenses necessary to do business at that particular location. The agreement should indicate that you're an independent contractor, not an agent, partner, or employee of the franchiser. This means you can't incur any liability for the franchiser, and that you bear the cost of defense of any claims.

Franchise agreements have arbitration clauses wherever applicable. Some states won't allow this and won't recognize them, but they do provide a basis for settling disputes without having to go to litigation. These clauses sometimes provide for binding arbitration; whatever the arbitrators decide dictates the final agreement.

The agreement also defines the term "franchisee" to include not only you but also your successors. There is a disclaimer that you agree to assume certain risks, that the success of the business isn't guaranteed, and that the success of the business depends on your ability as a franchisee.

INTERVIEW FRANCHISERS AND FRANCHISEES

Once you've received all the documents from the franchiser, you'll begin preliminary negotiations. At this time, you'll meet a representative for the franchiser and conduct interviews with as many franchisees as possible to evaluate the franchise package. This provides an opportunity for both you and the franchiser to see if you want to proceed further.

The representative of the franchiser may be one of three people: the franchise owner or company president, an in-house salesperson, or a franchise broker (an outside salesperson retained by the franchiser to act as a representative).

The franchiser is going to want to know about your financial status, your experience, and your general background. Be prepared with questions about the company. You might want to have your attorney present or have him or her highlight areas of the franchise agreement and UFOC that should be questioned. Don't leave until you've received all the information you need. This could take anywhere from a few hours to all day. Your primary goal is to eliminate your doubts so that you feel comfortable with the data supplied by the franchiser.

Take notes during all your meetings and conversations on the phone. Write down from whom you received the information, the person's title, the date the conversation took place, and so on.

During your meeting with the franchiser, concentrate on the following key areas to determine the strength of the franchise:

- Ask what the pretax net profits of existing operations are and compare this figure to the one on the earnings statement or pro forma that the franchiser has already supplied you with.
- Find out specifically what's included in the training program, field assistance, store design, facility construction, site selection, and feasibility studies.
- Will any additional working capital be required after the initial fee and investment and if so, how much?
- How will the franchiser arrange to get product to the business? Ask to see a current price sheet.
- Ask the franchiser to detail exactly what the territorial restrictions and protections are.

- Find out how many franchises have been sold during the past twelve months to investors in the state you will be operating in and how many have opened a franchised business in that time.
- Ask if the company has any plans for further expansion in your state. Has it identified any locations it plans to develop?
- If purchasing a current franchise, ask to see the operating books and records of the business for the past two years.
- What type of support will the franchiser provide once your franchise has opened its doors?
- Find out if any current lawsuits are pending against the franchiser. Get details on these and any past judgments.
- Will the franchiser assist in site selection?

Don't be afraid to ask questions, as the franchise agreement and the UFOC are complicated documents. If, for any reason, you run across a franchiser who is reluctant to pass along a list of current franchisees, makes promises of earning a fortune on your investment, insists on deposits for holding a franchise unit, tries to convince you to sign before someone else does, or is full of empty rhetoric when answering your questions, then head for the door. These franchisers are out for your money.

Check and double-check all the information supplied. Are the franchiser's claims backed by performance? Are the advertising claims true? Are the profitability claims justified? You can check this information by contacting as many franchisees as possible. If a franchisee doesn't want to talk to you, that might be an indication that he or she isn't doing nearly as well as expected.

Do all you can to convince franchisees to talk to you. Stress that the conversation will be kept confidential and be as candid as possible to establish a good rapport. Remember, franchisees aren't required to provide any information. The more amiable and up-front you are with them, the better your chances of obtaining information. However, if a franchisee continues to be uncooperative, move on to the next person on your list.

Ask the franchisees questions that will let you know whether or not the franchiser has given you the whole story. These questions might include:

- Are the franchisees happy with their investment, support from the franchiser, and entry into the business?
- Would the franchisees purchase a second franchise if it became available in their market area?
- Do the franchisees feel they were well-trained for the challenges of the business?
- What are their income and expenses? Compare those against the sample pro forma provided by the franchiser. Do the franchisees have any cash-flow problems?
- What are their sales patterns? Are they seasonal? Have them describe the busy season.
- What type of ongoing assistance have they received from the franchiser?
- Are their advertising fees reflected in the marketing support (for example, co-op advertising) received?
- Are the franchise and royalty fees fair and competitive with other franchises in the same industry?
- Is local market penetration in line with national figures?
- Were equipment, signage, logos, and so on provided without charge or at an additional cost?
- What hidden costs, if any, have been incurred by franchisees?
- What degree of autonomy are franchisees allowed? How tightly regulated are they by the franchiser?
- Is there a franchise owner's association? Are there any disputes that are the subject of discussion among franchisees?
- What are the actual costs of the products, and are they competitive in the marketplace?
- Have franchisees had any problems with product supply? Do they have any complaints about the franchiser?
- What were their initial start-up costs? What major hurdle(s) did they experience during the first few months of start-up? How did they finance the business?
- How long have they been a franchisee, and would they renew their contracts?
- Have franchisees encountered clauses in the franchise agreement that have been problematic?
- How long are their workdays and do they take vacations?

You'll gain lots of valuable information from the franchisees, but don't stop there. Check out all the bank references supplied by the franchiser to determine financial strength. Run a credit check on the company. Check out any references supplied by the franchiser. Call the Better Business Bureau to find out whether any complaints have been lodged against the company. Have Dun & Bradstreet deliver a status report on the firm through its subscriber service.

After you've completed a thorough evaluation of the franchiser, you can then make a truly informed decision and begin serious negotiations. Make sure your attorney is present at this time.

FINANCIAL REQUIREMENTS

There are many sources of investment capital—banks, credit unions, your own savings and investments, friends, family, venture capitalists, and even franchisers. Before approaching any lender, determine your net worth by using a personal balance sheet. Refer back to Figure 1.2 and list both your assets—what you own—and liabilities—what you owe. Under assets, include cash on hand, checking accounts, saving accounts, real estate (current market value), automobiles (whether paid off or not), bonds, securities, insurance cash values, and other assets. Then total them up. Follow the same steps for your liabilities. List your current bills, all your charges, your home mortgage, auto loans, finance company loans, and so on. Total up your liabilities and subtract them from your assets. What's left over is your net worth.

Next, take a look at your credit rating. All potential lenders look for these things in a credit rating: character, stability, income, and track record.

Most lenders are interested in how long you've been at a certain job or lived in the same location and whether you have a record of finishing what you start. If your past record doesn't show a history of stability, then be prepared with good explanations.

Not only is the amount of income you earn important, but so is your ability to live within that income. Some people earn $100,000 a year and still can't pay their debts, while others can budget on $60,000 a year. Most lending institutions look at your income and the way you live within that income for one very good reason. If you can't

manage your personal finances, chances are that you won't be able to manage those of a business.

The last element lenders look for is your track record—how successful you've been in paying off past debts. If you have a record of delinquent payments, repossessions, and so on, get them cleaned up before you apply for a loan.

Most lenders will contact a credit bureau to look at your credit file. You should check it as well before you try to borrow. Under the law, credit bureaus are required to give all the information they have on file about your credit history. Once you have a copy of your credit report, correct any wrong information, or at least make sure your side of the story is on record. For instance, a ninety-day delinquency would look bad. But if that ninety-day delinquency was caused by being laid off or by illness, then that is taken into consideration.

After you've determined your net worth and your credit rating, it's time to put together your business plan (see Chapter 8). A well-thought-out business plan can make the difference between having your loan application accepted or rejected. A complete business plan should always include a thorough study of the business you plan to go into, accurate pro formas and cost analyses, estimates of working capital, a carefully-researched marketing plan, and a description of your background and skills.

There are two types of funding available: debt and equity. Debt financing means paying the loan back over an agreed period of time, whereas equity financing means giving up a piece of your company.

The good news about debt financing for a franchise is that it can be easier than getting a loan for an independent business, thanks largely to the franchiser's established track record. In fact, the Small Business Administration (SBA) often leans toward franchisees when considering loan applicants because their success rate is generally higher than that of independent small business.

Traditionally, the first place franchisees turn to for financing is the franchiser. Almost all franchisers in the country provide debt financing. Some carry the entire loan or a fraction thereof through their own finance company.

In addition, the loans made by the franchiser can be structured a number of ways. Some offer loans based on simple interest, no principal, and a balloon payment five or ten years down the road. Others offer loans with no payment due until after the first year. Instead of financing the entire start-up cost, franchisers may have financing plans for portions of the entire cost such as for equipment, the franchise fee, operational costs, or any combination thereof.

In addition to financing a portion of the start-up costs, the franchiser usually has arrangements to lease franchisees the necessary equipment. This can be a significant area for financing since capital costs for equipment often make up between 25 and 75 percent of a franchise's total start-up costs.

If the franchise you're considering doesn't offer equipment leasing, look into non-franchise, non-bank companies that specialize in equipment leasing for franchises. These types of financing companies will often provide asset-based lending to finance franchisees' furniture, equipment, signs, and fixtures, and allow franchisees to purchase the equipment at the end of the lease. Keep in mind that you may lose some tax advantages, such as depreciation, if you lease that equipment. But if your financial resources are limited, leasing is one way to make your dollars stretch farther. Ask your CPA which arrangement works best for your business.

Franchisers usually provide assistance with business plans, loan applications, and introductions to lending sources. In many cases, franchisers serve as guarantors of the loan.

After you've determined the extent of financing available from the franchiser, make a list of all available sources of capital. Most experienced business owners use the following sequence of contacts: friends and relatives, home mortgages, veterans' loans, bank loans, SBA loans, and finance companies. A complete discussion of finance sources can be found in Chapters 14 and 24.

Often banks that aren't willing to work with you based on your financial profile become more amenable if you suggest working with an SBA loan guarantee, which pro-

tects loans up to 90 percent. Small businesses simply submit a loan application to the lender for initial review, and if the lender finds the application acceptable, it forwards the application and its credit analysis to the nearest SBA office. After SBA approval, the lender closes the loan and disburses the funds; the borrower makes loan payments to the lender. For more information on SBA loans, see Chapter 15.

Other options would be to take out a home equity line of credit or a second mortgage on your home. Be careful with this type of financing, however, since both are secured by your home. If you can't repay the amount you borrow using this source, you risk losing your home.

You can also use assets such as stocks, bonds, and mutual funds to secure a loan so long as they are not part of a qualified retirement plan, like an IRA or profit-sharing plan. If you're over age fifty-nine and have a lot of money tied up in an IRA, however, you could use it for part of your financing requirements. Although you will have to pay taxes on the amount used, not to mention the loss of income from interest, an IRA can be a good financing tool under certain circumstances.

If you're under age fifty-nine and your IRA is one of your largest assets, you still may be able to take advantage of this avenue without accruing the 10 percent penalty associated with early withdrawal. By taking substantial equal periodic payments spread over a minimum of five years, based on your life expectancy and a set of annuity tables published by the IRS, you can eliminate the 10 percent penalty, although the funds are still taxable.

There are many other sources of financing available to help you launch the franchise of your dreams. Be sure you understand the requirements of your cash investment and make sure you have a "cushion" of working capital to protect the business through its ups and downs. Do your homework thoroughly, work closely with your banker and accountant, and make sure your attorney is well-versed in franchise law.

CHAPTER 13

Buying a Business Opportunity

Remember when your elementary-school teacher was explaining that a square is also a rectangle but a rectangle isn't necessarily a square? The same relationship exists between business opportunities, independent businesses for sale, and franchises. While all franchises and independent businesses for sale are business opportunities, not all business opportunities meet the requirements of being franchises, nor are they in the strictest sense independent businesses for sale.

WHAT ARE BUSINESS OPPORTUNITIES?

Making matters somewhat complicated, not every state with a business opportunity law defines the term in the same manner. However, most of them use the following general criteria.

- A business opportunity involves the sale or lease of any product, service, equipment, and so on, that will enable the purchaser-licensee to begin a business.
- The licenser or seller of a business opportunity declares that it will secure or assist the buyer in finding a suitable location or provide the product to the purchaser-licensee.

- The licenser-seller guarantees an income greater than or equal to the price the licensee-buyer pays for the product when it is resold and that there is a market present for the product or service.
- The licenser-seller promises to buy back any product purchased by the licensee-buyer in the event it cannot be sold to prospective customers of the business.
- The licenser-seller of the business opportunity will supply a sales or marketing program for the licensee-buyer that many times will include the use of a trade name or trademark.

The laws covering business opportunity ventures usually exclude the sale of an independent business by its owner. Rather, they are meant to cover the multiple sales of distributorships or businesses that do not meet the requirements of a franchise under the Federal Trade Commission (FTC) rules passed in 1979. This act defines business offerings in three formats:

1. Package franchises
2. Product franchises
3. Business opportunity ventures

To be considered a business opportunity venture in accordance with FTC rules, four conditions must be met.

1. The individual who buys a business opportunity venture, often referred to as a licensee or franchisee, must distribute or sell goods or services supplied by the licenser or franchiser.

2. The licenser or franchiser must help secure a retail outlet or accounts for the goods and services the licensee is distributing or selling.

3. There must be a cash transaction between the two parties of at least $500 prior to or within six months after starting the business venture.

4. All terms and conditions of the relationship between the licenser and licensee must be stated in writing.

You can readily see that selling a business opportunity as defined by FTC rules is quite different from selling an independent business by a real estate agent. When you're dealing with the sale of an independent business, there are no obligations of the buyer to the seller. Once the sales transaction is completed, the buyer can subscribe to any business operations system he or she prefers. No continued relationship is required by the seller.

COMMON TYPES OF BUSINESS OPPORTUNITY VENTURES

Business opportunity ventures, like franchises, are businesses where the seller makes a commitment of continuing involvement with the buyer. The FTC describes the most common types of business opportunity ventures.

Distributorships

A distributorship involves entering into an agreement to offer and sell the product of another, without being entitled to use the manufacturer's trade name as part of the agent's trade name. Depending on the agreement, the distributor many be limited to selling only that company's goods or may have the freedom to market several different product lines or services from various firms.

Rack Jobbing

This involves selling another company's products through a distribution system of racks in a variety of stores that are serviced by the rack jobber. In a typical rack-jobbing business opportunity, the agent or buyer enters into an agreement with the parent company to market their goods to various stores by means of strategically located store racks. Under the agreement, the parent company obtains a number of locations in which it places racks on a consignment basis. It's up to the agent to maintain the inventory, move the merchandise around to attract the customer, and do the bookkeeping. The agent presents the store manager with a copy of the inventory control sheet, which indicates how much merchandise was sold, and then the distributor is paid by the store or location that has the rack, less the store's commission.

Vending Machine Routes

These are very similar to rack jobbing. The investment is usually greater for this type of business opportunity venture since the businessperson must buy the machines as well as the merchandise being sold in them, but here the situation is reversed in terms of the payment procedure. The vending machine operator typically pays the location owner a percentage based on sales. The secret to a route's success is to get locations in high-traffic areas and as close to one another as possible. If your locations are spread far apart, you waste time and traveling expenses servicing them, and such expenses can spell the difference between profit and loss.

What, you might ask, is really the difference between a franchise and a business opportunity venture? As a rule of thumb, a franchisee receives more support from the parent company, gets to use its trademarked name, and is more stringently controlled by the franchiser. Business opportunities, on the other hand, don't receive as much support from the parent company, generally aren't offered the use of a trademarked name, and are independent of the parent company's operational guidelines.

There are numerous forms of business opportunity ventures. Some are even turnkey operations similar to package format franchises. These business opportunities provide everything you could possibly need to start a business. They help select site location, provide training, offer support for the licensee's marketing efforts and supply a complete start-up inventory. Unlike a package format franchise, however, these types of business opportunity ventures aren't trademarked outlets for the parent company. Decisions concerning the company's name, logo and how it is legally operated are left solely to the licensee. Many times, the only binding requirement between the seller and buyer is that inventory be purchased solely through the parent company. All these stipulations are outlined in the disclosure statement and contract.

For more information on the FTC and business opportunities, go to www.ftc.gov/bcp/conline/pubs/alerts/bizopalrt.htm.

BUSINESS OPPORTUNITY VENTURES AND FTC REGULATIONS

Any business offering falling under the FTC definition of a business opportunity venture must meet all franchise disclosure regulations. That means the seller has to supply the buyer with a prospectus or circular and a copy of the agreement outlining the terms and conditions of the offering.

Some business opportunity ventures are exempt from FTC rules altogether. A common way for a business opportunity venture to exempt itself to take advantage of the *minimal investment rule.* For instance, many business opportunity ventures set their initial fee at less than $500, which technically places them outside the FTC restriction (although if consumer fraud is involved, the FTC will take action).

Other exemptions include *fractional franchises* in which an established distributor adds a franchised product line to its existing line of goods; *leased departments* where a retailer sells its goods from space rented from a larger retailer; *oral agreements; employer-employee* and *general partnership arrangements; agricultural cooperatives,* and *retailer-owned cooperatives.*

THE ADVANTAGES OF BUSINESS OPPORTUNITY VENTURES

Federal and state laws are meant to protect unsophisticated purchasers from investing in a business opportunity—after reading a puffed-up advertisement or listening to a slick sales pitch—without knowing all the facts about the business and the background of the seller. If you live in a state that regulates business opportunities and are thinking about buying one, you'll be protected in case you don't get what you paid for. These strict laws have helped regulate an industry where some offerings were created especially to exploit buyers. Under these disclosure requirements, the buyer knows exactly what the offering covers and what the relationship will be with the parent company.

The advantages of buying a business opportunity are:.

- *A lower initial fee than that required for a franchise.* Although the number of low-investment franchises has increased, the fee to get into a business opportunity is still considerably less. While the FTC requires a $500 minimum investment for it to be considered a business opportunity, there are many offered for less.
- *A proven product or system of operation.* Systems that are tried and true maximize efficiency and minimize problems.
- *Intensive training programs.* A solid business opportunity venture can eliminate most trial-and-error learning experiences through an intensive training program.
- *Better financing options.* Many times, the parent company offering the business opportunity—because of its financial resources and contractual agreements—can arrange better financing than that which could be obtained by an individual.
- *Professional advertising and promotion.* Most independent small-business owners don't spend enough money on advertising. When they do, their efforts are not always well thought-out and consistent. Many business opportunity ventures supply buyers with print advertising slicks, radio ads, and television storyboards to improve marketing efforts. Some business opportunity ventures even have a cooperative advertising agreement that splits the cost of print, radio, or television advertisements. This marketing help is beneficial in large metropolitan areas where the cost of media is prohibitive to the one-shop owner.
- *Ongoing counseling.* Most business opportunity ventures offer support not only through training but also through counseling from a staff of experts who offer assistance that no independent could afford. Legal advice is available to a certain degree. The most

efficient accounting systems—perfect for that particular business—have been designed by experts in the field. Some licensers offer free computer analysis of records, and through comparison with other units, can pinpoint areas of inefficiency or loss as well as profitable aspects of the business that are being neglected.

- *Assistance with site selection.* Experts in site selection and marketing choose locations based on quantifiable market research, rather than the "I've-got-a-hunch" method. Professional negotiators arrange leases and contracts to the best advantage.
- *Purchasing power.* Many times, the parent company's tremendous buying power and expertise can bring products, equipment and outside services to the licensee at a cost lower than an independent could ever get.
- *No ongoing royalties.* In a business opportunity venture, there are no ongoing royalties to the seller. The profits are all yours. You're not making money and putting it in someone else's pockets.

THE DISADVANTAGES OF BUSINESS OPPORTUNITY VENTURES

Most companies sell business opportunities because it allows them to expand their distribution channels without requiring additional capital. Under ideal conditions, business opportunities are a low-investment way to get into business with minimum risk and a good chance for success. But there are some pitfalls to beware in certain circumstances:

- *Poor site selection.* The majority of business opportunity ventures are consumer-oriented retail operations that rely on good location, visibility, and easy access to the establishment. Most buyers of business opportunity ventures casually accept the location chosen for them. Don't! Hire a marketing consultant to evaluate the site for you and make your argument to the parent company. Location has a very significant effect on your business profits.
- *Deficient lease/contract agreements.* Business opportunity companies must keep their costs in line. They can't afford to have an employee spend a week wandering around a city looking for bargains.

- *Lack of ongoing support.* There is usually no requirement for the business opportunity seller to offer ongoing support of any kind. If the seller decides not to supply information or guidelines that could help you once you're in operation, you may not have many resources available.
- *Exclusivity clauses.* Are you restricted to selling only the manufacturer's merchandise? If this is the case and you deviate for any reason whatsoever, you run the risk of the licenser canceling your agreement. If you buy from other sources, it will be very hard to hide. Most parent companies will require that you open your books for examination at certain periods. Any irregularities will be spotted at that time. Most smart buyers of business opportunities will negotiate the small print in the agreement stipulating sources of supply, in case product quality is inconsistent or the service becomes bad.
- *Parent-company bankruptcy.* Another pitfall is the possibility of the parent company becoming overextended and going bankrupt. While this is not as serious in a business opportunity as it would be in a franchise, you still run the risk of losing the business because your property contracts may have been financed through the parent company.

Carefully check any business opportunity venture you're considering. Get a list of operators from the parent company and call them. Have a lawyer with expertise in this area look over any agreement drafted by the parent company. Make sure you receive a disclosure statement. Then carefully evaluate the licenser. Don't let anyone rush you.

CHOOSING THE BUSINESS OPPORTUNITY

If you're thinking about buying a business opportunity, first make sure it's registered in your state, if required, and complies with your state's business opportunity statutes. Next, see whether the business opportunity is required by FTC rules to provide an offering prospectus to buyers.

When choosing a business opportunity, keep in mind that established concepts, with a sizable number of outlets and a minimum of three years in business, are more expensive than many new enterprises. If the business opportunity you're interested in is a new offer, study the parent company's history and evaluate its success and track record in its field of operation.

If you were to ask a business consultant how to know that you've found the "right" business opportunity, he or she would tell you to take the following steps:

- *Make an honest evaluation of yourself and your abilities.* If you've been working with kids for many years, will you be happy calling on businesspeople and selling them a product or service?

- *Be enthusiastic about the business you'll be operating.* Will you be happy introducing a new product or service that the public knows nothing about?

- *Be knowledgeable about the product or service with which you're involved.* If the parent company gives you little or no training, be wary. A good sign is a licenser-seller who's put together a manual with information about operations gained through years of experience in the business.

- *Make a market evaluation of the product or service to be offered.* Is the time right to introduce it to the public? Is there a need for this product or service, and what is its potential? Determine what type of advertising program is available from the licenser, on both a local and national level, if that applies. Will that advertising program work for you?

- *Analyze market trends.* When Medicare was introduced, the time was right for medical and dental assistant schools, doctors' collection services, and so on.

- *Find out how many buyers have been in business successfully for a respectable period.* A legitimate business opportunity will provide you with phone numbers of other buyers over the past several years, so you can verify that they're generally satisfied with the business opportunity and that the seller is capable of fulfilling his or her promises.

- *Check the skills required to run the business properly.* Is there a suitable curriculum of training? How broad is the scope of training? Does your background complement its requirements?

- *Calculate the business opportunity's profitability and financial leverage ratios.* Can you make more money in another type of business? Are you getting value for your initial purchase price? Examine the list of equipment, fixtures, inventory, and operating sup-

plies, and call a few suppliers dealing in these items. Compare their prices to those of the business opportunity. You may be able to purchase everything, including inventory, for less money than you could by affiliating with the licenser. Get all earnings claims in writing.

- *Determine how much time you need to spend to earn what you do now.* Can you invest the same amount in the particular business opportunity yet operate a larger operation and get a better return on your investment?

- *Check with current operators to see how they're doing.* Are they happy with their business? Do they have any problems in common with other units sold?

- *Get the history of the offering company's operation.* Are the seller's claims backed by performance? Do the claims that the seller makes when advertising products, for example, stand up at the store level? Are the profit claims that the seller makes confirmed by the current operators you've talked to?

- *Learn about the service personnel of the parent company.*

- *Examine the financial standing of the parent company.* Check out the bank references given by the licenser-seller and discuss the company's financial strength with the appropriate manager(s).

- *Evaluate the policies and plans of the company with the associations and business groups in which the parent company or seller is involved.* If the business opportunity involves selling products from well-known companies, call the legal departments of those companies and ask whether the company has ever threatened trademark action against the business opportunity.

- *Find out whether complaints against the company have been registered with the Better Business Bureau.*

- *Get a status report on the firm from Dun & Bradstreet.*

- *Have your attorney, CPA, or business consultant evaluate the business opportunity.* At the very least, your attorney should go over the contract to purchase the business opportunity so you understand what you're signing. Your accountant should review the financial statements to check out the company's financial strength and determine whether or not the business is a viable investment.

- *Visit the licenser-seller's office at your earliest convenience.* Talk to the personnel director to learn about their employees—what their skill levels and salaries are, and whether there are any binding agreements or contracts with any of them.

With any business opportunity, never overextend yourself financially. Operating a business without sufficient capital reserves and working capital is a big mistake.

ANALYZING THE BUSINESS OPPORTUNITY

A disclosure statement contains everything there is to know about the business opportunity and the seller's company. It includes information about the promoter's financial strength, how many operating units there are, and the buyer's total financial obligations so that there are no hidden fees. The two purposes of the disclosure statement are to protect the licensee and to eliminate unscrupulous licensers.

In most of the 23 states that require disclosure statements and registration for business opportunities, a licenser can't even offer a business opportunity for sale or send any literature unless the company registers with the state and files a copy of the disclosure statement, pays a fee, and posts a bond. The state will approve or disapprove the offer based upon whether the business opportunity appears to be legitimate and whether the seller has the financial strength or the operational capabilities to benefit licensees.

In addition to the states that require disclosure statements, there are also business opportunity laws on the federal level. The most significant is the FTC rule requiring full disclosure of the business opportunity in all states where the licenser is offering the opportunity. The rule doesn't require a registration but does require a disclosure that follows a specific format. The penalties for violation of state and federal laws, where applicable, are substantial. The rules, which are designed to prevent misrepresentation of a business opportunity offering, state:

- *Who the licenser is.* The history of the parent company needs to include the identity and business experience of any persons affiliated with the licenser, whether the company has had any litigation, whether

it has been bankrupt, what the initial fee is that a licensee would have to pay and if there are any other payments or fees so that there are no hidden costs.
- *Obligations of the licenser.* If there are any financing arrangements, they have to be revealed in the disclosure statement. If the buyer is obligated to buy from any supplier, it needs to be stated up front. The disclosure statement also details the obligations of the licenser. It describes what the parent company will have to provide in terms of equipment, training, and ongoing services.
- *What the licenser promises to deliver.* The disclosure statement should indicate whether the buyer would get an exclusive area or a territory as a licensee. Any trademarks, service marks, trade names, logo types, and commercial symbols that you're going to be able to use, and are a part of what you are buying, need to be identified in here, as well as any patents or copyrights that you can use.
- *Obligation of the licensee.* If the licenser indicates that you must personally operate the business, that needs to be stated. Restrictions on goods and services offered by the licenser are covered, as are provisions for renewal and termination, repurchase, or modification. The disclosure statement also has to list the current licensees and their addresses so you have the opportunity to contact these people.
- *Public figure relationships.* If the business opportunity is identified with a given person, such as Roy Rogers' Restaurant, it should indicate what arrangements have been made with that person. Is that person active in the business, or receiving a royalty out of the proceeds?
- *The financial status of the company.* Nearly every state requires an audited financial statement prepared by a CPA, which gives buyers a solid indication of the seller's financial strength. There is usually a letter from the accountant indicating that the books have been audited and are available for prospective buyers to study.

States' disclosure requirements are similar to the federal standards of information that must be supplied to the buyer. In addition, states' disclosure statements often include information giving the buyer three to seven days after executing the purchase documents to rescind the agreement.

Information on the bond posted by the seller is also included in many state disclosure statements. Generally, these bonds are posted with the state to ensure that the buyer can recover any damages suffered due to violation by the seller of the business opportunity laws. There's also a statement to the effect that the state does not endorse the business opportunity in any way. If a seller fails to comply with a federal or state business opportunity law, he or she will be subject to criminal and civil penalties. In addition, an injunction may be obtained that will stop further sales offerings.

A purchaser of a business opportunity who learns—after operating the business for a while—that the seller has misrepresented the business in some way may file a lawsuit against the parent company to recover damages. In some states, the regulating agency will also initiate proceedings against the seller. Though business opportunity laws are meant to protect buyers, the best way to avoid problems is to conduct your own thorough investigation. Carefully review all the seller's promotional material and statements by sales personnel. The federal and state laws are designed to promote full disclosure, but they don't promise or imply that any state investigation has been made concerning the potential or validity of the business opportunity.

BUSINESS OPPORTUNITIES AND FTC RULES

In spite of FTC rules and aggressive action at the state level, there are business opportunity sellers who seek every possible means to escape regulation. Neither the FTC rule nor state regulations guarantee freedom from fraud.

Every prospective buyer of a business opportunity must receive the FTC disclosure statement at least 10 business days prior to signing a binding contract or paying money to the seller. The 10-business-day requirement is minimal. If you meet face-to-face with the licenser or a representative to discuss proposed sale or purchase of the business opportunity and if the conversation results in a sales presentation, the licenser must provide you with a disclosure document at that time.

Whenever you receive the documents, which should include a copy of the standard purchase agreement, the seller should request that you sign an acknowledgment-of-receipt form. If you haven't received an FTC disclosure document, don't sign anything or pay any money, even if the seller claims that it is refundable.

If the seller doesn't give you a disclosure document, he or she is violating federal law and may also be violating state law. If the salesperson claims that the offering is exempt from FTC requirements, demand to see an opinion letter from counsel before continuing any dealings with the company. Also, ask the salesperson for the telephone number of the local state agency or FTC office that has advised the company that it is exempt.

Very few business opportunity offerings are exempt. The only major exemptions are those where the total initial payment within the first six months is under $500, or where payment made is only for initial inventory sold at a bona fide wholesale price.

FINANCES: YOURS AND THEIRS

The most common type of financing owners of business opportunities deal with is equipment financing. Equipment financing is usually based on what the banks assess as the useful life of the equipment. For example, banks usually figure a seven-year amortization period on equipment in the restaurant industry. They offer a seven-year loan on equipment at about an 8 percent add-on. Eight percent a year times seven years is 56. The bank will add 56 percent to the equipment price, divide it by the number of months in seven years, and assess that much of a payment per month, as opposed to simple interest, which is based on a declining balance. This is an expensive, but accepted, procedure with equipment financing and is usually readily available. You'll want to see a licenser's audited statement of what that company is doing. You'll know you're getting a legitimate financial statement because CPAs will not sign or stamp a statement that hasn't been properly audited and certified.

Have your CPA compare at least two years of statements to see the direction of the company. Are sales increasing? Is the company becoming more profitable? More efficient? The balance sheet, which shows the company's assets and liabilities at a given point in time, is another measure of the company's financial strength.

Companies may give you pro forma projections to show what you can expect to earn in this particular business opportunity. These projections take the costs for a unit doing, say $200,000, $300,000, or $400,000 a year in sales, and show you what you can expect to earn at each of those sales levels. Some states have outlawed the use of pro forma statements except for currently operating units because they do not always accurately reflect earning potential. Operating statements audited by a CPA will give a realistic sense for what a company is doing.

CHAPTER 14

Start-Up Financing

The old saw that "it takes money to make money" certainly pertains to entrepreneurs. You need money to get your business off the ground, market products or services, pay vendors, meet payroll, and buy equipment. If you've done the necessary research and written a well thought-out and thorough business plan, then you should know how much money you need to begin your venture and the most likely places to get it.

Small businesses have often had a hard time getting start-up funds from outside investors. That's why this book stresses the importance of planning. If you present an air-tight case and have a respectable credit history and track record, lenders will be more likely to talk with you and less risk-averse in considering a loan.

Lenders will always want to know how much money you need, how long you'll need it, what it will be used for and how it will be repaid. By providing clear answers, you'll be able to determine the best source for the type of money you need.

EVALUATING YOUR FINANCIAL SITUATION

New entrepreneurs frequently tap their personal savings to get their business going. Other financial resources they typically use are credit cards, home-equity loans, and loans from family and friends. If your personal credit history is good and the amount of money you're looking for is small, you might be able to get an unsecured loan from a bank. The difference is that the bank will look to you, not the business, for repayment of the loan.

However, if your personal debts are high, you may not be able to get the long-term financing you want. You may, then, have to look at equity financing, which means giving up a portion of ownership in your business. Your CPA can help you chart the course that's right for you and your business. To plan your financial needs, begin by answering a few basic questions:

1. How much money do you need?

2. When are you going to repay it?

3. Can you afford the cost of the money?

A lender's fee is added to the principal of the loan in the form of interest. Make an accurate, three-year profit-and-loss projection and then add in the interest on the money you're borrowing. This is how you determine whether you can afford the cost of money (question 3, above).

Although you make a good profit-and-loss projection with strong estimates and forecasted profits, you can still get into trouble if you don't show a good cash-flow projection. A cash-flow projection will indicate whether or not you can truly afford the loan by subtracting the actual money you pay out from the money you take in. When the prime rate of interest hit 20 percent in the early 1980s, there was not a lot of lending going on at banks. Businesses were forced to curtail their expansion because the cost of money was outrageously high.

Many business owners generate profit-and-loss projections and balance sheets, or have them prepared by their bookkeeper or CPAs every three months or so to see where they stand. Unfortunately, few use the cash-flow projection, which is an equally important and handy tool. For example, the interest you pay will show on your profit-and-loss statement, while the principal payments will show on your cash-flow statement.

Your banker will look at these projections to make sure that you can repay the loan from the profits of the business. He or she is also going to check the cash-flow projection to see that you have enough to cover your own salary, unless you have a separate income.

Keep in mind that it typically takes twelve months before you can break even. Some businesses may be located where foot traffic is heavy (for example, in a mall) and begin to immediately generate a positive cash flow. But for your own business, ask suppliers and others in the business how soon you can realistically expect cash flow to become positive.

The experienced business owner knows that financial statements are one part of the package. Your character is another. Bankers, investors, and suppliers all want to see what kind of person you are. Have you repaid your debts? Do you have a reputation of stability and reliability? If you can't answer a resounding "Yes!" to both of these questions, make sure you have a ready explanation why.

When evaluating your financial situation, see if you can sell any assets to free up cash. Take a good look at your personal expenditures to see whether you might be spending more than you should. Know where you can cut back and do so.

What Investors Are Looking For

Your ability to attract money depends as much on lenders' perception of your character as on the effectiveness of your paperwork. In a sense, lenders view all busi-

ness loans as personal loans because they look at your:

- *Stability.* Lenders want to know how long you've worked at a particular job, how long you've lived at a particular residence, and so on. If you've moved several times or changed jobs for better opportunities, be ready with answers to these questions.
- *Income.* Do you live within your means? Some people make a lot of money but don't manage it effectively. A lender will deduce that a person who can't manage his or her personal finances effectively will not be able to manage the finances of a growing business.
- *Debt management.* Lenders will look at your track record for paying off debts. Do you pay your credit card bills on time? Or do you have a lot of late-payment penalties? Do you make your mortgage and car payments on time? Ever late with your rent check? If you've had problems in this area, be prepared with a ready explanation.

Since a lender has immediate access to your credit report via his or her computer, make sure you've reviewed your credit history before applying for a loan. If any errors have been made, have them corrected ASAP. Credit bureaus like Equifax (www.equifax.com, 800-437-4619) or Experian (www.experian.com, 888-397-3742) can send you a copy of your credit history. Fees for these reports will vary.

Sometimes the reports are a little confusing. If so, make an appointment with the credit company and have someone explain to you the unfavorable items. They may not like the idea of having to do this, but the law is very clear on this point. You may be able to go directly into, say, a department store credit office and ask them to help you with a problem you may have with your store account. Let's say it was a late payment on a department store account. Go to the department store and explain that you've paid off the money and you'd like to have them remove that late-payment comment from your record. Have them send a note to the credit bureau saying your record is clean.

SOURCES OF MONEY

There are two types of capital for a business: internal and external. Internal funding means relying on money from operations, while external funding sources include banks, suppliers, commercial finance companies, and other investors.

When planning to raise money, consider all your internal options before searching for an external lender. Even if you can't generate all your capital requirements internally, at least you'll offset the amount of money required so that only a portion has to be raised through external sources. What's more, bankers will have more confidence in your management ability if you show you can make the most out of your internal financial resources.

Owner Financing

Many times, using personal assets is the only way to get a business started. Many lenders and investors won't put their money on the line unless you already have. If you're unwilling to commit a good portion of your funds to starting your business, then perhaps you should rethink the idea of being an entrepreneur.

You may have heard or read a supposed business expert saying, "Why risk your own money when you can use someone else's?" This line of reasoning is folly—why should someone invest in you if you're not willing to invest in yourself?

By using your own money, you risk your finances but your reward is maintaining control of your company. You'll reduce your debt service, and you'll look more attractive to outside financing sources because you've shown you have confidence in your business by investing your own funds.

To determine just how much money you have to invest in a business, refer to the personal balance sheet in Chapter 1. Compute your assets-to-liabilities ratio by dividing asset by liabilities (line A divided by line B). The ratio will look something like 2:1, or, if you carry a lot of debt, 1:2. This is generally referred to as the "acid-test ratio" or "quick ratio." If your assets exceed liabilities, you should be able to keep the creditors from knocking on your door. The Personal Financial Statement shown in Figure 14.1 is another way of presenting your assets and liabilities.

To help you gain control of your personal finances, consider the cash flow statement (Figure 14.2). Many cash flow statements are computed by the month. First, enter your expenses. Next tally your net income, which should include monthly salary, your spouse's salary, and any extra money you earn (e.g., income from rentals or investments). Subtract expenses from income to arrive at your disposable or discretionary income.

Debt Financing

Debt financing includes both secured and unsecured loans. Security involves a form of collateral as an assurance that the loan will be repaid. If the debtor defaults on the loan, that collateral is forfeited to satisfy payment of the debt. Most lenders will ask for some sort of security on a loan. Few, if any, will lend you money based on your name or idea alone.

Here are some types of security you can offer a lender.

- *Guarantors* sign an agreement stating they will guarantee the payment of the loan.
- *Endorsers* are the same as guarantors except for being required, in some cases, to post some sort of collateral.
- *Co-makers* are in effect principals, who are responsible for payment of the loan.
- *Accounts receivable* allow the bank to advance 65 to 80 percent of the receivables' value just as soon as the goods are shipped.
- *Equipment* provides 60 to 65 percent of its value as collateral for a loan.
- *Securities* allow publicly held companies to offer stocks and bonds as collateral for repaying a loan.
- *Real estate,* either commercial or private, can be counted on for up to 90 percent of its assessed value.
- *Savings accounts* or certificates of deposit can be used to secure a loan.
- *Chattel mortgage* applies when equipment is used as collateral—the lender makes a loan based on something less than the equipment's present value and holds a mortgage on it until the loan is repaid.
- *Insurance policies* can be considered collateral for up to 95 percent of the policy's cash value.
- *Warehouse inventory* typically secures up to only 50 percent of the loan.
- *Display merchandise* such as furniture, cars, and home electronic equipment can be used to secure loans through a method known as "floor planning."
- *Lease payments* can be assigned to the lender, if the lender you're approaching for a loan holds the mortgage on property that you're trying to lease.

| FIGURE 14.1 | Personal Financial Statement |

Statement of Financial Condition as of _____, 20__

Individual Information	Coapplicant Information
Name	Name
Home address	Home address
City, state & zip	City, state & zip
Name of employer	Name of employer
Title/position	Title/position
Years with employer	Years with employer
Employer address	Employer address
City, state & zip	City, state & zip
Home phone Business phone	Home phone Business phone

Source of Income	Totals	Contingent Liabilities	Totals
Salary (applicant)		If guarantor, comaker, or endorser	
Salary (coapplicant)		If you have any legal claims	
Bonuses & commissions (applicant)		If you have liability for a lease or contract	
Bonuses & commissions (coapplicant)		If you have outstanding letters of credit	
Income from rental property		If you have outstanding surety bonds	
Investment income		If you have any contested tax liens	
Other income*		If you listed an amount for any of the above, give details:	
Total Income			

*Income from alimony, child support, or separate maintenance income need not be revealed if you do not wish to have it considered as a basis for repaying this obligation.

Assets	Totals	Liabilities	Totals
Cash, checking, and savings		Secured loans	
Marketable securities		Unsecured loans	
Nonmarketable securities		Charge account bills	
Real estate owned/home		Personal debts	
Partial interest in real estate equities		Monthly bills	
Automobiles		Real estate mortgages	
Personal property		Unpaid income tax	
Personal loans		Other unpaid taxes and interest	
Cash value–life insurance		Other debts–itemize	
Other assets–itemize			
		Total Liabilities	
		Net Worth	
Total Assets		Total Liabilities and Net Worth	

FIGURE 14.2 Personal Cash Flow Statement

Statement of Financial Condition as of _____, 20__

Monthly Variable Expenses		Totals
Grocery purchases		
Automobiles: gasoline, repairs, servicing		
Utility bills: electricity, water, phone, etc.		
Clothing		
Medical, dental, prescriptions		
Entertainment		
Other monthly variable expenses–itemize		
Total Variable Expenses	**A**	

Monthly Fixed Expenses		Totals
Rent or mortgage payment		
Auto loan: car 1		
Auto loan: car 2		
Credit card payment 1		
Credit card payment 2		
Credit card payment 3		
Credit card payment 4		
Major store accounts		
Donations		
Insurance payments		
Home improvement loans–itemize		
Total Fixed Expenses	**B**	
Total Monthly Expenses (A + B = C)	**C**	

Monthly Income		
	Gross income	**D**	
	Payroll deductions	**E**	
	Net income (D–E)	**F**	
	Disposable income (F–C)	**G**	

You can also try to acquire debt financing through an unsecured loan. In this type of loan, your credit reputation is the only security the lender will accept. You may receive a personal loan for several thousand dollars, or more if you have a good relationship with the bank. But these are usually short-term loans with very high rates of interest.

Most outside lenders are very conservative and are unlikely to provide an unsecured loan unless you've done a tremendous amount of business with them in the past and have performed above expectations. Even if you do have this type of relationship with a lender, you may still be asked to post collateral on a loan due to economic conditions or your present financial condition.

In addition to secured or unsecured loans, most debt will be subject to a repayment period. There are three types of repayment terms.

1. *Short-term loans* are typically paid back within six to 18 months.

2. *Intermediate-term loans* are paid back within three years.

3. *Long-term loans* are paid back from the cash flow of the business in five years or less.

The most common source of debt financing for start-ups often isn't a commercial lending institution, but family and friends. When borrowing money from your relatives or friends, have your attorney draw up legal papers dictating the terms of the loan. Why? Because too many entrepreneurs borrow money from family and friends on an informal basis. The terms of the loan have been verbalized but not written down in a contract. Lending money can be tricky for people who can't view the transaction at arm's length; if they don't feel you're running your business correctly, they might step in and interfere with your operations. In some cases, you can't prevent this, even with a written contract, because many state laws guarantee voting rights to an individual who has invested money in a business. This can, and has, created a lot of hard feelings. Make sure to check with your attorney before accepting any loans from friends or family.

One of the most popular avenues of obtaining start-up capital is credit cards. Although most charge high interest rates, credit cards provide a way to get several thousand dollars quickly without the hassle of paperwork, as long as you don't overextend your ability to pay back the money in a timely fashion. Interest payments on credit-card debt add up quickly.

If you have three credit cards with a credit line on each card of $5,000 and you want to start a small business that you think will require approximately $8,000, you could take a cash advance on each card and start that business. Within six months, if you build up a profitable business and approach your local bank for a $10,000 loan at about 10 percent interest; then you could use this money to pay off your credit-card balances (which most likely have 18-percent annual rates). After another six months, you could pay off the bank loan of $10,000.

A small-business loan usually costs a little more than a loan at the regular prime rate, which is the rate that banks charge their most favored customers. Small businesses usually pay one to three percentage points above that prime rate. Most small businesses owners are more concerned with finding the right loan at the right terms than with the current interest rate. Shop around.

Banks tend to shy away from small companies experiencing rapid sales growth, a temporary decline, or a seasonal slump. In addition, firms that are already highly leveraged (a high debt-to-equity ratio) will usually have a hard time getting more bank funding.

Equity Financing

With equity financing, you sell a portion of your business to investors who may or may not actively participate in the management of the company. The main concern is how much control to give up. During start-up, you might have to give up as much as 50 percent of the equity in the company. If you have capital to invest in the company, you can receive the same proportion of equity for your funds. However, equity investors are beginning to provide capital for a minority share in the business by placing an equity value on proprietary knowledge such as patents or specific operating information. You can negotiate a value for this knowledge and receive a proportionate amount of equity for that contribution.

In a limited partnership arrangement, your goal is to recruit investors to become partners in your company on a limited basis. Sometimes referred to as "syndications," limited partnerships consist of a general partner who manages the money raised to actively operate the business, while the investors are limited partners. Should the venture meet with misfortune, the partners' liability is "limited" to what they've invested.

As the general partner, you assume the obligation of running the venture on a day-to-day basis. Limited partners, by their legally constituted role, serve as passive investors rather than active managers and are not responsible for producing profits. These net profits are divided among the partners. If the business succeeds, the partners can reap profits larger than those they are likely to get as conventional stockholders

Rules governing limited partnership capitalization vary from state to state and must be strictly observed. In many states, you cannot advertise or publicly offer limited partnership participation without formal registration as a security offering. Meeting these standards requires the services of an experienced securities lawyer.

In many states, you can secure exemption from registration if the offering is limited to a preset number of investors and is not trumpeted to the public. For instance, you could hold a cocktail party at which you approach the potential limited partners of your venture, but you couldn't advertise in the local newspaper for limited partners to join your venture. Find out what the rules are in your state with respect to forming limited partnerships and follow them.

You can also form a corporation to raise equity financing. Partners forming a corporation can divide ownership into shares, selling this private stock to equity investors; responsibilities can be defined in the corporate minutes, and a partner who wants to leave can be accommodated without much legal hassle or dissolution of the business. Stock can be used as collateral (in a partnership it cannot), while death of one shareholder doesn't kill the business (in a partnership it sometimes does).

The Subchapter S corporate structure allows you to take on passive investors who will contribute money to your business in return for stock in the corporation. Like a limited partnership, a Sub S corporation gives you full operational responsibilities while taking on investors within the company.

Unlike limited partnerships, however, a Sub S corporation is still a corporation with all the privileges except

one: Sub S corporations are not taxed like traditional, or C, corporations. Instead, the shareholders of a Sub S corporation include their proportionate shares of corporate profits and losses on their individual tax returns. Sub S corporations are excellent devices for allowing small businesses to avoid the double corporate taxation of profits (once as dividends, again as personal income). If your company produces a substantial profit, forming a Sub S corporation may be wise because the profits are added to your personal income and taxed at an individual rate that may be lower than the regular corporate rate on that income. You can find more information on Sub S corporations in Chapter 5.

Professional investors, such as venture capitalists, can be good sources of funds for larger small businesses. Many venture capital firms have capital available for new and relatively risky enterprises.

Venture capitalists expect two things from the companies they finance: high returns and a way to exit. Since venture capitalists hit the jackpot with only a small percentage of the companies they back, they must go into each deal with the possibility of a return of five to ten times their investment in three to five years if the company is successful. This may mean that they will own anywhere from 25 to 70 percent or more of your company. Each situation is different, and the amount of equity the venture capitalist will hold depends on the stage of the company's development at the time of the investment, the risk perceived, the amount of capital required, and the background of the entrepreneur.

What kinds of businesses do venture capitalists invest in? Venture capitalists invest primarily in technology-related industries and tend to specialize in a particular industry. The largest areas of investment for venture capitalists are usually computer-related communications, electronics, genetic engineering, and medical/health-related fields. There are, however, a number of investments in service and distribution businesses and even a few in consumer-related companies.

The key to attracting venture capital is the company's growth potential. If your company does not have the potential to be a $30- to $50-million company in five to seven years, forget raising money from most venture capitalists. They do not invest in mom-and-pop operations;

they invest in large businesses that are small because they're just getting started.

Before approaching venture capitalists, do your homework. Find out if your needs match their preferred investment strategy and what strengths the venture capitalist has that may help you in building your company. There are a number of directories that list the investment preferences of venture capitalists. For more information on the industry, visit the National Venture Capital Association's web site at www.nvca.org and click on the link to the American Entrepreneurs for Economic Growth www.aeeg.org. The AEEG works to inform its members about investment trends, entrepreneurial experiences, and noteworthy events.

When you've narrowed the field to ten or so companies, the best way to contact them is through an introduction from a third party, such as another entrepreneur, a lawyer, a CPA, a banker or anyone who knows you and the venture capitalist well enough to get his or her attention. The first meeting with the venture capitalist is very important. How you present your business plan, your appearance, your conduct, what you say, and how you say it are all of utmost importance. Be prepared. You'll be asked many questions about your business plan.

If the venture capitalist decides to finance your company, the actual investment is negotiable and can take on a variety of forms, ranging from a straight, common-stock purchase, to debentures with conversion features, to straight loans. Venture capitalists typically use a combination investment instrument to structure a deal that will be most beneficial to both parties.

Regardless of whether you're a spectacular success or a catastrophic failure, there will come a time when the venture capitalist will want out, or when you will want him or her out. This "exit" will have been discussed in depth when you negotiated the original deal. You will either take your company public, repurchase the investor's stock, merge with another firm, or, in some circumstances, liquidate your business.

Another type of professional investor, called a small business investment corporation (SBIC), operates under the auspices of the federal government's Small Business Administration (SBA). SBICs are privately owned and managed firms that make capital available to small business through loans or investments. SBICs make only long-term loans or equity investments and work with companies whose net worth is less than $18 million with average after tax earnings of less than $6 million.

A second type of SBIC, known as the specialized SBIC (SSBIC) or 301 (d) SBIC, is privately capitalized and invests in small businesses owned by women and minorities, as well as those in economically depressed areas. For information and a directory of active SSBICs, contact the National Association of Investment Companies at www.naicvc.com or 202 289-4336.

Small Business Development Companies (SBDCs) provide yet another avenue for financing. Typically located on college campuses, SBDCs are a cooperative effort among the SBA, the academic community, the private sector, and state and local governments. There are SBDCs in every state, and your local SBA office can give you the location nearest you.

Like SBICs and SSBICs, SBDCs invest for the long run. Don't approach them if you're trying to finance a short-term equipment purchase or need an overnight loan. That's why banks exist.

Trade Credit

Once you're a regular customer, a supplier will normally extend your credit for 30 to 90 days without charging interest. However, when you're first starting out, suppliers are not going to give you trade credit. They'll make every order COD until you've established that you can pay your bills on time. To show good faith and attempt to negotiate with suppliers during start-up, prepare a financial plan.

When you visit your supplier to set up your order during start-up, ask to speak directly to the owner of the business if it's a small company. If it's a larger business, make an appointment to speak with the chief financial officer or any other person who approves credit. Explain that you need to get your first orders on credit in order to launch your venture. The owner or CFO may give you half the order on credit with the balance due on delivery. Of course, the trick here is to get your goods shipped to you and sell them before you have to pay for them yourself. Avoid borrowing the money to pay for inventory because you'll pay interest on that money.

CHAPTER 15

SBA Loans

As one of the best friends to business owners who don't qualify for loans from traditional sources, the Small Business Administration (SBA) was established in 1953 by the Department of Commerce to help entrepreneurs secure capital to start a business or expand operations. The SBA is authorized to make loan guarantees through participating banks and other institutions, but in some rare cases will extend direct loans to new and existing businesses. With a portfolio of business loans, loan guarantees, and disaster relief worth more than $45 billion, along with a venture capital portfolio of $30 billion, the SBA is the nation's largest single financial backer of small businesses.

Among the services offered by the SBA are financial assistance through guaranteed loans, counseling services, help in getting government contracts, management assistance through programs like SCORE (Service Corps of Retired Executives), and low-cost publications. The SBA even maintains a registry to help franchisees and prospective franchisees receive expedited loan processing. There are also special services for businesses owned by ethnic minorities, women, veterans, and others with special needs and circumstances.

To find the SBA office nearest you, look in the white pages of your phone book under the general heading "United States Government," or visit the SBA web site at www.sba.gov.

TYPES OF SBA LOANS

SBA financing programs vary depending on a borrower's needs. SBA-guaranteed loans are made by a private lender and guaranteed up to 80 percent by the SBA, which helps reduce the lender's risk and helps the lender provide financing that's otherwise unavailable at reasonable terms.

7(a) Guaranteed Loan Program

The SBA's primary business loan program is the 7(a) General Business Loan Guaranty Program. It's generally used for business start-ups and to meet various short- and long-term needs of existing businesses, such as equipment purchase, working capital, leasehold improvements, inventory or real estate purchase. These loans are generally guaranteed up to $750,000. The guaranty rate is 80 percent on loans of $100,000 or less and 75 percent on loans more than $100,000.

The guidelines for SBA guaranteed loans are similar to those for standard bank loans. In addition, your company must qualify as a small business according to SBA standards, which vary from industry to industry.

The interest rate charged on SBA guaranteed loans is based on the prime rate. While the SBA does not set interest rates, since it is not the lender, it does regulate the amount of interest that a lender may charge an SBA borrower. If the loan has a term of seven years or more, the SBA allows the lender to charge as much as 2.75 percent above the prevailing prime rate. If the loan has a term of less than seven years, the surcharge can be as much as 2.25 percent.

You can use the following assets as collateral for an SBA guaranteed loan:

- Land and/or buildings
- Machinery and/or equipment
- Real estate and/or chattel mortgages
- Warehouse receipts for marketable merchandise
- Personal endorsement of a guarantor (a friend who is able and willing to pay off the loan if you are unable to)
- Accounts receivable
- Savings accounts
- Life insurance policies
- Stocks and bonds

504 Local Development Company Program

The 504 Loan Program provides long-term, fixed-rate financing to small businesses to acquire real estate, machinery, or equipment. The loans are administered by Certified Development Companies (CDCs) through commercial lending institutions. 504 loans are typically financed 50 percent by the bank, 40 percent by the CDC, and 10 percent by the business.

In exchange for this below-market, fixed-rate financing, the SBA expects the small business to create or retain jobs or to meet certain public policy goals. Businesses that meet these policy goals are those whose expansion will benefit a business district revitalization (such as an Enterprise Zone), a minority-owned business, or rural development.

The MicroLoan Program

Established in 1992, the SBA's MicroLoan Program offers anywhere from a few hundred dollars to $25,000 for working capital or the purchase of inventory, supplies, furniture, fixtures, machinery, and/or equipment to businesses that cannot apply to traditional lenders because the amount they need is too small. Proceeds may not be used to pay existing debts or to purchase real estate. These loans are not guaranteed by the SBA but are rather delivered through intermediary lenders, such as nonprofit organizations with experience in lending.

The MicroLoan Program is offered in 45 states through community-based, nonprofit organizations that have qualified as SBA MicroLoan lenders. These organizations receive long-term loans from the SBA and set up revolving funds from which to make smaller, shorter-term loans to small businesses. According to the SBA, the average loan size in 2006 was $13,000, with many going to minority-owned businesses and women-owned companies, groups that have historically had the most difficulty obtaining conventional small-business loans.

The SBA also facilitates other types of loans to help owners of small businesses. Loans are available to help small businesses comply with the federal air and water pollution regulations and with occupational safety and health requirements. Other loans can offset problems caused by federal actions, such as highway or building construction or the closing of military bases. There are loan programs targeted to relieving economic injuries suffered by a small business as a result of energy or material shortages or temporary economic dislocations.

In addition to these loans, the SBA offers the following programs:

- *State Business and Industrial Development Corporations (SBIDCs)* are capitalized through state governments. They usually offer long-term loans (from five to twenty years) for either the expansion of a small business or for the purchase of capital equipment. Lender requirements and rates of interest vary from state to state. Some SBIDCs will commit funds to very high-risk ventures, whereas others will look for minimal risk.
- *504 CDC Loans* provide fixed-asset financing through Certified Development Companies (CDCs). These nonprofit corporations are sponsored by private-sector organizations or by state and local governments to contribute to economic development. The 504 CDC

Loan Program is designed to enable small businesses to create and retain jobs—the rule of thumb is one job for every $35,000 provided by the SBA.

- *Community Adjustment and Investment Program Loans* aim to create new, sustainable jobs and preserve existing jobs in businesses at risk as a result of changing trade patterns with Canada and Mexico.
- *Energy and Conservation Loans* are for small businesses engaged in engineering, manufacturing, distributing, marketing, and installing or servicing products or services designed to conserve the nation's energy resources.
- *The Export Working Capital Program* provides short-term loans to small businesses for export-related transactions.
- *Export-Import Bank (EXIMBANK)* provides working capital for smaller companies to finance export and foreign marketing operations.

- *Small Business Innovation Research Program (SBIR)* offers an exciting opportunity for small businesses to benefit from more than $1 billion in federal grants or contracts. The SBIR Program (a result of the 1982 Small Business Innovation Development Act) promotes research and development for American-owned small businesses with 500 or fewer employees.

TYPES OF LENDERS

The SBA uses three primary types of lenders to fund loans:

1. *Infrequent participant lenders* are bank and non-bank lending institutions that deal with the SBA on a sporadic basis. An infrequent lender sends the SBA all paperwork involved with any particular loan guarantee situation. The SBA does an independent analysis of the plan and determines whether it will guarantee

LOWDOC LOAN PROGRAM

The Small Business Administration has a program that makes applying for a loan somewhat easier. Called the LowDoc Loan Program, it combines a simplified application process with a more rapid response from SBA loan officers (perhaps two or three days), reducing red tape from the loan process.

The LowDoc Program was created in response to complaints that the SBA's loan application process for smaller loans was needlessly cumbersome for both borrowers and lenders that participate in the SBA's 7(a) General Business Loan Guaranty Program. The process tended to discourage borrowers from applying and lenders from making loans of less than $100,000.

LowDoc streamlines the loan application process for guaranteed loans under $100,000. The approval process relies heavily on a lender's experience and judgment of a borrower's credit history and character. The primary considerations are the borrower's willingness and ability to repay debts, as shown by their personal and business credit history, and by past or projected cash flow. No predetermined percentage of equity is required, and lack of full collateral is not necessarily a determining factor.

The application form for loans under $50,000 consists of a single page. Applications for loans from $50,000 to $100,000 include that short-form application plus the applicant's income tax returns for the previous three years and personal financial statements from all other guarantors and co-owners of the business. Commercial lenders are likely to require additional paperwork to satisfy their own requirements. Other documents required by legislation, regulation and executive order are dealt with at the loan closing.

Eligibility

Any small business eligible under the regular 7(a) loan program can apply under LowDoc if its average annual sales for the previous three years is $5,000,000 or less and it employs 100 or fewer individuals, including the owner, partners or principals.

the loan that the institution is going to give the borrower.

2. *Certified lenders* are lending institutions that participate with the SBA on a regular basis and have a staff trained and certified by the SBA. Under this program, the lender reviews all the paperwork and decides whether the borrower merits a loan but gives the SBA the final word. Only after the lender has approved the loan does the SBA review the documents, and then they have only three days to do so.

3. *Preferred lenders* are certified lenders that have graduated to the top of the list based on performance. The SBA designates its "best and most reliable lending partners" as preferred lenders and gives them final approval on loans.

Not all banks are eligible for either the Bank Certification Program or Preferred Lenders Program. Indeed, most preferred lenders tend to be major commercial banks that may have specialized SBA divisions in their organization. Each bank must meet four criteria.

1. *Experience.* A minimum of ten years' SBA lending is required.

2. *Prudence.* A good record shows few loans bought back by the SBA.

3. *Community lending.* A solid record of loans to local borrowers, especially to minorities and to women, is needed.

4. *Assistance to small business.* The bank shows a record of helping local small firms.

SBA LOAN RESTRICTIONS

To be considered for any loan funded by or through the SBA, whether you are starting a new business or obtaining capital for an existing one, you must first meet certain criteria. First of all, the business requesting SBA financing must be independently owned and operated, not dominant in its field, and must meet employment or sales standards developed by the agency. Loans cannot be made to speculative businesses, media-related businesses, businesses engaged in gambling, lending or investing, recreational or amusement facilities, or non-profit enterprises.

Loans may not be used to

- Pay off a creditor who is adequately secured and in a position to sustain loss
- Provide funds for distribution to the principals of the applicant
- Replenish funds previously used for such purposes
- Encourage a monopoly or activity that is inconsistent with the accepted standards of the American system of free competitive enterprise
- Purchase property that will be held for sale or investment
- Relocate a business for other than sound business purposes
- Effect a change of ownership unless it will aid in the sound development of the company or will engage a person hampered or prevented from participating in the free enterprise system because of economic, physical, or social disadvantages
- Acquire or start another business besides the present one
- Expand to an additional location
- Create an absentee-ownership business
- Refinance debt of any kind

Be fully prepared to prove to the SBA that your company has the ability to compete and be successful in its field. Whether you're seeking a loan for a new concept or an established one, do not underestimate the importance of the category into which the SBA groups it. The success or failure of your application may rest on the classification assigned by the SBA. Determine which field or area your business can best compete in, state this in your application, and be prepared to back up your claim.

To help you address the issue of classification, be aware of how the SBA formulates its guidelines. A key publication it relies on is the Standard Industrial Classification (SIC) Manual, published by the Bureau of the Budget in Washington, D.C. The SBA also uses published information concerning the nature of similar companies, as well as your description of the proposed business. The SBA will not intentionally work against you, so it's up to you to steer the agency in the direction most beneficial to you. The standards used by the SBA for judging the size of a business for purposes of qualifying for a loan vary from one industry to another.

TABLE 15.1	Documents Needed for SBA Loans

Documents to Prepare for a New Business

- Loan request statement, describing loan amount and a detailed account of the type of business you are starting
- Your resume and the resumes of key managers you plan to employ
- Statement of your investment capabilities
- Current financial statement of all personal liabilities and assets
- Projection of revenue statement
- Collateral list

Documents to Prepare for an Existing Business

- Balance sheet, with all liabilities and assets listed
- Income statement of previous and current year-to-date incomes
- Personal financial statement, with each owner itemized
- Collateral list
- Loan request statement, describing loan amount and purpose

SBA LOAN STRUCTURES

Product classification and size are not the only things the SBA will want to know about your business. Whether you're applying for a loan to finance a new start-up or fund an existing business, the SBA will want to know the following about you and your business:

- A description of the business you plan to establish
- Your experience and management capabilities
- How much money you plan to invest in the business and how much you will need to borrow
- A statement of your present financial position showing all personal assets and liabilities
- A detailed projection of what your business will earn in its first year of operation
- The collateral you can offer as security for the loan and an estimate of its current market value

Accuracy is of utmost importance. Keep notes on everything that goes into the loan package as backup in the event you are called on to explain or prove a figure or statement on any of the documents. Table 15.1 lists the documents to prepare for a new or existing business.

The Personal Balance Sheet

The personal balance sheet lists all personal assets and liabilities and must be prepared for each major stockholder (one who has at least 20 percent ownership), partner, officer, and owner of the business. These balance sheets must be current (not more than ninety days preceding the date of your loan application) and must accurately portray each person's financial position. The SBA may reject your application if it finds any misrepresentation with inflated entries.

The Financial Plan

Every business, large or small, new or old, needs to have a financial plan to guide it. The SBA wants to know what your potential profit or loss and your cash flow will be during the first twelve months of operation. Making these estimates will probably be the most difficult part of preparing your loan package, and you may want to ask your CPA for help. If your projections show that you'll gross more than $250,000 during the first year, then a pro forma balance sheet should be made for the end of the first-year forecast.

Take the time necessary to prepare a reasonable and realistic projection of your month-to-month sales, expenses, profits, and cash flow. A reasonable and realistic estimate is based on fact—it is an educated guess, not a wish that cannot be substantiated. The more documented proof you can get to back up your estimates, the better your chance will be of securing the funding you requested. In addition, the exercise of putting all these numbers together will make you more knowledgeable about your business, and this will increase your chances of success.

The first month in your projection should be the month in which your business is fully operational. This could very well be two to three or more months after you receive your loan funds. Make sure to include the following items in your projection:

- *Total sales (net)* includes both "cash" and "on-account" sales. Net sales are total sales minus returns and refunds. If your business has separate profit-making departments, estimate sales for each department separately.
- *Cost of sales* should include the cost of merchandise sold and freight or transportation charges you pay on incoming inventory. If any of your employees will be paid a sales commission, the amount of commission should be included in your cost of sales.
- *Gross profit,* sometimes called gross margin, is the difference between net sales and cost of sales.

The second half of your financial plan projections deals with expenses. These are costs incurred on a monthly basis in order to operate your company.

- *Salaries* are actually your estimated payroll cost and do not include your own salary compensation.
- *Payroll taxes and benefits* include all state and federal obligations. In addition, any company-paid benefits you provide your employees, such as vacation, sick pay, health insurance, etc., should be included.
- *Outside services* are any services necessary to operate your business on a monthly basis such as janitorial, pest control, and so on.
- *Supplies* include all items purchased for office and operating use in the business (not for resale) This could include cleaners, paper towels, light bulbs, cash register tapes, ashtrays, stationery supplies, business cards, as well as pens, pencils, staplers, typewriter ribbons, and so on. Also include postage expenses here.
- *Repairs and maintenance* include all repairs to equipment used in the operation of the business as well as any maintenance contracts or regularly scheduled service work.
- *Advertising* is your budgeted cost for marketing your company, product or service, and should include any special promotions or grand-opening events.
- *Cars, delivery, and travel* include any costs incurred by you or your employees for air fare, meals, lodging, vehicle rental or lease payments, gas and the mileage allowance set forth by the IRS for company owned or operated vehicles.
- *Accounting/legal* are costs generated to maintain your accounting records, prepare year-end financial statements and tax returns, or consult with an attorney.
- *Rent* includes monthly rent, lease, or mortgage payment on the use of operating facilities.
- *Phone* includes monthly costs incurred for all telecommunications service such as phone, fax machines, cellular phone, and so on.
- *Utilities* include the cost of electricity, gas, or oil for heating water, garbage collection, and sewer charges, if applicable.
- *Insurance* includes property, product, and liability coverage. Don't forget to include any special coverage needed for your particular business. Do not include life insurance in this category.
- *Taxes and licenses* include all applicable taxes and licensing fees, such as business licenses, inventory tax, sales tax, excise tax, and personal property tax. Do not put income or payroll tax in this category.
- *Interest* applies only to business debts. Do not include the portion of your payment that covers principal repayment of your loan.

- *Depreciation* is what, for tax purposes, the IRS will allow you to deduct a certain percentage of the cost of various fixed assets.
- *Other* should include any miscellaneous expenses that do not appear in the preceding categories.
- *Total expenses* are the total of all the preceding expenses.
- *Profit before taxes* is difference between the gross profit of your business and the total expenses is the profit before taxes.

In making your projections, understand that sales, profits, and cash are not the same thing. Obviously they are related, but it is not unusual for a business to encounter periodic shortages of cash even though sales and profits may be booming. For this reason, it's necessary to prepare a cash-flow projection month by month for a twelve-month period.

A cash flow projection will enable you to manage receipts and disbursements so that cash is always available to meet expenses as they become due. Therefore, pay close attention to timing in your projection, taking into account the time lag between sales and the collection of receivables and between expenses and the due dates for their payment. Figure 15.1 shows a sample cash flow form.

In preparing your cash flow projection, include the following items:

- *Cash sales*: a monthly total of all cash and credit card sales.
- *Accounts receivable* : the percentage of sales on credit accounts that can be collected within a given month.
- *Other*: all other sources of cash inflow, including funds from family members, stock offerings, and any other loans except start-up funding.
- *Total cash available*: the total money on hand before making any monthly disbursements.
- *Owner's draw*: the monthly stipend(s) received by the owner(s).
- *Loan principal repayments*: principal only, and should not include any interest payments.
- *Cost of sales.*
- *Total expenses.*
- *Capital expenditures*: all costs associated with the purchase of equipment, fixtures, tools, leasehold

improvements, vehicles, and other capital assets in the first month.
- *Reserve for taxes*: a reserve fund for future income tax.
- *Other*: any miscellaneous disbursements that do not appear in the preceding categories.
- *Total disbursements.*
- *Monthly cash flow*: total available cash after meeting all disbursements.
- *Cumulative cash flow*: the yearly total on the monthly cash flow.

Capital Requirements

If you're requesting a loan to start a new business, you'll need to consider all your start-up costs in launching your business, how much of these costs you can meet from your personal funds, and how much will come from your loan.

Keep all your notes and worksheets to show how you determined each of the figures on the statement. Obtain written price quotations on all items you plan to purchase. With equipment, estimate the amount of money you'll need for repair and maintenance of all pieces. Get bids from three reliable contractors for the cost of building improvements. For inventory, budget enough money to carry you through your opening period and the first few months. Prepare a list of your major suppliers, and for each one, get information on their prices, delivery schedules, and terms of payment.

Estimate your working capital needs from your cash flow projection. Your goal is to have enough cash at all times to cover three months' expenses and inventory replenishment. It's unlikely that your business will generate enough cash flow to meet this target; the shortage will be covered from the loan funds.

The SBA will expect you, as an owner, to make a considerable investment in the business, preferably 20 percent or more. Your investment can be in any form that benefits the business—cash, furniture, equipment, and so on.

You'll also need to prepare a brief description of your business. This does not have to be as involved as the one described in "The Financial Plan" section. You merely need to describe your business and include a paragraph outlining the expected benefits you'll receive from the loan.

FIGURE 15.1 Cash Flow Projection Form

								MONTH						
	1st	2nd	3rd	4th	5th	6th	7th	8th	9th	10th	11th	12th	Total
1. Sales														
2. Cost of sales														
3. Gross profit														
EXPENSES														
4. Advertising														
5. Automobile														
6. Bank discounts														
7. Depreciation														
8. Dues & subscriptions														
9. Insurance														
10. Interest														
11. Office supplies														
12. Payroll taxes														
13. Professional services														
14. Rent														
15. Repairs & maintenance														
16. Salaries														
17. Supplies														
18. Taxes/licenses														
19. Utilities/phone														
20. Miscellaneous														
21. Total expenses														
22. Profit before taxes														
23. Cash sales														
24. Accounts receivable														
25. Other														
26. Total cash available														
DISBURSEMENTS														
27. Owner's draw														
28. Loan repayment														
29. Cost of sales (line2)														
30. Total expenses (less line 7)														
31. Capital expenditures														
32. Tax reserve														
33. Other														
34. Total disbursements														
35. Monthly cash flow														
36. Cumulative cash flow														

Collateral

Collateral is an important criteria by which the SBA judges a loan application. Prepare an itemized list and accurately describe the collateral you're prepared to offer—see SBA Form 4, Schedule A. You can get SBA forms from your bank, the nearest SBA office or at the SBA's web site at www.sba.gov. Get three copies of the required forms: one for preparing a draft, one for the final copy, and a spare one in case you need an extra in a hurry.

The Loan Application

The loan application form is the last document you should fill out. Much of the information on that form is a summary of the data just described and listed in the financial plan. If you have prepared this plan correctly, it should contain all the required information about your proposed or existing business and the start-up financing it needs.

There are two sides to the application form. The front side is divided into six sections and includes full instructions for completing the information requested. The sections are as follows.

1. *Applicant.* Include all relevant information about yourself and your business in this section, such as your full legal name, fictitious name statement if applicable, trade name of borrower, street address, employer's ID number, type of business, date the business was established, number of employees, and the bank for your business account.

2. *Management.* List the name and home address of each person who will assume responsibility for managing the business.

3. *Use of proceeds.* This is similar to the "Use of Funds" statement. List all expenditures and estimated costs such as land acquisition, new plant or building construction, building expansion or repair, building or property acquisition, capital equipment, inventory, working capital, as well as all debt services including the SBA, total loan requested and term of loan.

4. *Summary of collateral.* This is a summary of the assets you wish to use as collateral for your loan.

5. *Previous government financing.* Describe government loans that you, any principals or affiliates have requested.

6. *Indebtedness.* Include all outstanding debts, such as installment contracts.

An applicant for an SBA business loan should have his or her attorney, accountant, appraiser, or other representative help prepare and present the application. Such representation is not mandatory, but if a loan is approved, the services of an attorney may be necessary to prepare closing documents, title abstracts, and so on. The SBA allows payment of reasonable fees or other compensation for services performed by consultants assisting applicants.

OTHER GOVERNMENT AGENCIES OFFERING FINANCING TO SMALL BUSINESSES

The SBA isn't the only government resource for small business financing. Congress requires that federal agencies set aside 23 percent of their contracts for small businesses. Among the agencies making loans to small businesses are:

1. *Farmers Home Administration (FmHA) of the U.S. Department of Agriculture.* Applicants must be residents of cities or areas with a population of 50,000 or less, outside major metropolitan areas. FmHA loans are guaranteed long-term loans backed 90 percent by the FmHA. They can be used as a source of start-up or working capital, new equipment purchases, refinancing, or expansion (including purchase of real estate). Loans for real estate and major construction are available for up to thirty years. Equipment and machinery can be financed for up to fifteen years or their depreciable life, if shorter. Capital funds can be obtained for six-year terms. There is no limit on the amount you can borrow. Approval depends solely on need and the way you plan to use the money.

2. *Economic Development Administration (EDA) of the Department of Commerce.* This agency makes loans and loan guarantees to new and existing businesses in depressed areas (regions with high unemployment and low-to-average income levels). Loans may not be granted to cover working capital or to purchase fixed assets. Working capital loans extend up to seven years, while loans for fixed assets may extend up to twenty-five years. The loan applicant is expected to provide 15 percent of the required funding. Interest

rates vary according to the prevailing prime rate of interest at the time the loan is granted.

3. *Department of Energy.* DOE offers a loan program geared toward firms developing methods to increase domestic energy efficiency through conservation, alternate energy sources, or new methods of energy utilization.

4. *Department of Housing and Urban Development.* HUD has several programs for the construction of commercial and residential buildings to rehabilitate needy areas in targeted cities. Funds are channeled through local officials in cities and towns, who make loans or grants to entrepreneurs to develop properties.

5. *Department of the Interior.* DOI has a program though which it makes grants for the restoration of rundown properties that have been declared historic sites by a state agency.

PART 2

Managing Your Business

O nce your dream of starting a business becomes a reality, the next step is to get serious about managing your business. Business management can be challenging for entrepreneurs because they typically:

- *Lack attention to detail.* Since they're concept-oriented, entrepreneurs are often not in tune with the details of handling day-to-day business operations. Many entrepreneurs have great ideas and are hard working and motivated, but their greatest strengths can become liabilities once the business is up and running.

- *Don't want to delegate control.* Entrepreneurs often feel no one can do as good a job as they can, so they have a hard time delegating effectively. A business owner who tries to do everything may experience a high employee turnover because of their unrealistic expectations for work performance.

- *Lack management expertise.* Some entrepreneurs manage their businesses by trial and error because they've never learned any other way, while others have knowledgeable, competent employees but fail to empower them.

The chapters in this section cover areas every business owner needs to address for effective—and profitable—small business management.

CHAPTER 16

Record Keeping

Your business needs accurate and up-to-date records for two reasons. First is that records are required by law, to determine the business' tax liabilities. Second, records are useful to you as the business' manager. Information about your business' financial condition helps you identify and correct small problems before they become big ones.

Regardless of the type of bookkeeping system you use, your records must be permanent, accurate, and complete. They must also clearly establish income, expenses, credits, employee information, and anything else specified by federal, state, and local regulations.

When you start a business, figure out the type of bookkeeping that best suits you and your business, keeping in mind the type of taxes for which the business is liable and when they fall due. If this is not your area of expertise, get help from your CPA. Setting up a good record-keeping system needs to be done only once, and doing it right the first time makes things easier down the road.

ACCOUNTING METHODS

Two systems of accounting are used for record-keeping purposes: the cash basis and the accrual basis.

Which one is best for your business depends on your sales volume, the legal form under which your business operates, and whether you extend credit.

Cash Basis

In cash-basis accounting, you do business and pay taxes according to your real-time cash flow. Cash income begins as soon as you ring it up on the register or receive it by check. Expenses are paid as they occur. Both income and expenses are put on the books and charged to the period in which they are paid or received.

You can defer income to the following year as long as it isn't actually received by you in the present year. A check you receive in the present year but don't cash until the following year is still income for the present year. Therefore, if you want to shift income to the following year, you'll either have to delay billing until the following year or bill so late in the present year that a present-year payment is unlikely.

If you want to accelerate expenses to the present year, pay bills received and enter them as the present year's expenses. An expense charged to your credit card will count as an expense in the year it was charged and not when you pay the card company. Be careful about paying next year's expenses in advance. Generally, expenses prepaid in excess of one month have to be prorated over the specified payment period. However, dues and subscriptions can be deducted currently if you prepay them for the upcoming year.

Accrual Basis

With accrual basis accounting, income and expenses are charged to the period to which they apply, regardless of whether money has been received. For instance, if you're a contractor using accrual-basis accounting and have done work for which you haven't yet been paid, you recognize all expenses incurred in connection with that contract during the period in which it was supposed to have been completely paid and expensed. If an employee works for you this month but you haven't paid him or her, you still take the deduction for the expense because that person has earned the money.

CLASSIFICATION OF LEDGER ACCOUNTS

INCOME

Retail sales

Wholesale sales

Sales—services

Miscellaneous income

EXPENSES

Salaries and wages

Contract labor

Payroll taxes

Utilities

Insurance

Telephone

Rent

Maintenance expense

Office supplies

Postage

Insurance

Interest

Depreciation

Travel expense

Entertainment

Advertising

Dues and contributions

Miscellaneous expenses

ASSETS

Cash in bank

Petty cash

Accounts receivable

Inventory

Materials and supplies

Prepaid expenses

Deposits

Land

Buildings

Accumulated depreciation—
   buildings

Tools and equipment

Accumulated depreciation—
   tools and equipment

Automotive equipment

Accumulated depreciation—
   automotive equipment

Furniture and fixtures

Accumulated depreciation—
   furniture and fixtures

Organization expenses

LIABILITIES

Accounts payable

Notes payable

Sales taxes—payable

FICA taxes—payable

Federal withholding taxes

State withholding taxes

Unemployment taxes

Long-term debt—
   mortgage payable

Miscellaneous accruals

NET WORTH

Retained earnings

Source: Small Business Administration—Office of Business Development

You must use the accrual method to track purchases and sales if your business involves an inventory. According to the Tax Reform Act of 1986, if your gross sales exceed $5 million per year and your business is a corporation, partnership, or trust, the IRS requires you to use the accrual method of accounting. Several exceptions to this rule permit some businesses to use the cash method of accounting no matter how large the gross receipts. These businesses are farming operations, partnerships without corporate partners, sole proprietorships, and qualified personal service corporations. These include corporations performing services in the fields of health, law, accounting, actuarial science, and consulting.

In accrual-basis accounting, it doesn't matter when you receive or make accrual payment. Income is reported when you bill. Expenses are deductible when you are billed, not when you pay. This accounting method has more tax benefits for a company with few receivables and large amounts of current liabilities. Advance payments to an accrual basis taxpayer are considered taxable income in the year received.

If you run two or more businesses at the same time, you may use different accounting methods for each business.

BOOKKEEPING

The cardinal rule of bookkeeping is to keep your system as simple as possible. Your time is valuable and if your records are too complex, you'll spend too much time maintaining them. In addition, you may have to hire an accountant or bookkeeper to maintain more complicated records.

Bookkeeping Systems

Whether you automate your bookkeeping with software like Intuit's QuickBooks (http://quickbooks.intuit. com) or do your bookkeeping with pencil and paper, double-entry bookkeeping is the preferred method for keeping business records. First you enter transactions in a journal, then post monthly totals of the transactions to the appropriate ledger accounts. There are five categories of ledger accounts:

1. Income
2. Expenses
3. Assets
4. Liabilities
5. Net Worth

The Classification of Ledger Accounts sidebar provides a breakdown of the various ledger accounts found within the categories listed above.

Figures 16.1 and 16.2 show examples of two ledger accounts and how a transaction is posted and cross-referenced against each account. The transactions from these ledger accounts are then posted in the general journal, shown in Figure 16.3. At the end of each fiscal year or accounting period, accounts are balanced and closed. The income and expense accounts are transferred to the income statement for use in the summary of revenue and expenses. The asset, liability, and net worth accounts are used to provide figures for the balance sheet.

Although single-entry bookkeeping is not as complete as the double-entry method, you can still use it effectively for your small business, especially during its early years. A single-entry system can be relatively simple. The flow of income and expenses are recorded through a daily summary of cash receipts, a monthly summary of receipts, and a monthly disbursements journal (such as a checkbook). This system is adequate for the tax purposes of many small businesses.

RECORDS TO KEEP

Your business will generate four types of records to track:

1. Sales records
2. Cash receipts
3. Cash disbursements
4. Accounts receivable

Sales records include all income derived from the sales of products or performance of services. They can be grouped in one large category called gross sales or into several subcategories depicting different product lines so that you know what is doing well and what isn't. Figure 16.4 shows an example of a sales journal.

Cash receipts account for all funds generated through cash sales and the collection of accounts receivable. This is actual income collected and doesn't include earnings from your sales records unless you choose to operate a

FIGURE 16.1 General Ledger (Entry 1)

Account Cash

Month of August

Account number 123

Page number 1

Date	Item	Transaction		Balance	
		Debit	**Credit**	**Debit**	**Credit**
August 3	Jones Janitorial Payment	$500		$500	

FIGURE 16.2   General Ledger (Entry 2)

Account Jones Janitorial   **Month of** August

Account number 987   **Page number** 1

Date	Item	Transaction Debit	Transaction Credit	Balance Debit	Balance Credit
August 3	Payment from Cash	$500		$500	

FIGURE 16.3 General Journal

Month of _____

Number _____

Date	Account Debited	Account Number	Amount	Account Credited	Account Number	Amount
August 3	Cash	123	$500	Jones Janitorial	987	$500

FIGURE 16.4   Sales Journal

Month of _____

Number _____

Date	Invoice Number	Description	Account Debited	Acct. No.	Amount Receivable	Account Debited	Acct. No.	Amount Sales Tax	Amount Other

FIGURE 16.5	Cash Receipts Journal

Month of _____

Number _____

Date	Account Credited	Acct. No.	Sales	Amount Receivable	Other	Account Debited	Acct. No.	Amount		
								Cash	Discounts	Other

cash-and-carry business. In a cash-and-carry business, your cash receipts theoretically match your sales records. Figure 16.5 shows an example of a cash receipts journal.

Cash disbursements are sometimes referred to as operating expense records or accounts payable. All disbursements should be made by check so that business expenses can be well documented for tax purposes. If you need to make a cash payment, include a receipt for it, or at least an explanation of it, in the business records. All canceled checks, paid bills, and other documents that substantiate your entries should be filed and stored in a safe place. Breaking the cash disbursement headings into different categories such as rent, maintenance, and advertising may be easier to deal with than one large category. Figure 16.6 shows an example of a cash disbursement journal.

Set up a petty cash fund to disburse cash for expenses that are immediate and small enough to warrant payment by cash. The Small Business Administration suggests that you account for petty cash by cashing a check for petty cash and placing the money in a safe or lock-box. Record items purchased from the petty cash fund on a form listing the date of purchase, the amount, and the purpose of the expenditure. When the petty cash fund is almost depleted, total the cost of all the items and write a check to replenish the account. Figures 16.7 and 16.8 show examples of a petty cash voucher and a petty cash journal. Requests for petty cash are made using the voucher and are then recorded in the journal.

Accounts receivable are sales made by extending credit. Maintain these records on a monthly basis so you can age your receivables and determine how long your credit customers are taking to pay their bills. If an account ages beyond sixty days, start investigating the reasons why the customer is taking so long to pay. (Credit extension and collection are the subject of Chapter 22.) Figures 16.9 and 16.10 are examples of journals where receivable and payables can be tracked.

BALANCING ACCOUNTS AND BANK STATEMENT RECONCILIATIONS

The SBA recommends that you balance every page of sales, cash receipts, and disbursements to ensure the accuracy of your records and that every month you reconcile your checkbook with your bank statement to make sure your records match those of the bank. Make any necessary corrections and immediately report any errors. If there's a bank error, you notify the bank within 14 working days after receiving the bank statement.

OTHER RECORDS TO KEEP

Records supporting entries on your federal tax return should be kept until the statute of limitations (ordinarily three years after the return is due) expires. Keep copies of federal income tax returns forever.

In addition to the four basic records and your tax documents, make sure to keep records for three other important items:

1. Capital equipment

2. Insurance

3. Payroll

Capital Equipment

Keep records for major equipment purchases so you can determine what your depreciation expenses will be for tax purposes. Don't keep records on small items like staplers, tape recorders, and answering machines. Don't list leased equipment in this section. Records pertaining to leased equipment belong under the category of cash disbursements. Leased equipment is a liability payable each month.

Maintain records only on capital equipment you've purchased, whether outright, on a contract basis, or through a loan. Major equipment you've purchased is considered an asset, even though you've financed it. As you pay off your loan, you build equity in the equipment that you can enter as an asset on your balance sheet.

Your equipment records should include the following information: date of purchase, the vendor's name, a brief description of the item, how it was paid for, the check number if appropriate, and the full amount of the purchase.

Insurance

Keep all records pertaining to your company's insurance policies including auto, life, health, fire, and any special coverages you may obtain. List the policy carriers and the underwriting agents who issued the coverages. Also

FIGURE 16.6   Cash Disbursements Journal

Month of _____

Number _____

Date	Check No.	Payee	Account Credited	Acct. No.	Cash	Account Discounts	Other	Account Debited	Acct. No.	Amount Payable	Amount Other

FIGURE 16.7   Petty Cash Voucher

Date _____

Voucher number _____

For	Account Debited	Account Number	Amount
		Total	

Approved by _____

Received by _____

Date _____

Voucher number _____

For	Account Debited	Account Number	Amount
		Total	

Approved by _____

Received by _____

FIGURE 16.8 Petty Cash Journal

Reporting period _____

From _____ **To** _____ **Balance on hand** _____

Date	Voucher Number	Account	Account Number	Payee	Approved By	Total	Balance

Total Voucher Amount	
Total Receipts	
Cash on Hand	
Overage/Shortage	
Petty Cash Reimbursement	
Balance Forward	

Approved by _____

Received by _____

FIGURE 16.9	Aging of Accounts Receivable

Reporting period _____

From _____ **To** _____

Date	Invoice Number	Account	Account Number	Description	Amount			
					30 Days	60 Days	90+ Days	Total

FIGURE 16.10   Aging of Accounts Payable

Reporting period _____

From _____   **To** _____

Date	Invoice Number	Account	Account Number	Description	Amount			
					30 Days	60 Days	90+ Days	Total

maintain records on any claims made against your policies to resolve any misunderstandings that may arise.

When updating your records, enter all information about the payment of premiums, including the date the check was written, the amount, and which policy it was written for. This will help you in case payment disputes arise and for tax purposes.

Payroll

Payroll records present another set of problems. An employer, regardless of the number of employees, must maintain all records pertaining to payroll taxes (income tax withholding, Social Security, and federal unemployment tax) for at least four years after the tax becomes due or is paid, whichever is later. Altogether, twenty different kinds of employment records must be kept just to satisfy federal requirements.

Income Tax Withholding Records

1. Name, address, and Social Security number of each employee
2. Amount and date of each payment for compensation
3. Amount of wages subject to withholding in each payment
4. Amount of withholding tax collected from each payment
5. Reason that the taxable amount is less than the total payment
6. Statements relating to employees' nonresident alien status
7. Market value and date of non-cash compensation
8. Information about payments made under sick-pay plans
9. Withholding exemption certificates
10. Agreements regarding the voluntary withholding of extra cash
11. Dates and payments to employees for non-business services
12. Statements of tips received by employees
13. Requests for different computation of withholding taxes

Social Security (FICA) Tax Records

1. Amount of each payment subject to FICA tax
2. Amount and date of FICA tax collected from each payment
3. Explanation for any difference

Federal Unemployment Tax (FUTA) Records

1. Total amount paid during calendar year
2. Amount subject to unemployment tax
3. Amount of contributions paid into the state unemployment fund
4. Any other information requested on the unemployment tax return

Payroll for a small firm is a simple task with a good one-write system. Any office supply store can show you samples of one-write systems, which most accountants recommend because they reduce errors and save time in making payroll entries.

Business Papers

Carefully preserve all purchase invoices, receiving reports, copies of sales slips, invoices sent to customers, canceled checks, receipts for cash paid out, and cash register tapes. They're not only essential to maintaining good records but also may be important if legal or tax questions are ever raised.

HOW LONG TO KEEP RECORDS?

The accounting firm PricewaterhouseCoopers LLP offers the following guidelines.

- Income tax, revenue agents' reports, protests, court briefs and appeals should be retained indefinitely.
- Annual financial statements should be retained indefinitely; monthly statements used for internal purposes should be kept for three years.
- Books of account, such as the general ledger and general journal, should be retained indefinitely.
- Cash books should be retained indefinitely, unless posted regularly to the general ledger.
- Subsidiary ledgers should be retained for three years. (Ledgers refer to the actual books or the magnetic

tapes, disks, or other media on which the ledgers and journals are stored.)

- Canceled, payroll, and dividend checks should be retained for six years.

- Income tax payment checks should be retained indefinitely.

- Bank reconciliations, voided checks, check stubs, and check register tapes should be retained for six years.

- Sales records such as invoices, monthly statements, remittance advisories, shipping papers, bills of lading, and customers' purchase orders should be retained for six years.

- Purchase records, including purchase orders, payment vouchers authorizing payment to vendors, and vendor invoices should be retained for six years.

- Travel and entertainment records, including account books, diaries, and expense statements should be retained for six years.

- Documents substantiating fixed asset additions, such as the amount and dates of additions or improvements, depreciation policies, and salvage values assigned to assets should be retained indefinitely.

- Personnel and payroll records, such as payments and reports to taxing authorities, including federal income tax withholding, FICA contributions, unemployment taxes, and workers' compensation insurance should be retained for four years.

- Corporate documents, including certificate of incorporation, corporate charter, constitution and bylaws, deeds and easements, stock, stock transfer and stockholder records, minutes of board of directors' meetings, retirement and pension records, labor contracts, licenses, patents, trademarks, and registration applications need to be retained indefinitely.

RECORDING TRANSACTIONS

In a manual, or one-write, system of recording financial transactions, each check you enter is recorded automatically in the cash disbursements journal. This is popular with many small businesses because it saves time. If you only write a few checks each month, it makes sense to use a manual or one-write system. Maintaining your general ledger on a regular basis should give you all the financial information you need to make good business decisions.

If you write a large number of checks each month, consider batch processing your general ledger postings. Data processing services will handle this for you. You'd need to develop expense codes for the types of checks you write. Then make an adding machine tape of the totals and send that to the data processing center. You'll then get a computer printout of your general ledger, with all your checks listed according to expense code.

If you spend a lot of money in cash, list these expenditures on an expense report form. Such forms are readily available at stationery stores and are designated by category, such as travel, entertainment, office supplies, and so on. Attach the receipts to the entry on the form corresponding to the expenditure. The bookkeeper then adds the expense codes and writes you a check for reimbursement of expenses. Ultimately, all cash disbursements are handled by check—even out-of-pocket expenses. For example, you spend $200 out of pocket, fill out an expense report, and pay yourself for what you spent. This way you know those expenses were entered into your bookkeeping system. Figure 16.11 shows an example of an expense report.

Try to pay as much as you can by check, as you have an instant record of all debits from your company. And try to work out of one checkbook for the business, if at all possible. Nothing is more annoying to an accountant than tracking inter-account transfers.

In some lines of business, legal restrictions preclude using just one checkbook for your business. Lawyers and collection agents are usually required by law to maintain trust accounts on behalf of their clients. These accounts represent money held in trust on the client's behalf until it is disbursed in the form of client receipts (for example, court-awarded damages or collection monies) or, ultimately, service fees.

PROFESSIONAL FINANCIAL ADVISORS

If you choose your banker wisely, you'll have at your service a skilled professional consultant who will not, under normal circumstances, charge for his or her services. You'll also require the help of other specialists, including

FIGURE 16.11   Expense Report

Date	Breakfast	Lunch	Dinner	Tips	Lodgings	Phone	Travel	Parking/Tolls	Gas/Oil	Entertainment	Miscellaneous	Daily Total

Name _____   **Start date** _____

Purpose _____   **End date** _____

	Subtotal	
	Less Advance	
	Total Amount Due	

a CPA, an attorney and one or more consultants who are experts in your field. You'll rely on some of these experts only occasionally, such as during start-up or when problems arise. Your CPA, however, will work with you on a regular basis.

Discuss fees as soon as possible with all professional financial experts and consultants, making certain you understand what services you'll receive for the agreed-upon fee. Fees charged by professionals vary enormously, depending in large part on their experience and their expertise in the field.

Accountants

A knowledgeable and experienced CPA is a small-business owner's best ally. Once you're in operation, he or she can help you decide whether your volume warrants a full-time bookkeeper, an outside accounting service, or merely a year-end accounting and tax-preparation service. When you borrow money, your bank manager will want to see your balance sheet and other financial statements. If a reputable CPA prepares these statements, they'll be more credible than if you prepare them yourself. (If you're borrowing less than $500,000, many banks will accept unaudited financial statements prepared by a public accountant.)

A knowledgeable and experienced CPA can help you organize the data concerning your business, determine future strategies based on past performance, and advise you on your overall financial strategy for purchasing, capital investment, and other matters related to your business goals. He or she can also help:

- *If you're organizing a corporation.* Your accountant should counsel you during the start-up phase to determine how you can minimize your tax liabilities.
- *If you're starting a sole proprietorship or a partnership.* Ask your CPA to set up the chart of accounts for your bookkeeping system.

In addition to these tasks, accountants help business owners comply with a number of laws and regulations affecting their record-keeping practices. If you spend your time trying to find answers to the many questions that accountants can answer more efficiently, you'll take time away from managing your business. Spend your time doing what you do best and delegate the rest to those with the appropriate expertise.

Choosing and Using a CPA

Where do you find a good accountant? Ask other small-business owners, your banker, or your lawyer for recommendations. See if the chemistry is good between you and your prospective CPA before you decide to hire him or her. You must feel comfortable with the person who will help direct your business and personal finances. To find out if you'd be comfortable working with a particular CPA, arrange for an initial interview, which most firms provide without charge.

Ask for a list of services available and make sure the firm offers those services you need. Equally important is the CPA's experience, particularly in your type of business.

Another factor to consider is the CPA's standing in the business community. An accountant's connections and professional relationships can benefit you. If you need a business loan, the whole process will be easier if the CPA is respected by members of the local banking and investment community. To assess a CPA's professional standing, inquire into his or her certification, license status, educational background, and involvement in professional organizations. A CPA's reputation is a good indicator of performance. Take the time to question peers, clients, associates, and others.

How much does a good accountant charge? Their fees, like those of lawyers, doctors, and other professionals, vary widely. But a good CPA is worth his or her weight in gold, especially when he or she winds up saving you more money than their cost for fees or helps you avert catastrophes or avoid headaches.

Once you've found a CPA who can meet your needs, ask for a reasonable assessment of what his or her services will cost. Then ask for a proposal letter to find out what kind of work needs to be done and what it will cost to do it. Also look for a firm that offers sufficient personnel to meet your needs if the principal CPA is not available.

When to Use National Accounting Firms

Whether you use a local CPA or a national firm depends on how large you expect your business to grow, and on what type of business you'll operate. If you have a small shoe shop and don't plan to build a chain of stores, then stay with a local CPA. If you have an investment business and expect your customers to look closely at your financial stability, you may need an audited statement prepared by a national firm.

Large accounting firms used to be reluctant to work with small companies. But as the number of corporate giants has decreased due to mergers and acquisitions, some of the nation's largest accounting firms have aggressively gone after the small-business market. That's good news for entrepreneurs who can now get those firms' resources at competitive prices.

Calling in a CPA before it's time to do the books could help improve a company's bottom line. An audit is essentially conducted after the fact, and some things can't be changed, no matter how skilled or experienced the accountant may be. For example, how a company obtains a piece of equipment—whether it's rented, leased, or bought—determines how it's taxed. Acquiring an asset one way can cause you to lose tax benefits you'd enjoy if you got it another way. Ask your CPA's advice before you make any major purchasing decisions.

Streamline Your Accounting System

You can make efficient use of your accountant's time, and reduce his or her fees, if you handle a number of routine bookkeeping tasks yourself. Do you produce neat, efficient records for monthly accounting work and taxes? If not, you're probably paying for more accounting hours than you should. Perhaps you should hire someone on a part-time basis to get—and keep—your records in order.

Ask your accountant for a list of the specific records required for routine accounting work. If you've organized your accounting system correctly and have an orderly filing system for important documents, your records of assets and depreciation, income and expenses, capital gains and losses, inventory, and costs of goods sold should be ready at tax time.

CHAPTER 17

Financial Controls

George Bernard Shaw's quip, "The lack of money is the root of all evil," certainly holds true for business owners. More start-ups fail by undercapitalization than any other problem. If your new business has sufficient working capital, along with a cash reserve to cover unforeseen expenses, your chances for success soar.

Managing that capital requires special skills. Your goal is for your investment in your business to yield a higher rate of return than that earned from a government security with a guaranteed rate of interest. Entrepreneurs often get so caught up in the day-to-day affairs of running their businesses that they neglect the longer-term planning and management of their finances.

That could be a fatal mistake. Lack of planning and financial controls are the scourge of small business. Even if your accountant prepares financial statements, you still need to know how to interpret them and how to use them. Otherwise, you're playing Russian roulette.

Financial control starts with a comprehensive record-keeping system that produces thorough accounting records on a day-to-day basis—the subject of Chapter 16.

Three reports are financial-management cornerstones for all types of businesses:

1. The income statement
2. The balance sheet
3. The cash-flow statement

These reports track assets, liabilities, working capital, and equity to evaluate a business' financial performance, which is expressed in terms of dollars and percentages. A company's past performance as well as its current performance can be evaluated using financial ratios and comparing them to industry standards. This type of financial analysis points out strengths and weaknesses of a business as well as any recurring trends that help business owners manage their resources better from a strategic planning viewpoint.

Through effective financial controls, you'll be able to avoid financial crises and:

- Prevent excessive investment in fixed assets
- Have a better understanding of investor and banking relationships
- Maintain receivables and net working capital in proper proportion to sales
- Steer clear of excessive (and expensive!) inventories

THE FINANCIAL STATEMENTS

The best preventive medicine, financially speaking, is to read and analyze your financial statements on a timely and regular basis. This way, you're assured of making better-informed and more sound decisions regarding your business. If the language of finance is Greek to you, get help from someone at SCORE (the Service Corps of Retired Executives, an SBA program) or take a class at a community college or adult education center. This investment in yourself and your business will pay dividends forever.

The Balance Sheet

A balance sheet is a snapshot of your business' financial position at a given point in time. It's a measure of what you own less what you owe (your assets minus your liabilities), but it doesn't indicate whether your business is making or losing money. A balance sheet is typically generated when books are closed after a specific period, either monthly or quarterly. Figure 17.1 shows a sample balance sheet.

By comparing the most current balance sheet against past balance sheets covering the same reporting period, you can identify changes in the business' financial condition. These changes point out any fluctuations within assets, liabilities, working capital, and equity. For instance, if you had excess cash but an undue amount of capital tied up in loans and other claims against the company, you'd have a business with strong liquidity but low debt capacity. Most companies in this type of situation use their excess cash to pay down debts and improve their debt-to-equity ratio.

A comparative analysis of balance sheets points out increases in the rate of receivables compared with cash, an overabundance of inventory compared with sales, decreasing book values of capital assets, inconsistency in maintaining long-term investments, increases in current liabilities in proportion to current assets, and declining returns on investments compared with increasing long-term liabilities payable. It also shows whether the owner's equity, or net worth, is increasing or decreasing in value.

When you prepare a balance sheet, the top portion lists your company's assets. Assets are any classified as current assets and long-term or fixed assets. Current assets can

easily be converted to cash or will be used by the business in a year or less and include the following.

- Cash is all income derived from cash sales as well as those assets that have been converted to cash during the accounting period, and generally refers to all cash in checking, savings, and short-term investment accounts.
- *Accounts receivable* is income generated through the extension of credit that has yet to be collected at the end of the accounting period, less an allowance for bad debt.
- *Inventory* is finished products and supplies, if your business is a wholesale or retail operation. With service businesses, inventory refers to supplies only. For manufacturers, inventory includes raw materials, work in progress, and finished goods and supplies. The value of all inventories should be stated less an allowance for inventory loss.
- *Notes receivable* are all promissory notes extended by the company that are due and payable within a year. If a note is payable in full beyond a year, it should be classified as a fixed asset.
- *Marketable securities* are all the company's short-term investments in stocks and bonds that can easily be converted into cash in a period of a year or less.

Other assets that appear on the balance sheet are called long-term or fixed assets because they're durable and will last more than one year. Examples of long-term assets include:

- Equipment is the book value of all equipment less depreciation.
- *Buildings* are the appraised value of all buildings the business owns less depreciation.
- *Land* is the appraised value of all land owned by the business.
- *Long-term investments* are all investments by the company that cannot be converted to cash in less than one year. For the most part, companies just starting out will not have accumulated long-term investments.
- *Miscellaneous assets* are all other long-term assets that do not fit into the preceding categories. These might include patents, trade investments, or even

FIGURE 17.1 Balance Sheet

Statement of Financial Condition as of _____, 20_____

ASSETS		
Current Assets		**Totals**
Cash		
Accounts receivable		
Inventory		
Total Current Assets	**A**	

Fixed Assets		**Totals**
Capital/plant		
Investment		
Miscellaneous assets		
Total Fixed Assets	**B**	
Total Assets (A + B)	**C**	
Total Assets	**A**	

LIABILITIES		
Current Liabilities		**Totals**
Accounts payable		
Accrued liabilities		
Taxes		
Total Current Liabilities	**D**	

Long-Term Liabilities		
Bonds payable		
Notes payable		
Total Long-Term Liabilities	**E**	

Total Liabilities (D + E)	**F**	
Owner's Equity (C–F)	**G**	
Total Liabilities/Equity (F + G)	**H**	

goodwill, at least to the extent that it was purchased. Such assets are generally referred to as "intangible assets."

The bottom half of the balance sheet lists the business' liabilities and the amount of equity or capital you've accumulated. Liabilities are the obligations of the business to creditors. Like assets, liabilities may be classified as current or long-term. Debts that are due in one year or less are classified as current liabilities, while those due in more than one year are considered long-term.

Current liabilities indicate short-term cash requirements since they must be paid with cash within a year. Examples of current liabilities are:

- *Accounts payable* are owed to suppliers of goods and services, and payable in a year or less.
- *Accrued liabilities* are expenses such as operating costs, sales commissions, and property taxes that will be incurred by the business but haven't been billed at the close of the reporting period.
- *Notes payable* are all promissory notes taken out by the business that are due and payable within one year. If a note is payable in full beyond a year, it should be classified as a long-term liability.
- *Taxes* are owed for business income, taxable sales, real property, and employee withholding.

Long-term liabilities are obligations of the business that will not be due for at least a year, including:

- *Bonds payable* are publicly held debts that have been offered for sale by the company. All bonds at the end of the year that are due and payable over a period exceeding one year should be listed.
- *Mortgage payable* is the amount owed to a bank or lending institution on real property. The mortgage payable is that amount still due when the books close for the year.
- *Notes payable* are all promissory notes taken out by the business that are payable in a year or more.

Net worth represents the claim that the business owner has on the assets of the business. This is also referred to as owner's equity. Capital is not money in an accounting sense. For example, if a person has a car worth $5,000 (asset) and owes the bank $3,000 (debt), then his equity in the car (the capital claim) is $5,000 − $3,000 =

$2,000. The $2,000 is not cash but rather the monetary value of the owner's claim on the car.

The Income Statement

Also known as a profit-and-loss (P&L) report and operating statement, the income statement measures the economic performance of a business during a specific period—usually a month, quarter, or year. Basically, it determines the profitability of an operation by summarizing revenue and expenses to arrive at the company's net profit.

Although the basics of an income statement are the same from business to business, there are notable differences between services, merchandisers, and manufacturers when it comes to the accounting of inventory.

For service businesses, inventory includes supplies or spare parts—nothing for manufacture or resale. Retailers and wholesalers, on the other hand, account for their resale inventory under cost of goods sold, also known as cost of sales—see Figure 17.2 (a). This refers to the total price paid for the products sold during the income statement's accounting period. Freight and delivery charges are customarily included in this figure. Accountants segregate costs of goods on an operating statement because it provides a measure of gross profit margin when compared with sales, an important yardstick for measuring the firm's profitability.

For a retailer or wholesaler, cost of goods sold is equal to total inventory at the beginning of the accounting period plus any merchandise purchased, including freight costs, minus the inventory present at the end of the accounting period. This is your total cost of goods sold.

Although manufacturers account for cost of goods sold in the same manner as merchandisers—by reporting beginning and ending inventories, as well as any purchases made during the accounting period—their approaches are also different because they track inventory through three phases:

1. Raw material is purchased to create a finished product.
2. Work-in-progress is inventory that is partially assembled.
3. Finished products are inventory fully assembled and available for sale.

FIGURE 17.2 Cost of Goods Sold—Merchandiser

(a) Cost of Goods Sold (Merchandiser)		
For Period Ending December 31, 2006		Totals
Net Sales		$155,000
Beginning inventory, January 1, 2006	$29,367	
Merchandise purchases	$74,190	
Freight	$4,637	
Cost of Goods Available for Sale		$108,194
Less ending inventory, December 31, 2006	$30,913	
Cost of Goods Sold		$77,281

(b) Cost of Goods Manufactured		
For Period Ending December 31, 2006		Totals
Work in process inventory, January 1, 2006	$2,318	
Inventory, January 1, 2006	$20,866	
Purchases	$35,549	
Freight in	$1,545	
Cost of Materials Available for Use		$57,960
Less inventory, December 31, 2006	$22,412	
Cost of Materials Used		$35,548
Direct Labor		$20,093
Indirect labor	$3,091	
Factory utilities	$12,365	
Factory supplies used	$3,091	
Insurance & taxes	$773	
Depreciation	$4,637	
Total Manufacturing Overhead		$23,957
Total Manufacturing Costs		$79,598
Total Work in Process During Period		$81,916
Less work in process inventory, December 31, 2006	$4,635	
Cost of Goods Manufactured		$77,281

Associated with this process are other costs, such as direct labor and factory overhead. To account for all of these costs, manufacturers usually report them on a separate statement called the cost of goods manufactured (see Figure 17.2b). This statement is formed by first listing the work-in-progress inventory at the beginning of the accounting period. The next listed are raw material and direct labor. The total cost of materials available for use includes inventory at the beginning of the accounting period plus new purchases and freight charges. Subtract the raw material inventory present at the end of the reporting period from the cost of material available for use to determine the cost of materials used. Add direct labor and manufacturing overhead to this amount. This results in your total manufacturing costs. Add the work-in-progress beginning inventory present at the end of the accounting period. This supplies you with the cost of goods manufactured.

In the income statement for manufacturers, cost of goods manufactured is added to the finished goods inventory at the beginning of the inventory, resulting in total cost of goods available for sale. The finished goods inventory present at the end of the reporting period is subtracted from this amount to produce the cost of goods sold (see Figure 17.3).

Aside from cost of goods, the rest of the income statement is the same from business to business and is based on the following format (see Figure 17.4).

- *Income* is all revenue generated by the business minus any discounts and returns.
- *Cost of goods.*
- *Gross profit margin* is the difference between revenue and cost of goods. Gross profit margin can be expressed in dollars, as a percentage of revenue, or both.
- *Operating expenses* are all overhead and labor expenses associated with the operations of the business.
- *Net profit* is the difference between gross profit margin and operating expenses.
- *Depreciation* is the decrease in value of capital assets used to generate income.
- *Net profit before interest* is the difference between net profit and depreciation.
- *Interest* includes all interest accrued from both short-term and long-term debts.
- *Net profit before taxes* is the difference between net profit before interest and interest.
- *Taxes* include all taxes on the business.
- Profit after taxes is the differences between net profit before taxes and the taxes paid, the ultimate bottom line of any company.

Figure 17.5 shows an example of an income statement for a service business. Notice that there is no cost-of-goods sold. Since many service businesses do not maintain an

---

FIGURE 17.3   Cost of Goods Sold—Manufacturer

Cost of Goods Sold (Manufacturer)		
For Period Ending December 31, 2006		**Totals**
Net Sales		**$155,000**
Finished goods inventory, January 1, 2006	$29,367	
Cost of goods manufactured	$77,281	
Cost of Goods Available for Sale		**$106,648**
Less ending inventory, December 31, 2006	$29,367	
Cost of Goods Sold		**$77,281**

FIGURE 17.4   Income Statement (Manufacturer and Merchandiser)

Income Statement		
(Manufacturer and Merchandiser)		
For Period Ending December 31, 2006		Totals
Income		$155,000
Cost of goods sold	$77,281	
Margin %	50%	
Gross Profit	$77,719	
Payroll	$34,100	
Rent	$545	
Utilities	$1,285	
Office supplies	$920	
Insurance	$1,770	
Advertising	$15,272	
Professional services	$855	
Travel	$4,655	
Maintenance and repair	$1,117	
Packaging/shipping	$12,328	
Miscellaneous	$65	
Total Expenses		$72,912
Net Profit		$4,807
Margin %	3%	
Depreciation	$123	
Net Profit before Interest		$4,684
Margin %	3%	
Interest	$118	
Net Profit before Taxes		$4,566
Margin %	3%	

FIGURE 17.5 Income Statement (Service Business)

Income Statement		
(Service Business)		
For Period Ending December 31, 2006		Totals
Income		$155,000
Payroll	$34,100	
Rent	$545	
Utilities	$1,285	
Office supplies	$920	
Insurance	$1,770	
Advertising	$15,272	
Professional services	$855	
Travel	$4,655	
Maintenance & repair	$1,117	
Packaging /shipping	$12,328	
Miscellaneous	$65	
Total Expenses		$72,912
Net Profit		$82,088
Margin %	53%	
Depreciation	$123	
Net Profit before Interest		$81,965
Margin %	53%	
Interest	$118	
Net Profit before Taxes		$81,847
Margin %	52%	

inventory from which sales are made, there is no cost of goods sold that can be expensed.

The income statement is used by companies to evaluate operating performance. It will let you know whether or not you've met some of your financial goals, such as to increase sales, decrease the cost of goods sold, or reduce overhead.

When comparing several income statements over time, you can chart trends in your operating performance. This helps you chart future goals and strategies for sales, inventory, and operating overhead.

The Cash Flow Statement

Your financial picture isn't complete unless you can relate all this information to the actual flow of cash through your business, which is shown in the cash flow statement (see Table 17.1).

The cash flow statement summarizes the operating, investing, and financing activities of the business as they relate to the inflow and outflow of cash. This translates to either positive or negative cash flow and shows whether your investment and financing endeavors are increasing or draining cash resources. Just like the balance sheet and income statement, the cash flow statement charts a business' performance over a specific accounting period— monthly, quarterly, semiannually, or annually. Most companies prepare monthly cash flow statements and summarize them through an annual report for year-end meetings.

With its focus on liquidity rather than profitability, the cash flow statement is the single most important financial tool for businesses. If insufficient income is being generated from operating revenue to meet expenses, then the business' liquidity is at risk. Additional revenue will have to be obtained either through financing or from the sale of investments. The cash flow statement provides a clear picture of how quickly cash is leaving the business compared with how promptly it is coming in.

Keep in mind that the cash flow statement doesn't reveal a profit or a loss. Just because a company has a positive cash flow doesn't mean it's generated more income from operating activities than it spent meeting its obligations. Additional revenue may have been obtained from investment and financing activities, both of which add to the business' cash position but not to its profitability.

On the other hand, a negative cash flow doesn't mean the company is unprofitable. For example, a seasonal business like a beachfront resort may have a negative cash flow six months of the year but a strongly positive one during the other six months of the year.

The cash-flow statement begins with the income section, showing all revenue coming into the company.

- *Cash sales* are derived from sales paid for by cash.
- *Receivables* are derived from the collection of sales made by credit.
- *Investment income* is derived from investments, interest on loans that have been extended, and the liquidation of any assets.
- *Financing income* is derived from interest-bearing notes payable.

The next section includes all cash disbursements, such as:

- *Material/merchandise* refers to the raw material used in the manufacturing of a product (for manufacturing operations only) or the cash outlay for merchandise inventory during the accounting period (for merchandisers). In some cases, the material inventory used in a service will be included under this category.
- *Direct labor* is the labor required to manufacture a product or the cost to service a client if this expense is not included under payroll.
- *Overhead* includes fixed and variable expenses required to operate a business. For manufacturing operations, the overhead costs related to production are included here as well.
- *Marketing and sales* include salaries, commissions, and other direct costs associated with marketing and sales.
- *R&D* refer to labor expenses required to support the research and development operations of the business.
- *G&A* are labor expenses required to support the general and administrative functions of the business.
- *Taxes* include all taxes, except payroll, paid to the appropriate government institutions.
- *Capital* refers to the capital requirements needed to obtain any equipment for the generation of income.

TABLE 17.1 Cash Flow Statement (Service Business)

	Jan.	Feb.	Mar.	Apr.	May	Jun.	Jul.	Aug.	Sept.
Cash sales	17,113	25,670	34,226	51,339	59,896	68,452	72,730	81,287	85,565
Receivables	0	0	25,670	38,504	51,339	77,009	89,844	102,678	109,096
Other income	0	0	0	0	0	0	0	0	0
Total income	**17,113**	**25,670**	**59,896**	**89,843**	**111,235**	**145,461**	**162,574**	**183,965**	**194,661**
Material	0	0	0	0	0	0	0	0	0
Direct labor	7,800	11,700	15,600	23,400	27,300	31,200	33,150	37,050	39,000
Overhead	0	0	0	0	0	0	0	0	0
Marketing and sales	8,250	9,900	11,550	11,550	12,045	12,705	13,530	15,345	17,325
R&D	3,500	4,200	4,900	4,900	5,110	5,390	5,740	6,510	7,350
General and Admin.	1,750	2,100	2,450	2,450	2,555	2,695	2,870	3,255	3,675
Taxes	0	0	40,528	0	0	40,528	0	0	40,528
Capital	3,430	3,430	3,430	3,430	3,430	3,430	3,430	3,430	3,430
Loans	25,000	25,000	25,000	25,000	25,000	25,001	25,002	25,000	25,000
Total Expenses	**49,730**	**56,330**	**103,458**	**70,730**	**75,440**	**120,950**	**83,720**	**90,590**	**136,308**
Cash Flow	**−32,617**	**−30,660**	**−43,562**	**19,113**	**35,795**	**24,511**	**78,854**	**93,375**	**58,353**
Cumulative cash flow	**−32,617**	**−63,277**	**−106,840**	**−87,727**	**−51,932**	**−27,421**	**51,433**	**144,808**	**203,160**

The third section of the cash flow statement deals with the net and cumulative cash flow of the business. Net cash flow is the difference between income and expenses. When this amount is carried over to the next reporting period, it becomes cumulative cash flow. To determine cumulative cash flow, the net cash flow of the current period is added to the cumulative cash flow from the previous period.

COMPARATIVE FINANCIAL RATIO ANALYSIS

Financial ratios are handy tools used by business owners to spot trends (both good and bad), get a better handle on cash management and forecast the effect of operations on profitability. Ratios compare values from the balance sheet and income statement, and provide information that's more meaningful than just looking at dollar amounts. Financial ratios give business owners benchmarks from which to gauge the financial strengths and weaknesses of their business' operation—and a basis for determining which course of action to take to correct a problem. They also indicate a company's competitive strength in relation to similar businesses in that industry.

Financial ratios generally measure two areas within a company:

1. *Liquidity ratios* indicate a company's ability to meet current obligations on time. A company with liquidity problems has trouble paying its bills and needs more capital, better management, or both.

2. *Profitability ratios* measure management's performance regarding the business' ability to generate revenues, net income, and an acceptable return on investment.

Liquidity Ratios

The various measures of liquidity tell you how much cash you have on hand, the amount of assets that can readily

TABLE 17.1 Cash Flow Statement (Service Business), continued

	Oct.	Nov.	Dec.	2000	1st Qtr	2nd Qtr	3rd Qtr	4th Qtr	2005	2006
Cash sales	98,400	124,070	136,904	855,652	164,247	200,747	255,496	291,995	912,485	1,021,730
Receivables	121,931	128,348	147,600	892,019	458,720	261,317	323,540	398,190	1,441,767	1,552,160
Other income	0	0	0	0	0	0	0	0	0	0
Total income	**220,331**	**252,418**	**284,504**	**1,747,671**	**622,967**	**462,064**	**579,036**	**690,185**	**2,354,252**	**2,573,890**
Material	0	0	0	0	0	0	0	0	0	0
Direct labor	44,850	56,550	62,400	390,000	91,806	95,979	112,671	116,844	417,300	467,376
Overhead	0	0	0	0	0	0	0	0	0	0
Marketing and sales	17,325	17,490	17,985	165,000	38,841	40,607	47,669	49,434	176,550	197,736
Brewery ops. R&D	7,350	7,420	7,630	70,000	16,478	17,227	20,223	20,972	74,900	83,888
General and admin.	3,675	3,710	3,815	35,000	8,239	8,614	10,112	10,486	37,450	41,944
Taxes	0	0	40,529	162,113	41,538	41,538	41,538	41,538	166,150	186,451
Capital	3,430	3,430	3,430	41,164	11,018	11,018	11,018	11,018	44,072	49,361
Loans	25,000	25,000	25,000	300,000	75,000	75,000	75,000	75,000	300,000	300,000
Total expenses	**101,630**	**113,600**	**160,789**	**1,163,277**	**282,920**	**289,982**	**318,230**	**325,292**	**1,216,422**	**1,326,756**
Cash flow	**118,701**	**138,818**	**123,715**	**584,394**	**340,048**	**172,082**	**260,807**	**364,894**	**1,137,830**	**1,247,134**
Cumulative cash flow	**321,861**	**460,679**	**584,394**	**584,394**	**924,442**	**1,096,524**	**1,357,331**	**1,722,224**	**1,722,224**	**2,969,358**

be turned into cash, and generally how quickly you can do so. The most widely known and frequently used ratio is the current ratio, which is your current assets divided by current liabilities—a measure of your company's ability to meet current debt. As a rule of thumb, this ratio should be 2:1, because some of the assets (particularly inventory) take time to turn to cash. And, if the receivables are old and uncollectable, the ratio would not be accurate.

Look for current assets and current liabilities on your balance sheet. For instance, suppose your current assets are $300,000 and your current liabilities are $100,000. The current ratio would be:

$$\frac{\$300,000}{\$100,000} = 3$$

Compare your current ratio with those of similar companies in your industry by referring to surveys conducted by various trade associations and marketing companies. If you think your current ratio is too low, you can use a number of strategies to increase it. For instance, you may be able to add to your current assets by raising capital through equity or debt financing. If you choose to borrow money, make sure the loan has a maturity of at least one year in the future. You can increase your current ratio by paying off some of your debts that appear as current liabilities, or by turning some of your fixed or miscellaneous assets into current assets. As a last resort, you can always funnel profits back into your business.

Another common ratio is the acid test or quick ratio, which measures your business' ability to meet current obligations. Total all your liquid assets such as cash on hand plus any government securities and receivables, then divide these assets by your current liabilities.

Suppose your current liquid assets are $30,000 cash, $50,000 in receivables, and another $20,000 in securities for a total of $100,000. You've determined your current liabilities are $50,000; your quick ratio would be:

$$\frac{\$100,000}{\$50,000} \ = \ 2$$

For most businesses, a quick ratio of 2.0 or better is more than sufficient. If, however, something's slowing up payment of receivables or the due dates on your receivables exceed the amount of time you have for your payables, then you'll need a ratio higher than 2.0.

Try to keep your quick ratio at a level sufficient for your needs. Remember: good financial management entails the optimum use of your assets to increase your business' profitability. If you have large amounts of cash, receivables, and inventories that are out of line with your needs and lying idle, they are not working for you. Astute financial management necessitates walking a tightrope between too much liquidity and not enough.

To determine the right amount of liquidity for your business, figure out the average collection period of your receivables. You can do this by first taking your net sales found on your P&L or income statement and dividing this number by the days in your fiscal accounting period. This will provide you with your average sales per day. Now divide your accounts receivables by your average sales per day to determine your average collection period.

For example, say your annual net sales are $850,000, your fiscal accounting period is 365 days and accounts receivable are $50,000. This would result in the following:

$$\frac{\$850,000}{365} \ = \ \$2,328.77 \ \text{(your average sales per day)}$$

$$\frac{\$50,000}{\$2,328.77} \ = \ 21.5 \ \text{(your average collection period)}$$

The average collection period in the preceding example shows 21.5 days. If the credit terms are 30 days, then your accounts, or the people to whom you extend credit, are very dependable. However, if your average collection period is 60 days, then you need to review your credit policies and institute a tighter credit collection strategy. Chapter 22 provides more information on collections of accounts receivable.

Inventory turnover is another measure to determine the amount of liquidity you should maintain, in particu-

lar the amount of capital invested in inventory to meet your operation requirements. Turnover represents the number of times per year your inventory investment revolves.

$$\text{Inventory turnover} \ = \ \frac{\text{Net sales (or cost of goods)}}{\text{Average value of inventory on order and on hand}}$$

This ratio measures the efficiency of funds invested in materials and inventory and shows how often inventory is liquidated. To illustrate inventory turnover, let's say your cost of goods sold is $500,000, and the average value of inventory is $45,000. To arrive at inventory turnover, you'd divide $500,000 by $45,000. This results in an inventory turnover of 11.1.

If the inventory turnover ratio is lower in relation to the average for the industry (or in comparison with the average ratio for your business), it's likely that some obsolete or otherwise non-salable inventories are being carried. On the other hand, if the turnover is unusually high compared with the average figure, your business may be losing sales because of lack of adequate stock on hand.

Determine the turnover rate of each item in stock so you can evaluate how well they're moving. You may even want your inventory turnover to be based on periods more frequent than a year. For food-service operations with inventory that includes perishable items, calculating turnover periods based on daily, weekly, or monthly periods may be necessary to ensure products' freshness.

Profitability Measures

If your company isn't profitable, why put yourself through the headaches and long hours that being in business entails? You could be working for someone else and feeling financially secure with a weekly paycheck and benefits and less stressed out because of more free time.

But if you're in business, it's your job to make money. By taking a look at ratios that compute your company's asset earning power, return on owner's equity, net profit on sales, investment turnover, and return on investment (ROI), you'll learn:

- How much money you're making
- Whether your present resources are maximizing the profit potential of your business

- Whether you're losing money or just breaking even

Asset earning power measures how well your assets are performing for you. This measure looks at the earning power of your total assets, not just your liquid assets. The asset earning power is a ratio that is calculated by taking your earnings before taxes and interest and dividing that number by your total assets. If you had total earnings before taxes and interest of $100,000 and total assets of $300,000, you would have an asset earning power of .33 or 33 percent. This shows you that your total assets are earning you 33 percent of present marketable value.

The ratio known as return on owner's equity is used to determine what the return from the business is on the amount invested in your business. Equity in a company is usually based upon capital investment and includes not only initial capitalization but ongoing as well. You can also include intangible assets, such as patents or trade secrets that have been contributed to the business in exchange for equity. If you're the only investor in your company, total equity belongs to you.

To compute the return on the owner's equity, first calculate what your average equity investment in the business has been over a twelve-month period. You can find this number on the balance sheet. Now divide your net profit by the equity to determine your return on owner's equity. For example, if you have equity in the business of $75,000 and your net profit is $50,000, your return on the owner's equity would be .66 or 66 percent.

Net profit on sales is the ratio that shows the profitability of your business. It measures the difference between your net sales and what you spend to operate your business. To determine the net profit on sales, divide the net profit by the net sales. If we use the net profit of $50,000 from the preceding example and have net sales of $300,000, your net profit on sales would be .17 or 17 percent.

Most experts agree that if your percentage of net profit to net sales doesn't exceed the amount of money that can be earned from interest or dividends in securities, then you're not making the most of your assets. In this example, you're earning 17 cents on every dollar the company spends—a very good return for most businesses. Check the average ratios of similar businesses in your industry and compare your net profit on sales to theirs. If your net profit on sales is substantially lower, look carefully at those areas in your business that could be contributing to this reduced earning power. Those areas might be high operating costs or a price point that may not be producing sufficient profit or is not competitive enough.

Like inventory turnover, investment turnover can be used to determine the amount of times per year that your total investment or assets revolve. To calculate your investment turnover, divide total annual net sales by total assets. If your net sales are $500,000 and your total assets are $300,000, your investment turnover would be 1.6. Compare your investment turnover with that of similar businesses within the industry. In fairly investment-intensive businesses, your investment turnover may be lower than ones that don't require heavy capitalization.

ROI is the most common profitability ratio. There are several ways to determine ROI, but the most frequently used method is to divide net profit by total assets. If your net profit is $100,000 and your total assets are $300,000, your ROI would be .33 or 33 percent.

Return on investment is not necessarily the same as profit. ROI deals with the money you invest in the company and the return you realize on that money based on the net profit of the business. Profit, on the other hand, measures the performance of the business. Don't confuse ROI with the return on the owner's equity. This is an entirely different item as well. Only in sole proprietorships does equity equal the total investment or assets of the business.

You can use ROI in several different ways to gauge the profitability of your business. For instance, you can measure the performance of your pricing policies, inventory investment, capital equipment investment, and so forth. Some other ways to use ROI within your company are by:

- Dividing net income, interest, and taxes by total liabilities to measure rate of earnings of total capital employed.
- Dividing net income and income taxes by proprietary equity and fixed liabilities to produce a rate of earnings on invested capital.
- Dividing net income by total capital plus reserves to calculate the rate of earnings on proprietary equity and stock equity.

Industry Averages

In addition to using financial ratios to get a better fix on your company's strengths and weaknesses, you can compare them to industry averages prepared by third-party companies. You can use operating ratios as well as liquidity and profitability ratios. Operating ratios express the expenses of a firm as a percentage of net sales and indicate any imbalances in the present performance of the business, enabling business owners to plan more efficiently.

There are several sources for financial and operating ratios, but the best-known is Risk Management Association's (RMA, which was formerly known as Robert Morris Associates) *Annual Statement Studies.* These are available in the reference section of most business libraries and at your bank's lending department. For more information on RMA, visit their web site, www.rmahq.org.

Trade publications are another source of financial and operating ratios. The government also publishes a number of studies with financial and operating ratios such as the *Statistics of Income Bulletin,* published by the Internal Revenue Service. You can find the bulletin at www.irs.ustreas.gov/prod/tax_stats/index.html.

CHAPTER 18

Bootstrapping

Anyone who's started a business on a shoe-string is adept at bootstrapping or stretching resources, both financial and otherwise, as far as they can. But bootstrapping is not limited to start-up. It's a valid way for business owners to treat valuable resources at any stage of their business' growth.

Bootstrapping is one of most effective and inexpensive ways to ensure a business' positive cash flow. Among its advantages:

- Less money has to be borrowed.

- Interest costs are reduced.

- The balance sheet is strengthened, which is more attractive to lenders and investors when the time comes to borrow money.

TRADE CREDIT

Trade credit is one way to maximize your financial resources for the short term. Normally, suppliers extend credit to regular customers for 30, 60, or 90 days, without charging interest. For example, suppose that a supplier ships something to you and you have trade credit. Your terms might be net sixty days from the receipt of goods, in which case you'd have thirty extra days to pay for the items.

However, when you first start your business, suppliers will want every order COD (cash or check on delivery) until you've established that you can pay your bills on time. While this is a fairly normal practice, in order to raise money during start-up you're going to have to try to negotiate a trade credit basis with suppliers. One of the things that will help you in these negotiations is having a written financial plan.

Using trade credit on a continual basis is not a long-term solution. Your business may become heavily committed to those suppliers who accept extended credit terms. As a result, the business may no longer have ready access to other, more competitive suppliers who might offer lower prices, a superior product, and/or more reliable deliveries.

Depending on the terms available from your suppliers, the cost of trade credit can be quite high. For example, say you make a purchase from a supplier who decides to extend credit to you. Terms the supplier offers are two percent cash discount within ten days and a net date of 30 days. Essentially, the supplier is saying that if you pay within ten days, the purchase price will be discounted by two percent. On the other hand, by forfeiting the two percent discount, you're able to use your money for 20 more days, and it will only cost you that two percent discount.

Cash discounts aren't the only factor to consider. There are also late payment or delinquency penalties, should you extend payment beyond the agreed-upon terms. These can usually run between one and two percent on a monthly basis. If you miss your net payment date for an entire year, that can cost you as much as 12 to 24 percent in penalty interest.

Effective use of trade credit requires intelligent planning to avoid unnecessary costs through forfeiture of cash discounts or the incidence of delinquency penalties. But every business should take full advantage of trade credit available without additional cost in order to reduce the need for capital from other sources.

FACTORING

Factoring involves selling your receivables to a buyer, such as a commercial finance company, to raise capital and is very common in the clothing industry, where long receivables are part of the business cycle. Factors usually buy accounts receivable at a rate that ranges between 75 and 90 percent of face value, and then add a discount rate of between two and six percent. The factor assumes the risk, and task, of collecting the receivables. If your prices are set up to take factoring into account, you can still make a profit.

LETTERS OF CREDIT FROM CUSTOMERS

Customers can help you obtain financing by writing you a letter of credit. For example, suppose you're starting a business manufacturing industrial bags, and a large corporation has placed an order for a steady supply of cloth bags. The major supplier that you'll source the material through is located in India. In this scenario, you obtain a letter of credit from your customer when the order is placed, and the material for the bags is purchased using this letter of credit as security.

In your personal financial dealings, you may have had a builder ask for money up front in order to buy materials for your job. That contractor used your money to get started on the job—you actually helped finance his business.

REAL ESTATE LOANS

If your business needs to buy its facility, your initial cost may be high but the building's cost can be financed over a long-term period of fifteen to thirty years. The loan on the facility can be structured to make optimum use of your planned growth or seasonal peaks. For instance, you can arrange a graduated payment mortgage that initially has very small monthly payments with the cost increasing over the lifetime of the loan. The lower monthly payments give your business time to grow. Eventually, you can refinance the loan when time and interest rates permit.

Another advantage is that real estate appreciates over time and creates a valuable asset called equity. You can borrow against this equity—lenders often loan up to 75 or 80 percent of a property's appraised value.

This applies to any personal real estate you own. Home equity loans are a popular financing device for new business owners because there's often substantial equity tied up in a home and the loans are easy to come by. However, for most people, their home is their biggest asset and losing it would be devastating, which could happen if the business were to fail and the loan was called.

LOANS FROM EQUIPMENT SUPPLIERS

If you spend a lot of money on equipment, you may find yourself without enough working capital to keep your business going in its first months. Instead of paying cash for your equipment, the manufacturer can effectively loan you the money by selling you the equipment on an installment basis. This helps conserve your working capital while allowing you to use the equipment in your business.

Two types of credit contracts are commonly used to finance equipment purchases:

1. *The conditional sales contract.* The purchaser does not receive title to the equipment until it is fully paid for.

2. *The chattel-mortgage contract.* The equipment becomes the property of the purchaser on delivery, but the seller holds a mortgage claim against it until the amount specified in the contract is paid.

LEASING

Leasing is a way to avoid financing the entire purchase of high-ticket items like equipment, vehicles, furniture, computers, and even employees. With leasing, you pay for only that portion you use, rather than for the entire purchase price. When you're just starting out in business, it might make sense to shop around and get the best leasing arrangement possible. For example, you could lease a photocopier for several hundred dollars a month rather than financing the entire $3,000 purchase price, or you could lease your automobile or van instead of shelling out $25,000 or more.

There are many ways that a lease can be modified to increase your cash position. These modifications include:

- A down payment lower than 10 percent or no down payment at all.
- Maintenance costs that are built into the lease package, thereby reducing your cash outlays. If you needed a repairperson to do maintenance on purchased equipment, it would cost you more than if you had leased it.
- Extending the lease term to cover the entire life of the property (or use of the property for as long as you wish to use it).
- A purchase option that allows you to buy the property after the lease period has ended. A fixed purchase price can also be added to the option provision.
- Lease payments that can be structured to accommodate seasonal variations in the business or tied to indexes that track interest to create an adjustable lease

MANAGING CASH FLOW

Bootstrap financing really begins and ends with your attention to careful management of your financial resources. Be aware of what you spend and keep your overhead low. If you need to go the top-dollar route, make sure you can justify the expense. Don't choose an overly expensive office or location unless it's really going to pay off in increased sales. Take a look at secondhand furniture—if it works for your office, buy it. Barter for goods and services when appropriate. Buy on promotion, to take advantage of better prices offered for a limited time.

Keep a close watch on operating expenses. If interest rates are high, it won't take too many unpaid bills to wipe out your profits. At a 12 percent interest rate, carrying an unpaid $10,000 of bills will cost you $120 per month. Tight margins mean it's more costly to accumulate bills than increase production.

Positive cash flow results when you:

- Identify billable events, other than delivery
- Set payment due dates
- Establish penalties for late payment
- Determine the place of payment

Be prepared to consider these steps before accepting an order. Time invested in obtaining favorable cash flow terms and conditions can mean added profits and higher returns on your investments. Take steps to get the best available payment terms.

Identifying a Billable Event

Try to bill before delivery. There are three ways you can issue an invoice before you ship the final product.

1. *Milestone billing* is fairly common where heavy, up-front investment is required for a new product or job. In this case, the completion of a certain event or milestone (placing a subcontract, passing a critical design review, completing a set of tests or receiving a large amount of material), is given a billing value. This authorizes you to issue an invoice when the event occurs—often long before completion of a deliverable item.

2. *Progress billing* is fairly common in the defense and aerospace industries and allows you to invoice costs, as incurred, on a routine, bimonthly or monthly basis. This way, your customer finances your inventory, thereby reducing your need for working capital. In effect, your costs are recovered before you deliver anything, even though your customer has a lien against the inventory.

3. *Sub-line-item billing* is fairly common in the construction industry as it recognizes the times when an

entire item cannot be completed but main elements of it are. Examples of sub-items are foundation, plumbing, frame, and roof. The advantage here is that as each major supplement is completed, an invoice can be issued, thus strengthening the contractor's cash flow.

Setting Payment Dates

Define when you'll be paid by setting payment dates. Why take an order if you don't make an effort to assure payment? Bear in mind that extending credit to customers has a real cost to you and be sure your contract (and price) provides for that cost. Sales to poor credit risks should be COD. Discounts can be offered but tied to the shipment date, customer acceptance date, your invoice date, or a calendar date. Once the payment date is established in your contract (purchase order, etc.), you have a legally enforceable document.

Establishing Late-Payment Penalties

Enforcing penalties for late payment helps you get timely payment. What happens today if a customer pays you 30 days late? Do you collect interest or are you just happy to get paid? If your terms and conditions require a penalty for late payment, you improve your chances for timely payment—and, based upon the terms of your contract, you have recourse for legal action should you need it.

Determining Place of Payment

The place of payment can make a two- to five-day difference in cash receipts. Firms that sell throughout the United States use geographically dispersed deposit lockboxes. Each order requires payment to the lockbox closest to the customer. Other firms require payment directly to their bank. This makes the money more readily available.

Having the right payment provisions will help your company hold on to the profits it earns.

CHAPTER 19

Insurance

One of the smartest moves any business owner can make is having enough of the right kinds of insurance. Not only does this protect the business' assets from risks that could very well reduce them to nothing if a catastrophe struck—it also safeguards a business owner's personal assets, which are often on the line, from a liability point of view.

What kind of risks should you be concerned about? If you have employees, you're obligated to:

- Provide a safe place to work
- Employ individuals reasonably competent to carry out their tasks without endangering others
- Warn employees of danger
- Furnish appropriate and safe tools
- Set up and enforce proper rules of employee conduct as they relate to safe working procedures

You also owe a degree of safety and concern to your customers, clients, and the public—not only for their physical well-being when they're doing business with you but also to protect their property.

Insurance, provided your carrier is a solid company, is a safe bet worth taking. By paying a relatively small amount as a premium, you're guaranteed a quick recovery from certain perils, should they occur.

To find the right coverage for your business, work with an agent who's familiar with a variety of carriers. For more information on insurance providers, contact Insurance Information Institute at www.iii.org.

MANAGING RISKS

Let's face it: Starting and running any type of business has risks. Recognizing the risks in all areas of your business—management, marketing, contracts, personnel, and the particular ramifications of your product or service on customers and the market—is the first step in effective risk management. Follow these steps before talking to an insurance representative:

- Make a list of risks that your business faces.
- Evaluate your liabilities from your customers' point of view.
- Chart the customers' path as they come into contact with your shop—across the sidewalk, through the door, under the ceiling fan, up to your counter, and so on.

After identifying the risks inherent to your business, estimate the probability of financial loss in various situations that could go wrong. Develop a worst-case scenario and put a price tag on it—shop damage, employee injuries, harm to a customer because of your product or service. Next, decide the most economical way to handle the possible losses, considering the following avenues:

- *Assumption* means assuming the risk and the accompanying financial burdens. Sometimes absorbing a risk is prudent. If you're a one-person graphic-design business, no employees are going to be injured on the job. Nor are you likely to be sued for personal injury if clients infrequently visit your office. However, if you own a bakery that employs 30 people, you'd best not assume any risks pertaining to employees getting injured on the job or a customer tossing their cookies because of eating one of yours.

- *Avoidance* means removing the cause of risk. If a caustic material is making employees hesitant and fearful, replace it with a non-hazardous substance. The cost is small compared to what you'd pay if an accident happened. An organized company safety program that implements suggestions from employees and insurance safety representatives can also help eliminate potentially dangerous situations in your business.

- *Loss reduction* is the transfer of the risk to another party altogether. When your own delivery service has problems—tardiness, damaged goods, mechanical breakdowns, and employee hassles—consider contracting a delivery service to take all the headaches away. Similar circumstances include contracting for maintenance, electrical, plumbing, carpentry, bookkeeping, landscaping, and security. Such actions are a form of insurance because you have shifted the risk and responsibility to another party for a negotiated fee. However, shifting the risk and responsibility does not necessarily shift the liability. When the new landscaping crew improperly installs a sprinkler head causing water damage to the inside of a nearby Jaguar, you can hold the landscaping firm liable. But the man who falls into the cactus plant growing by the front office and injures himself will hold you liable for planting it there.

Know what your potential liabilities are and make sure you're covered.

- *Self-insurance* entails setting aside a specified amount of money into a reserve fund each year to cover any losses incurred. The owner holds the cash in this reserve fund, rather than paying premiums to an insurance company. In practice, this method is risky for small firms that could experience a large loss. If the reserve fund is not large enough to cover that loss, the company will be sunk. A growing business with several geographically diverse units is more suited for self-insurance, as are big nonprofit organizations like school systems.

These methods can be used to offset some of risks a business faces. Some areas of risk, however, require the transfer of that risk through insurance, to make sure your business is protected and not overly exposed.

Sound insurance planning requires attention on all fronts. The usual, plain-vanilla insurance packages need to be complemented by additional special coverages relevant to your business. See Figure 19.1 for a sample Business Insurance Planning Worksheet that you can fill out after reading this chapter.

Cover your largest loss exposure first—the lives and health of you and your employees, the most valuable assets your company has.

LIFE INSURANCE

Life insurance is one of the lowest-cost benefits you can offer your employees. For a small additional fee, health insurance providers allow you to purchase a life insurance plan, either from them or from another company. Specialized life insurance options include:

- *The survivor-income plan* provides the deceased employee's family with monthly income.

- *Key-employee insurance* indemnifies you against losses resulting from the death or disability of a key employee in your firm, including yourself or your partners. By taking out an insurance policy on his or her (or your) life, you (or your beneficiaries) will have ample funds to recruit a successor. To avoid negative tax consequences, ask your CPA to help you decide whom you should name as the beneficiary of your policy.

FIGURE 19.1	Business Insurance Planning Worksheet

Types of Insurance	Required (Yes/No)	Yearly Cost	Cost Per Payment
General liability insurance			
Product liability insurance			
Errors and omissions liability insurance			
Malpractice liability insurance			
Automotive liability insurance			
Fire and theft insurance			
Business interruption insurance			
Overhead expense insurance			
Personal disability			
Key-employee insurance			
Shareholders' or partners' insurance			
Credit extension insurance			
Term life insurance			
Health insurance			
Group insurance			
Workers' compensation insurance			
Survivor-income life insurance			
Care, custody, and control insurance			
Consequential losses insurance			
Boiler and machinery insurance			
Profit insurance			
Money and securities insurance			
Glass insurance			
Electronic equipment insurance			
Power interruption insurance			
Rain insurance			
Temperature damage insurance			
Transportation insurance			
Fidelity bonds			
Surety bonds			
Title insurance			
Water damage insurance			
Total Annual Cost		$	$

Partnership Plans

A partnership usually dissolves when one partner dies, unless the partners have provided otherwise with a well thought-out and adequately financed buy-and-sell agreement. This agreement provides for the purchase of the deceased partner's share of the business at a prearranged price.

A partnership-insurance plan for two partners is straightforward, as it involves purchasing a life insurance policy on the other partner. Each partner in return pays the premiums.

Where there are three or more partners, it's common to have the firm buy a policy on the life of each partner. The trick lies in trying to set up a formula to determine the future value that will be paid by the partners and partners' heirs. The simplest plan sets an arbitrarily agreed upon value for each partner's interest in advance. More complex systems are necessary for small business partnerships that are growing.

In order to disburse the partnership's assets, an independent appraisal must be done. Sometimes three independent appraisals are performed, and an average value is chosen.

Corporate Plans

The death of a major stockholder or founder of a small, incorporated firm can be costly in terms of relations to investors, loss of business, or damage to employee morale.

If the deceased had a controlling interest in the company, the estate administrator could name a new director to take over control of the firm. Sometimes, this could be the deceased's spouse or other heir, who may have no knowledge of or experience in running the business. That's why the importance of a buy-sell agreement cannot be overstated. A carefully planned buy-sell agreement determines in advance what will be done upon the death of a stockholder and makes funds immediately available, through life insurance proceeds, for accomplishing those tasks.

The main benefit of a buy-sell agreement is continuity of the management team. This guarantees that business will proceed uninterrupted and that no outsiders can come into the business unless agreed upon in advance.

Stock repurchase agreements, the most common cause

of family disputes, are ironed out in an equitable manner, usually with a guaranteed minimum price. The insurance benefit is normally a lump sum payout with some extended payments over time, which relieves the bereaved family of concerns about the business.

HEALTH INSURANCE

Life insurance often comes with group health insurance, in economically attractive packages specifically geared toward small businesses. Every insurance company has a different definition of a small group—twenty-five people, or fifteen or fewer.

Two questions small business owners face when considering health insurance are "What kind of benefits should I buy?" and "How much should I pay?" Regarding the first, buy the benefits that will protect you, your employees, and your families in case of emergency. Regarding the second, it depends on your age (and your employees' ages), gender, and whether families will be considered.

Choosing the most suitable and cost-effective selection of medical benefits can be time-consuming. A workforce that's married with children will have considerably different needs, such as maternity and dental coverage, than groups of single workers. People who work outdoors or workers who spend their days at a computer may prefer an optical program for eye care, safety glasses, and sunglasses.

Take a look at your workforce to determine:

- How many workers fall into each age group
- How many heads of households there are
- Where they live
- How big their families are
- Any other pertinent information

Your medical insurance costs may be determined solely on the basis of your company's experience, such as the aggregate number and dollar value of claims submitted by your employees. In other cases, you'll be a part of a larger statistical group that the insurance company or health-care provider uses in calculating your premiums.

Make sure to explore the wide range of options available in health-care coverage today, including:

- *Fee-for-service* provides the eligible employee with the services of a doctor or hospital with partial or total reimbursement depending on the insurance company. Most insurance companies offer 80/20 plans; the insurance company pays 80 percent of the bill, and the employee pays 20 percent. The employee can go to any doctor he or she chooses, and the plan covers any service that is defined as medically necessary and specified in the plan.

- *Health maintenance organizations (HMOs)* provide a range of benefits to employees at a fixed price with a minimal contribution (or sometimes no contribution) from the employee, as long as employees use doctors or hospitals specified in the plan. Usually, HMOs are set up so that patients go to the managed-care plan facilities. If a patient goes to a doctor or hospital outside the plan—except in case of an emergency or if the individual was traveling outside the plan's service area—no benefits are paid at all. Make sure the HMO has facilities near where your employees live and get feedback on the HMO's reputation in the community.

- *Preferred provider organizations (PPOs)* are considered managed fee-for-service plans because some restrictions are put in place to control the frequency and cost of health care. Under a PPO, arrangements are made among the providers, hospitals and doctors to offer service at an alternative price—usually lower. Many times there is a co-pay amount, which means that the employee pays $15 or $20 for each visit to doctors specified in the plan, and the insurance company pays the rest. The PPO differs from an HMO in that if an employee goes to a doctor not specified by the insurance company, the plan still partially covers it. There is usually a higher co-pay amount or a deductible with varying percentages.

- A *"flexible-benefit"* plan allows employees to choose from different fringe benefits. If your workforce is largely white-collar, they may appreciate a health program that encompasses an executive fitness program. Other health programs include vision care plans and rehabilitation for alcohol and substance abuse.

- *Health-care savings accounts (HSAs)* were created in 2003 through a Medicare bill to help people save for future qualified medical and retiree health expenses on a tax-free basis. HSAs are often coupled with high-deductible plans and contributions to them are tax-deductible; interest earned on the accounts is tax-free and withdrawals for qualified medical expenses are tax-free. Since these accounts, like IRAs, are required by law to have trustees or custodians to administer them, talk to your bank, credit union, or insurance company about setting one up.

Aside from being concerned about the cost of your health-insurance plan, also look into the creditworthiness of the insurance provider. Make sure it's rated A or better by A.M. Best (www.ambest. com), an insurance industry rating service whose rankings are available online and at your library. Go with the highly rated, established company, even if its cost is a little higher. That way, you can protect yourself from "insurer flight"—when an insurance carrier packs up its bags and leaves rather than meeting new mandates in your state.

If you've narrowed your choice down to two HMOs, ask each to name a private firm you can speak to that's already using their services. Given equal price and medical services, maybe one HMO has a simpler billing method or a superior consumer service division than the other does.

Growing enterprises need to know that government legislation requires businesses to offer continued coverage in health insurance benefits even after an employee has left. The Consolidated Omnibus Budget Reconciliation Act (COBRA) calls for this privilege to be extended to any worker in a firm with 20 or more full-time employees. Signed into law in 1986, COBRA demands compliance in both union and nonunion plans. Only two groups are exempt from complying with COBRA: churches or church-operated, tax-exempt organizations and federal or District of Columbia employees.

You, the employer, need only offer continued coverage. Any ex-employee who elects to continue coverage must pay the full cost of that coverage. This includes both the employer's and employee's share. Employees may elect to remain covered under the firm's plan up to 19 months, and dependents can maintain coverage up to 36 months.

COBRA has imposed additional administrative burdens and potentially higher plan costs on virtually all group insurance plans. Managing and monitoring COBRA compliance procedures are necessary to avoid costly financial penalties involved with noncompliance.

One penalty is loss of the corporation's tax deduction for its group insurance plan. The plan administrator, in a small firm, is subject to a personal fine for failing to notify an employee of his or her COBRA rights at each step of the termination or hiring process. COBRA provisions include advising all new and terminated employees, and all spouses, of their COBRA continuation rights in writing. Be sure that those electing continued coverage are removed from the plan as soon as they become covered under a new plan.

As you might have anticipated, COBRA presents two problems for small-business managers: more complicated administration and inevitably higher insurance costs. This has spawned a whole new industry of independent administrators and management programs that offer employers relief from the paper logjam.

LIABILITY INSURANCE

Customers, employees, repair people, delivery people, and anyone else who comes in contact with your business property can hold you liable for your failure to take the proper degree of care. This can be as simple as keeping your sidewalk swept or shoveling the snow on your front walk. If someone is injured as a result of your negligence, the court will generally find in favor of the injured party, even if your negligence was only slight.

Basically, there are two types of liabilities against which you have to insure yourself and your business: liabilities to nonmembers of the firm and liabilities to members of the firm (employees and partners). Most of the liabilities toward outsiders will be covered under a comprehensive general liability (CGL) policy. A CGL policy covers the following four risks:

1. Payments due to accidents and injuries that might happen on your premises or to your employees

2. Any immediate medical expenses necessary at the time of the accident

3. The attorney fees and expenses for investigation and settlement

4. The cost of court bonds or other judgments during appeal.

The limits to liability are determined on a per-accident and per-person basis. Additional limitations may include a total on bodily injury or property damage.

A CGL policy does not protect you against all liabilities, however. These include:

- Liability caused by an employee automobile accident while on the job
- Liability related to products manufactured or sold, or services offered, by your company
- Liability insurance covered under workers' compensation laws

Other liability insurance policies take up where general comprehensive leaves off; they will be covered in more detail later.

Automotive Liability

The same type of policy you purchase for your personal use is also necessary for your business. Be certain that all employees with an active driver's license in your state are listed on the policy. And, beware of coverage gaps between owned, non-owned, and hired vehicles.

Never cut corners on automotive liability coverage. Minimal packages of 25/50/25 (per person bodily injury/ total accident coverage / property damage) are available; however, hitting an expensive sports car can quickly wipe out the insurance company's coverage. Pay the extra few dollars for higher coverage of 100/300/100. Most states have laws concerning uninsured motorists coverage. Supplement the standard auto policy, as the costs are minimal.

As a businessperson, meetings and seminars may take you out of town. The daily price of rental-car insurance for collision has reached astronomical levels. The addition of a relatively inexpensive endorsement to your company auto policy can save money and prevent headaches on the road. This also gives you the advantage of rate shopping with the major rental agencies. Without this endorsement, the costs of collision damage waiver (CDW) offered by the major car rental companies can tack on up to $10 per day for car rentals. Failure to purchase the CDW results in the renter carrying full responsibility for any damage to the car. Ask your insurance carrier if this coverage is automatically included or if there's an extra fee.

Most states have an insurance watchdog agency to oversee the industry as a whole. They release comprehensive studies citing rates for some typical drivers in average cars, driving safely for a set number of miles. It will have information on the premiums your state's insurance firms charge for the same standard and is an excellent tool for determining the maximum coverage at the minimum costs.

Product Liability

In manufacturing, and in certain sectors of retail trade, you may have an assumed product liability: You are responsible for knowing if a product is defective. In a service business, product liability may be a factor if you're in the repair business and inadvertently cause an accident or injury.

As a result of strict judicial interpretations, companies have been held accountable for injuries to those using a product fifteen or twenty years after its manufacture or sale. Manufacturers or vendors who defend themselves by saying that the product met all known standards of safety at the time of construction or sale are usually ruled against by the court.

Consult an insurance representative who knows product liability well, as premiums vary widely. If you manufacture ski-lift parts, your premiums will be considerably higher than the firm that makes the lenses for snow goggles.

Workers' Compensation

Workers' compensation insurance mandates unlimited medical coverage during the course of employment on all job-related injuries incurred on company property or in pursuit of an employee's livelihood. An injured delivery person could receive compensation if he or she were hurt while unloading your goods at another site.

As with any insurance coverage, rates for workers' compensation can be modified higher or lower, depending upon the company's accident record. The safer the workplace and the better the accident record, the less expensive your company's coverage will be.

Concentrate on your overall risk management planning. Take note of those risks that you will assume and those where systematic avoidance can heighten the safety standards and performance of your employees.

COMPREHENSIVE PROPERTY INSURANCE

Make sure to get a policy written on an all-risk basis rather than on a named-peril basis. While the latter only covers the specific perils named in the policy, an all-risk policy will cover you for virtually anything (except for a few specific enumerated exclusions). The all-risk policy will allow you to:

- Eliminate duplication and overlap
- Avoid gaps in trying to cover your liabilities through a number of specialized policies
- Encourage quicker settlements by working with one agent and one attorney
- Reduce the expense of having many different policies

If your area is inclined toward a specific calamity, you may consider additional insurance or pay an additional premium to insure against fire, flood, earthquake, nuclear risks (if you're near a nuclear plant), hail, windstorm, vandalism, or crime.

An experienced agent or broker may roll many overages into a business owner's policy (BOP)—a ready-made program for small businesses—or a special multiple-peril plan.

Replacement Cost Property Insurance

Replacement cost insurance will replace your property at current prices, regardless of what you paid for it, and thus protect you against inflation. However, there's usually a provision that your total replacements can't exceed the policy cap. For example, if you have a 40,000-square-foot facility that would cost $40 per square foot to replace, the total replacement cost ($1.6 million) may exceed your $1 million policy limit. To protect yourself, buy replacement insurance with an insurance guard, which adjusts the cap on the policy to allow for inflation. If this isn't possible, simply review your policy limits from time to time to make sure you have adequate coverage.

Co-insurance

With co-insurance, the owners of a building can actually share the potential loss with the insurance company if they're willing to share the premium cost. These terms are crucial if you are on either end of a leasing agreement. A common percentage of market value of buildings used in co-insurance is 80 percent, with the owner bearing the cost of the other 20 percent in the event of a complete loss.

SPECIAL COVERAGE

Your business will require its own set of special coverages for the risks inherent in your industry. Sometimes these can be added as endorsements to your policy, or you can buy them separately.

Care, Custody, and Control

This is a must for service industries, particularly those with customer goods in their control anytime during the business transaction. Should an accident happen, the insurance company would reimburse you (and the customer). This is especially useful to businesses that provide services such as framing pictures, furniture repair, bicycle assembly, dry cleaning, and so on.

Basically, if you have a customer's goods in your control at any time during the business transaction, you're liable for the full value should an accident happen. You're held liable even for the most insignificant handling of the customer's property—holding and losing athletic shoes while your customer is roller-skating is considered an accident.

Consequential Losses

This clause should be inserted into a standard property or fire insurance policy. For an extra premium, you can insure the extra expenses of obtaining temporary quarters, relocation, and incidental expenses.

Business Interruption

This specialized insurance reimburses the business owner for future profits lost and fixed charges as a result of damages due to perils specifically accounted for in the policy. Weather damage is the most common cause. Other causes (e.g., a labor strike or material shortage) are not covered. The inclusions (e.g., tornado, hurricane) and exclusions (e.g., mudslide or tidal wave) differ, depending on your geographic location.

Predicting a company's profitability at a particular point in the future can be tricky. If the company was operating at a loss, then only the fixed expenses that it incurred may be reimbursed. However, if your company is operating at a profit, then good records (which underscores the importance of keeping duplicate records at another site) will support your case. If all the records have been destroyed in a fire, the previous year's tax records can help.

Business-interruption coverage is particularly crucial for restaurants, as they risk complete loss of income in the event of fire while still being obligated to make rental and loan payments.

There are even more specialized provisions with business-interruption insurance. Under the terms of an extended period of indemnity, the period of loss is defined as the period necessary to return to normal business operation. Otherwise, the payments are only made until the business can physically reopen (even if in a makeshift pattern).

Peak season endorsements, which are even more specialized, cover those service industries that make all their money during a particular season. If your company is located in a snow belt, a specialized form of business-interruption insurance can provide funds for a temporary source of heat until a new boiler arrives. Depending on the provisions you insert, the coverage may also take care of the costs of the new machine.

Profit Insurance

Unlike business-interruption insurance, which covers future profits, profit insurance covers the loss of goods already manufactured but destroyed before they could be sold. This specialized coverage is aimed at manufacturers.

Credit Insurance

If your business extends credit to another party, person, partnership, or corporation, you could encounter losses stemming from:

- Bankruptcy
- Closure of a financial institution
- Death or physical disability
- Destruction of accounting records
- Political instability in a foreign country

The two major classifications for credit insurance are:

1. *General coverage,* which applies to those losses incurred during the one-year policy caused from sales made during the year prior to the starting date.

2. *Forward coverage,* which covers the insured for losses resulting from accounts that were created by sales made during the policy term.

General policies account for the lion's share of the credit policies in force. They cover all debtors falling into given classes of credit ratings on a blanket basis. The policy specifies dollar limits on debtors according to classifications set by Dun & Bradstreet credit ratings. Various levels of blanket coverage can be assigned depending on the size of the company. Automatic coverage on unrated accounts can also be provided.

Money and Securities Insurance

You may need additional insurance to cover those peak cash holding periods during the business day such as closing, after lunch, or payday. Check to see if your policy covers money in transit, money or securities on the premises during business hours and after hours, and money at home (when you're just too tired to go to the bank).

Glass Insurance

Businesses have the option of purchasing a comprehensive policy insuring breakage of plate glass, neon signs, and showcases from any source except fire or nuclear reaction. This includes weather, riots, vehicles, or sonic boom. Determine whether this coverage includes damage to stock by broken glass. Some policies include the costs of replacing lettering and other ornamentation.

Electronic Equipment

Electronic equipment can be insured for fire, theft, malicious damage, accidental damage, mechanical breakdown, or electrical breakdown. A separate electronic data-processing (EDP) policy can cover hardware as well as software. Should fire occur in the computer room, the standard property insurance policy might pay you the price of replacing a blank roll of computer tape—an EDP policy could compensate you for the cost of reconstructing the data. These items and coverage are above and

beyond the normal scope of business property insurance unless you have a comprehensive policy.

Power Interruption

A power interruption endorsement is available on a machinery contract to provide coverage for losses from interruption of electricity, gas, heat, or other energy from public utilities. This is critical for those businesses in the perishable food industry or specialized sectors such as an ice warehouse.

Rain

Rain insurance is designed to cover losses at a certain percentage, for example 60 percent of the gross revenues on the last day not affected by rainfall. Swap meets, carnivals, auctions, and sporting events would consider this coverage.

Temperature Damage

In the same vein, this insurance is needed by businesses such as bakeries, dairies, and greenhouses that require the maintenance of a certain temperature to prevent loss of valuable inventory.

Transportation

Transportation insurance indemnifies your materials in transit. Common carriers like United Parcel Service are liable for most shipping damages to your goods. They are not liable for unforeseeable "acts of God" such as floods or lightening.

Land shipments most frequently use an inland transit policy. This would include a train derailment but exclude a labor strike or riot. Also excluded are breakage and leakage, however, the common carrier is generally liable for these damages.

Truck shipments can be covered by a blanket motor-cargo policy. Federal interstate trucking laws require minimum coverage that may not offer you full protection.

Fidelity Bonds

Fidelity bonds protect the firm from losses incurred by employee thefts. It is often difficult to establish losses, and only established losses are reimbursed. These bonds have been used to cover cash losses rather than merchandise losses, even though it's well known that losses from stolen merchandise far exceed those from cash losses. If applicable to your business, fidelity bonds should be used more widely to cover losses of both cash and merchandise.

Surety Bonds

A surety bond protects your company against losses incurred as a result of the failure of others to perform on schedule. If you're familiar with the construction industry, you know the importance of this insurance contract. Surety bonds, otherwise known as performance bonds, guarantee that a person or corporation will perform the service agreed on. The bond guarantees that you have the financial capacity to perform your duties, and it also backs your credit. Because your work is guaranteed, you're able to compete and bid on jobs with firms that are considerably larger than yours. Keep in mind that surety bonds may require extensive credit information and collateral.

Title Insurance

Title insurance is available for a nominal fee and should always be requested for real estate purchases. In cases in which the title is not conveyed, even though the purchasers thought they had such a title, they are reimbursed.

Water Damage

Different than flood insurance, water damage insurance covers risks from leaking pipes, sprinkler system, backed-up toilets, bursting water tanks, and a leaking roof.

Other Specialized Packages

Specialized packages include an "errors and omissions rider clause" for owners and managers who are in the business of giving professional advice. A director and officer's liability policy is available if you serve on the board of directors of a corporation. A garage owner's policy covers any damage to vehicles in your care if you are customizing or repairing automobiles. There is also "special liquor legal liability" insurance for claims that stem from auto accidents caused by patrons who drink too much at a restaurant or tavern. Companies that use or produce chemicals, drugs, or industrial pollutants are wise to carry specific endorsements for these hazards. If you or your employees work or travel overseas, a special worldwide liability policy is available. This may or may not include kidnap and extortion coverage.

Very special circumstances, including non-business risks, can be purchased from Lloyd's of London. Almost any type of risk can be insured against, but the question is: How much can you afford to pay in insurance premiums?

BUYING INSURANCE

Whether you deal with an independent agent, insurance broker, or directly with an insurance company, make sure comparison shopping is your first order of business.

Just as it may not always be the best idea to buy your business products from a single supplier, neither should you necessarily one-stop shop for your insurance. Like a backpacking trip, your goal is to outfit yourself with adequate provisions and seamless protection—coverage that has no gaps. High-quality insurance provides the best protection. Cutting corners doesn't make sense—it can be risky, and you might end up paying more in the long run. Overlapping insurance policies result from poor planning and often indicate spending more money than necessary.

Depending on which type of insurance you're purchasing, various factors affect the price of your insurance premium. For life insurance, your age, gender, health, and family health history are all factored in to determine your rates. Regardless of your health, if your family has a history of heart disease, your rate may be slightly higher. Do not misrepresent this information, as the entire policy could be invalidated if you have misrepresented anything on the application.

Auto insurance rates are determined by the type of car or truck you drive, your age, your marital status, the number of drivers, how long you've lived in the state, and the number of miles you drive back and forth to work each day.

Property insurance rates vary depending on the location of your building. Factors such as the local crime rate, the type of your industry, and the condition of the building are all computed into the final rate you're quoted.

Regardless of the type of insurance you're purchasing, as long as you take the highest deductible you can afford, the premium should be affordable.

Your application for insurance is evaluated by the company you have contacted, after which you're given a firm price quotation. Auto insurance quotes can normally be given on the spot. Life, health, and property insurance rates may take the insurance representative longer to study. Be aware of the lag time if you're considering changing policies.

Insurance firms are somewhat flexible with payments. The norm is every three months. You can pay monthly, but there is a slight surcharge for this arrangement.

Educate yourself in insurance terminology so you can have a fruitful discussion with the insurance representatives. The four basic sections of insurance policies are:

1. *Declarations page* names the policyholder, describes the property or liability to be insured, states the coverage, and specifies the maximum the insurer will pay in case of loss.

2. *Insurance agreement* describes both sides' mutual responsibilities while the policy is in force. Often this section tells the policyholder when, how, and why claims should be filed and the insurers alerted.

3. *Conditions of the policy* spell out in detail what is covered and what is required of both parties in case of a loss.

4. *Exclusions* list specific perils, property, and losses that are not covered.

A fifth section, endorsements and coverage expansions, can be added to show the coverage allowed, but it is not standard.

Agents, Brokers, and Direct Writers

Direct writers are employed by a specific firm and may have a specialty in the field of insurance. Though tied to one firm, the direct writer insurance representative can still handle any number of insurance lines: auto, home, health, and life. The commission paid to the salesperson should be somewhat lower as a result of purchasing it "factory direct."

An agent is an independent businessperson who usually deals with a variety of different coverages and handles any number of different insurers. The independent agent may have gathered a greater breadth of knowledge across many different fields of insurance. This interaction with many firms and policies increases the agent's scope and awareness of cost-effective coverage. Though the commission for an independent agent is generally higher, he or she may strive to give you the best service possible so that you're a happy customer who returns again and again.

Insurance brokers, such as Alexander & Alexander or Marsh & McLennan, make it their business to negotiate with different insurers for different types of policies. The broker represents the insurance buyer, not the insurance company, in dealing with a variety of insurers. They're particularly adept in business dealings, and thus, their costs may be higher.

Determining which professional to go with can be frustrating. The insurance companies' true area of expertise is underwriting. The direct writer may not be as knowledgeable as the field agent in customizing an individual package for your company within a specialized field. In any case, an experienced, thorough, conscientious broker or insurance agent has an incentive to customize a plain-vanilla insurance policy so that it meets all your needs.

Finding an insurance representative who you can trust and who will keep your business information confidential is key. Look for a concerned insurance representative who's interested in you and your business, who will be with you for the long run, and who will structure deductibles to suit your budget.

Almost every insurance company has a few specialists within your specific field. If in doubt, call one or two major insurance companies' public relations offices and ask them to give you the name of an all-star.

An advanced agent will certainly have the designation CLU after his or her name. This stands for Certified Life Underwriter and is the industry's most recognized designation of excellence. An even more advanced seal of approval, ChFC or Chartered Financial Consultant has been initiated in the field.

Evaluating Insurers

The general axiom of insurance is that the lower the premium, the higher the deductible, and vice versa. The difficulty lies in comparing apples with apples. Some firms have better track records in paying dividend and claims.

Their reputation in this matter can be difficult to evaluate, though important. This reputation generally is acquired through word-of-mouth within the community. Ask your peers, associates, or even the trade association in your state.

Do your homework and consider the following five questions when selecting an insurer:

1. *Does the insurer have knowledge about your industry?* You want an agent for the long haul, one who understands the issues unique to your industry. This is not the time for on-the-job training!

2. *Does the insurer offer all the coverages you need?* If you need specialized coverages, can the insurance company provide the endorsements or extra coverages at a reasonable cost, or can they work with another insurer to do so?

3. *What kind of service will the insurer provide?* Will the agency go beyond offering an 800-number to answer claim questions? And how often will an agent be in touch with you? Under normal circumstances, an agent should meet with you at least twice a year, and for more complex situations, monthly. Also important are loss-control services to help you reduce claims in the long run. Does the insurer offer fire-safety or employee-risk-reduction programs?

4. *Is the insurance priced competitively?* Does the insurer participate in any premium-reducing programs? Compare deductibles and premiums between the insurers you're considering and don't ignore other options, such as pooling your resources to purchase insurance with a group of other businesses.

5. *How would you rate the financial stability of the agency?* If you suspect that an agency could be bought out, don't select it. Factors to consider are the size of the agency, the owner's age, and whether there's a successor.

Deciding on the Deductible

The general rule is to take the highest deductible you can afford without overextending your cash flow. Research the average claim in your industry to get a ballpark figure of what to expect.

Buying first-dollar coverage against accidents that may never occur is not necessarily a good idea.

Accepting a moderate risk will result in a lower deductible and premium. Many insurers tend to charge disproportionately for low-level deductibles, so retain the amount of risk that you can afford. Setting deductibles too low means that your company simply pays the insurer to process more paper and pay for losses that actually may be routine. Find the limit that works for your business.

Tax Tips

Insurance premiums for fire, casualty, and burglary coverage on business property are all deductible for tax purposes as bona fide business expenses. If a business self-insures, payments into the self-insurance reserve would not be deductible for tax purposes, but actual losses incurred by the taxpayer would be.

Insurance premiums for life-insurance coverage as a fringe benefit are tax deductible. But premiums for a life-insurance policy covering the life of an officer or other key person are not deductible if the business is a direct or indirect beneficiary under the policy. Premiums paid on a life insurance policy where the business is a beneficiary are not deductible because life insurance proceeds would not have to be included in taxable income when received by the company.

Guidelines for Purchasing Insurance

The following list provides some basic guidelines for purchasers of insurance. In addition, Table 19.1 will help you identify the special needs of your business. Here are some points to keep in mind:

- Before speaking with an insurance representative, write down a clear statement of what your expectations are.

- Do not withhold important information from your insurance representative about your business and its exposure to loss.

- Get at least three competitive bids using brokers, direct agents, and independent agents. Note the interest that he or she takes in loss prevention and suggestions for specialty coverage.

- Avoid duplication and overlap in policies; don't pay for insurance you don't need.

TABLE 19.1   Choosing Small Business Insurance

Life Insurance	Health Insurance	Liability Insurance	Property Insurance	Special Coverage
Retail **Sole Proprietorship** Owner and all employees are covered under survivor-income and accidental death and dismemberment plans.	Owner, all employees, and dependents have medical, dental, and vision coverage.	Comprehensive general liability, automotive liability, product liability, and workers' compensation.	All-risks, replacement cost insurance.	Consequential losses have been added to the property insurance policy.
General Partnership **(Consulting Service)** Owner and all employees are covered under survivor-income and accidental death and dismemberment plans. Partners, in addition, are covered under a partnership insurance plan.	Owner, all employees, and dependents have medical, dental, and vision coverage.	Comprehensive general liability, automotive liability, product liability, and workers' compensation.	All-risks, replacement cost insurance.	Consequential losses, errors and omissions.
Food Service Business **Restaurant** Owner and all employees are covered under survivor-income and accidental death and dismemberment plans. Head cook is covered under key-employee insurance, as well.	Owner, all employees, and dependents have medical, dental, and vision coverage.	Comprehensive general liability, automotive liability, product liability, and workers' compensation.	All-risks, replacement cost insurance.	Consequential losses, business interruption, money and securities, glass, electronic equipment, power interruption, special liquor legal liability.
Manufacturing **Business Corporation** Owner and all employees are covered under survivor-income and accidental death and dismemberment plans.	Owner, all employees, and dependents have medical, dental, and vision coverage.	Comprehensive general liability, automotive liability, product liability, and worker's compensation.	All-risks, replacement cost insurance.	Consequential losses, business interruption, profit, transportation.

- Entire insurance packages for small businesses do exist in certain sectors. Ask for a BOP (business opportunity plan).
- Ask whether the insurance firm is an "admitted insurance company." If so, make sure it has a solvency fund should a catastrophe put the insurance company in danger of going under.
- Mutual employer trusts are another form of insurance. Though rates may be attractive, check the backing of funds and note the lack of legislation or guarantees in some arenas.
- Get your insurance coverage reassessed on an annual basis. As your firm grows, so do your needs and potential liabilities. Under-insurance is one of the major problems growing firms face. Get an independent appraiser to place a value on your property—if it's been more than five years since the previous appraisal, you might be surprised.
- Keep copies of your insurance policies and complete records of premiums paid, itemized losses, and loss recoveries. This information will help you get better coverage at lower costs in the future.

Insurance Losses

If your company has to report a loss, take these four steps:

1. *Notify your insurer in a timely fashion.* Virtually all policies require notification of an accident within 24, 48, or 72 hours of the incident. The claim itself does not necessarily have to be filed at this time, but the loss must be reported. Failure to do so may nullify your right to recovery.

2. *Have adequate proof of loss.* You will have a reasonable period to provide documentation, if necessary.

3. *Know how you'd like to be reimbursed.* The insurer usually has three options to fulfill the terms of a replacement policy: paying cash, repairing the insured item, or replacing the insured item with one of similar quality. Don't hesitate to let your insurer know what your preference is.

4. *Use arbitration if necessary.* Disputes regarding the amount of the settlement are put to arbitration, with an independent appraiser acting as judge in the conflict. If a compromise cannot be reached, then a lawsuit can be initiated.

CHAPTER 20

Tax Planning

To stay on good terms with Uncle Sam, small business owners need a crackerjack CPA and a basic understanding of the tax system. You don't need to know every detail in the tax code—that's your CPA's job—but you do need to know when to ask your CPA's advice so you can maximize deductions, tax credits, and savings, and adapt to changes in the federal and state tax codes.

TAXATION BASICS

Who's often hardest hit when taxes rise? Typically it's businesses and their employees. That's why you need to be savvy in your tax planning. By all means, pay your fair share but do everything possible to minimize your tax liabilities.

Taxes You Collect

As a business owner and employer, you're responsible for collecting various state and federal taxes and remitting them to the proper agencies. In addition, you're required to pay certain taxes yourself. When reading the following sections, remember that at the time this book went to press, all tax information reflected current law. But Congress passes tax legislation on a regular basis. Therefore,

check with your CPA before making any decisions that could affect your personal or business tax planning.

Employer Tax Identification Number

If you have one or more employees, you're required to withhold income tax and Social Security tax from each one's paycheck and remit these amounts to the appropriate agency. To do so, you need to obtain an employer tax number from the federal government using IRS Form SS-4, and if your state has an income tax, from the state as well. Call your local IRS office, which will send you a tax ID number along with charts to determine payroll tax deductions, quarterly and annual forms, W-4 forms, tax-deposit forms, and a manual on filling out forms. No advance fees or deposits are required.

Income Tax Withholding

The amount of "pay-as-you-go" taxes you must withhold from each employee's wages depends on the employee's wage level, the number of exemptions he or she claims on the withholding exemption certificate (Form W-4), marital status, and length of the payroll period. The percentage withheld is figured on a sliding basis, and IRS percentage tables are available for weekly, biweekly, monthly, semi-monthly, and other payroll periods.

Social Security (FICA) Tax

The Federal Insurance Contributions Act, or FICA, provides for a federal system of old-age, survivors, disability, and hospital insurance. The old-age, survivors, and disability insurance part is financed by the Social Security tax. The hospital insurance part is financed by the Medicare tax.

FICA requires employers to match and pay the same amount of Social Security tax as the employee does. Currently, the FICA tax for both employers and employees is 6.2 percent for wages up to $94,200 (in 2006), and 1.45 percent each from employer and employee for Medicare on all earnings.

Charts and instructions for Social Security deductions come with the IRS payroll forms. Congress has mandated requirements for depositing FICA and withholding taxes, and failure to comply with these regulations subjects a business to substantial penalties. Four different reports must be filed with the IRS regarding payroll taxes (both FICA and income taxes) that you withhold from your employees' wages:

1. Quarterly return of taxes withheld on wages (Form 941);

2. Annual statement of taxes withheld on wages (Form W-2);

3. Reconciliation of quarterly returns of taxes withheld with annual statement of taxes withheld (Form W-3);

4. Annual Federal Unemployment Tax return (Form 940).

In addition, employers who pay compensation of $600 or more to independent contractors must report the payments to the IRS by filing Form 1099MISC for Miscellaneous Income. Form 1099MISC is similar to the W-2 form employers give to employees. Businesses are required to send the Form 1099MISC to the contractor by January 31 of the year following the payment and must also transmit the information to the IRS by February 28 along with a summary sheet, Form 1096, Annual Summary and Transmittal of U.S. Information Returns.

State Payroll Taxes

Almost all states have payroll taxes of some kind that you must collect and remit to the appropriate agency. Most states have an unemployment tax that's paid entirely by the employer. The tax is figured as a percentage of your total payroll (up to a specified limit of annual wage per employee) and remitted at the end of each quarter. The actual percentage varies from state to state and by employer.

Some states impose an income tax that must be deducted from each employee's paycheck. As an employer, you have the responsibility of collecting this tax and remitting it to the state. A few states have a disability insurance tax that must be deducted from employees' pay; in some states, this tax may be split between employee and employer.

Most states have patterned their tax-collecting system after the federal government's. They issue employer numbers and similar forms and instruction booklets.

Independent Contractors

Hiring independent contractors requires filing an annual information return (Form 1099) to report payments totaling $600 or more made to any person for services performed in the course of trade or business during the calendar year. If this form is not filed, you could be subject to penalties. Be sure your records list the name, address, and Social Security or Employer Identification Number (EIN) of every independent contractor you hired, along with the dates they worked, the nature of their work, and how much they were paid.

Other than licensed real estate agents and insurance agents, only a few people who perform services for your business qualify as independent contractors. If the IRS feels an individual should have been treated as an employee, you'll be liable for payroll taxes that should have been withheld and paid, plus penalties and interest.

Some factors taken into account by the IRS to determine if an individual is an independent contractor include:

- Whether the person has his or her own business license
- Whether the person has cards, stationery, and a real business address

- Whether the person has a business bank account
- Whether the person sells services regularly to various clients/customers
- Whether the person has control over his or her schedule

Personal Income Tax

Operating as a sole proprietor or partner, you will not be paid a salary like an employee; therefore, no income tax will be withheld from money you draw from your business. Instead, you're required to estimate your tax liability each year and pay it in quarterly installments on Form 1040. Request the necessary forms and instructions for filing estimated tax returns from your local IRS office. When applying for the forms, also ask them to send the Tax Guide for Small Business (Publication 334).

At the end of the year, you must file an income tax return as an individual and compute your tax liability on the profits earned in your business for that year. Partnerships are required to file a partnership return (Form 1065). Each partner's share of the net income or expense of the partnership is reported to the partner on a Schedule K-1.

Corporate Income Tax

If your business is organized as a C corporation, you'll be paid a salary like other employees. Any profit the business makes will accrue to the corporation, not to you personally. At the end of the year, you must file a corporate income tax return. Corporate tax returns may be prepared on a calendar- or fiscal-year basis. If the tax liability of the business is calculated on a calendar year, the tax return must be filed with the IRS no later than March 15 each year; however, the corporation may file a request for extension of due date. Businesses that work within a fiscal year must file their returns by the fifteenth day of the third month following their year end.

Reporting income on a fiscal-year cycle is more convenient for most businesses because they can end their tax year in any month they choose. A corporation whose income is primarily derived from the personal services of its shareholders must use a calendar-year end for tax purposes. In addition, most Subchapter S corporations are required to use calendar-year ends.

Sales Taxes

Sales taxes are levied by many cities and states at varying rates. Most provide specific exemptions, as for certain classes of merchandise or particular groups of customers. Service businesses are often exempt altogether. Contact your state and/or local revenue offices for information on the law for your area so that you can adapt your bookkeeping to the requirements.

Levying taxes on all states would present no major difficulties, but since this is not the case, your business will have to identify tax-exempt sales from taxable sales. Then you can deduct tax-exempt sales from total sales when filing your sales tax returns each quarter. Remember, if you fail to collect taxes that should have been collected, you can be held liable for the full amount of uncollected tax, plus penalties and interest.

Advance Deposits

Some states may require an advance deposit on future taxes to be collected. In lieu of a deposit, some states will accept a surety bond for that amount from your insurance company. If you have a fair credit record, the bond is usually simple to obtain through your insurance agent. The cost varies according to the amount and the risk—5 percent is a rule of thumb, but 10 percent is not unusual for small dollar amounts.

If your state requires a deposit or bond, you can keep the amount down by estimating sales on the low side—a wise strategy, especially for new business owners who tend to be overly optimistic when it comes to estimating their business' sales.

TAXES ON PROPRIETORSHIPS, PARTNERSHIPS, AND CORPORATIONS

The first tax issue business owners face is the legal form of your business. You can be a sole proprietor, a general partner, or the head of your corporation. Your choice has a big impact on your tax liability, so make sure to get your CPA's advice first.

Sole Proprietorship Taxes

A sole proprietorship is a one-owner business, which has many or few employees. This form of organization is simple and requires no fancy legal work. You name your business in accordance with licensing laws, you apply for a federal EIN number if you have employees, and you're all set. A sole proprietor's income is included on his or her personal tax return.

Suppose a husband and wife file a joint return. The husband has his own business, while the wife works part-time for the government and makes $50,000 a year. The husband's gross income from his business was $100,000, and his business made $20,000 in profits after business expenses were deducted. His $20,000 profit is included on the individual return, along with his wife's $50,000. The business income is considered personal income for the sole proprietor, and there are no special business-income taxes other than self-employment taxes.

Partnerships and Taxes

A partnership is a business with two or more owners and, like a sole proprietorship, a partnership is not a taxable entity. For tax purposes, the income or loss from a partnership is considered the personal income of the individual general partners.

If Owner A and Owner B are in a partnership that makes $80,000, and they divide everything evenly, the $40,000 Owner A gets and the $40,000 Owner B gets are included on each individual return with whatever other income they have. Itemized deductions and credits are taken from that figure.

A partnership agreement must be well defined regarding capital investment, return, salaries, duties, responsibilities, losses, and so on. What if you're in a partnership with someone who isn't as reliable and hardworking as you are? Whatever mistakes your partner makes, you are also liable because of the rule known as "mutual agent." Mutual agent means that you are responsible for the actions of your partner because he or she is an agent for the partnership. If your partner does something that costs a lot of money or causes your business to suffer great losses, you will bear the consequences equally. The same is true if your partner does something that results in an additional tax liability for your company. You could sue your incompetent or unscrupulous partner, but that is a separate matter.

Taxes on Corporations

Most corporations determine their tax by using the following tax rate schedule:

- Up to $50,000: 15 percent
- $50,000 to $75,000: $7,500 plus 25 percent of the amount over $50,000
- $75,000 to $100,000: $13,750 plus 34 percent of the amount over $75,000
- $100,000 to $335,000: $22,250 plus 39 percent of the amount over $100,000
- $335,000 to $10 million: $113,900 plus 34 percent of the amount over $335,000
- $10 million to $15 million: $3.4 million plus 35 percent of the amount over $10 million
- $15 million to $18,333,333: $5.15 million plus 38 percent of the amount over $15 million
- $18,333,333 and above: 35 percent

Your corporation may be subject to several other taxes, such as the personal-holding-company tax or the accumulated-earnings tax. An additional tax of 39.6 percent is applied to undistributed personal-holding-company income. Ask your CPA if any special taxes apply to your corporation.

A corporation's income is taxable and any distribution of income to individual stockholders, known as dividends, is taxable a second time as ordinary dividend income. If General Motors earns $1, it will in theory pay 34 cents in federal tax, and the remaining 66 cents will be distributed as dividends. If you're a stockholder, you pick up that 66 cents as dividends-and-interest income on Schedule B of your 1040 and pay tax accordingly. Dividends received from qualified U.S. corporations are taxed at the 15 percent tax rate.

Subchapter S Corporations Taxes

The disadvantage of double taxation is effectively eliminated if you file a Subchapter S election with the IRS. The qualifications for electing Subchapter S status were amended in 1982 when the Subchapter S Revision Act liberalized many of the old rules. The new flexibility of these corporations makes them popular with small and medium-sized businesses. Subchapter S allows profits or losses to flow directly through the corporation to you and other shareholders. If you earn other income during the first year and the corporation has a loss, you can deduct the loss against the other income, thereby reducing or completely eliminating your tax liability.

To qualify under Subchapter S, the corporation must be a domestic corporation, must not have more than 100 shareholders, must have only individuals or estates as shareholders, and must not have a nonresident alien as a shareholder. Under current law, an unlimited amount of passive income from rents, royalties, and interest is now allowed. When profits exceed 25 percent of the gross receipts, Subchapter S corporations may be taxed on passive income, according to Section 1375(a) of the Internal Revenue Code (IRC). Pension restrictions have been eased.

Call the IRS at 800 829-3676 for the appropriate forms to select for your business entity or download them from the IRS web site at www.irs.ustreas. gov/prod/forms_pubs/index.html.

The Fiscal Year

A corporation may elect any day of the year as its year end. Why is this so important for tax-planning purposes? Many people begin their small business operating as a sole proprietorship or partnership and later choose to incorporate. They gain some flexibility in reporting the income of the business by having a corporate year different from the calendar year, which ends on December 31.

There are two restrictions on the year end a corporation may choose:

1. If a corporation derives most of its income from the personal services of its shareholders/employees, it must use a calendar year end. This applies to accounting firms, legal practices, insurance agencies, and so on.

2. A Subchapter S corporation must generally use the same year end as its shareholders, which, if they are individuals, will be the calendar year end. As an alternative, the Subchapter S corporation can show a business purpose for a different year end if the IRS approves.

Tax Planning for Corporations

It's not unusual for a new company to lose money in the first year or two. This is why it might make sense to set up a Subchapter S when your corporation is first formed. The corporation's losses appear on your tax return to the extent of your investment in the corporation and any loans you made to it. If the business becomes profitable and you and your accountant feel you should switch to the conventional C corporation form, the conversion is simple. The only catch is that once you switch from Subchapter S to C corporation, it's usually disallowed to switch back again.

There are other techniques for reducing your tax liability if your small business is incorporated. You may set up a fiscal year that's different from the calendar year by which individuals are typically taxed. You may accrue or defer income between the corporation and yourself so that you can consistently stay in the lower tax bracket. You can also zero out the company's income by making sure the corporation doesn't have any income outstanding at the end of the year.

How can you achieve this? Pay salaries that will absorb whatever profits there are in the company. There's a limit to how much of this you can do, and in most states, you have to document this process with appropriate resolutions and director meetings. But for most small companies not making a tremendous amount of money, it makes sense to pay income out of the corporation in the form of salary. There may come a time when you'll want to take advantage of a lower tax break by splitting income between corporate and individual, especially if you're reinvesting the money for expansion purposes. Employing such a strategy requires advice from your CPA and attorney.

Other items that may be deducted from a corporation's tax bill include group life insurance that is purchased on the lives of major employees or medical plans for all personnel and their families. Perhaps the most significant benefit in this area is the deduction for contributions to pension or profit-sharing plans, along with the costs for setting up and administering those plans.

Business veterans know that there are many reasons to form a corporation aside from tax savings. One is that a corporation limits the legal, personal liability of its principal shareholders. Suppose you've invested $100,000 to start a business that you incorporate. Should your company get sued or suffer irreversible losses, the liability extends only to the assets of the company with one big caveat. If you've assigned no other personal assets as collateral for loans, your home and other personal assets and investments would be protected from any litigation against the corporation. That's not true of a sole proprietorship or a partnership, in which your liability extends to everything you own.

In some instances, even though you form a corporation, you cannot assume that your personal assets will always be protected. Often, a lawsuit or losses come up in connection with fraud or product liability. If this occurs, lawyers will sometimes sue you as an individual and claim that there was some irregularity in the way you maintained the company. Thus they "pierce the corporate shield" and go after you personally. To avoid this problem, keep detailed corporate minutes and records, keep personal assets separate from corporate assets, be certain your corporation is sufficiently capitalized, and have adequate insurance to protect your assets.

STANDARD BUSINESS DEDUCTIONS

One of the big advantages of owning a business is that your costs of doing business are deductible to the full extent of the law. Your CPA can help you figure out which costs fall into this category.

General and Administrative Expenses

Deductible general and administrative (G&A) expenses include telephone, utilities, office rent, salaries, legal and accounting expenses, professional services, dues, and subscriptions to business publications.

If you work out of your home, investigate whether a home-office deduction makes sense for you. Remember that you can only claim this deduction if your home office is your principal place of business and that office is used for no other purposes other than your business. If you have another office somewhere else, you may not be able to deduct the cost of a home office as well. You can deduct business-related telephone charges made from your home number, as well as business equipment and supplies, but you will not be able to deduct any part of your rent or depreciate any part of the property as a business expense.

Home-office expenses that are eligible for deduction include all normal office expenses plus interest, taxes, insurance, and depreciation on the portion of your home used exclusively for business. Allocation of home-office expenses is generally made on the basis of the ratio of square footage used exclusively for business to total square footage of the residence.

If the business didn't make enough money to absorb the home-office deduction, you can deduct the excess from income earned on a 9-to-5 job, if you still have one, or from your spouse's income, if you file a joint return. However, there is a limit to what you may deduct. All your home-office expenses are deductible if they are less than your gross income from the business use of your home. If they're greater, you can carry them over to the following year.

Automobile Expenses

Business-related automobile mileage is deductible at the rate of 44.5 cents a mile in 2006. To calculate the deductions you could make based on straight mileage is very simple. Suppose you drive a car 20,000 miles a year. Of those, 12,000 were for business purposes. Your deduction would be 44.5 cents x 12,000 miles, or $5,340.

What constitutes a business mile? The distance you drive from your home to your place of business is not deductible, but mileage you drive from your place of business to any other location for business purposes is. Meeting with a prospective client or doing something to promote your business is considered business mileage. Just make sure to keep a log of your business-related travel for tax purposes; at the end of each day enter the miles you drove on your appointment calendar.

There's another method for deducting the cost of driving using actual operating expenses. Typical deductions include gasoline, maintenance, insurance, and depreciation. For example, assume that your depreciation deduction is $2,800. Add to this the following expenses for operating your car: insurance, $400; maintenance, $500; gasoline, $1,600. You have $5,300 in deductions. Take this number and multiply it by the fraction of business miles over total miles driven: 12,000 business miles divided by 20,000 total miles, or 60 percent business mileage. Sixty percent of $5,300 is $3,180. If you elect the second method, then, you get a deduction of $3,180 for the same mileage versus the $5,340 for straight-mileage calculation.

If you use this second method, you must stick with it for the life of the car you use for business. If you sell the car for a profit, you have to take the depreciation off its cost to determine its tax basis. If you sell it for more than its base, you'll have a gain that's taxable at your regular income tax rate.

Generally, straight mileage is best if you're driving an older car many miles. If you're driving a fairly new car with a fairly high cost, the operating expenses/depreciation method might result in higher deductions. Ask your CPA to help you figure out which method makes most sense for you.

Entertainment and Travel

If you entertain clients to promote your business, maintain a log for deductible entertainment, travel, and related expenses. Use a standard appointment calendar to write in whom you were entertaining, the nature of the business, where you were, and how much you spent. Contrary to popular belief, you do not need receipts for entertainment expenditures under $75, but you must maintain a log. In certain instances you can even claim business-related entertainment at home—as a precaution, have clients or prospects sign a guest log. If you prepare a meal or serve drinks, your expenses are deductible as part of the cost of doing business.

Currently, only 50 percent of entertainment expenses are deductible. The remaining 50 percent are not deductible, even if your business is incorporated. For entertainment expenses, these five elements must be recorded:

1. The amount of expenditure

2. The date of expenditure

3. The location and type of entertainment

4. The reason for entertainment and the nature of the business discussion that took place

5. The occupation of the person being entertained

A deduction is not permitted for travel, food, and lodging expenses incurred in connection with attending a conference, convention, or seminar related to investment activities such as real estate investment or stock investments. However, the cost of the actual seminar is still deductible.

Travel deductions include the cost of air, bus, and auto transportation; hotels; meals; and incidentals including dry cleaning, tips, and taxis. However, you must stay overnight to claim travel-incidentals deductions.

Things you do to increase your expertise in your field of business are tax deductible. While deductions are allowed for convention expenses, rules limit the amount that can be deducted for attending conventions in foreign countries. Also, there are limits on the deductibility of conventions held on cruise ships. The cost of getting to and from the convention and the cost of your stay are deductible, but if you stay three days after the convention ends, those expenses are not deductible. Deductions for your spouse are not allowed unless he or she is active in the business.

RECORD KEEPING FOR TAX PURPOSES

If you fail to keep the necessary records, you risk losing deductions and credits that can minimize your tax bill. Although your time may be consumed by setting up shop, getting new clients, and making sales, you also need to focus on setting up a proper accounting system. The biggest benefit is that it will help your business be more profitable in the long run.

Payroll Records

It's essential to keep accurate employee compensation records. Be particularly vigilant about your payroll tax returns. Information you need in this area is contained in the IRS's *Employer's Tax Guide*. The guide also has a tax calendar showing exactly when various forms are due. The paperwork can be annoying and time-consuming, but do not ignore it.

With respect to Social Security (FICA), federal unemployment insurance (FUTA), state unemployment insurance, federal withholding, state withholding, and state disability taxes, you're responsible for collecting and withholding from employee paychecks all relevant amounts, contributing whatever the employer's portion may be, and depositing those amounts monthly with the appropriate agency. You must also file quarterly state and federal tax returns. If you file late, penalties and interest may be assessed.

Whatever financial pressures may be upon you, don't ever get behind on payroll taxes. If you do and wind up shuttering your business, you'll owe that money until it's paid to the appropriate government agencies. Remember that it never belonged to you, and that until you remit it, interest and penalties continue to accrue.

DEPRECIATION

Depreciation is defined as the decrease in value of property over the time that the property is being used. Wear and tear, age, deterioration, and obsolescence are a few of the reasons why property depreciates in value. By taking a deduction for depreciation on your tax return, you can recover the cost of certain property or equipment you use in your business or for the production of income.

If you buy a piece of equipment, depreciation of its original cost should be included as an expense on your monthly operating statement. If you lease a piece of equipment, the monthly lease payment is part of your monthly operating expenses (cash-value depreciation is frequently figured into the cost of an equipment lease and need not be figured separately by you).

Many equipment-leasing agreements have a clause providing for what is known as a "depreciation reserve." This consists of setting aside money commensurate with the declining value of the vehicle. When the lease is up, the equipment is sold to either the lessee or another third party. If it goes for a price over and above its depreciated value, the difference can be refunded to the lessee. If, however, the equipment is sold for a price under its depreciated value, the lessee must pay the difference to the lessor. This is where the depreciation reserve comes in handy.

Straight-line or uniform depreciation is the most frequently used method of depreciating new equipment for financial statements. In straight-line depreciation, the equipment loses an equal part of its total value every year of its life. For your tax return, though, your accountant will most often use a tax-approved depreciation that gives you the largest deduction on your tax return and goes farther in minimizing your taxes.

Suppose you buy a $15,000 piece of equipment with a ten-year useful life, according to your accountant's schedule. The straight-line depreciation rate is calculated by dividing its ten years of useful life into the $15,000, or $1,500 a year. If you're in the 28 percent tax bracket, $1,500 in depreciation will save you $420 in taxes. Suppose you only need 20 percent down to buy a $15,000 machine. Suppose, too, that you financed your equipment on the installment plan. The interest you pay on any amount owed is going to be another deduction for you. So if you have a $12,000 loan that costs $1,200 in interest, you'll wind up with another $336 (in the 28 percent bracket) in savings.

Keep in mind that many states have different sets of rules than those used on your federal income tax return for allowable depreciation methods on state tax returns.

You can learn the rules for depreciation of assets used in your trade and business by ordering Publication 946, *How to Depreciate Property*, from your local IRS office, or by downloading it at www.irs.gov.

Section 179 Expense Election

Section 179 of the Internal Revenue Code (IRC) allows you to deduct all or part of the cost of certain qualifying property in the year you place it in service. You can do this instead of recovering the cost by taking depreciation deductions over a specified recovery period. However, there are limits on the amount you can deduct in any given year.

Under current federal tax laws in 2006, you can write off $108,000 of business-related equipment purchased for use in your business that qualifies for Section 179. If a piece of equipment costs more than $108,000, the additional amount can be depreciated over a five- to seven-year life as provided by the IRS tax code. Keep in mind that sport utility vehicles are limited to a maximum deduction of $25,000 per vehicle.

A qualified enterprise-zone business may be able to claim an increased Section 179 deduction, but it cannot be more than the cost of the property placed in service that year.

Real Estate

If you're depreciating real estate used in your business or held for investment, the time period over which it's depreciated depends on whether it's residential or commercial property. While both use the straight-line method, residential real property is depreciated over 27.5 years, while commercial real property is depreciated over 31.5 years.

Personal Property Used in Business

Remember that personal use of business property isn't deductible. If you spend $2,000 on a computer that will be used 80 percent of the time for free-lance word processing, you can probably deduct $1,600 on Schedule C of your tax return, where business income is reported. To keep the record straight, maintain a handwritten or computer-generated log that documents your use of the computer.

For the final word on what is and what isn't deductible, consult with your CPA.

PENSION AND RETIREMENT PLANS

One of the most important ways your business can take care of you is by having a qualified retirement plan. Generally speaking, these plans meet IRS requirements for tax-favored treatment, which often makes today's dollars worth more tomorrow.

There are four major advantages of qualified retirement plans.

1. Employer contributions are tax deductible for the company.

2. Employee's income tax liabilities are postponed until funds are distributed from the plan.

3. Income realized on invested retirement funds accumulates tax-free until distribution.

4. Distribution of funds at retirement is usually on a tax-favored basis.

Individual Retirement Accounts

One type of retirement plan that's available to all people who earn current income is the Individual Retirement Account (IRA). An IRA is an investment for your retirement with two tax benefits, one immediate and one long-term. First, your contribution to a regular (not Roth) IRA

is tax deductible, subject to certain limitations if you're covered by other retirement plans. It's deducted from your gross income, thereby lowering your net taxable income. Second, the interest or dividends earned on your IRA investment grow on a tax-deferred basis. You pay federal taxes on you IRA investment earnings only when you withdraw the money.

When you consider that most people's tax brackets drop appreciably at retirement, you understand the benefits of an investment that accumulates compounded, untaxed interest over the years, and then is taxed at the rate for the lower retirement tax bracket. All in all, an IRA is a great way to build a retirement nest egg.

A taxpayer with earned income can now make a fully deductible contribution to an IRA if his or her adjusted gross income (AGI) is less than $30,000 per year for a single person or is less than $50,000 on a joint return (AGI on a joint return includes income earned by the spouse).

You can open an IRA at any point before age 70, and you may begin to withdraw your savings at age 59. But you must begin to withdraw by age 70½ or face stiff penalties. If you're married, filing jointly, and only one of you earns income from a job, you can open a second IRA (called a "spousal IRA") to cover the non-wage-earning partner. The maximum contribution in 2006 for the two IRAs is $8,000—that's $4,000 allowed the wage-earning spouse plus an additional $4,000 for the non-working spouse. If both of you are employed, you may each contribute up to $4,000 to an IRA every year and deduct $8,000 from your combined gross income at tax time. If you are more than fifty years of age, you are allowed a "catch-up" contribution of an additional $1,000 per taxpayer in 2006.

Your contributions to an IRA don't have to be regular. If money is tight, you can skip a year, or contribute less than $4,000. With many investments, you have the option of monthly contributions if contributing the $4,000 in a lump sum is a hardship. If you happen to contribute more than the maximum allowed, the IRA would fine you a percentage of the amount you contribute over its limit and also assess taxes on that amount.

The Roth IRA is a relatively new kind of IRA designed for low- to middle-income taxpayers. The rules that apply to traditional IRAs generally apply to Roth IRAs except that contributions are not deductible. But the advantage is that qualified distributions are not taxable. Your CPA can help you figure out which type of IRA makes the most sense for you.

If you face a financial emergency, there are certain circumstances in which you may tap your IRA funds. The IRS typically levies a 10-percent penalty on the amount you withdraw prematurely from your IRA, and you're also liable for the taxes on that money. If you're more than age 59, the IRS does not charge the 10 percent penalty. Some investments, however, charge fees for early withdrawal of IRA funds. Be sure to read the fine print on your depositor or shareholder agreement.

In an emergency, another approach is to exercise the IRA's rollover option and use that money without penalty for 60 days. With a rollover, you receive a check made out to you for the amount of your investment to date. You have 60 days to reinvest that money somewhere else before the IRS penalizes you 10 percent in addition to assessing taxes due on that money. A rollover may be exercised only once a year, but there are times when it may be a useful option.

You can open an IRA at a bank, savings and loan institution, federal credit union, mutual fund company, brokerage firm or insurance company, choosing among bank certificates or accounts, mutual funds, stocks, bonds, annuities or any number of different investments. There's no limit on the number of IRAs you can open or the combination of investments, as long as you do not exceed the maximum annual allowable contribution.

A prudent choice for an IRA are investments held for the long term, with a reasonable amount of stability, and most important, ones you're comfortable with. An option worth considering is a mutual fund that invests in a mix of stocks and bonds, a diverse, so-called "growth-income fund" that provides a buffer against the swings of inflation and the market.

You can switch your IRA investment to another type of investment if you're not happy with its performance. Simply request a transfer form from the sponsoring institution of the new investment you have chosen, and notify the custodian (usually a bank or trust company) of your present IRA investment. You may transfer your IRA between investments as often as you wish. The difference

between this type of transfer and the rollover is that with a transfer you never actually receive a check for the amount of your IRA investments. The IRA simply changes custodians.

Fees for maintaining your IRA can range up to $35 annually. Brokerage firms often charge an additional fee (up to $30) to open an IRA. Some mutual funds charge an up-front fee (or "load") to invest in their fund, and banks often charge a withdrawal penalty on CDs cashed in early. These fees and penalties can take a bite out of your investment, so be sure to read the fine print in your agreement.

SEP Plans

Simplified Employee Pension (SEP) plans allow employers to make contributions of up to $44,000 or 25 percent of compensation to employee's IRAs. Not only are these contributions tax deductible to both the employer and the employees—employees can make an additional deductible contribution to their own IRAs. An added bonus is that there are no minimum annual contribution requirements, which gives business owners flexibility when their income fluctuates.

Keogh Plans

Keogh plans are for owners of unincorporated businesses. There are two types of Keogh plans: defined contribution plans and defined benefit plans. Contributions may be made either on a profit-sharing or money-purchase (the same dollar amount every year) basis.

The maximum contribution to a defined benefit Keogh plan is $35,000, or 25 percent of annual compensation, whatever is less. If you adopt a defined-benefit Keogh plan, the maximum contribution is the lesser of $135,000 or 100 percent of the average of your three highest years of compensation. Your earned income from which you may make and deduct a Keogh plan contribution does not include investment income or salary received as an employee. Directors' fees are considered self-employment income from which you can make Keogh plan contributions.

The most common way to contribute to a Keogh plan is on a profit-sharing basis. This type of plan permits you to determine the amount of contribution you make each year based on the profits of your business as shown on your tax return prior to deducting the Keogh plan contribution. While you're limited in the amount you may contribute, you're not required to contribute to these plans in years when the business does not show a profit.

Keoghs that are defined-benefit plans require an actuary to calculate the amount of contribution needed to yield a desired amount of savings at the time of retirement. The actuary bases this amount on the participant's remaining years until retirement and the expected earning of the contributions. This type of plan is usually the most expensive to administer due to the additional cost of the actuary.

While a Keogh must be established by December 31, you need not make the actual cash contribution until the due date of your tax return. Many stockbrokers, insurance companies and some banks offer Keogh plans for nominal set-up charges and modest annual administration fees. The earnings of the Keogh plan also grow tax-free until withdrawn by the participants.

Generally, Keoghs must cover all employees who are at least 21 years old and who have one year of service with the employer. You can usually exclude part-time employees from your plan. Benefits of the plan must be nondiscriminatory.

Plans that benefit owners to a much greater extent than they do employees are deemed to be "top-heavy" by the IRS and must be avoided. Review your plan with a retirement planning expert to make certain it meets all the requirements.

SIMPLE Plans

Another option is the Savings Incentive Match Plan for Employees, or the SIMPLE plan, which was created under the Small Business Jobs Protection Act in 1996. Under the plan, which is relatively inexpensive to set up and easy to administer, a business owner and the employees can save up to $10,000 in 2006.

A big benefit of SIMPLE plans for small companies is that nondiscrimination rules (assuring that a certain percentage of lower-paid employees can participate in the plan) don't apply.

SIMPLE plans allow a "catch-up" contribution for participants more than fifty years of age of $2,500 in addition to the above limits.

Solo 401(k) Plans

The Solo 401(k) Plan is available to self-employed individuals or business owners with no employees other than a spouse. Sole proprietorships, partnerships, and corporations qualify. Provisions for these plans allow a small business owner to deduct $44,000 a year in 2006. Additionally, a $5,000 "catch-up" contribution is allowed for owners who are fifty years of age or older by the end of the tax year. The Solo 401(k) plan is easy to set up and inexpensive to maintain—administration is minimal.

The Small Business Employer Start-up Credit

Small business employers who adopt a new qualified defined benefit or defined contribution plan may claim a non-refundable credit. This credit is equal to 50 percent of any administrative or retirement-related education expenses incurred for the plan for each of the first three plan years. The maximum credit allowed is $500 per year. This credit is allowed only to employers who employ less than 100 employees in the preceding year.

Corporate Pension Plans

Corporate pension plans are like Keogh plans. Contribution need not be made until the due date of your corporate tax return, the plans may be defined contribution or defined benefit, and contributions may be made on a profit-sharing or money-purchase basis. The same maximum contribution rules that govern Keogh plans apply to corporate plans.

Plans may be designed so that they are integrated with benefits employees will receive from Social Security, ensuring that higher-paid or key employees receive greater benefits than others. However, plans must comply with all the rules governing top-heavy plans.

Other types of plans available to corporations include Employee Stock Ownership Plans (ESOPs), in which the contributions are the employer corporation's stock, and Section 401 (k) plans, in which an employee may elect to defer up to $15,000 of his or her earnings per year tax-free in 2006. With a 401(k) plan, the employee generally has the option to direct the type of investment in which the deferred amount is placed. The "catch-up" provisions for employees more than fifty years of age also apply to 401(k) plans, with an additional contribution of $5,000 allowed in 2006. A 401(k) plan can now include a qualified Roth contribution program, which allows participants to elect to have all or part of their deferrals treated as contributions to a Roth IRA.

When choosing a pension-services administrator, make sure the institution is capable of designing a plan to meet the financial needs of both you and your business. If the institution's investment choices are limited, it may structure a plan to accommodate only those investment vehicles it has to offer.

Choosing the Plan

Which type of plan is right for your business? Your CPA can help you decide. There are myriad options to choose from when structuring a plan and different costs associated with those choices. Make sure you get the best and most thorough advice you can before making any final decision on setting up a retirement plan for your business.

A fee-only financial planner can help you choose investments that you're comfortable with. These planners are objective, are typically paid by the hour and have nothing to sell you. Take advantage of their expertise. Software like Quicken Financial Planner is also helpful.

TAX PLANNING

The cardinal rule of business is to always pay Uncle Sam. If you don't, you risk being liable for penalties and interest, which can amount to exorbitant sums over time. If you haven't paid sufficient amounts of estimated income tax, you may be able to avoid or reduce penalties for underpayment by increasing the amounts withheld from paychecks remaining in the present year. All withheld income tax is treated as if spread equally over the calendar year, even if a disproportionately large amount is withheld in December.

Accounting Methods

Without incurring any additional expense, you can save taxes by your choice of accounting method. In cash-basis accounting, you report the income in the year you receive payment or have an unrestricted right to it. Generally, you can deduct an expense in the year you pay it. If you send payment on December 31, 2006, the expense is deductible in 2006 even though your payment won't be received until 2007.

In accrual basis accounting, it doesn't matter when you receive or make actual payment. Income is reported when you bill. Expenses are deductible when you are billed, not when you pay. This accounting method has more tax benefits for a company with few receivables and large amounts of current liabilities. Advance payments to an accrual-basis taxpayer are generally held to be taxable income in the year received.

Equipment Purchases

Due primarily to tax incentives, the yearend is the time to consider buying business equipment. Under Section 179 of the IRC, the $108,000 deduction is not prorated for the period of the year that you hold and use the equipment. Consequently, you will get the same deduction whether you buy and put into service the equipment at the beginning or the end of the year. You can only take this deduction for tangible property used in your business—not real estate or automobiles.

Inventory Valuation

You don't automatically get a deduction for purchasing inventory for your business. You must reduce the amount paid for inventory by the value of the inventory at the end of the year. For example, if you paid $10,000 for merchandise in one year and your inventory at the end of the year was $7,000, you could only deduct $3,000 for purchases in the year, even though you paid $10,000.

How you determine a value for your inventory has tax implications. The FIFO (first in, first out) method assumes the items you purchased or produced first are the first items you sold or consumed. The items in inventory at the end of the tax year are matched with the costs of similar items that you most recently purchased or produced. The LIFO (last in, first out) method assumes the items of inventory you purchased or produced last are the first items you sold or consumed. Items included in closing inventory are considered to be from the opening inventory in the order of acquisition and from those acquired during the tax year.

Each method produces different income results, depending on current price levels. In times of inflation,

LIFO produces a larger cost of goods sold and a lower closing inventory. With FIFO, the cost of goods sold will be lower, and the closing inventory will be higher. In deflationary times, the opposite is true.

The rules for using the LIFO method are complex. Once you adopt it, IRS approval is required to return to FIFO. Since the value of your inventory is a major factor in determining your taxable income, get your CPA's help so you use the method that works for your business.

Employing Family Members

Employing your spouse or children in your business has tax advantages, especially if your business is not a corporation.

If you're self-employed and pay wages to your spouse, or to a son or daughter under age 21, these wages are not subject to Social Security taxes and federal unemployment taxes. Wages paid to your children are taxable to them at their tax bracket, which is normally lower than yours. As long as their wages are reasonable and for actual services rendered, you can deduct their wages as a business expense.

If your children are under age 18 and have unearned income (income not derived through the child's employment), that unearned income will be taxed at your rate. Unearned income includes interest and dividends, and must exceed $1,700.

Postponing Taxes on Compensation

If you're employed by someone else and expect to receive a year-end bonus or other additional compensation, you may want to defer it until the next year, especially if you expect to be in a lower tax bracket. This is often the case with a first-time entrepreneur who has quit his or her job and doesn't have a steady income during the time needed for their new business to break even. If your employer uses the accrual method of accounting, the bonus should still be deductible in the current year, provided it is fixed by yearend and paid shortly thereafter.

As to compensation for future services, you may want to negotiate an agreement with your employer whereby part of your earnings will be deferred and paid either in one or several future years. Since the employer has the use of the funds during the deferral period, an interest factor may be added. If certain requirements are met, deferred compensation will generally not be taxed to you or be able to be deducted by your employer until it's actually paid.

Tax-Postponed Investment Income

Waiting to report taxable income is almost always advantageous since it enables you to defer taxes and use those funds for an additional period of time. However, you must make sure the funds are available for paying taxes when needed and evaluate whether deferring payment has implications on your future tax liabilities.

The following are widely-used methods for postponing investment income:

- *Treasury bills and bank certificates.* Businesses and individuals who invest in short-term securities can shift interest income into the next year by buying Treasury bills or certain bank certificates of deposit that mature in that next year.
- *Savings bonds.* U.S. savings bond holders can elect to postpone taxes on the interest until the bonds are cashed in, which may be 30 years or more if the Treasury continues to extend maturities as it has in the past. Another option for reducing or eliminating bonds' income tax is to give the bonds to minor children in low tax brackets and have them report the interest currently. If you have untaxed savings-bond interest that's accumulated for many years, you can continue postponing taxes if you exchange the bonds for Series HH bonds, which pay interest semiannually.
- *Deferred annuities.* Taxes can be postponed on earnings from capital put aside for long-range goals by purchasing a deferred annuity. Annuities are arranged by contract with an insurance company. While there is no tax deduction for the amount contributed, all interest earned and compounded is tax-free until withdrawn, which may be as late as age seventy for some plans. Deferred annuity purchases may be made in installments or with a single payment. Early withdrawals are deemed taxable to the extent the cash value of the contract exceeds the investment in the contract. Only after any excess has been withdrawn as taxable income is it possible to receive nontaxable early withdrawals of principal.

Distributing Expenses and Profits

If you start a business this year and incur expenses but your business does not become active, can you write off your expenses? The answer is both yes and no. If the expenses are related to the organization of the business, you must capitalize and amortize those expenses as you would other assets over a five-year period. If, for example, you spend $2,000 to incorporate your business, that expense is not deductible as a single legal fee in the first year of business. It is considered a start-up cost and is amortized over a five-year period. You'd thus take a $400 deduction this year.

Even if you don't actively engage in business your first year, many items are considered write-offs, provided you're in business the next fiscal year. However, you must carefully document your write-offs as well as be judicious in your approach to them. Some things you might do are to get the fictitious-name statement, open a business bank account, and make business-related disbursements out of that account.

Showing a new business with deductions but no income can raise a red flag for IRS auditors. The IRS could attempt to disallow your loss deduction using the "hobby loss" rules that limit deductions if your business does not make a profit in three out of every five years of business. To avoid this label, you must show that you've started your business with the intent to make a profit and not just to reduce your taxes. You can overcome the "hobby loss" presumption by having a business license, business cards and letterhead, a bank account, an office, sales literature, a business phone and advertising.

Partnerships have special concerns in the area of expenses and profits. If two people form a partnership, losses may be allocated in any manner agreed upon between the partners, subject to restrictions and rules in the tax code. If Partner A does not have a tax problem and Partner B does, and if the partnership is going to lose money that year, Partner B can take the entire loss for tax purposes. That doesn't mean Partner B has to pay all the money—just that he or she could take the entire loss.

Whether or not such an arrangement is successful for tax purposes requires the services of an expert tax attorney or CPA to structure your partnership agreement so that it successfully allocates all the partnership losses to one partner.

Partnership agreements also have to address how income is going to be distributed. Suppose Partner A puts up $100,000 but is not going to be active in managing the business. Partner B is going to do all the work. Do they split profits evenly? Suppose Partner A claims that if it weren't for him the business wouldn't be going at all and that he should get a bigger share than Partner B. Partnerships can raise some pretty complex and thorny issues.

Tax Adjustments

If the IRS wants to look at one of your tax returns, it must do so within three years of your filing that return. Allegations of fraud are an exception to this rule. In such cases (e.g., deductions claimed with the intent to defraud the government out of tax revenues, or unreported income), the IRS may look at tax returns that have been filed at any time. Assuming, however, that you're keeping accurate records and tracking your tax credits and liability, the IRS has three years to look at your records.

The statute of limitations for assessment of taxes starts from the date you file your tax return. If you fail to file your tax return, the statute does not start to run. If you omit from gross income an amount in excess of 25 percent of the gross income reported on your return, the statute of limitations for an audit and assessment is six years from the date the return was filed or accepted.

Conversely, this means you have three years to straighten out tax matters as they arise. If you discover something that results in a change in your taxable income in any of three previous years, you may file a one-page amended return form, known as a 1040X, and indicate whatever changes there are on the amended return. It may mean you'll be paying more taxes. On the other hand, if you had business deductions you didn't take, you can file an amended return and claim a refund—plus interest.

Tax Advisors

Most small business owners should see a CPA twice a year: once when getting ready to prepare their tax returns and again at midyear to do tax planning for the rest of the year. Additionally, many business veterans believe that a CPA should prepare quarterly financial statements, which are handy for preparing a business tax return or applying for a bank loan.

CHAPTER 21

Pricing

Pricing often presents a quandary to small business owners because there are no hard-and-fast rules as to what to charge for a product or service. Do you charge a percentage above costs? The same price as your competitors? Whatever the market will bear? Since pricing is such an important component of your marketing, take time to research and strategically determine the appropriate price for your product or service in your market.

Costs and profit are two components of price. What your competition is charging and how your customers perceive your price are two other elements that bear serious consideration.

This chapter is designed to familiarize you with the various fundamentals involved in pricing and the methods for determining price. Keep in mind, though, that pricing is subjective. What works for one company may not be the answer for another. You've got to figure out what's best for your business.

PRICING GUIDELINES

Whether your company sells a product or provides a service, the price you charge your customers or clients will have a direct effect on the success of your business. Though pricing strategies can be complex, the basic rules of pricing are straightforward:

- All prices must cover costs and profits
- The most effective way to lower prices is to lower costs
- Review prices frequently to assure that they reflect the dynamics of cost, market demand, response to the competition, and profit objectives
- Prices must be established to assure sales

The Relationship Between Prices and Costs

Before setting a price for your product or service, you have to know the costs of running your business. If the price for your product or service doesn't cover costs, your cash flow will be cumulatively negative, you'll exhaust your financial resources, and your business will ultimately fail.

To determine how much it costs to run your business, include property and/or equipment leases, loan repayments, inventory, utilities, financing costs, and salaries/wages/commissions. Don't forget to add the costs of markdowns, shortages, damaged merchandise, employee discounts, cost of goods sold, and desired profits to your list of operating expenses.

Most important is to add profit in your calculation of costs. Treat profit as a fixed cost, like a loan payment or payroll, since none of us is in business to break even.

Pricing and Re-pricing Considerations

Because pricing decisions require time and market research, the strategy of many business owners is to set prices once and "hope for the best." However, such a policy risks profits that are elusive or not as high as they could be. When is the right time to review your prices? Do so if:

- You introduce a new product or product line
- Your costs change
- You decide to enter a new market
- Your competitors change their prices
- The economy experiences either inflation or recession
- Your sales strategy changes
- Your customers are making more money because of your product or service

Your creativity in merchandising, flair for the inventive, product selection, and management style are other factors in how the market perceives your product or service vis-à-vis those of your competitors. Keep tabs on your marketing activities to see how they relate to your overall costs and final prices. If costs outweigh the benefits, revise your marketing strategy to lower your costs.

PRICE, QUANTITY, AND THE THEORY OF DEMAND

What's the relationship between the price you set for your product or service and the quantity of goods you can sell at that price? A cardinal rule of economic theory is that the higher the price, the lower the customer demand will be for that product at that price. Business people refer to this rule, pictured in Figure 21.1, as the demand curve because it shows how revenue (price x units sold) fluctuates as price changes.

Many new business owners automatically infer from the demand curve that the only way to stimulate higher sales volume is to lower prices. But this is not always the

case. Changes in the market can also affect the demand curve.

Occasionally, these changes may enable a particular company to both charge more and sell more, which seems to violate the theory. Actually, it does not. If consumers think that a particular product has a significant value, they'll generally be willing to pay more for that product. For example, a fleece jacket from Saks Fifth Avenue may be four times as expensive as the one at Old Navy, even though the fleece for both jackets was made at the same Malden Mills factory near Boston.

PRICING METHODS

Prices are generally established in one of four ways:

1. Cost-plus pricing
2. Demand pricing
3. Competitive pricing
4. Markup pricing

Cost-Plus Pricing

Many manufacturers use cost-plus pricing. The key to being successful with this method is making sure that the "plus" figure not only covers all overhead but generates the percentage of profit you require as well. If your overhead figure is not accurate, you risk profits that are too low. The following sample calculation should help you grasp the concept of cost-plus pricing:

Cost of materials	$ 50.00
+ Cost of labor	30.00
+ Overhead	40.00
= Total cost	**$120.00**
+ Desired profit (20% on sales)	30.00
= Required sale price	**$150.00**

Demand Price

Demand pricing is determined by the optimum combination of volume and profit. Products usually sold through different sources at different prices—retailers, discount chains, wholesalers, or direct mail marketers—are examples of goods whose price is determined by demand. A wholesaler might buy greater quantities than a retailer, which results in purchasing at a lower unit

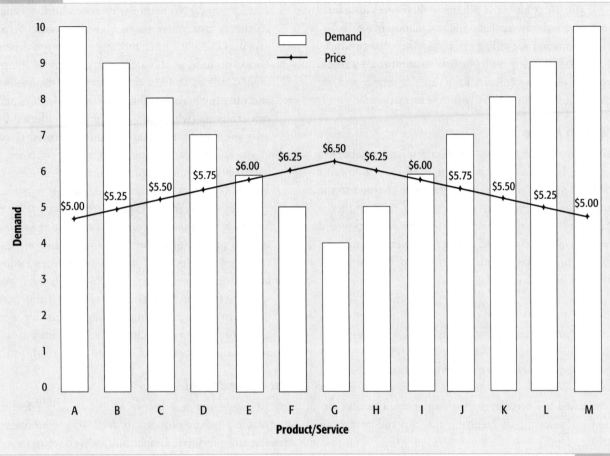

FIGURE 21.1 Demand Versus Price Game

price. The wholesaler profits from a greater volume of sales of a product priced lower than that of the retailer. The retailer typically pays more per unit because he or she is unable to purchase, stock, and sell as great a quantity of product as a wholesaler does. This is why retailers charge higher prices to customers.

Demand pricing is difficult to master because you must correctly calculate beforehand what price will generate the optimum relation of profit to volume.

Competitive Pricing

Competitive pricing is generally used when there's an established market price for a particular product or service. If all your competitors are charging $100 for a replacement windshield, for example, that's what you should charge. Competitive pricing is used most often within markets with commodity products, those that are difficult to differentiate from another. If there's a major market player, commonly referred to as the market leader, that company will often set the price that other, smaller companies within that same market will be compelled to follow.

To use competitive pricing effectively, know the prices each competitor has established. Then figure out your optimum price and decide, based on direct comparison, whether you can defend the prices you've set. Should you wish to charge more than your competitors, be able to make a case for a higher price, such as providing a superior customer service or warranty policy. Before making a final commitment to your prices, make sure you know the level of price awareness within the market.

If you use competitive pricing to set the fees for a service business, be aware that unlike a situation in which several companies are selling essentially the same products, services vary widely from one firm to another. As a result, you can charge a higher fee for a superior service and still be considered competitive within your market.

Markup Pricing

Used by manufacturers, wholesalers, and retailers, a markup is calculated by adding a set amount to the cost of a product, which results in the price charged to the customer. For example, if the cost of the product is $100 and your selling price is $140, the markup would be $40. To find the percentage of markup on cost, divide the dollar amount of markup by the dollar amount of product cost:

$$\$40 \div \$100 = 40\%$$

This pricing method often generates confusion—not to mention lost profits—among many first-time small-business owners because markup (expressed as a percentage of cost) is often confused with gross margin (expressed as a percentage of selling price). The next section discusses the difference in markup and margin in greater depth.

PRICING A PRODUCT

To price products, get familiar with pricing structures, especially the difference between margin and markup. As mentioned, every product must be priced to cover its production or wholesale cost, freight charges, a proportionate share of overhead (fixed and variable operating expenses), and a reasonable profit. Factors such as high overhead (particularly when renting in prime mall or shopping center locations), unpredictable insurance rates, shrinkage (shoplifting, employee or other theft, shippers' mistakes), seasonality, shifts in wholesale or raw material, increases in product costs and freight expenses, and sales or discounts will all affect the final pricing.

Overhead Expenses

Overhead refers to all non-labor expenses required to

operate your business. These expenses are either fixed or variable.

- *Fixed expenses.* No matter what the volume of sales is, these costs must be met every month. Fixed expenses include rent or mortgage payments, depreciation on fixed assets (such as cars and office equipment), salaries and associated payroll costs, liability and other insurance, utilities, membership dues and subscriptions (which can sometimes be affected by sales volume), and legal and accounting costs. These expenses do not change, regardless of whether a company's revenue goes up or down.
- *Variable expenses.* Most so-called variable expenses are really semi-variable expenses that fluctuate from month to month in relation to sales and other factors, such as promotional efforts, change of season, and variations in the prices of supplies and services. Fitting into this category are expenses for telephone, office supplies (the more business, the greater the use of these items), printing, packaging, mailing, advertising, and promotion. When estimating variable expenses, use an average figure based on an estimate of the yearly total.

Cost of Goods Sold

Cost of goods sold, also known as cost of sales, refers to your cost to purchase products for resale or to your cost to manufacture products. Freight and delivery charges are customarily included in this figure. Accountants segregate cost of goods on an operating statement because it provides a measure of gross-profit margin when compared with sales, an important yardstick for measuring the business' profitability. Expressed as a percentage of total sales, cost of goods varies from one type of business to another.

Normally, the cost of goods sold bears a close relationship to sales. It will fluctuate, however, if increases in the prices paid for merchandise cannot be offset by increases in sales prices, or if special bargain purchases increase profit margins. These situations seldom make a large percentage change in the relationship between cost of goods sold and sales, making cost of goods sold a semi-variable expense.

Determining Margin

Margin, or gross margin, is the difference between total sales and the cost of those sales. For example:

PRICING YOUR PRODUCT

How do you price a new product or service? This is one of the most important questions to answer as you start your business.

You know your costs. One easy way is to decide "Because this widget cost me two dollars to make, I will retail it for five times its cost, or ten dollars." Although this is easy to calculate, when you determine your prices according to how much the parts cost you, you forget about your consumer. In determining prices, user benefits are a better criterion.

To illustrate this point, many products consist of inexpensive parts, but they have an important use. For example, a heart valve may contain less than $20 worth of parts. However, because of its use, the valve is priceless to the patient and the surgeon. If you own a computer and you need a piece of software to solve a problem, that software becomes very precious.

To know how much to price an item, do a lot of consumer testing. Try different prices in isolated geographic areas. Because you'll incur extra start-up costs, start high as you enter the market. It's easier to lower your prices later. However, because every product competes for your customers' hard-earned dollars, it is necessary to accurately measure the value of your product.

Ask these questions:

- Is my product faster, cleaner, smaller?

- What will the customer pay for the benefits my product offers?

If you have a reseller, ask:

- What margins does the reseller need?

Finally, if you are the manufacturer, you need to know:

- What about warehousing, transportation, and packaging?

- What kind of warranties and return policies should I have?

- How much will liability insurance, credit, labor, advertising, and sales cost me?

As you can see, there are a lot of questions to answer when you prepare to price your product. If you answer these questions through research, marketing, and testing, you can anticipate how much people will pay to become your customers.

$$\text{Total sales} = \$1,000$$
and
$$\text{Cost of sales} = \$300$$
then
$$\text{Margin} = \$700$$

Gross-profit margin can be expressed in dollars or as a percentage. As a percentage, the gross-profit margin is always stated as a percentage of net sales. The equation:

$$\frac{(\text{Total sales} - \text{Cost of sales})}{\text{Net sales}} = \text{Gross-profit margin}$$

Using the preceding example, the margin would be 70 percent.

$$\frac{(\$1,000 - \$300)}{\$1,000} = 70\%$$

When all operating expenses (rent, salaries, utilities, insurance, advertising, and so on) and other expenses are deducted from the gross-profit margin, the remainder is net profit before taxes. If the gross-profit margin is not sufficiently large, there will be little or no net profit from sales.

Some businesses require a higher gross-profit margin than others to be profitable because the costs of operating different kinds of businesses vary greatly. If operating expenses for one type of business are comparatively low, then a lower gross-profit margin can still yield the owners an acceptable profit.

The following comparison illustrates this point. Keep in mind that operating expenses and net profit are shown as the two components of gross-profit margin; that is, their combined percentages (of net sales) equal the gross-profit margin:

	Business A	Business B
Net sales	100%	100%
Cost of sales	40	65
Gross-profit margin	60	35
Operating expenses	43	19
Net profit	17	16

Computing Markup

Markup and (gross-profit) margin on a single product, or group of products, are often confused. The reason for this is that when expressed as a percentage, margin is always figured as a percentage of the selling price, while markup is traditionally figured as a percentage of the seller's cost. The equation is:

$$\frac{(\text{Total sales} - \text{Cost of sales})}{\text{Cost of sales}} = \text{Markup}$$

Using the numbers from the preceding example, if you purchase goods for $300 and price them for sale at $1,000, your markup is $700. As a percentage, this markup comes to 233 percent:

$$\$1,000 - \$300 \div \$300 = 233\%$$

In other words, if your business requires a 70 percent margin to show a profit, your average markup will have to be 233 percent.

You can now see from the example that although markup and margin may be the same in dollars ($700), they represent two different concepts as percentages (233% versus 70%). More than a few new businesses have failed to make their expected profits because the owner assumed that if his markup is X percent, his or her margin will also be X percent. This is not the case.

Table 21.1 shows what the markup on cost must be to give the desired margin in a number of more common cases. To use this table, find your margin or gross profit percentage in the left-hand column. Multiply the cost of the article by the corresponding percentage in the markup column. Add this result to the cost to give you the correct selling price.

PRICING A SERVICE

How should you set fees or prices for your service business? Procedures depend upon the business, but the same three elements must be considered for every service business:

1. Labor and material costs

2. Overhead

3. Profit

These factors must be considered not only during start-up, but also during growth. Table 21.1 also works to determine the markup cost that gives the desired margin for service businesses.

Labor and Materials

Labor costs are wages and benefits you pay to employees and/or subcontractors who perform, supervise, or manage your service business. If you as the owner are involved in a job, then include the cost of your labor in the total labor charge. The cost of your labor will be quite significant during start-up, when most new business owners pour lots of time and energy into their businesses.

Labor costs are usually expressed as an hourly rate. Check in your library's reference room for government publications giving national and state salary ranges for different occupations. The editors of trade publications also might have similar information. Current rates are often cited in classified newspaper ads or available from your local chamber of commerce.

Labor can also be subcontracted—such workers are not on the payroll as employees. When labor is purchased for each job on a contract basis, the full cost is agreed upon in advance, which helps keep your costs fixed. The key is to carefully estimate the labor time it will take to accomplish each job on which you bid.

TABLE 21.1 Markup Table–Pricing a Product or Service

Margin % of Selling Price	Markup % of Cost	Margin % of Selling Price	Markup % of Cost	Margin % of Selling Price	Markup % of Cost	Margin % of Selling Price	Markup % of Cost
4.8	5.01	18.0	22.0	32.0	47.1	50.0	100
5.0	5.3	18.5	22.7	33.3	50.0	52.4	110
6.0	6.4	19.02	23.5	34.0	51.5	54.5	120
7.0	7.5	20.0	25.0	35.0	53.9	56.5	130
8.0	8.7	21.0	26.6	35.5	55.0	58.3	140
9.0	10.0	22.0	28.2	36.0	56.3	60.0	150
10.0	11.1	22.5	29.0	37.0	58.8	61.5	160
10.7	12.0	23.0	29.9	37.5	60.0	63.0	170
11.0	12.4	23.1	30.0	38.0	61.3	64.2	180
11.1	12.5	24.0	31.6	39.0	64.0	65.5	190
12.0	13.6	25.0	33.3	39.5	65.5	66.7	200
12.5	14.3	26.0	35.0	40.0	66.7	69.2	225
13.0	15.0	27.0	37.0	41.0	70.0	71.4	250
14.0	16.3	27.3	37.5	42.0	72.4	73.3	275
15.0	17.7	28.0	39.0	42.8	75.0	75.0	300
16.0	19.1	28.5	40.0	44.4	80.0	76.4	325
16.7	20.0	29.0	40.9	46.1	85.0	77.8	350
17.0	20.5	30.0	42.9	47.5	90.0	78.9	375
17.5	21.2	31.0	45.0	48.7	95.0	80.0	400

Profit

Profit is the amount of income earned after all costs for providing the service have been met. When calculating the price of a service, profit is applied in the same number as markup on the cost of a product. For instance, if your labor costs for a job are $210 and you plan to net 21 percent before taxes on your gross sales, you'll need to apply a profit factor of about 25 percent to your labor and overhead to achieve your goal.

For example, say you have:

Subtotal of operating costs	$324
Profit	81
Price you quote your customer	$405

If you compare the price of $405 with the cost of labor ($210) already estimated, you'll notice that one figure is more than double the other. Some contractors use this ratio as a basis for determining price: They estimate their labor costs and then double that figure to arrive at a bid price. Pricing can be time-consuming, especially if you don't have a knack for it. Some contractors seem to have a sixth sense when it comes to pricing and they "guesstimate" on what they need to quote to make a job profitable to them.

If you're just starting out, you obviously won't have the skill of a seasoned pro. If your quote is too low, you'll either rob yourself of profits or be forced to lower the quality of your work to meet the price. If you estimate too high, you may lose a contract, especially if you're in a competitive bidding situation. Make it your business to learn how to estimate labor time accurately and how to calculate your overhead properly so that when you quote a price, you can be competitive, profitable, and successful as a business.

CHAPTER 22

Credit Management

You may have seen a sign in a store that says, "In God we trust. All others pay cash." It points to the difficult choice business owners face when they consider granting credit to customers.

Many businesses rely on extending credit for a large portion of their sales without realizing the impact that decision has on their cash flow and profits. It doesn't matter what type of business you're in but if you allow your customers or clients to settle their accounts over time, you are, in effect, loaning them money. Any time goods or services are not paid for with cash, your customer is getting the use of your money interest-free.

Extending credit to customers can be chancy. How will you know if the customer is a good credit risk? How can you tell if extending credit will actually increase your bottom line? Will it cost extra to sell on credit? Make sure you know the answers to all these questions.

THE ADVANTAGES OF EXTENDING CREDIT

Cash and carry is the most efficient way to do business. It eliminates the need for credit checks and costly monitoring of receivables, and it minimizes the chances of operating losses.

By their very nature, certain types of business—custom manufacturing, professional service providers, convenience stores—demand straight cash transactions. Other businesses—construction contractors and clothing manufacturers—must offer credit to customers. Offering credit can

- Encourage customers to spend more, which can result in increased sales if receivables are turned to cash

- Increase customer goodwill and build good customer relations

- Make your customers less sensitive to price and more focused on the services you offer

To illustrate these points, consider a small bookstore in Minnesota that sold books to college students on a cash-only basis. After one year of operation, the store had fallen 60 percent below its projected first-year volume and was facing a loss of thousands of dollars.

Then the owner did a simple study of the store's customers and discovered that most operated on a monthly budget; funds were provided either from scholarships or from home. In this market, people traditionally sent money to their children on the first of the month.

For three or four days around the first, sales volume and foot traffic were good. But for the remaining days, sales bottomed out. The owner tried everything—more advertising, sales promotions, discount offers—but nothing worked.

In the bookstore's second year of operation, the owner began granting credit to students. Business zoomed, and his first-quarter sales were up more than 200 percent.

THE DISADVANTAGES OF EXTENDING CREDIT

Certain costs are involved in granting credit. The major gamble is that the customer might not pay. Statistics indicate that 97 to 98 percent of all credit bills in America are paid on time. However, that remaining 2 to 3 percent can sink some small businesses.

Credit costs you money. When you offer credit, you're selling an item you've already paid for on the premise that you'll be paid by the buyer tomorrow. The dollars to pay for the product come from operating capital that you then don't have on hand to reinvest in your business.

Your customer is, in effect, using your product on loan while your operating costs and cash needs continue to mount. If you decide that you can safely carry receivables of $20,000, then one way or another you're going to have to replace that $20,000 in your cash flow.

Credit costs you time. For most small business owners, time is a precious and finite commodity. When you add credit decisions to your workload, you spend time making those choices instead of spending time running other aspects of your business.

Other major disadvantages of offering credit are the potential losses when a customer fails to pay or takes a long time to pay and the additional expense of credit checking, credit-bureau memberships and fees, discounts on sales, and costs of collection agencies and lawyers.

When all is said and done, however, your competitors may simply force you to offer credit. You may have to provide credit not just to increase sales but to maintain them.

EXTENDING CREDIT

When you offer credit, you make four basic assumptions:

1. That your customer has every intention of paying;

2. That your customer is able to pay;

3. That nothing will happen to prevent payment;

4. That your judgment about the character and integrity of your customer is accurate.

Credit data and a past history gives you an initial indication of your customer's intention and ability to pay (see Figure 22.1). Past payment history helps with the third assumption. The fourth assumption can only be dealt with by calling on your experience in business, your knowledge of human behavior, and what you know about your customers.

Verifying credit is fairly easy. On your credit application form, request three trade references and the name and branch of the applicant's bank. Call the bank, give your name and company name, and ask for a credit rating on your customer. Ask how long the account has been open, the average balance and whether the bank has credit experience with this account.

Contact each of the trade references and tell whoever answers that you'd like a credit rating on one of their customers. Ask how long the account has been open, the highest amount of credit that's been granted, and how the customer pays. Once you've reached the bookkeeper, you usually don't even have to ask these questions—the necessary information will be volunteered. You might also obtain membership in your local credit bureau and draw reports on each account or utilize one of the financial rating services for businesses such as Dun & Bradstreet. This way, if the customer has any judgments against him or her or a record of slow payments with anyone, you will know.

RETAIL CREDIT

Businesses offer credit in three different ways, each of which has its own risks:

1. Check cashing

2. Credit cards

3. Installment loans

Check Cashing

How can you minimize your risks when accepting checks? The answer is with careful screening and by using modern technology. It's possible to get insurance against bad checks from check-verification and guarantee serv-

FIGURE 22.1 Consumer Credit Application

NAME/ADDRESS

Last	First	Middle initial	Social Security Number
Address			
City	State	Zip	Telephone

EMPLOYMENT HISTORY

Employer	Job title
Address	Supervisor
City State Zip	Salary
Telephone	Date from Date to
Employer	Job title
Address	Supervisor
City State Zip	Salary
Telephone	Date from Date to

SOURCE OF INCOME	TOTALS	EXPENSES	TOTALS
Salary		Loans	
Bonuses & commissions		Charge account bills	
Income from rental property		Monthly bills	
Investment income		Real estate mortgages	
Other income		Other debts–itemize	
Total Income		**Total Expenses**	

BANK REFERENCES

Institution name	Institution name	Institution name	
Checking account no.	Savings account no.	Home equity loan no.	Loan balance
Address	Address	Address	
Phone	Phone	Phone	

STATEMENT OF ACCURACY AND PERMISSION TO VERIFY

I hereby certify that the information contained in this credit application is complete and accurate. This information has been furnished with the understanding that it is to be used to determine the amount and conditions of the credit to be extended. Furthermore, I hereby authorize the financial institutions listed in this credit application to release necessary information to the company for which credit is being applied for in order to verify the information contained herein.

Signature: _____ Date: _____

ices such as Telecheck Services, Inc., and Equifax. A number of smaller services also offer verification-only services or verification and guarantee.

These companies will verify checks by phone, simply with one identification: either the customer's driver's license or state ID (from United States or Canada), or a military ID. Most merchants use some kind of check verification service—it's too risky not to. The amount spent, say $24 for a $600 check, is often worth the risk of losing the whole $600. Usually the fee will be lower than the merchant's discount rate (fee) for accepting credit cards.

Whether or not you use a verification service, take these steps any time a check is presented to you or one of your staff:

- Make sure the check is drawn on a local bank.
- Check the date for accuracy.
- Do not accept a check that is undated, postdated or more than 30 days old.
- Be sure the written amount and the numerical amount agree.

Post your check-cashing procedures in a highly visible place. Most customers are aware of the problem of bad checks and are willing to follow your rules if they know what they are.

Your main reason to ask for identification is so you can locate the customer if something is wrong with the check. The most valid and valuable piece of identification is a driver's license, which, in some states, includes a picture, signature, and address. Make sure the signature, address, and name agree with those listed on the check.

The driver's license is a useful ID, thanks to computer technology. In each state, the license is recorded and registered on a computer system. Each driver's license is also registered in a series of computers that can tell instantly whether it is valid, stolen, or has been connected with some fraudulent credit or check procedures.

If you're not signed up with a check-verification provider, you may want to ask for a second piece of ID, such as a major credit card or department store credit card. Keep in mind, though, that in many states it is now illegal to copy down any numbers off credit cards. You can only ask to see them. Retail merchants' associations often provide lists of stolen drivers' licenses and credit

cards so if the customer is unknown to you, it makes sense for you to check the list.

The following pieces of ID will not help you determine whether or not a check is good:

- Social Security cards (anyone can apply for one by mail)
- Business cards (anyone can have them printed)
- Club cards (membership does not imply honesty)
- Bank books (easily forged or stolen)
- Birth certificates (they don't prove that this is the person standing in front of you)
- Voter registration cards (they simply prove that the customer lives or lived at a certain location)

Without a check-verification service, don't accept the check if you have any question about the validity of the ID. Remember, it's your working capital that's on the line here, and you don't want to take unnecessary risks just to increase sales. Increasing profitability is what really counts and if a check is bad, your bottom line will suffer.

Credit Cards

While most of us have at least one Visa or MasterCard, did you know that they're not actually credit card companies but rather clearinghouse systems for the credit-card activities of their bank members?

When you accept credit cards, you make it easy for your customers to buy from you because you're offering convenience and the chance for the customer to buy on "float." Yet the money isn't coming out of your pocket—quite.

A kitchenware store in Atlanta might take a Visa card purchase from a customer who lives in Milwaukee. The sales slip is deposited along with the other receipts in the store's bank account.

The Atlanta bank credits the amount of the sale less a handling fee, generally 4 to 7 percent. Assuming the sale was $20 and the handling fee is 5 percent, the Atlanta storeowner actually receives only $19. The loss of the one dollar is built into the store's pricing and profit structure and passed along to the customer.

Then the Atlanta bank transfers the debt to the customer's Milwaukee bank, which stands behind the debt and transfers the necessary funds to the Atlanta bank. The

Milwaukee bank then bills the customer for the $20, plus interest if payment isn't received by a certain date. The bottom line is that the storeowner in Atlanta offered credit without much risk, the Milwaukee customer received the merchandise, and the banks in both cities made money.

Since the credit card companies are shouldering the risks in granting credit, they expect merchants to help them cut their losses. Both Visa and MasterCard publish regular lists of card numbers that are unacceptable for some reason, and they expect you to look at this list before granting credit.

American Express, Discover, and Diner's Club are credit cards you may decide to accept. They differ considerably from bankcards because their credit requirements are generally higher. Most bankcards grant credit if a person has a job, a permanent residence, and no questionable information in a computer credit file.

These so-called "entertainment cards" generally have a higher credit ceiling. Bankcards will put a credit line to a customer's account and hold the person to that limit. Entertainment cards are geared to the more affluent consumer with lots of discretionary dollars to spend.

The final difference is that entertainment card companies expect to be paid in full each month, while the bank cards give the customer two options: Pay the balance in full or pay 3 percent of the total balance plus interest monthly.

With high rates of interest, banks profit handsomely if cardholders don't pay off their entire credit card bill at once.

If you haven't already been approached by one of the major credit card representatives, approach them. Their sales associates work on commission and are happy to pitch the advantages of the various programs.

Offering a credit card program eliminates the time you waste handling credit sales. When you consider that certain costs of credit are fixed (posting accounts, billing, etc.) and will cost you the same for a $10 sale as for a $500 sale, this argument also makes sense.

A marketing benefit that helps your advertising sales is the automatic mailing list the credit-card sales slip provides you with. You can (if you ask customers to fill in their name and address) have a day-by-day record of that customer's purchases and use your mailing list to promote future sales by mail.

Another benefit the sales personnel will tout is the security of credit card sales. You will (if you follow the credit card company's guidelines) be able to collect your money even if the cardholder skips town. The credit card operation assumes the risk and pursues collection, which helps you spend your time more profitably running your business.

Installment Credit

Certain kinds of businesses demand installment credit. Companies selling high-ticket items like cars and RVs, major appliances, televisions, computers, cameras, sound equipment and carpet are all examples.

Basically, installment credit means that your customer is willing to sign a contract agreeing to pay, over a set period of time, the purchase price plus accrued interest and carrying charges. The contract makes your customer liable for full payment of the debt and gives you the power to take legal action to collect overdue payments. If you don't want to spend time and money managing an installment credit program, you could sell your credit contracts to a factor, a company that purchases qualified accounts receivable.

Installment credit is more risky than checks or credit cards. At the same time, it allows tremendous volume growth for sales of high-ticket items. The secret to profitable installment credit is careful, step-by-step management.

Being in business, you've undoubtedly filled out dozens of credit applications in the past. But unless you're involved in professional credit management, you probably never realized the wealth of information a credit application obtains—what most credit experts call the "three C's of good credit":

- Capacity (to repay)
- Character
- Collateral

Armed with the credit application your customer filled out, you can learn a lot about his or her creditworthiness. First, confirm employment by phoning the employer. Don't ask for the exact salary, but rather phrase the question in terms of range: "Does he earn in the low to mid-80s?"

If the switchboard operator has trouble recognizing the name, then check the "length of time employed" line on the credit application. If the customer says he or she's been employed for two years but the person you're talking with has trouble recognizing the name, that's a red flag.

Next, call the bank(s) the customer listed. A bank's first obligation is to its customers, but it will provide certain information. You might hear that a customer's average checking balance is an "L-3 or an "H-4." This translates to "low three figures" or "high four figures." A low three-figure balance would be in the $100 to $300 range, while a high four-figure balance would fall in the $7,000 to $9,000 range.

Several experts suggest that you involve your bank in this process. Tell your banker you need a credit "suggestion" on a certain customer. Banks tend to speak more freely with one another, and you can get a fairly realistic appraisal, not only on general balances but also of any trends such as slow payments or insufficient funds.

After you've made preliminary investigations, then enlist the aid of one of the major credit reporting houses. Experian (www.experian.com) is a company where giant computers store millions of records on millions of customers. For a fee, you can receive an in-depth credit history (if available) that will greatly help in your decision. See Figure 22.2 for a sample application from Experian.

Your analysis of an individual's creditworthiness should help you decide the kind and amount of credit to offer. Experts generally agree that you should be cautious about going into the installment credit business yourself, unless you have done your homework. Here's why:

- Your need for working capital will increase. This happens because you've already paid for the merchandise you're selling on credit. Installment credit involves an initial cash drain. For instance, assume you buy a refrigerator for $400. Depending on your credit arrangements with the manufacturer, you will have to put $200 down for that refrigerator. If you mark that refrigerator up to $900 and sell it for that in cash, you will have a guaranteed cash flow. You pay the manufacturer the other $200, and you reinvest your $500 profit. But if you sell that refrigerator in

twelve monthly installments, you'll have one-twelfth of the $900 plus interest in the till at the time of the sale. You'll have to pay the manufacturer the full $400 before you collect all the money from your customer.

- Offering credit costs more. By adding interest and carrying charges to the purchase of the $900 refrigerator, you'd arrive at a financed price of around $1,100 (figuring in 18 percent interest, insurance and overhead charges). That will increase your profit from your original projection, but that increase is going to cost you. You'll need to hire someone to handle the administration and paperwork—the bookkeeping, mailing statements to the customer, and collecting the receivable.

TRADE CREDIT: TIPS AND TRAPS

How'd you like an interest-free business loan without the hassle of credit checks and filling out papers? Sound too good to be true? Well, businesses do it every day by using payables financing, otherwise known as trade credit or commercial credit.

Your Credit Policy

The biggest problem most small businesses face with their credit policies is that they have none. Credit decisions—whether asking for credit or granting it—are generally made on a whim, at the spur of the moment, relying on a gut feeling or imitating what competitors are doing. But sharp businesspeople realize that credit is one of the most important aspects of business financing. It must be managed with a carefully thought-out game plan, and it must address what you'll do as a borrower as well as a lender.

The first step in determining your long-range credit policy is to get a fix on the exact status of your credit rating. Just as you turn to consumer credit bureaus to get a picture of the customer, so can other businesses turn to financial rating services to get a picture of you. Dun & Bradstreet (www.dnb.com) is just one major company, among others, that produces various reports on businesses.

These reports provide detailed pictures of a business, including types of credit offered, payment history, size of operation, capitalization, and so on. Ask these agencies for copies of their reports on you. If you're not listed, take steps to make sure you are so you can successfully use trade credit to make your business grow.

If there is any inaccurate information in these reports, have it corrected immediately.

Types of Trade Credit

There are two types of trade credit.

1. *Promises.* These, also known as "promises to pay," are invoices and promissory notes. Any time you order goods and don't want to lay out the cash at that time, you get them on an invoice. If the amount of goods involves a high price, you may, on occasion, be asked to sign a promissory note guaranteeing payment.

2. *Orders.* These are also known as "orders to pay" and differ from promises in that you sign a document specifying the rate of payment, the dates of payment and the method of transaction. Once an order to pay is accepted, it then becomes known as a trade acceptance. This allows the company that's granting you credit to use your trade acceptance as a guaranteed source of receivables income. This practice generally occurs when the amount of cash is considerable, usually more than $10,000.

When you order goods, you'll probably receive them with an invoice. This simply means that the supplier has checked your credit, believes you to be creditworthy, and has decided to let you have the goods. Many small businesses slip up at this point by not specifying their terms when ordering.

It also makes sense to request shipping terms. Many business owners ignore the money-saving aspect of FOB, which stands for "Free on Board," and designates who pays the freight. If you request in your order "FOB destination," the supplier pays the freight. If you don't specify this, chances are you'll pay.

FOB terms are always negotiable. Remember, most suppliers want your business and will make exceptions. This is a point worth discussing.

Spell Out Credit Terms

Precisely spell out credit terms so there's no chance for confusion. Most businesses, on one hand, will ask for "FOB destination," and on the other hand will reject or renegotiate any orders coming with that term. Their view is that no one else should use their money even though they want to use that of others!

Make sure that all the credit you grant is "EOM," otherwise known as "end of the month." This is generally written up as "net 15 EOM"—you expect the customer receiving your goods to pay you by the fifteenth of the following month. If you ship radios out on June 20, using this phrase guarantees payment by July 15. In other words, you've cut the maximum time someone else can use your money down to 25 days.

To see just how important this aspect is, consider this: If you carry someone for three months, you've lost 10 percent of your net profit. Carrying them for four months results in a 14 percent loss; five months brings the loss to 19 percent. Generally, if a bill is not paid in five years, you can write it off as a 100-percent loss.

To eliminate any potential loss of business revenue, spell out your credit terms and stick to your guns. If someone else is using your money, cut your risks to a minimum.

Expensive Discounts

Often a customer will ask if there's a cash discount for fast payment. Although this is a standard practice, you don't have to offer it as it's an expensive proposition. If you give a customer terms of "2 percent 10, net 30," then that customer can deduct 2 percent from the cost of goods if they pay you within ten days. If you go along with this, then you are letting the customer use your money for a very low interest rate.

In effect, the customer is paying you only $2 interest for the use of $98, based on a $100 order. On the other hand, quick-paying customers will boost your cash flow and cut down on your bookkeeping chores.

If a customer applies for credit and your research tells you that their credit history is bad but the business picture looks bright, then you will move from "promises to pay" into the realm of "orders to pay."

Get the customer to sign a promissory note that on a certain date, a specified amount of cash is due. Businesses signing these documents know you have recourse. If all else fails, you can have your bank draft an order to pay, which

FIGURE 22.2   Sample Credit Report

experian®

About Experian | Careers | Press | Privacy

United States   CONSUMER KNOWLEDGE CENTER   BUSINESS SERVICES

Search

CAPABILITIES | YOUR MARKET | PRODUCTS | E-COMMERCE | SMALL BUSINESS | B2B | CRM

⊠ Bankruptcy, tax lien and judgment sample reports

BANKRUPTCY DETAIL REPORT

Filing Number:	00000009404102JM

Filing Date:	04/15/2005
Filing Location:	U.S. BANKRUPTCY COURT - SOUTHERN - SAN DIEGO 325 WEST F STREET SAN DIEGO, CA 92189

Filing Date:	04/15/2005
Discharge Date:	06/19/2005
Filing Type:	Chapter 11
Liabilities:	$550,005
Assets:	$80,000
Exempt:	$10,000
Debtor:	SAMPLE COMPANY 123 MAIN STREET ANYWHERE, IL 91919

Additional Debtor:	JONES COMPANY 456 SAMPLE STREET SOMEWHERE, IL 90909

STATE TAX LIEN DETAIL REPORT

Filing Number:	0922179729
Filing Date:	11/23/2003
Release Date:	10/15/2006
Liability Amount:	$30,576
Filing Location:	LOS ANGELES COUNTY RECORDER ROOM 1007 12400 EAST IMPERIAL HWY NORWALK, CA 90650

Debtor:	SAMPLE COMPANY 123 MAIN STREET ANYWHERE, CA 99999

http://www.experian.com/product/pubrec/cprsample.html

Page 1 of 2

FIGURE 22.2   **Sample Credit Report,** continued

| Additional Debtor: | SAMPLERS UNLIMITED
456 WEST EAST STREET
ANYWHERE, CA 99999 |

JUDGMENT DETAIL REPORT

Original Filing Number:	0000000094C00958
Original Filing Date:	6/28/2005
Satisfaction Date:	8/3/2005
Liability Amount:	$9,564

| Filing Location: | LOS ANGELES COUNTY
MUNICIPAL COURT
10025 EAST FLOWER
STREET
BELLFLOWER, CA
90706 |

| Defendant Name: | SAMPLE COMPANY
123 MAIN STREET
LAKEWOOD, CA 90712 |

| Additional Defendant: | JONES COMPANY
2929 BAKER STREET
LAKEWOOD, CA 90712 |

| Plaintiff Name: | JOHNSON
CORPORATION
988 BLOCK AVENUE
ANYWHERE, CA 90909 |

| Additional Plaintiff: | BUCKNER SERVICES
383 CORONEL ROAD
ANYWHERE , CA 90909 |

Please note: Not all information may be available for all businesses. Some successful bankruptcy, tax lien and judgment searches may generate reports with no data at all. **An "empty" report still gives you valuable information.**

For more information on credit reports from Experian, call 1-888-EXPERIAN or visit www.experian.com.

is then transferred to the other business' bank. Businesses don't like this to happen because it tips off the bank that the customer isn't paying bills when they are due.

Establishing Credit

The best credit managers have predetermined lines of credit available to their customers. This simplifies bookkeeping and makes it easier for credit arrangements. If a certain store has a $1,000 line of credit with a manufacturer, then goods up to that $1,000 can be ordered and shipped out quickly. Figure 22.3 shows a sample credit application for a business.

When developing your credit policy, make sure to establish a good line of credit with your suppliers by paying according to the terms of the agreement during your first six months of operation. Because of the unpredictability of the mail, mail early and date the check for the date the payment is due. If the check is dated after that, your creditor will correctly assume that you've not met your obligation.

Once your credit line is established, you can begin using other businesses' money. The key to doing this is to make sure that you keep in touch with your creditors. If you're going to be late in paying, let them know ahead of time. If you can't make full payment the first month, make a partial payment. Always let the creditors know what your plans are.

The availability of trade credit helps you reduce the amount of cash you have to borrow. Since no interest is charged for such credit, this amounts to free money.

COLLECTIONS

The moment you decide to extend credit to your customers—whether to consumers or to another business—you automatically inherit another hat to wear, that of bill collector. Most business owners realize that bad debts cost money, but few realize exactly how much. If your business averages 7 percent net profit after taxes, and you have $100 in bad receivables, you have to increase sales by $1,429 to make up for it.

Bill collecting is a combination of the right financial controls and good management. The first step is to set up a clear and thorough collection policy. Will you be rigid and expect 100 percent payment on the exact date due, or

will you use a more flexible approach, taking into consideration the many possible reasons for slow payment?

Your policy should fall somewhere between these two extremes. If you're dealing with perishable products, you need a strict policy. If you're dealing with products that have a long shelf life, then you can have a more relaxed policy. The most important thing is to think your policy through, then make sure all your employees understand it. This will save you time in the long run since you won't have to be called to solve every collection problem.

A full 80 percent of collection and payment problems are due to invoicing difficulties. Costly mistakes on invoices occur in several areas. The major errors are wrong addresses, wrong person billed, payment terms not spelled out, and due dates not clearly specified.

The invoice you send out should always be typed or computer-printed. Illegible handwriting accounts for many of the errors. It should be written in terms that everyone understands (see Figure 22.4).

If you invoice a customer on an irregular basis, always have the payment terms spelled out. If you do regular business with a customer, keep a "statement of account" that you send out monthly. A statement of account is simply a recap of all the invoices sent to a customer during a given month. This statement should list each invoice by number, date shipped and amount due.

Whether using a computerized or a manual system, be sure to stay organized and know how your system works. In a manual system, many business people lump all the invoices together, then spend time at the end of the month sorting them out. This system presents several problems. If you are a one- or two-person operation, there's a chance of losing an invoice or facing additional end-of-the-month bookkeeping problems that delay your invoicing. Remember that if you don't promptly bill your customers, they have the luxury of using your money interest-free.

Aging Receivables

There are many different techniques for setting up an aging system for your receivables. You can either purchase the appropriate accounting software or set up your own manual system with code letters, different colored folders, and so on. The key is to make sure that everyone in your

FIGURE 22.3   Business Credit Application

NAME/ADDRESS

Last	First	Middle initial	Title
Name of business			Tax ID number
Address			
City	State	Zip	Telephone

COMPANY INFORMATION

Type of business		In business since
Legal form under which business operates	Corporation ☐ Partnership ☐ Proprietorship ☐	
If division subsidiary, name of parent company		In business since
Name of company principal responsible for business transactions		Title
City	State Zip	Telephone
Name of company principal responsible for business transactions		Title
City	State Zip	Telephone

BANK REFERENCES

Institution name	Institution name	Institution name	
Checking account no.	Savings account no.	Loan no.	Loan balance
Address	Address	Address	
Phone	Phone	Phone	

TRADE REFERENCES

Company name	Company name	Company name
Contact name	Contact name	Contact name
Address	Address	Address
Phone	Phone	Phone
Account open since	Account open since	Account open since
High credit	High credit	High credit
Current balance	Current balance	Current balance

STATEMENT OF ACCURACY AND PERMISSION TO VERIFY

I hereby certify that the information contained in this credit application is complete and accurate. This information has been furnished with the understanding that it is to be used to determine the amount and conditions of the credit to be extended. Furthermore, I hereby authorize the financial institutions listed in this credit application to release necessary information to the company for which credit is being applied for in order to verify the information contained herein.

Signature: _____   Date: _____

FIGURE 22.4 Sample Invoice Form

Bill to _____   **Date** _____

_____   **Invoice no.** _____

_____   **Salesperson** _____

_____

P.O. No.	Quantity	Description	Price	Discount	Total

Subtotal	
Sales tax	
Total	

STATEMENT OF ACCOUNT

Payments				
Balance				
Current charges				
New balance				
Current	30 days	60 days	90+ days	

business can tell at a glance the status of any account at any given time.

Experienced business owners have their accountants provide them with recaps of receivables on a monthly basis, so that they can structure their collection efforts in an orderly way. Current receivables can quickly turn into overdue ones if you're lax, and from there, into collection problems and losses while you're preoccupied with other aspects of running your business.

Make informed decisions by keeping track of each customer's credit history. Then you'll be able to spot problems sooner rather than later. If a customer traditionally pays ten days after a due date, that person is probably taking advantage of an implied grace period. You'd see this reflected on their payment ledger and know that there's no cause for worry.

On the other hand, if a customer has traditionally been prompt with payments and suddenly one is overdue, you have a problem. Problems with overdue accounts seldom go away by themselves. The farther behind you let a customer get, the greater the risk is that you'll never collect.

If a bill isn't paid when it's due, you lose money. Even levying a 1-percent surcharge doesn't begin to compensate for the staff hours and costs you face when trying to collect. Adding a service charge can serve as a warning to the slow payer. It lets the customer know you aren't going to allow your business to be treated in this manner. If the customer continues to do so, they're going to have to pay more.

Before proceeding with firm collection procedures, find out why your customer has been slow to pay. The customer could be delinquent for reasons beyond his or her control. Give him or her the benefit of the doubt but take action quickly.

A negligent customer has the money and the intention to pay but needs a reminder that the bill is past due. Companies often instruct their employees not to process bills until "past due" notices are sent. To speed up payment of these accounts, mail the past due notices early.

Not-at-fault delinquent customers have faced some sort of disaster—fire, flood, earthquake, loss of a key employee, and so on. If this is the situation, don't press for payment but let the customer know that you'll carry the account for a reasonable time.

THE COLLECTION PROCESS

The collection process is a step-by-step procedure that starts with friendly reminders, then firm requests, then demands for payment, and finally threats of legal action. Each step has proven techniques that will pay off. The important thing to remember is to organize your approach, then follow through with your stated action.

The most effective course of action is to begin with written reminders, followed by collection letters, followed by phone calls. If you run your business by yourself, your first reaction probably is, "I can't take time out to write collection letters. I don't even have a secretary." That's too bad, but if you don't take the time to write a brief, to-the-point letter, you send the signal that not paying your bill is acceptable.

The first step in your letter-writing campaign is to send another copy of the bill along with a handwritten note on the bill saying, "In case you forgot," or "past due." This reminds the customer without questioning the person's creditworthiness. It gives the customer the benefit of the doubt. The tone of the letters gradually moves from one of friendly persuasion to one of firm demand.

Personalized Letters

With accounts that are three months old, you'll have to adopt a slightly tougher policy. This is an area where form letters aren't as effective as personalized letters. Make sure your letter is:

- *Concise.* Letters that appear long and complicated go to the bottom of the stack or to the "circular file." State the reason you're writing right up front.
- *Clear.* When your reader can't grasp right away what your letter is about, he or she will ignore it.
- *Accurate.* Nothing destroys the effectiveness of a collection appeal faster than being wrong. The letter must have the correct invoice (or statement) number, date, and amount. It should also accurately reflect the status of the account on the date it was written.

On the Phone

To save time and money, many business owners turn to the telephone. If you decide to do this, have all the facts and figures at hand. It also doesn't hurt to have the points you'd like to make written down. When you call, speak in a cordial yet firm voice. And make sure to listen.

Here's a list of excuses you might hear, along with suggestions on how to respond:

- *"I paid the bill."* Ask for a copy of the canceled check, money order receipt, or any other receipt that can prove payment.

- *"I never got a bill."* Verify the address to make sure it corresponds to the one you have on record.

- *"Business is slow right now."* Find out when business is expected to pick up.

- *"I sent it yesterday."* Ask who mailed the payment and from where it was mailed. Find out if it was a personal check or money order. If it was a money order, ask where it was purchased and the receipt number.

- *"The insurance company was supposed to pay for this."* Ask for the name of the insurance company and what type of policy was supposed to cover these expenses. If it was a group policy, get the name of the employer and the name of the insured employee, which may be different from that of the person you're talking with. Also ask for the name of the insurance agency, the policy number, and any other identifying or claim number. Then try to find out why the insurance company didn't pay.

- *"I didn't get what I ordered."* Ask what was wrong with the merchandise and try to resolve the situation.

- *"The balance is wrong."* If you cannot resolve the dispute at the time, advise the debtor that you'll send an itemized statement and a copy of the payment record. Check the debtor's mailing address to be sure it is correct. Send the statement by registered mail, return receipt requested.

If a customer still hasn't paid after collection letters and phone calls, then it's time to turn the account over to a collection agency. Most agencies have a minimum amount for bills they'll accept, so some business owners wait until they have several overdue accounts before turning them over to a collection agency.

As soon as you start offering credit, familiarize yourself with reputable collection agencies in your commu-

nity. You may want to find out if they are affiliated with a reputable national organization, such as the ACA International (www.acainternational.org), formerly the American Collectors Association, a trade group for the credit and collection industry.

Small Claims Court

An alternative to working with collection agencies is to file a complaint in small claims court. This is a simple procedure that forces a hearing between you and the person or company who owes you money, and generally results in a judgment in the creditor's favor. In many states, debts up to $1,000 can be handled in this manner, but policies vary from state to state. Check with your state attorney general's office to determine the best way to handle small claims accounts.

Laws on Collection

Like most consumer-oriented legislation, laws on credit and collection tend to be complex in their wording. The following is a brief summary of the main points of some of the most important laws:

- *The Robinson-Patman Act (1936)* makes it illegal for chain stores to purchase goods at lower prices than other retailers.

- *The Assignment of Claims Act (1940)* permits the assignment of proceeds from contracts to institutions solely involved in banking or financial activity. In effect, this allows businesses to replenish their supply of operating capital immediately on shipment of a product and opens the door to receivables financing.

- *Uniform Commercial Code (1972; frequent revisions)* provides the basis for all commercial transactions.

- *The Consumer Credit Protection Act (1968)* is also known as the Truth in Lending Act and protects consumers from unfair credit practices.

- *The Fair Credit Billing Act (1975)* regulates the methods and procedures firms may use in billing credit card accounts and other revolving accounts with a finance charge.

- *The Fair Credit Reporting Act (1970; added to the Truth in Lending Act)* regulates consumer credit information regarding confidentiality, accuracy, relevancy, and proper utilization of customers' credit histories.

- *The Equal Credit Opportunity Act (1977)* prohibits discrimination on the basis of gender or marital status in granting credit.

- *The Fair Debt Collection Act (1978)* eliminates abusive collection practices by debt collectors.

- *Postal regulations* require that no words, illustrations, or codes identifying an addressee as delinquent in payment of a debt may appear on the outside of an envelope or postcard where they might be seen by a third party.

- *Internal Revenue Service* governs writing off bad debts.

CHAPTER 23

Legal Matters

While state laws vary, there are certain federal regulations that affect all business owners. Violating those laws, either by accident or deliberately, is a sure-fire way to put your hard work, reputation, and large sums of money on the line. Make sure you work with an experienced business attorney and don't hesitate to contact him or her if you have questions about any of the areas covered in this chapter.

RAISING MONEY

Loans from investors—banks, credit card companies, or state or federal agencies—are either secured or unsecured. If the loan is secured, you'll be required to sign a security agreement in addition to your promissory note. The security agreement typically requires you to put up some form of collateral. If you sell the specified collateral, the agreement usually allows the lender to take whatever new collateral you may have received for the old. For example, if you put up a car as collateral then sell it for another car of more value, the new car becomes the collateral. If it's worth more, you must receive credit for the difference if the lender seizes your new car and sells it in order to be paid.

Raising equity capital involves selling shares in a corporation or units in either a general or limited partnership. To prevent fraud, the government has stepped in with some regulations. At the federal level, the Securities and Exchange Commission (SEC) regulates selling securities, including shares of stock and partnership interests. At the state level, "blue sky" laws that protect consumers from buying fraudulent securities are enforced by the attorney general's office.

If a company decides to "go public," it must register its securities, which involves attorneys, accountants, underwriters, and hundreds of thousands of dollars. This company must prepare a prospectus—in essence, a business plan that meets the SEC requirements—and a subscription that explains the details of the investment to prospective investors.

The government recognized how onerous its rules and regulations are, so it carved out a series of exemptions depending on how much money is to be raised in a certain time frame, how many investors are involved, how sophisticated the investors are, and how closely related to the business owner the investors are. The process becomes very simple if investors all reside in one state.

The most common exemption is the federal government's Rule 504, which is compatible with most state laws. It permits a company to raise $1 million in a 12-month period by filing a few simple forms. Your local SBA office can help with the process.

MARKETING LAWS

If your company's product is unique, think about protecting it from unauthorized duplication in one of the following ways.

Patents

A patent is a government grant of the exclusive right to make, use, or sell an invention. A U.S. patent is good for either fourteen to seventeen years, depending on the type. A design patent is good for up to fourteen years on new, original, ornamental shapes or configurations.

Generally speaking, the following are excluded from patenting: printed matter, naturally occurring substances, methods of doing business, ideas, scientific principles, and mental processes. You must file for patent protection before exposing your product to the marketplace or you run the risk of someone copying it.

Some examples of what's patent-able include certain types of computer software, fabric designs, furniture designs, a drink holder with a unique configuration to prevent spillage, or an automated machine that analyzes blood components.

Patents are the best form of protection for your product because even if someone challenges you because he or she invented it first, your application will take precedence. The Patent and Trademark Office (www.uspto.gov) in Washington, D.C., can provide a basic search for prior patents for a similar invention. However, these searches are not extensive and can therefore produce misleading results. If a large sum of money is at stake, it's best to have a patent attorney conduct a thorough search through the Patent Office.

Trademarks

Trademarks and service marks are applied to a manufacturer's or a seller's products and services to distinguish them in the marketplace—a valuable marketing tool, in some circumstances. A trademark or service mark prevents another person from offering a product or service confusingly similar to yours. If you don't register your trademark, you may be prohibited from using it by someone who has.

Copyrights

A copyright does nothing more than protect against unauthorized duplication of certain classes of original works, including writings, toys, art, films, photography, music, and computer software. The federal copyright law does not protect individual words and may or may not protect character configurations, depending on the focus. For example, the courts held that the Disney character Mickey Mouse was protected by copyright, since they viewed Mickey Mouse as a work of art.

Place the symbol "©" with the year and the words "all rights reserved" on your materials to provide your company with minimal protection. Registering your copyright with the Library of Congress (www.loc.gov) will be necessary if you want to file suit for infringement.

CONSUMER LAWS

Various states adopt laws in response to customers who have been taken advantage of by misleading advertising, bogus products or services, and other rip-offs. Unfortunately, these laws then add to the cost of sales for honest and ethical business owners. The following sections describe the most common areas in which business owners are caught off guard when they assume that the logical way to do business is the legal way of doing business.

Truth in Advertising

Especially in retail businesses, competitive advertising can be cutthroat. Often you'll see companies refer specifically to their competitor's product in pointing out deficiencies, comparing prices, or making their own grandiose claims about the superiority of their products.

Advertising is regulated primarily by the Federal Trade Commission (FTC, www.ftc.gov), and by various state laws too numerous to mention. Often, complaints against your company for false or misleading advertising will originate from a disgruntled customer or from your competitor. The FTC will see if you can substantiate your claims in an objective way (lab tests, etc.) and review your lab results for adequacy in both scientific principles and consistency of implementation of test studies.

Direct Mail

In addition to general advertising rules, business owners who send products through the mail must comply with direct-marketing laws. The U.S. Postal Service controls this area with a criminal mail fraud statute and can issue an order to terminate the distribution of your product through the mail.

If you must delay a shipment, send a postage-paid return notice offering the buyer the option of either terminating the order or extending the time for shipment to a revised shipping date. If the buyer cancels, you must send a prompt refund (within seven business days).

Product Liability

Product liability is a special area of the law that implies that just the mere manufacturing and distribution of your product makes you responsible to the consumer who buys it. Getting the word out about a product's problem is crucial to minimize your risks. For example, an elaborate customer-oriented recall program on parts that you manufacture may save you thousands of dollars dealing with government intervention and consumer lawsuits because you'll be held responsible if your customer is injured.

CONTRACTS

Relationships between businesses and consumers are controlled by contracts, either verbal or written. Contracts clarify what each party expects and what each party is willing to give in exchange for the expected results.

Agency

"Agency" is the theory that people who work for you or represent you are you in the eyes of the law. For example, assume your secretary signs a one-year contract for a postal machine. It seems like a small expense, at less than $100 per month, and it saves the secretary from regular trips to the post office. Unfortunately, you now find you can't afford this luxury (in your eyes, not hers). You try to cancel the agreement and are informed that it's a one-year commitment. Do you have an out?

Agency theory says that if the secretary was in a position of apparent authority and had a history of signing other documents on your behalf, then you are responsible for her actions. However, if you're a corporation with clearly written policies that state only corporate officers can bind the company, then you have a case that the secretary was acting outside the scope of her authority, and you may be able to get out of the contract.

Another area in which agency comes into play is when one of your staff leaves work in the morning to pick up doughnuts for the employees and has an accident on the way back. The car he hit can sue your company because he was acting in the scope of his employment—his negligence is your negligence. This is where your company liability insurance comes to the rescue—unless it has a specific exclusion, you'll be covered for the damage related to the lawsuit.

Warranties

Warranties are either express or implied. Express warranties are those in writing or directly given by you to your customer or client. Examples of express warranties are "Parts and labor warranted for ninety days on moving parts." Implied warranties are not expressly stated but can be derived from advertisements and literature. Examples are "You'll never have to paint again if you use this product," or "Use this rust-free compound to save you time and money." The implication is that no rust will form on the item and that you'll never have to redo your project. From a business owner's point of view, it's important to make sure that the person writing your advertising or brochures doesn't inadvertently give a warranty that you can't pay for. Breaches of warranties usually mean that you have to give the cost of the product back or at least replace or repair it. This can be very costly.

PURCHASING A BUSINESS OR FRANCHISE

There are four questions to get answered when purchasing a business.

1. *Which debts are truly accounts receivable?* How many are collectible, and how many are really bad debts?

2. *How many business relationships are committed to in writing?* Ask the seller to send a letter to the customers verifying that the terms the seller has represented to you about the customers are what the customer understands to be true.

3. *Are there any liabilities that the seller may have forgotten about, such as unpaid sales tax, payroll taxes, and amounts due on open-ended leases of equipment?* Arrange for 15 to 25 percent of the purchase price to be paid six months to one year after closing in an escrow account.

4. *Have you done due diligence on the company's assets?* Your research should include a Dun & Bradstreet search, a credit search and information from the local courthouse, the secretary of state, the Department of Motor Vehicles, and the county recorder.

Some parties prepare a "letter of intent" outlining the transaction. In most states, while letters of intent are not contracts, they do make it easier for an attorney to draft a purchase and sale agreement.

The purchase and sale agreement is usually accompanied by a series of exhibits that form the due diligence of the purchase. These exhibits include actual sales contracts, employment contracts, inventory lists, customer lists, equipment lists, tax clearance certificates, and rental contracts.

Purchasing a franchise has other requirements—see Chapter 12 for more information.

NEW WAYS OF DOING BUSINESS ON THE INTERNET

Laws governing internet commerce are still being developed and debated. There's been a high incidence of plagiarism, both intentional and not. As a result, copyright holders now have to be more vigilant in protecting what's rightfully theirs.

The good news is that present intellectual property laws protecting materials through patents, trademarks, and copyrights are flexible enough to give the kind of protection business owners need for electronic materials. Make sure your agreements limit the media for which rights are granted.

THE NORTH AMERICAN FREE TRADE AGREEMENT AND EXPORTING

The North American Free Trade Agreement (NAFTA) was designed to create a single trade entity among the United States, Mexico, and Canada. Through NAFTA, import duties that affect the flow of goods from the United States to both Canada and Mexico have been eliminated.

Remember that even though trade barriers have come down with NAFTA, basic exporting principles remain the same. You must verify that a difference in culture will not require changes in your product formula, packaging, or marketing.

There are myriad books and seminars about NAFTA. Check out the SBA's guide at www.sba.gov/nafta. The U.S., Canadian, and Mexican embassies and consulates are other good sources of information.

One issue to be aware of is that the Export SBDC recommends letters of credit with one of the better-known Mexican banks. In a letter-of-credit situation, a bank acts as an escrow agent holding money pending delivery and acceptance of merchandise. The customer's bank verifies with the seller's bank that the funds are available. It is important to ask for an "irrevocable letter of credit."

KEY EMPLOYEE PROMISES

Some small business owners make the mistake of offering key employees shares in their company in lieu of cash when money is tight. What happens if the business grows rapidly and outgrows those key employees, yet they own a fairly significant portion of the business? Such a scenario can be avoided if you follow these rules:

Rule 1. Never underestimate how large your business will grow and in how short a time.

Rule 2. Never give away more than 10 percent of your company unless you have a strategic plan and a business plan that specifies otherwise in detail. The more successful you are, the more working capital you'll need for your growth. That's typically how you end up with investors who are also your key employees. They embrace your vision, they see the company growing, and they want to be part of it. A cavalier promise made during a time when everyone is working hard can end up as a lawsuit. Even though it's unlikely your key employee will prevail based on an oral promise, you must still go through the cost and emotional drain defending a lawsuit.

Rule 3. *Don't give away anything without a written document that's reviewed by your attorney.* There's a big difference between profit sharing, giving up equity interest in a company and giving stock either as a bonus or through a stock option plan. If you want your key employees to receive a portion of your company's profits, see your CPA and then your lawyer to draft a plan that's structured properly.

Rule 4. *Make your promises contingent upon continued performance.* If a key employee has stopped performing in the manner he or she is supposed to, document it in writing immediately. Don't handle it informally.

Rule 5. *Use employment agreements.* Employment agreements for key employees and executives help clarify what their positions require. Consult with a labor or business attorney to make sure your bases are covered.

THEFT OF INFORMATION

Example 1. You've spent $10,000 to develop a special mailing list. Since your business is in a highly competitive industry, you hire salespeople to saturate the market with your product information in order to gain market share. You've also spent thousands on new graphics, and you're poised for success when an aggressive sales rep starts a competing business with your information.

Example 2. You learn a method of doing business that no one else knows and begin to achieve major success. Your partner of five years becomes disillusioned with your business philosophy and starts a business competing with yours, using that same method.

Example 3. Your number-one competitor hires away one of your popular computer software programmers, who happens to be familiar with the design and code of an existing product that has paid your overhead for many years. Three more of your programmers go work for the competitor, leaving your programming staff cut in half.

These problems address issues all business owners must be knowledgeable about: non-competition, non-solicitation, nondisclosure, unfair business competition, and a duty of loyalty.

Business partners who split up are entitled to prohibit each other from competing with a non-competition clause in the buy-out contract. If the partner sets up a competing business, you can—presuming the contract is drafted correctly—obtain an injunction against your previous partner to prevent him or her from competing for the time specified. The geographic area of non-competition and the time period must be reasonable for your particular business and the industry.

Employees are a different matter. There's a presumption in the law that all people are entitled to gainful employment. Companies that have tried to pay their former employees not to compete have been unsuccessful unless they were paid the equivalent of their salary not to work. Even then, an employee can choose to not receive the payment and find a job elsewhere. The employee does owe the owner a duty of loyalty while employed. This means that if the employer finds the employee calling about another job while still employed, or trying to solicit coworkers to work somewhere else, the employer has a right to damages if the case can be proven. However, the day after the employee leaves, he or she can call coworkers on the phone and solicit them.

But how about those customer lists—do former employees have the right to take those with them? The law states that former employees are entitled to use their skills and resources at a new job. However, employees are not entitled to steal confidential trade information from a previous employer. The most common reason that business owners lose these cases against former employees is that the owner never identified the company's confidential or secret information. The receptionist on the computer network has access to the customer lists. None of the computers has a password. Anyone walking by can sit down to a computer and retrieve the information.

A former employee does not have the right to steal company confidential information or trade secrets that are identified as such; however, the ownership of information developed through company procedures must clearly differentiate what belongs to the employee and what to the company. The easiest way to accomplish this is through nondisclosure agreements.

Nondisclosure Agreements

Nondisclosure agreements should be signed by anyone who has access to sensitive company information: consultants at the start of a business relationship, new employees prior to starting (their signing is a condition of employment), and clients before receiving unpublished information about the future direction of your company.

A nondisclosure agreement identifies confidential information by category, states what actions will be required to maintain confidentiality, and identifies ownership rights in the material disclosed. It is not a substitute for establishing a hierarchy of access to sensitive information. Prudent measures include allowing sales reps to have access only to the territory that they're responsible for, instituting passwords for computer access, hiring outside consultants to assemble certain portions of information so that no one person has the entire picture except you, intentionally putting misspelling in some parts of your documentation so it's easy to prove unauthorized copying, and always using copyright and trademark symbols to establish ownership.

LAWSUITS

Lawsuits are costly. Even the prevailing party, if attorney's fees are paid and judgment received, loses a lot in emotional energy and in actual time spent for various aspects of litigation. As a result, alternatives such as arbitration and small claims court have become popular ways of resolving these situations.

Litigation and the Court System

Attorneys rely on published cases to prove that your facts match the facts of the case in which your equivalent party prevailed. Only cases that have been appealed from the trial court to the appellate or supreme court are published. This means that many of the most common cases decided in the lower courts are never recorded, which in turn means that it is very important to have a trial attorney who has experience in your local court system.

Arbitration

The difference between arbitration and a lawsuit is primarily in formality. For example, in arbitration the formal rules of evidence do not apply. Each side can go on and on with narrative discussions, drawings, and charts, and the arbitrator will take in all of it and make a decision. There are no juries in arbitration. Instead, usually one to three people specially trained in the subject matter of the arbitration hear the case. Arbitrations are heard much sooner than lawsuits can be scheduled. This can be either good or bad, depending on which side you're on.

Unless specified as such in a contract's arbitration clause, arbitrations are not final and binding. Either party can decide that they do not like the outcome. Once an arbitration award is made and a binding clause is in the contract, a court will make the arbitration award an enforceable judgment.

Mediation

Mediation is never final or binding and is heard in front of a person who is an expert on the subject matter in question. The mediator can share the law in a way that allows both parties to have their day in court, vent their position and work toward a resolution, so that the relationship is not lost over the threat of a lawsuit. Mediation is very effective in situations where there's an ongoing relationship between two companies.

Small Claims Court

Small claims court can resolve differences quickly and efficiently. Attorneys are not permitted to be present until the appeal stage. Cases are usually heard within thirty days, and in some states the amount you can sue for has been raised to $5,000 under certain conditions. Each state—and often each county—has different rules about the allowable sum.

The following list outlines three steps in filing a small claims action.

1. Determine the jurisdiction's dollar limit on small claims actions.

2. Find out in which jurisdiction the defendant resides or does business. This is the jurisdiction in which you'll generally bring the action.

3. Visit the court clerk for the above jurisdiction. The clerk will give you the appropriate forms for filing the claim. Follow the instructions on these forms.

THE CORPORATE SHIELD

Don't be fooled by the statement, "If you're doing business as a corporation, your assets are untouchable." There are certain caveats you must be aware of.

A corporation is its own entity that can sue and be sued. If you have a validly established corporation, your personal assets are usually safe if a judgment is awarded against the corporation.

The first exception to the rule concerns personal guarantees. Sometimes when you apply for a bank line of credit, especially if your corporation is newly formed, the bank will require you to sign a personal guarantee. If you don't pay on your loan, although the bank will look first to the corporation to pay, you will be on the line personally as well. This also occurs with office and equipment leases. Before you sign on the dotted line, consider negotiating for the personal guarantee to be removed at some point in the first couple of years after you've established a record of paying promptly.

Another personal guarantee that is implied when you set up your corporation is the payment of taxes. The Franchise Tax Board will always hold you personally responsible for the payment of corporate taxes as an officer and director of the corporation. It is important to explain this potential liability to your directors.

Another exception is for specific statutes that hold directors and officers personally liable for the criminal acts of the corporation. Directors have been jailed for failing to correct workplace hazards for their employees, for gross negligence in toxic spills and for selling inexpensive items to the government for outrageous sums of money. If your corporation has committed a fraud, even if you're not directly aware of it, you may be held responsible.

And yet another exception is when a director or officer acts outside the scope of his or her duties. For example, a general contractor is angered by a homeowner and gets into a fistfight. The corporation cannot, in most cases, protect against an action of this sort.

Finally, if the corporation is not properly established and maintained, a plaintiff may claim that the corporation and you are one and the same, and therefore your personal assets can be used to satisfy the judgment. What constitutes "properly established and maintained?" First, you must have good standing with the secretary of state. That means that you've paid your taxes to date and that you've filed the requisite yearly forms. Second, your corporate minutes must be up-to-date, and bylaws regarding annual meetings and so on must be complied with. Third, you must have sufficient capital in the corporation to pay its bills.

In most states, the plaintiff must show that you set up the corporate shell with the intent to defraud creditors. This is usually proved by showing the commingling of assets and liabilities. Thus, you must keep your personal and corporate business separate. If you loan money to the corporation or borrow money from the corporation, complete written promissory notes that include your paying the going rate of interest and a reasonable payback schedule. Never write checks for personal debts, such as your house payment, out of your corporate account. Finally, when you sign documents, use this:

CORPORATE NAME

BY: _____

Your name, President

The word "BY" is important because it is your title.

Some plaintiff's attorneys will try to sue you personally, as a scare tactic. However, remember that the plaintiff cannot make fatuous claims and hope that something will show up to implicate you.

PART 3

Growing Your Business

Small businesses, particularly those in "hot" industries, often experience growth in spurts. If you're not prepared (i.e., you haven't foreseen this scenario and figured out what steps to take to capitalize upon your good fortune), your business can suffer. Employees can become overworked, burned out, and disgruntled. Their discontent will eventually spread to customers, who aren't receiving the service they need. The business can skimp on thoroughly exploring markets for their riches. Opportunities are lost—forever.

Growing your business can be like walking though a minefield if you haven't properly planned for expansion. Risks loom with every step forward. In your strategic planning efforts, map out your "best-case approach" by looking ahead to the possibility/probability of adding more staff, purchasing additional equipment, seeing that appropriate marketing support is in place, and having adequate financing lined up for when it's needed.

Although growing your business is challenging, the rewards can be great if you minimize your risks. Among the entrepreneurs who've achieved some pretty lofty goals are Bill Gates (Microsoft), Lillian Vernon (catalog sales), Dave Thomas (Wendy's), and Calvin Klein (clothing). They all started with a dream that they grew into large, thriving businesses, some of which dominate their industries.

This kind of entrepreneurial success comes not only from good ideas, opportune timing, and hard work but also from careful planning and a keen sense for recognizing growth opportunities. Part 3 of the Ultimate Small Business Advisor provides the information you'll need to take advantage of strategic opportunities while growing your business.

CHAPTER 24

Financing a Growing Business

Many successful businesses reach a point where they need more money in order to keep growing and improving their product or service. The key to getting those funds is to plan ahead. Know how much you'll need, why you'll need it, how it will be used to make more money for your business, and where to find the best sources for it. Don't wait until the last minute, when you're rushed and desperate—these are the circumstances under which poor, and often costly, decisions are made.

To avoid stressful surprises, review your business plan once a year (make revisions as needed), and make sure that your marketing plan is in sync. These planning tools not only help you refine goals and objectives—they also provide you with strategies for attaining them.

Armed with this knowledge, you'll be able to shop for a loan before you need it—instead of when you need it—exploring the type of financing available and comparing the terms being offered. This way, you can arrange the best deal and avoid being pressured to take whatever's available at the moment you need it. An added bonus is that your investors will be favorably impressed by your ability to project and plan ahead.

WHEN FINANCING CAN HELP GROW YOUR BUSINESS

A track record of profitability is important in order to secure financing. Profitability is a measure of the company's performance in relation to sales, cost of sales and overhead, all of which are included in a monthly income statement that charts the business' performance. However, while the income statement indicates the performance of the company, it doesn't denote the timing differences in cash flow.

Cash flow measures the actual investment in additional material to continue production (usually referred to as "cost of sales"), the outlay of capital to meet all payables and overhead, and the collection of receivables, all of which occur at different times during the cash flow cycle.

In order for businesses to meet customer demand, materials have to be purchased at predetermined times to replenish finished goods. Within 30 days of ordering goods, they must be paid for. Then you have to sell the product, which takes time, and then you have to get paid for that sale, which often takes thirty days—or sometimes longer.

Based on this scenario, you will have paid for the production of the product long before you collect any cash for it from a sale. In the meantime, you still have to meet overhead. If your working capital is not sufficient to cover the ebbs and tides of cash flow, you'll experience the dreaded cash-flow crunch. Many otherwise successful small businesses have succumbed to cash-flow crises that could have been averted had appropriate measures been taken in advance.

Plan for Expansion

Entrepreneurs often get so focused on the actual operations of the business that they fail to plan adequately for the future. Ideally, a business owner, president, or CEO should allot more than half of his or her time to planning.

Planning the goals and strategies of the company should be done annually by the executive management team. Large companies often hold off-site meetings where the entire executive group gathers to chart the company's strategy for the upcoming year and beyond. For smaller companies, where the executive management team consists of the owner and a few key people, the same principle applies.

The management team should take these steps at an annual meeting:

- *Set goals, both long-term and short-term.* These goals focus on market share, sales, profit, geographic expansion, staffing, internal management, or product expansion, among others.
- *Review company performance.* Year-end financial statements should be generated to provide a snapshot of the company's profitability, cash position, liquidity, and net worth. These figures can easily be retrieved from an income statement, cash flow statement, and balance sheet (see Chapter 17).
- *Evaluate operation requirements.* Meeting the company's goals requires an accurate appraisal of all components of the business: marketing, sales, production, administration, personnel and research and development.
- *Create a budget.* All goals and expectations have to be translated into numbers and budgets for planning purposes. These budgets are produced on the income, balance sheet and cash flow statements.

Both the business plan and marketing plan will be refined as a result of the annual meeting. The informa-

tion you generate will help you determine whether you can finance growth from operations or whether you'll need outside investors.

Using your business plan and marketing plan as foundations, you can refine your budget and determine time frames in which additional capital, personnel, and equipment are required.

The Importance of Cash Flow

A cash flow budget highlights the following figures:

- Sales/revenue
- Development expenses
- Cost of goods
- Capital requirements
- Operating expenses

Your cash flow projection is based on the past performance of your business. Start by breaking down projected sales over the next year according to the percentage of business volume generated each month. Divide each month's sales according to cash sales and credit sales. Cash sales can be logged into the cash flow statement in the same month they are generated. Credit sales are not credit card sales, which are treated as cash, but rather invoiced sales with agreed-upon terms. Refer to your accounts receivable records and determine your average collection period. If it's thirty days, then sales made by credit can't be logged into cash until thirty-five to forty days after they're made. (Although the collection period is thirty days, you still have to deposit the money and draw on another bank to receive payment.)

The next line item on a cash flow statement is "other income." Other income refers to any revenue derived from investments, interest on loans that have been extended and the liquidation of any assets. Total income is the sum of cash sales, receivables, and other income. In the first month of your cash budget it will usually consist of cash sales, other income, and any receivables from the previous budget that have aged to a point of collection during the first month of the current budget.

Also tied to the breakdown of sales is cost of goods and direct labor. To sell the product, you must first produce it. Since you already have broken down sales by month, you need to determine the cost in material and labor to produce those sales. Refer to your cost of goods table in your business plan. Determine how much direct labor will be for the year to produce your product. Divide that number by the percentage breakdown of sales. Direct labor can be logged into cash flow during the same month in which it is accrued.

Material costs, on the other hand, are a little different. You need to include the material cost in cash flow using a time frame that allows you to convert the cost of raw material in cash flow into finished goods for sale. Therefore, if it requires sixty days to convert raw material to finished goods, and your payable period is thirty days after delivery, then enter the cost of goods under material in cash flow thirty days before sales are logged.

Working capital can be determined from operating expenses. All personnel and overhead costs are tied to sales (see Chapter 8). You can figure out your working capital and payroll requirements by dividing marketing and sales, general and administrative, and overhead expenses by the total projected operating expenses. Divide that total by the percentage breakdown of sales for each month and apply that amount to the appropriate line items in the cash flow statement.

As for capital equipment, there are two lines of thinking. The first is to purchase and install the needed equipment at a point during the year where additional volume warrants the expenditure, thereby assuring sufficient cash flow to handle the additional debt service or the outright purchase of the equipment. The second method is to have the equipment purchased and installed at the beginning of the business year or quarter closest to the time when you'll actually need the equipment, allowing time for training and working out bugs before the equipment is placed into full production.

The avenue you choose depends on your cash flow. If you can service additional debt or purchase the equipment from operating expenses, then the latter method works best. If your cash flow is tight, then choose the former method. Either way, capital equipment costs are accounted for under the heading "capital."

In addition to the preceding costs, include your tax obligations and any long-term debt or loans. These figures are readily available on loan schedules and tax charts used to project these costs.

Once all these costs have been entered in the cash flow budget, add them up to produce total expenses.

When total expenses are subtracted from total income, the result is your cash flow—either a surplus or deficit. If it's a deficit, determine the minimum cash balance you wish to maintain, and then calculate the difference between the minimum cash balance and the cash-flow deficit. This result is the amount required for financing purposes.

When forming a cash-flow budget, any amounts financed within a given month need to be included in the cash flow under a projected repayment schedule. Consult with your accountant or banker when developing this repayment schedule.

Evaluating Your Financial Position

Although it's an important financial-management tool for every business, a cash-flow projection can't project a business' capacity to borrow money. That can be determined by analyzing an income statement and balance sheet and using financial ratios that measure liquidity.

The first test of liquidity is the current ratio, which compares assets to liabilities. This ratio provides lenders with a quick look at the business' ability to meet obligations within a short-term period. If you have strong assets compared with your liabilities, your capacity for shouldering additional debt is fairly good. Generally, a two-to-one current ratio is good. The same goes for the quick ratio, which compares current assets to current liabilities. Refer back to Chapter 14 for more information on these ratios.

Net profit on sales also helps to evaluate a company's borrowing capacity. To determine your net profit on sales, divide net profit before taxes, which can be found in your income statement, by net sales. The result indicates the profitability of your company, which you can compare to industry averages as a benchmark.

If you already have low current and quick ratios, taking on an additional short-term loan would further weaken your ability to meet current obligations. You could, on the other hand, take out a long-term loan to improve your liquidity because only the portion of that loan due and payable during the first year would appear as a current liability on the balance sheet.

Generally, a business should be as profitable as the amount of money that can be earned from interest or dividends in securities. If your profitability is strong, investors will want to lend money to your business.

The debt-to-equity ratio compares total liabilities to total equity in a company. Most businesses aim to have a ratio of one-to-one or below. It's not prudent to leverage your business so much that it has no room to maneuver when the unexpected hits. And, if you're already burdened by debt, you may not be able to get the long-term financing you want at a favorable rate. You may have difficulty finding a partner, limited partner, or a shareholder for your corporation.

SOURCES OF CAPITAL FOR GROWING BUSINESSES

The key to keeping your business on the growth track is finding the right type of financing for your needs. There are several types.

Bootstrap Financing

As discussed in Chapter 18, bootstrap financing takes advantage of opportunities in your company through wise financial management. It's a way, in effect, to pull yourself up by the bootstraps without the help of others. You finance your growth through current assets. One big advantage of bootstrap financing is that you don't have to pay for borrowed money, which improves your balance sheet.

Factoring is a financing method whereby you sell your accounts receivable to a buyer, such as a commercial finance company, to raise capital. In addition to reducing internal costs, factoring also frees up money that would otherwise be tied to receivables. This money can then be used to generate profits through other avenues of the company.

You can bootstrap real estate expenses by leasing, instead of purchasing, your facility. If your lease payments are not as high as a mortgage payment, you can reduce your cash outlay. You may even be able to structure payments on your lease so that they correspond to seasonal peaks or growth patterns of your business.

Equipment suppliers are another source of financing, particularly if you spend a lot of money on equipment. Instead of paying cash for your equipment, the manufacturers can extend credit and you can pay over a period of time, typically three to five years.

Debt Financing

If your company has a good track record, a solid customer foundation, and a strong financial position, banks and other investors will want to talk to you about your capital requirements. You're the perfect customer—you have collateral with which to secure a loan and the capacity to incur additional debt.

The advantages of debt financing for growing businesses are that it provides funds when you need them in a time frame suitable for your business and doesn't require any surrender of equity. Several forms of collateral are used to secure loans, and the type you'll need depends on one of the three kinds of loan you're requesting:

1. Working capital loans are usually short-term loans tied to the business cycle of a company. They can be secured or unsecured loans and are used to increase working capital to fund the purchase of inventory, meet overhead and increase the number of sales made on credit. Collateral used for working capital loans includes receivables and inventory.

2. Term loans are generally intermediate- to long-term loans used to finance the purchase of capital equipment, expand a facility, increase working capital, or acquire another business. Term loans aren't tied to the cyclical nature of a business but to projections of higher earnings and larger profit margins by the business. A specialized type of term loan is a capital loan, a long-term loan used for the acquisition of a fixed asset and secured by that asset.

3. Interim loans are a type of bridge financing, extended until repayment is made by either the borrower or from another creditor.

Loans can also be unsecured, in which case your credit reputation is the only security the lender has. Unsecured personal loans are available for several thousand dollars or more if you're on good terms with the bank. These loans usually have short terms and high interest rates.

Unsecured loans are typically arranged with a bank to provide a revolving line of credit to the business for meeting short-term needs, usually tied to the business cycle of the company. As a rule, the principal must be periodically paid off and a compensating balance, usually 10 percent of the outstanding balance, is held by the bank in a non-interest-bearing account.

Banks are the largest source of financing for small businesses and are known for being risk-averse. It's best that the banker receive any information about you and your company from you, not from somebody else, and that you're up-front about your company's financial condition. Falsifying information on a loan application can be a felony and intentionally concealing information will come back to haunt you.

Equity Financing and Venture Capital

Equity financing is selling off a portion of your business to investors who may or may not actively participate in the management of the company (see Chapter 14). Depending on how you raise equity capital, you may relinquish anywhere from 25 to 75 percent of the business.

Venture capital is a form of equity financing used to finance high-risk, high-return businesses. The amount of equity a venture capitalist holds is a factor of the company's stage of development when the investment occurs, the perceived risk, the amount invested, and the relationship between the entrepreneur and the venture capitalist.

Venture capitalists usually invest in businesses of every kind. Many individual venture capitalists, also known as angels, prefer to invest in industries that are familiar to them. The reason is that while angels do not actively participate in the day-to-day management of the company, they do want to have a say in strategic planning in order to reduce risks and maximize profits.

On the other hand, private venture capital partnerships and industrial venture capitalists like to invest primarily in technology-related industries, especially applications of existing technology such as computer-related communications, electronics, genetic engineering, and medical or health-related fields. There are also a number of investments in service and distribution businesses, and even a few in consumer-related companies that attract venture capitalists.

In addition to the type of business they invest in, venture capitalists often define their investments by the business' life cycle: seed financing, start-up financing, second-stage financing, bridge financing, and leveraged buyout. Some venture capitalists prefer to invest in firms only during start-up, where the risk is highest but so is the potential for return. Other venture capital firms deal only with second-stage financing for expansion purposes or bridge financing where they supply capital for growth until the company goes public. Finally, there are venture capital companies that concentrate solely on supplying funds for management-led buyouts.

Generally, venture capitalists like to finance firms during the early and second stages, when growth is rapid, and cash out of the venture once it's established. At that time, the business owner either takes the company public, repurchases the investor's stock, merges with another firm or, in some circumstances, liquidates the business.

There are several types of venture capital:

- *Private venture capital partnerships* are perhaps the largest source of risk capital and generally look for businesses that have the capability to generate a 30 percent return on investment each year. They like to actively participate in the planning and management of the businesses they finance and have very large capital bases—up to $500 million—to invest at all stages.

- *Industrial venture capital pools* usually focus on funding firms that have a high likelihood of success, like high-tech firms or companies using state-of-the-art technology in a unique manner.

- *Investment banking firms* traditionally provide expansion capital by selling a company's stock to public and private equity investors. Some also have formed their own venture capital divisions to provide risk capital for expansion and early-stage financing.

- *Individual private investors,* also known as angels, can be friends and family who have only a few thousand dollars to invest, or well-heeled people who've built successful businesses in a similar industry and want to invest money as well as their experience in a businesses. Sponsored by the SBA's Office of Advocacy, the Angel Capital Network (ACE-Net, www.sba.gov/advo/acenet.html) is a nationwide, internet-based listing service that allows angel investors to get information on small, growing businesses looking for $250,000 to $5 million in equity financing.

- *Small Business Investment Corporations (SBICs)* are licensed and regulated by the SBA. SBICs are private investors that receive three to four dollars in SBA-guaranteed loans for every dollar they invest. Under the law, SBICs must invest exclusively in small firms with a net worth less than $18 million and average after-tax earnings (over the past two years) of less than $6 million. They're also restricted in the amount of private equity capital for each funding. Being licensed and regulated by a government agency distinguishes SBICs from other private venture capital firms, but other than that, they're not significantly different from those firms. For a complete listing of active SBICs, contact the National Association of Small Business Investment Companies (www.nasbic.org) at 666 11th Street NW, Suite 750, Washington, D.C. 20001, or call 202 628-5055.

- *Specialized Small Business Investment Companies (SSBICs)* are also privately capitalized investment agencies licensed and regulated by the SBA. They are designed to aid women- and minority-owned firms, as well as businesses in socially or economically disadvantaged areas, by providing equity funds from private and public capital. As with SBICs, SSBICs are restricted in the amount of their private funding. For information and a directory of active SSBICs, contact the National Association of Investment Companies at www.naicvc.com or call 202 204-3001.

- *Small Business Development Companies (SBDCs)* offer business counseling, training, and technical assistance. Located on college campuses, SBDCs are a cooperative effort among the SBA, the academic community, the private sector, and state and local government. There are SBDCs in every state ask your local SBA office for the location nearest you.

Before approaching any investor or venture capital firm, do your homework and find out if your interests match their investment preferences.

The way to contact venture capitalists is through an introduction from another business owner, banker, attorney, or other professional who knows you and the venture capitalist well enough to approach them with the proposition.

Merging Your Company with Another

Another way to grow your company is to sell it to another business, one that can provide the financial, distribution, marketing, operational, or whatever expertise you need to take your company to the next level of growth. While mergers can ensure that a brand remains intact or that a market expands, these opportunities can be tricky for small business owners—both financially and emotionally (see Chapter 30, "Selling Your Business").

The big advantage of having your company acquired by another is that it might make you, your key employees, and your investors rich. The big disadvantage is that entrepreneurs give up their ownership stake and independence—two of the main reasons we like to go into business for ourselves in the first place. There's only so much room for unconventionality in corporate culture—remember when Unilever gobbled Ben & Jerry's? The Vermont-based ice cream maker was founded in 1978 by childhood friends Ben Cohen and Jerry Greenfield with a $12,000 investment, $4,000 of which was borrowed. When Ben & Jerry's sold for $326 million and made the former hippie founders multimillionaires, staff wondered what would happen to fringe benefits like three free pints a day and the self-imposed gap on the lowest-paid and highest-paid employees and stockholders knew they'd have to say goodbye to the world's craziest meetings.

But for those business owners who dream of building an even more successful company, and are ready to acknowledge their achievements and move on, merging with another company can present terrific opportunities. The key is doing your homework, knowing what your business is worth, finding the right acquiring company, and working with competent professionals (lawyer, accountant, business broker). Ask tough questions and get to know the acquiring company on all levels. Remember that to it you are entrusting your reputation, your years of hard work, your employees, and your shareholders. As far as your involvement in the business after the merger, be honest with yourself and do what's best for your business.

CHAPTER 25

The Marketing Plan

Many young, small businesses include their marketing plans in their business plans. However, as the company grows and its product or service line expands, its marketing strategies get more complicated. It becomes necessary to have a written marketing plan that's separate from, but compatible with, the business plan to address just how you'll achieve the marketing and sales goals for your products/services.

The advantages of writing a marketing plan are that it forces you to:

- Chart industry growth
- Define the market(s) you serve
- Define your customers
- Determine the strengths and weaknesses of the competition
- Project sales
- Establish strategies to achieve your marketing goals
- Establish a market niche
- Identify your capital equipment needs
- Decide to whom certain responsibilities get assigned

At the end of this chapter, you'll find an actual marketing plan (Figure 25.1) from a successful specialty yarn store, whose sales for 2007 are expected to double those of 2000. While its format is slightly different than that outlined in this chapter, this sample marketing plan covers all the information suggested below and will give you a good starting point as you think about preparing your own. The only section not included is financial projections, which the business owner preferred not to publish.

THE CONCEPT

Marketing plans generally include the following sections:

- Executive summary
- Product description
- Goals and objectives
- Market analysis
- Description of customers
- Analysis of competition
- Product development
- Marketing tactics
- Financial projections
- Summary

EXECUTIVE SUMMARY

The executive summary is a brief synopsis of the entire marketing plan. It provides a short description of your product or service and a brief explanation on how it differs from those of your competitors. Here, you also state your objectives and explain how much capital you need to meet those goals.

A well written, to-the-point executive summary is a marketing document in and of itself, especially if you're trying to raise money. It piques the reader's interest and assures that he or she will continue reading. It also provides busy investors and lenders with a quick view of your proposed idea. Your executive summary can be a few paragraphs and no more than a page and a half in length.

Write your executive summary after you've finished your marketing plan, when your ideas are fully formed and finalized. That way, you will understand the market and know exactly where your opportunities are. The goal of your descriptive summary is to grab the reader's attention so that he or she will move to the next section of the marketing plan.

PRODUCT DESCRIPTION

The product description is a detailed preface of your proposed project. The product description should communicate to readers the purpose of your plan, what your product or service is and what you intend to do with it.

Like the executive summary, the product description can be a few paragraphs to a few pages in length, depending on the complexity of your plan. If your plan is relatively simple, keep your product description short, describing your product or service in one paragraph and your objectives and strategies in another. While a lengthy product description may be necessary in some cases, a short product description that succinctly conveys the required information is most effective.

When writing your product description, make sure to credit any sources for statistics so the reader knows they weren't formed arbitrarily.

MARKET ANALYSIS

The market definition starts from a broad study of the industry and then focuses on the niche for your product or service. To analyze the market you're serving, chart items such as sales history, current demand, and future trends for your product or service based on the customer base you've targeted. From this information, draw conclusions regarding demand for your product or service: will it increase, level off, or decline? Also address how often, if ever, new products are introduced in your industry and what the trends are from a technological point of view.

In addition to defining demand, identify the customers who will buy your product or service. Address what motivates your customers to buy, along with how they buy your product/service. When do they buy it? Where do they buy it? And how often? If relevant, describe the customer's gender, marital status, occupation, financial status, age, and/or geographic location.

Having examined these demographic elements, look next to the industry. Is your product high-tech, low-tech, or no-tech? If high-tech, how often are new products introduced? This will have a direct bearing on the product's life cycle.

How do the products get to market? The distribution channels used in the industry should be described in detail, along with any applicable laws and regulations.

THE COMPETITIVE ANALYSIS

This section identifies your competitors and evaluates their strategies to determine their strengths and weaknesses relative to those of your product or service. With this evaluation, you can establish what makes your product unique, your so-called "Unique Selling Proposition (USP)."

As detailed in Chapter 3, evaluate your competitors by placing them in strategic groups according to how directly they compete for a share of the customer's dollar. For each competitor or strategic group, list the product or service, its profitability, growth pattern, marketing objectives and assumptions, current and past strategies, organizational and cost structure, strengths and weaknesses, and size (in sales) of the competitor's business. Answer questions such as:

- Who are your competitors?
- What products do they sell?
- What is each competitor's market share?
- What are their past strategies?
- What are their current strategies?

- What type of media are used to market their product or service?
- How many hours per week are purchased to advertise through the media used in this market?
- What are each competitor's strengths and weaknesses?
- What potential threats do your competitors pose?

PRODUCT DEVELOPMENT

This section details the development of the product or service by charting goals, placing time lines on those goals and associating costs with those goals. The product development section also needs to define the expertise required to develop the product or service and state whether it's currently available on staff or will require new hires.

First, detail the current status of the product or service. Explain exactly what stage of development your product or service is in.

Next, detail the goals associated with its development. When forming your goals, don't underestimate time lines, costs, and personnel requirements, or you may not adequately cover the expenses of production. If you say you can develop a product in three months but it will actually take closer to four months, that will raise costs beyond your specified requirement.

Your goals must also provide a set of general procedures with schedules and delegated personnel for each task to ensure completion of the goals by specific dates. The work assignments created from the broad procedures will break down the various tasks into stages in order to achieve goals outlined in this section. These stages usually include a completion date for delivery of the preliminary product, a time line for preliminary product review and revision, and final delivery of the product.

Within the product development section, present a development budget. When forming your development budget, take into account all the expenses required to develop the product, from prototype to production. As detailed in Chapter 8, these costs usually include:

- *Material.* All raw materials used in the development of the product.
- *Direct labor.* All labor costs associated with the development of the product.

- *Overhead.* All overhead expenses required to operate the business during the development phase such as taxes, rent, phone, utilities, and office supplies.
- *General and administrative costs.* The salaries of executive and administrative personnel along with any other office support functions.
- *Marketing and sales.* The salaries of marketing personnel required to develop promotional materials and plan the marketing campaign that should begin prior to delivery of the product.
- *Professional services.* Include consultation with accountants, lawyers, and business consultants.
- *Miscellaneous costs.* Costs that are related to product development.
- *Capital equipment.* Equipment requirements related to product development. To determine capital requirements, first establish the type of equipment you need, decide whether to acquire the equipment or use outside contractors, and finally, if you decide to acquire the equipment, whether to lease or purchase it.

The last element in the product development section is the amount of risk involved. Identifying and addressing these risks is important as it shows prospective investors or lenders that you've thought through the development process and have contingency plans in case crises or problems arise.

OPERATIONS

Start by listing all the various products or services your company offers, along with some background information on yourself and your management team. Include information on your experience, education, projects you've supervised, and so on. Make your investors confident of you and your management team, so they'll feel good about funding your project.

Also provide information on your business' financial resources, what type of expertise you have available to implement your marketing plan, and how you perceive your company's strengths and weaknesses.

As with your business plan, include tables showing operating expenses, capital requirements, and the cost of goods. Operating expenses should illustrate how the introduction of the new product will affect the company, while the capital requirements table shows what's needed for new equipment to produce the product. The cost of goods table is relevant for manufacturers, merchandisers, and service companies as it clarifies material, labor, and overhead expenses associated with the production of the product on a continuing basis.

Administration is in charge of overhead functions that support operations, such as accounting, legal, human resources, and other operations functions. The expenses for Softie Baby Care are illustrated in Table 25.5, divided according to the functional lines detailed earlier.

OBJECTIVES AND GOALS

Objectives are the foundation of a marketing plan because they define where your company is going. They also describe what success will look like when you achieve it. Objectives need to be measurable ($100,000 in sales, a 5 percent increase in market share) and set within a time frame (in six months, in three years).

Your objectives should spell out exactly what you intend to accomplish. Long-range objectives usually involve financial targets such as overall sales, return on investment, and increased profit margins, and can also include market share, personnel, productivity, research and development, and/or any other goal you deem suitable.

Short-term goals should be viewed as a series of building blocks that lead to achieving long-range objectives. Short-term goals let you know whether you're on the right course or whether any of your long-range objectives need to be modified. Well-conceived short-term goals take into account the various elements that need to be accomplished to achieve long-range objectives, such as an increase in production staffing, acquisition of modernized equipment, and increased productivity.

Start your objectives and goals section by stating your long-range objectives and then describing the various short-term goals that must be accomplished by a certain time period to reach your objectives. State the assumptions you used to formulate your objectives and include any relevant facts and figures that bolster your argument.

MARKETING TACTICS

Strategies to achieve your goals need to focus on what sets your product or service apart from those of your competitors. In this section of your marketing plan, detail your market strategy and explain how your competition will react. For every action you take, your competitors will respond with a countermove to maintain their present position in the market or expand it. Provide the reader with various scenarios of your competitors' reactions to your plans and how you propose responding to them.

To develop the information you'll need for this section, ask yourself the following questions and write down your answers in a notebook.

Product

1. What is your product or service?
2. How does your product or service differ from those of competitors?
3. What message will you include on your package?
4. What will be the size, shape, color, and material of the package?
5. What is your sales and production forecast?

Distribution

1. What channels will you use to distribute your product or service?
2. How will you time your distribution?

Price

1. What are your pricing objectives?
2. What will be your unit cost? Your unit price?
3. Will you offer a discount policy?
4. What do you project your revenue and profit to be?

Sales Promotion

1. What are your sales promotion objectives?
2. How will you position your product or service?
3. Will your promotions be coordinated with distribution schedules? How will you sell?
5. Who will do the selling?
6. Will you define sales territories?
7. How will you compensate your sales force?
8. What are your publicity objectives?
9. What type of publicity will you seek?

Advertising

1. What's the message in your campaign?
2. What benefits will you promote to customers?
3. What media do you plan to use? How frequently?
4. What's the cost of your campaign?
5. What's your advertising budget?

FINANCIAL PROJECTIONS

The financial projections section includes all the financial information relevant to the project. Most marketing plans benefit from a three-year income statement, a three-year cash flow projection, and a three-year summary of the balance sheet.

Through your research and from the body of the marketing plan, you should already have solid numbers on which to base your projections. Your financial information is not only important to investors to determine whether or not they want to fund the proposal but you need it to control costs.

For more information on financial controls, see Chapter 17. A three-year income statement is a month-by-month look at projected sales, fixed and variable expenses, and profits. It provides a quick look at how you believe you'll perform over a three-year period. Whereas the income statement takes a close look at sales and expenses, the cash flow projection summarizes this information and displays the availability of cash on a month-to-month basis. When expenses are subtracted from income, you wind up with a cash flow surplus or deficit.

The cash flow projection highlights when you'll need additional money to keep the project going.

A balance sheet is a snapshot of a business' assets and liabilities, along with owner's equity, at a given point in time. For the marketing plan, provide your balance sheets on an annual basis.

You may also want to include an implementation schedule in your marketing plan. The implementation schedule lists the major goals and tasks necessary to complete the project and the capital outlay for each period. You can base your schedule on weekly, monthly, or quarterly periods. If your project is a lengthy one with projec-

tions up to three years, base your schedule on quarterly periods. If it ranges between one year and three years, implement a monthly schedule. If it is a year or less, you may want to consider a weekly schedule.

Keep in mind while you're forming your projections that market potential, sales potential, and sales forecast all mean different things. Market potential pertains to the total potential sales for a product or service within a specific geographic area over a fixed period. Sales potential refers to the capability of the market to absorb the volume produced by a specific company within the industry, supposedly yours.

Your sales potential, however, is not the same as your sales forecast. Sales forecast is the actual sales you believe your company will generate during the year based on your market research.

There are reasons companies don't achieve the total sales potential within a market:

- Limited resources
- Margin of return on the investment
- Unforeseeable market factors

Perhaps the greatest reason, however, that companies don't achieve total sales potential is the law of diminishing returns. This means the more aggressive you are in achieving total sales potential, the greater your marginal cost will be for each additional percentage point above your sales forecast. Most companies won't be able to sustain this expenditure, and it's not wise to try to do so. The return on investment will decrease while your overhead increases; your break-even point will be extended dramatically, and you won't reach your profit goals. All this has to be considered when forecasting sales.

SUMMARY

The summary should highlight the significant points in your plan, such as the advantages your product has over your competitors, cost structure, and profits. Strongly emphasize the unique selling proposition of your product—something your product or service has that your competitors don't. It is the key to your marketing plan's success.

The summary doesn't have to be long. In a few paragraphs, encapsulate all the major points within your marketing plan so it is readily available for readers who bypass the body of the plan and go straight to the summary. Your summary statement should start off explaining the purpose of the marketing plan. If you write yours for the express purpose of raising capital, include how much you'll need to accomplish your goals. And then provide the reasons this investment is justified.

| FIGURE 25.1 | A Sample Marketing Plan |

Marketing Plan

THE ELEGANT EWE

71 South Main Street

Concord, New Hampshire 03301

www.elegantewe.com

603 226-0066

info@elegantewe.com

Mission Statement

The Elegant Ewe is an upscale retail yarn store founded in 1998 that offers a unique shopping experience with a vast selection of designer yarns, knitting and crochet accessories, and spinning supplies, as well as its own distinctive pattern line and custom yarns. The shop is known for its knowledgeable and pleasant staff that excels in helping customers find the project that fits their needs, making the shop a destination for many around the country.

History

The Elegant Ewe opened in June 1998. It was established as a sole proprietorship and initially open five days a week with two full-time employees. Now the shop is open six days a week in the summer and seven days a week the rest of the year with four full-time employees.

In 2001 the shop was featured as one of "America's Favorite Yarn Shops" in Knitter's Stash, a hardcover publication from Interweave Press. In 2003 the shop was featured as an editor's choice "must visit" shop in *Yankee Magazine's Travel Guide to New England.*

Sales in the first four years increased eightfold (800 percent) and sales in years 5 and 6 nearly doubled that increase due to a scarf craze that hit and lasted for almost two years. Sales of these expensive yarns were quick and easy with minimal "waste" yarn, customers required minimal knitting skill (thus pulling in a lot of new knitters with minimal work to teach them to knit), and repeat sales were very frequent and easy. We faced some challenges in ordering fast enough and keeping up with the workload, and later several yarns became unavailable with some orders taking six months to one year to get. We quickly adjusted, often creating our own one-of-a-kind yarn combinations with materials that were obtainable and our class schedule doubled in order to teach all of the new potential knitters. Even though we worked hard to capture and keep as many knitters as possible during this time, years 7 and 8 showed an expected 10 percent and 15 percent respective decrease in gross sales once the scarf fad began to diminish.

Marketing Goals

Our overall goal is to continue to distinguish ourselves from the competition in this time of heavy discounting and store closings not based on price, but rather on our unique features.

Our long-term goals are to:

- Explore the possibility of publishing a book with our store patterns in the summer of 2007, looking at a two-year time frame.
- Pursue selling our patterns wholesale to other shops, not so much as an income generator but to get our name out there with the hope that customers will come find us.
- Review a computerized tracking system for inventory.

Our short-term goals are:

- Reformat with new photographs of current pattern line (we are currently talking with a photographer) and update designs.
- Spend at least two hours per week updating our web site, to promote our pattern line and pattern kits as well as look at other potential promotional opportunities on the internet (making sure we are linked to distributors' web sites, etc).
- Submit a few store patterns in early 2007 for a soon-to-be-published book, One Skein Wonders.
- Continue to attend current vendor shows. We do not feel we can increase the number at this time without adding more staff.

Sales and Profit Goals

Overall our objective is to halt our current drop in sales and to continue to become more efficient with inventory and operation costs, with a modest 2.5 to 3 percent growth within two years.

In the long term, we hope to continue stocking no more than $150,000 in inventory during the busy season (in the past we have been up to $200,000). Sales are seasonal so that inventory fluctuates throughout the year. We want to continue to fine-tune the manual inventory system in place (all inventory orders are on a schedule in which inventory is counted and checked for selling trends) and keep our turns to as close as possible to three per year.

Products and Services

The majority of our sales (60 percent) are from yarn sales. Other items include needles, books, spinning supplies, bags, buttons, and music (which is also played during store hours). We are now designing our own patterns, which not only sets us apart from other yarn stores but also gives us a great profit margin. Some items have been dropped (rug hooking supplies, local gifts) that were not profitable in order to better focus on yarns.

The services we offer customers include sweater finishing and repair at $25 per hour. We also run between six and seven classes per week as well as "knitting clinics" that allow customers to come in for help on a drop-in basis while still paying for service.

Target Markets

The total number of customers based on our hard copy mailing list is approximately 4,000 with 800 (20 percent of the "serious customers") on the e-mail update list. Our customer segmentation according to mailing list is: 10 percent from Concord, 50 percent from New Hampshire other than Concord, 40 percent from out of state/country, 99.5 percent women, 30 to 50 years of age, and the majority working with some disposable income.

A group of customers whose numbers are currently dropping are the 18 to 24-year-olds who picked up knitting as a fad in 2004. A group whose numbers are increasing is those age 30 to

50 who also picked it up as a fad and those we are who we are trying to appeal to with classes and projects that make knitting a way of life.

Overall Strategy

Although experiencing a recent two-year decrease in sales, our net income has held steady; our final figures for 2006 may show a slight increase, due to reduced expenses and better inventory control. Although we had a 10 percent drop in sales in 2005 from 2004, we dropped expenses by 12 percent, leaving us with only a 3 percent decrease in net income. In other words, we are making more money with less sales due to less depreciation and no debt service or liabilities, creating our own inventory (our own pattern line, which is high profit margin) and higher pricing on unique items. In 2006 we dropped inventory by $50,000 as well as further reduced expenses.

Competition

Our biggest competition right now is the internet, which offers heavy discounting and ease of shopping from home but provides poor service.

Catalogue shopping also offers discounting and ease of shopping from home, but poor service.

Other nearby local shops include one in Nashua, New Hampshire (35 miles), another in Meredith, New Hampshire (40 miles), and a third in Lexington, Massachusetts (65 miles).

Advertising/Promotional Strategy

1. Word of mouth is huge for us, and it's free! Customers who have a positive experience tell others, especially on their blogs, and often will often refer or link customers to our web site.

2. We do two newsletter mailings and two postcard mailings a year to 4,000, at an approximate cost of $4,200.

3. Although primarily attended for the resulting sales, vendor shows are a great way of promoting our business out of our area. We are currently working five shows per year, which account for 10 percent of our annual gross sales: the New Hampshire Sheep and Wool Festival, Stitches Midwest in Chicago, Stitches East in Baltimore, the Knitting Guild Association in Philadelphia, and the Boston Knit Out (promotion only, no direct sales).

We began developing our web site as a promotional tool the latter part of 2004, when we realized the scarf trend would soon be over. We hired an employee to develop and maintain the web site, but that relationship did not work out. The web site is currently updated and maintained by the store manager and myself and is used mostly as a promotional tool. There is so much yarn discounting currently on the internet that we have decided to continue using the web site more as a promotional tool to get customers into the shop. Most hits to our web site come from links from distributors, blogs, and fiber source web site. The web site costs approximately $240 per year plus $500 staff time to update. Our e-mail newsletter is sent every one to two weeks to 800 "serious knitters" on our mailing list.

Yellow pages: At one time we were paying almost $200 per month for yellow pages ads, but found them not as effective as our customers were looking more on the internet. In 2004 we began to develop our web site.

Initially we ran ads in two national knitting magazines, but we have cut that back to one (*Interweave Knits*), which we feel is the better magazine since it fits better with the styles our shop promotes.

7. Our cargo van with our logo and shop information is very visible and frequently seen.

8. Book signings by noted authors are held whenever possible.

9. National/international designers visit the shop twice a year.

10. Fashion shows are held twice a year and they promote our store designs. Customers will often travel a long distance to come to some of these events and they also tend to save their money so they can spend a lot on these weekends. These events will sometimes get us free listings in our local newspapers.

11. We donate twelve to twenty items to local auctions/charities each year. This may not generate new customers, but builds on name recognition and customer loyalty while getting rid of older store model samples. It is also a tax deduction.

Pricing Strategy

We do not discount, except for a few select sale yarns (total discount sale yarn sales for 2006 was under 5 percent). Because we are in a high-rent downtown area (provides easy access), carry a large inventory (currently $150,000 wholesale), and have had increases in shipping fees as well as credit card fees and overhead, we have to charge over keystone (double our costs, which is standard in the knitting industry) for most items. We often look for unique items that we are able to make a better profit on when we do our purchasing in order to keep our more "common" yarns closer to keystone. We have gotten very creative in moving "slow sellers." Rather than discounting them, we work them into a different model or may even dye them, making them a hand-dyed yarn for which we can charge significantly more—then they sell. Unfortunately we do not feel that we can increase our service fees at this time, since many shops offer these services for free. Currently we charge $25 per hour for sweater finishing/repair and private lessons, and $50 for a four-class group lesson, a total of eight hours. We did increase class costs three years ago.

Marketing and Advertising Budgets

Although our current budget shows that we spend 2 percent of gross sales on advertising, we actually spend more than that since most of what we do involves marketing (vendor shows are very important marketing tools but are seen under other operating expense since they are direct sales). Newspaper advertising is very ineffective and expensive, although we have had a great response to free listings. Our in-store events also are important marketing tools—direct advertising is often done through the author/designer/publisher, making our cost minimal with a possible free press release along with it. Overall, our marketing is very streamlined. We do much more than the average yarn store to market ourselves with minimal cost.

Beginning in February 2007, we will add two to three staff hours per week to work on internet and publication promotions (approximately an additional $1,500 per year, but this cost will show up under wages).

Potential Problems

The knitting industry is currently undergoing a lot of change. Several new shops opened during the 2003-2004 scarf craze and are now having serious financial issues with the drop in sales and are closing, dumping inventory into the market at often well below wholesale. Several distributors, who now have warehouses overstocked with yarn, are also dumping inventory, again well below wholesale cost, to the general public. Other seasoned yarn shop owners I have talked to recently have experienced a much larger drop in sales than we have, one even up to 50 percent. We are expecting that these events will be short-lived, although the effects in the industry may last at least a couple of years.

CHAPTER 26

Advertising

Advertising is a powerful marketing tool as it provides a direct line of communication to your existing and prospective customers about your product or service. The purpose of advertising is to:

- Make customers aware of your product or service

- Convince customers that your company's product or service is right for their needs

- Create a desire for your product or service

- Enhance the image of your company

- Announce new products or services

- Reinforce salespeople's messages

- Make customers take the next step (ask for more information, request a sample, place an order, and so on)

- Draw customers to your business

Your advertising goals are established in your business plan. You may want to obtain a certain percentage of growth in sales, generate more inquiries for sales, or build in-store traffic. The desired result can simply be increasing name recognition or modifying the image you're projecting. Objectives vary depending on the industry and market you're in.

All products and businesses go through three stages, with different advertising goals for each one:

1. *The start-up business.* You're new in the market and need to establish your identity. Your company needs high levels of promotion and publicity to grab consumers' attention.

2. *The growing business.* Once your identity is established, you need to differentiate yourself from your competition. Convince buyers that yours is the service or product to try.

3. *The established business.* Remind consumers why they should continue buying from you.

No matter which stage your business is in, advertising follows these steps, according to the industry mnemonic, AIDA: "Awareness, Interest, Desire, Action." Your job is to make prospective customers aware that your product or service exists, pique their interest in what your product or service can do for them, make them want to try your product or service, and finally take action (asking for more information or actually buying the product).

When developing your advertising campaign, follow these four steps:

1. *Define your market.* Determine who your target market is, those customers most likely to buy your product or service. One magazine that's fun to read, interesting, and helpful in this regard is *Advertising Age* (711 Third Avenue, New York, N.Y. 10017, 212 210-0100, www.adage. com).

2. *Establish your budget.* Know what you can afford to spend to reach your target audience.

3. *Plan which media you'll use.* Figure out what's the best way to reach your prospective customers with your message.

4. *Create an advertising strategy.* Choose the most effective message and visuals for your advertising campaign.

DEFINING YOUR MARKET

To figure out who your target market is, ask yourself:

- *Who are my potential customers?* For example, for a retail business like a paint store or a doughnut shop, the market is typically within a five-mile radius of the business.
- *How many potential customers are there?*
- *Where are they located?*
- *Where do they now buy the products or services I want to sell them?*
- *Can I offer them anything they are not getting now?*
- *How can I persuade them to do business with me?*

Taking a single message and aiming it at as many buyers as possible is not the way to reach your target audience. This is what is often referred to as "the shotgun approach," which can miss targets, require lots of effort, and be costly. A much more effective tactic is "the rifle approach."

The "rifle approach" provides a clear, well-thought-out message that's focused on your target market. To craft such a message, you need accurate demographic information about your target market, including gender, age, income, and occupation (see the Demographic Comparison worksheet in Chapter 4). Other characteristics will be helpful, depending on the nature of your business.

Determine who your customers are, where they're located, and what media will reach them most effectively. For example, if your company sells satellite radios and your market research shows that the target audience is mainly men between ages 18 and 34, then the optimum place for you to reach them with your ad would be while they're in their cars, wishing they had a satellite radio to listen to! You can conduct your own market research to generate demographic information, or you can hire a professional marketing firm or ad agency to do it for you.

CREATING YOUR ADVERTISING BUDGET

How much should your business devote to an advertising campaign? Amounts—which typically vary from industry to industry, and from one business to another—are expressed as a percentage of gross revenue. Percentages range from more than 30 percent of gross revenue for direct-mail merchandisers to 1 percent for small manufacturers of specialty products.

Most companies base their advertising budget on a percentage of projected gross sales, usually anywhere from two to five percent. This is generally referred to as the "cost method," which theorizes that an advertiser can't afford to spend more money than they have. For example, if your business plan projects first-year gross sales of $260,000 and you use the cost method to determine the advertising budget (figuring five percent), you'd have $12,500, or $1,042 per month, to spend on advertising. For a grand opening, you might want to use twice your monthly amount, or $2,084 in this case, to promote your opening.

Although $12,500 might seem like a small amount for a year, and a drop in the bucket compared with what your competitor down the street spends, here's how to plan an effective, cost-efficient advertising campaign using that amount. If your target audience can be effectively reached using print and outdoor media, you can run an ad in a community weekly paper every other week all year (26 weeks). Say a two-column-by-five inch ad costs a total of $1,560 for the entire year. You can then buy transit advertising on the two buses that pass by your front doorstep for a year for, let's say, $960. Placing those ads on the back of the bus cards above passenger seats for 52 weeks will cost $480 for the year using the 10 buses that cover your neighborhood. You can do 2,000 pieces of direct mail for, let's say, 80 cents apiece, four times a year for about $6,400, including production. Budgeting $2,100 to cover freelance copywriting and design by qualified professionals brings the total expenditure up to $12,500. This is a comprehensive and effective advertising campaign.

While figures used for this sample advertising campaign are based on national averages for these particular vehicles, costs will vary from market to market. Large markets such as New York and Los Angeles will be much more expensive than smaller markets. Or, if you're planning on spending three or four percent of your gross sales on advertising instead of the five percent used in this sample, you'll need to adjust your figures to take that into account. Remember, if you don't have the budget to use all media effectively, it's best to dominate one or two media at a time rather than to spread yourself too thin.

Where can you effectively cut corners with advertising? Instead of hiring staff, use freelancers as much as possible.

Trading or bartering your products or services in exchange for media time or space (called "trade-outs") is another advantage to working directly with the media. This is particularly common with small radio stations, smaller television stations, and community weeklies. For example, a complete campaign for an automobile dealership can be financed by the trade of automobiles for the media time needed.

After you determine your advertising budget, consider what media is appropriate for your product and how much it will cost to advertise with those media.

MEDIA PLANNING

Choosing which media or type of advertising is tricky for small firms with limited budgets and know-how. Large-market television and newspapers are often too expensive for a company that services only a small area (although local newspapers can be used). Magazines, unless local, usually cover too much territory to be cost-efficient for a small firm, although some national publications offer regional or city editions. Metropolitan radio stations present the same problems as TV and metro newspapers; however, in smaller markets, the local radio station and newspaper may sufficiently cover a small firm's audience.

That is why it's important to put together a media plan for your advertising campaign. The three components of a media plan are:

1. *Defining the marketing problem.* Do you know where your business is coming from and where the potential for increased business lies? Do you know which markets offer the greatest opportunity? Do you need to reach everybody or only a select group of consumers? How often is the product used? How much product loyalty exists?

2. *Translating the marketing requirements into attainable media objectives.* Do you want to reach lots of people in a wide area (getting the most out of your advertising dollar)? Then mass media, like newspaper and radio, might work for you. If your target market is a select group in a defined geographic area, then direct mail could be your best bet.

3. *Defining a media solution by formulating media strategies.* Certain schedules work best with different media. For example, the rule of thumb is that a print ad must run three times before it gets noticed. Radio advertising is most effective when run at certain times of the day or around certain programs, depending on what market you're trying to reach.

Advertising media generally include:

- Television
- Radio
- Newspapers
- Magazines (consumer and trade)
- Outdoor billboards
- Public transportation
- Yellow pages
- Direct mail
- Specialty advertising (on items such as matchbooks, pencils, calendars, telephone pads, shopping bags, and so on)
- Other media (catalogs, samples, handouts, brochures, newsletters, etc.)

When comparing the cost and effectiveness of various advertising media, consider the following factors:

- *Reach*. Expressed as a percentage, reach is the number of individuals (or homes) you want to expose your product to through specific media scheduled over a given period of time.
- *Frequency*. Using specific media, how many times, on average, should the individuals in your target audience be exposed to your advertising message? It takes an average of three or more exposures to an advertising message before consumers take action.
- *Cost per thousand*. How much will it cost to reach a thousand of your prospective customers (a method used in comparing print media)? To determine a publication's cost per thousand, also known as CPM, divide the cost of the advertising by the publication's circulation in thousands.
- *Cost per point*. How much will it cost to buy one rating point for your target audience, a method used in comparing broadcast media. One rating point equals 1 percent of your target audience. Divide the cost of the schedule being considered by the number of rating points it delivers.
- *Impact*. Does the medium in question offer full opportunities for appealing to the appropriate senses, such as sight and hearing, in its graphic design and production quality?
- *Selectivity*. To what degree can the message be restricted to those people who are known to be the most logical prospects?

Reach Versus Frequency

Reach and frequency are important aspects of an advertising plan and are used to analyze alternative advertising schedules to determine which produce the best results relative to the media plan's objectives.

Calculate reach and frequency and then compare the two on the basis of how many people you'll reach with each schedule and the number of times you'll connect with the average person. Let's say you aired one commercial in each of four television programs (A, B, C, D), and each program has a 20 rating, resulting in a total of 80 gross rating points. It's possible that some viewers will see more than one announcement—some viewers of pro-

gram A might also see program B, C, or D, or any combination of them.

For example, in a population of 100 TV homes, a total of 40 are exposed to one or more television programs. The reach of the four programs combined is therefore 40 percent (40 homes reached divided by the 100 TV-home population).

Many researchers have charted the reach achieved with different media schedules. These tabulations are put into formulas from which you can estimate the level of delivery (reach) for any given schedule. A reach curve is the technical term describing how reach changes with increasing use of a medium. The media salespeople you work with or your advertising agency can supply you with these reach curves and numbers.

Now let's use the same schedule of one commercial in each of four television programs (A, B, C, D) to determine reach versus frequency. In our example, 17 homes viewed only one program, 11 homes viewed two programs, seven viewed three programs and five homes viewed all four programs. If we add the number of programs each home viewed, the 40 homes in total viewed the equivalent of 80 programs and therefore were exposed to the equivalent of 80 commercials. By dividing 80 by 40, we establish that any one home was exposed to an average of two commercials.

To increase reach, you'd include additional media in your plan or expand the timing of your message. For example, if you're only buying "drive time" on the radio, you might also include some daytime and evening spots to increase your audience. To increase frequency, you'd add spots or insertions to your existing schedule. For example, if you're running three insertions in a local magazine, you'd increase that to six insertions so that your audience would be exposed to your ad more often.

Gross rating points (GRPs) are used to estimate broadcast reach and frequency from tabulations and formulas. Once your schedule delivery has been determined from your reach curves, you can obtain your average frequency by dividing the GRPs by the reach. For example, 200 GRPs divided by an 80 percent reach equals a 2.5 average frequency.

Frequency is important because it takes a while to build up awareness and break through the consumer's selection process. People are always screening out messages they're not interested in, picking up only on those things that are important to them. Repetition is the key word here. For frequency, it's much better to advertise regularly in small spaces than it is to have a one-time expensive advertising extravaganza.

Word-of-Mouth Advertising

Word-of-mouth advertising is important for every business, as each happy customer can steer dozens of new ones your way. Make sure that business cards and/or fliers are always available for customers or clients to pass on to others. Successful business owners are active in their communities and become well-known by joining and leading civic organizations, attending charity events, speaking at seminars, getting involved in politics, and being present at openings of businesses and other special events. While running your business comes first, time spent developing contacts always pays off.

Print Media

Once you know what your goals and budget are, you can determine the best print media for reaching your target market. Effective print advertising may include a combination of different print vehicles, such as regional magazines, newspapers, direct mail, and the Yellow Pages. Take a look at your competition to see what they're doing and find out how well it works for them.

You can find publications that are appropriate for your advertising needs by looking through references such as the directories put out by the Standard Rate and Data Service (SRDS), 1700 Higgins Road, Des Plaines, IL 60018, 847 375-5000, www. srds.com. The SRDS directories list all the relevant information about consumer and trade publications, including a short description of each publication, its editorial content, who the publication goes out to and a breakdown of circulation figures. Using this information, you can compile a list of publications suitable for your advertising.

For more in-depth information, contact an ad representative at each publication you've chosen and request a media kit. These contain sample copies of the publication, detailed information about the editorial content, a breakdown of readers' demographics, the publication's ad

rates, and an audited circulation statement from the publisher.

There are two primary audits: the Audit Bureau of Circulation (ABC), and the Business Publications Audit (BPA). Audited circulations are sworn statements by the publisher, verified by an outside source, that the publication is distributed to the number of people claimed in the circulation figures.

With this information in hand, you can judge the cost-effectiveness of advertising in a publication by determining the relationship between its circulation and the ad rates. This ratio is your CPM, or cost per thousand. For example, if the circulation is 30,000 and the rate for a full-page ad is $1,500, divide $1,500 by 30. You'd see that advertising in this publication would cost $50 to reach each thousand readers.

As well as finding out each publication's CPM, inquire about what kind of deals you can work out with the ad rep from each publication. For example, you can sometimes negotiate for special positioning in the publication—inside the front cover, on the back cover, or within the first few pages of the book are prime locations for ads. Publications will often charge an additional 10 to 20 percent of the ad's cost for special positioning, but if you're a good negotiator, you can sometimes get it for no additional charge. Always ask for your ad to be placed in the first third of the publication (where readers are apt to read more closely) and on a right-hand page, which is not considered special positioning.

You can also negotiate with the ad rep on a frequency discount. If you run your ad three times, six times, or twelve times instead of just once, you'll get a reduced rate for each insertion. Publications have standard frequency discounts as listed in the Standard Rate and Data Service directory or on the rate card the ad rep gives you, but often the rep can give you an even better deal than the standard frequency discounts if you run your ad on a regular schedule and if the rep wants your business.

If your business' customers or clients are local, you'll find newspaper advertising valuable. A display or classified ad is not expensive compared with advertising on television or radio, and your exposure will be greater. In large metropolitan areas, some papers have created special, small-firm advertising sections and service directories where a dozen or more small-firm ads may appear on a single page.

Certain sections of the paper are more effective, depending on whom you want to reach. For example, the sports pages are better for men, feature sections are generally better for reaching women, and the business pages are best for businesspeople. Certain days of the week are better than others for specific groups—gardeners are known to carefully read the home or style sections of newspapers, frequently published on Thursdays. To reach your target audience effectively, you may want to request a certain section or day of the week as you see fit.

Whenever you're buying newspaper space, you'll get a discount based on the total number of lines that you run. Ask about special monthly runs or business edition specials within a certain industry sector. The rates for advertising in these sections are lower, making them more accessible to small businesses. By the same token, classified display ads, as they are called, cost less than display ads in many magazines, but not all magazines allow advertisers to take display ads in their classified sections. Certain frequent and larger-scale advertisers, like department stores and banks, are also able to take advantage of industry-related, below-rate-card rates.

Consider different types of magazines: consumer-oriented, women's, country living, home, gardening, food, travel, business, men's automotive, and sports. Most magazines on the market are targeted toward a specialized sector of readers. These publications help you focus on a particular market segment.

Newsletters are great vehicles for reaching specialized markets. Because circulations are typically small, rates for advertising in newsletters are very reasonable. Their circulations are also very targeted because of their specialized editorial content. In terms of cost-effectiveness, this is one of the best types of print media to purchase. But you have to be careful. Many newsletters aren't audited publications. They operate on a controlled-circulation basis, so you basically have to take the word of the publisher that the newsletter is distributed to the number of people he or she claims.

Trade journals may be the most effectively targeted medium, since their readers are narrowly grouped around a particular industry. Sometimes your advertising can be effective in a direct, but related, industry publication. For example, when a small firm that originally made miniaturized homes, buildings, and villages for architects advertised in a railroad hobby magazine, sales zoomed. The tiny structures were perfect for setting up around train sets. A manufacturer of a mobile car-washing compressor with an adjustable wand advertised in a window-care trade journal after finding that the compressor was ideal for washing mini-blinds.

Most local businesses promote their goods and services in the yellow pages with advertisements that may be illustrated and vary in size from simple one-line listings to half-page spreads. (See Figure 26.1, Yellow Pages Ad.) Since the phone company has specific categories with which they classify businesses, be careful to choose the most appropriate one(s) for your business. Sometimes it's worthwhile to advertise in more than one category. Whatever you decide, just be careful about making the Yellow Pages deadline for sending in your ad(s). Missing them can mean waiting a whole year until your ad runs.

Don't scatter your ads, as skipping from one publication to another seldom gets results. It destroys the effectiveness of consistent advertising and, most important, you lose privileges given to consistent advertisers.

Broadcast Media

The goal for radio and television commercials is to get the listener's attention. Good radio and television writing incorporates three elements:

1. *Meaningful content.* The listener has to believe the product provides a reward.

2. *Getting the listener or viewer's attention and keeping it focused on the message.* A commercial for a spaghetti sauce misses the boat, for example, if the listener starts thinking about the size of tomatoes in the garden instead of the possibility of having spaghetti for dinner.

3. *Reinforcing the product or service's benefits to the listener or viewer.* An effective commercial emphasizes benefits. Commercials for Advil focus on relief from muscle pain, while ads for Dove soap stress soft skin.

Creativity is essential for radio and television commercials, especially when you don't have funds to flood

FIGURE 26.1 **Yellow Pages Ad**

the marketplace for an extended period. Your ads must be well crafted and make an impact upon listeners and viewers. Make sure that what you're telling people isn't boring or dull; otherwise, they'll tune out or turn off in a big hurry.

Advertising on major radio stations presents the same problems for small business owners as advertising in metro newspapers. Such advertising may reach an audience far beyond the limits of a small business' trading area, and the cost may be prohibitive. But radio advertising on local stations can be effective and affordable. These stations have programs specifically designed to appeal to listeners in smaller markets.

To get the complete story on a radio station's advertising costs, ask one of the station's salespeople for the rate card. The Standard Rate and Data Service directory also furnishes information on costs.

Radio ads can work well for small-business owners, especially if they supplement those ads with other advertising. Radio is great if your product has mass appeal and especially if you're the exclusive provider of your product or if your competition isn't using radio.

Radio advertising can be relatively inexpensive and can reach different market segments than metropolitan newspapers. Ask your sales rep about merchandising packages or sponsorships to further increase your on-air exposure. An example of a merchandising program might be enlisting one of the station's disc jockeys to give away samples of, or coupons for, your product on the air. Or, you could "sponsor" the station's weather or traffic reports or some other program segment that might relate to your product.

Always negotiate the cost per radio spot with your salesperson before you agree to pay rate card rates. Put together a "package" of spots that you'd like to use as your schedule. A good one might be something like this:

Weekday	Spots per Week	Listening Time
Mon.-Fri.	5X, 6a.m.–10a.m.	morning drive time
Mon.-Fri.	4X, 10a.m.–3p.m.	daytime
Mon.-Fri.	5X, 3 p.m.–7 p.m.	evening drive time
Sat.	2X, 6 a.m.–10 a.m.	morning drive time
Sat.	2X, 10 a.m.–3 p.m.	daytime

Morning commuter time has the highest listenership in radio; afternoon and evening drive time are the next highest and may be less expensive than morning rates. Use your ideal schedule as a reference when negotiating with your salesperson, who may throw in some "overnight" spots (midnight–6 a.m.), which have low listenership but might give you a lower cost in morning drive time if you take them.

Television advertising has a reputation for being expensive. Far too many small-business owners are intimidated by stories of the high cost of television time. Major corporations spend millions on their advertising campaigns, but they need to reach millions of viewers.

However, on a smaller scale, TV costs can be surprisingly low. The price of television time depends on several factors: the size of the market area, the length of the ad, the time of day the ad appears, the rating of the program, and the quantity of advertising purchased. It's up to the advertiser to decide just how much money is available for television advertising and then have the sales rep structure the best deal.

At many stations, a grid system is used to price TV time. This means that there may be several prices possible for the same commercial at the same time of day. The higher the price, the higher the priority of the spot. A high-priority commercial will preempt one of lower priority.

One additional cost is producing a commercial. This can range from a low of a couple hundred dollars for a simple, station-produced announcement to thousands of dollars for a spot produced by professionals with on-air talent.

Local stations often package deals designed to give small businesses an opportunity to use TV effectively while keeping costs low. A station salesperson can explain options and opportunities for low-budget advertisers.

Your advertising should appear in programs relevant to your market. If your target audience is children, your best bet is advertising during Saturday morning programs. If sports fans are your target, try weekend sports. Your salesperson will offer other suggestions, and together you can come up with a schedule that fits your budget and meets your advertising needs.

Standard Rate and Data Service also offers an information sourcebook for television, listing stations in the market, some rate information, and so on. This can be helpful in choosing the stations to contact.

Your local cable television station is flexible, offering spots from 10 to 120 seconds in length. Prices depend on the number of subscribers to the channel. The cable salespeople can supply data on the numbers and demographics of their viewers, and the Nielsen ratings service can tell you which programs are most popular among viewers.

Take a look at advertising on national channels such as ESPN, MTV and CNN, which sometimes offer quality airtime at cost that's lower than that of regular television advertising.

And don't overlook underwriting on your local public radio or television station. Both media offer affordable options for reaching a wide range of listeners or viewers.

Fliers, Mailers, and Brochures

Fliers, mailers, and brochures are affordable ways to get marketing information to a select audience. To generate an effective printed piece, start with well-written copy. If you're not a professional business writer or copywriter, hire someone who is.

Crisp, pleasing graphic design is the other important component of successful, printed marketing communications. You want to be sure that prospects read your literature, and good design can ensure that at least they'll scan the pages. Using attractive, easy-to-read colors in a clean layout helps. Refrain from using reverse type—white type on a black background—for large blocks of text because it's hard to read. Use photos and other graphics to break up large blocks of text on a page. Pull callouts from the text that highlight important points about your product or service you want your reader to see, even if he or she doesn't read the entire piece from top to bottom.

Fliers, handbills, and postcards can be an inexpensive and highly effective form of advertising for small-business owners. They are especially useful for your grand opening announcement, for periodic reminders of the merchandise or services you offer and for promoting special sales. Ask your copywriter and designer for help with the flier's message, visual appeal and so on.

One of the most professional ways to describe your product or service is with a brochure (see Figure 26.2). Your company brochure does not have to be an expensive 16-page, four-color publication. To keep expenses down, you can go with one sheet of 8 1/2-by-11-inch stock printed in two colors on both sides and folded in thirds, which fits easily into a number-ten envelope. This makes it an ideal companion for your direct mail marketing efforts as well as an excellent handout.

Your brochure is a powerful marketing tool. Your logo should appear on it, and text and paper stock should match the colors and paper stock you use for your letterhead, business cards and other printed pieces. When you place all your company's printed pieces on a table, they should look like members of a family and it should be clear to anyone that they're all generated by the same company.

The beauty of using letters, fliers, postcards, or brochures for direct-mail advertising is that it's so easy to personalize your mailings. Letters should be addressed to "John Smith" instead of "Customer." But the most important element in every direct-mail campaign is the mailing list. If your letter, card, or package goes to the wrong person or the wrong address, you may as well throw your money in the trash. Make sure your list is accurate and up-to-date. Using first-class postage ensures that improperly addressed mail will be returned to you, allowing you to make corrections to your mailing list.

You can also buy lists of names from mailing list brokers (look in the yellow pages under "Advertising—Direct Mail") typically for 20 cents a name. How do you pick a list? Use the RFM formula: "R" stands for recent, "F" for frequency, and "M" for money. Because people and businesses move, a list that's been recently updated is vital to the success of a mailing. Frequency refers to how many times the people on the list purchased your product or service. And money refers to how much they spend.

Because the success of a direct-marketing campaign depends on the mailing list, buy lists only from reputable services. Ask how many times the list has been sold in the previous six months and get the names and telephone numbers of some of the buyers. Ask them what their response rate was (3 percent is acceptable for most direct-mail campaigns), how many pieces were returned because of bad addresses and whether the buyer thought the list was worth the cost.

Sometimes other businesses trade their lists with one other. Nonprofits often do this for fund-raising purposes, provided their focuses are in different areas.

There are several options for postage. Bulk rate requires filing an application with the U.S. Postal Service, paying a one-time application fee (remaining in force as long as you use the service as least once a year) and paying an annual fee, good from January through December. This means that if you pay the fee on December 10 and want to do a mailing on January 3, you'll have to pay another annual fee when the New Year begins. The advantage of bulk mailing is that the per-letter cost is discounted substantially from first-class rates. You must also meet minimum requirements regarding the number of pieces per mailing.

Sending by bulk requires bundling the mail according to ZIP codes, and any pieces unable to be delivered are tossed unless you state on the face, "Return postage guaranteed." Bulk is slow—local delivery can take five to seven days, and getting from one coast to the other may take two weeks or more. Postal workers deliver bulk mail only when they have room, after taking all other classes of mail.

The other disadvantage of bulk mail is that it's generally perceived as junk mail. If image is important to your business, it makes sense to use first-class mail because you need to make a favorable impression on prospective customers or clients.

Another form of direct mail is the coupon mailer, which features coupons from a group of businesses within a community. In most circumstances, coupons

| FIGURE 26.2 | Tri-Fold Brochure |

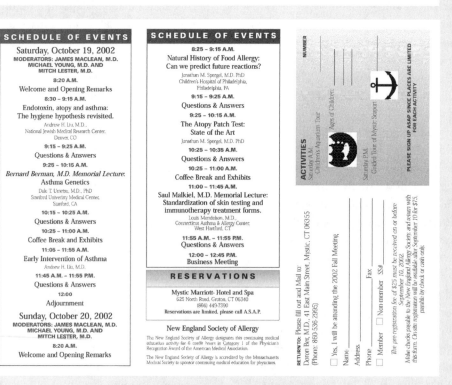

OBJECTIVES

In the initial presentation, participants will learn of the role of endotoxin as both a factor known to exacerbate existing allergy and asthma symptoms, as well as a factor that may drive immune development away from the T-helper lymphocyte type 2-mediated allergy and asthma profile. These roles of endotoxin will be discussed in the context of the 'hygiene hypothesis', which attributes the past century's rise in allergy and asthma to a reduction in microbial burden.

In the second lecture, the relevance of genes that may increase the likelihood of asthma disease expression will be will be reviewed. The final lecture of the first day of the program will educate participants on the role of early intervention as a potential disease modifying treatment modality in asthma.

On the second day of the program, participants will learn about new data that suggests that some individuals may become tolerant to foods that were thought to cause lifelong allergy. The mechanism of allergic sensation to food allergens and the natural history of food allergy will be reviewed as it is currently evolving. Participants will also learn of the atopy patch test that has developed into an additional tool in the diagnostic work-up of food allergy in infants and children. The utility of this test and its diagnostic accuracy in the evaluation of food allergy and atopic dermatitis will be reviewed.

Our final talk will examine initiatives by our national allergy societies to standardize allergy skin testing and treatment forms to improve the safety and transferability of medical records and of immunotherapy treatment extracts.

New England
Society of Allergy
www.neallergy.org

Fall 2002
Meeting

OCTOBER 18-20, 2002
MYSTIC, CT

SCHEDULE OF EVENTS

Saturday, October 19, 2002
MODERATORS: JAMES MACLEAN, M.D.
MICHAEL YOUNG, M.D. AND
MITCH LESTER, M.D.

8:20 A.M.
Welcome and Opening Remarks

8:30 – 9:15 A.M.
Endotoxin, atopy and asthma:
The hygiene hypothesis revisited.
Andrew H. Liu, M.D.,
National Jewish Medical Research Center,
Denver, CO

9:15 – 9:25 A.M.
Questions & Answers

9:25 – 10:15 A.M.
Bernard Berman, M.D. Memorial Lecture.
Asthma Genetics
Dale T. Umetsu, M.D., PhD
Stanford University Medical Center,
Stanford, CA

10:15 – 10:25 A.M.
Questions & Answers

10:25 – 11:00 A.M.
Coffee Break and Exhibits

11:05 – 11:55 A.M.
Early Intervention of Asthma
Andrew H. Liu, M.D.

11:45 A.M. – 11:55 P.M.
Questions & Answers

12:00
Adjournment

Sunday, October 20, 2002
MODERATORS: JAMES MACLEAN, M.D.
MICHAEL YOUNG, M.D. AND
MITCH LESTER, M.D.

8:20 A.M.
Welcome and Opening Remarks

SCHEDULE OF EVENTS

8:25 – 9:15 A.M.
Natural History of Food Allergy:
Can we predict future reactions?
Jonathan M. Spergel, M.D. PhD
Children's Hospital of Philadelphia,
Philadelphia, PA

9:15 – 9:25 A.M.
Questions & Answers

9:25 – 10:15 A.M.
The Atopy Patch Test:
State of the Art
Jonathan M. Spergel, M.D. PhD

10:25 – 10:35 A.M.
Questions & Answers

10:25 – 11:00 A.M.
Coffee Break and Exhibits

11:00 – 11:45 A.M.
Saul Malkiel, M.D. Memorial Lecture:
Standardization of skin testing and
immunotherapy treatment forms.
Louis Mendelson, M.D.,
Connecticut Asthma & Allergy Center,
West Hartford, CT

11:55 A.M. – 11:55 P.M.
Questions & Answers

12:00 – 12:45 P.M.
Business Meeting

RESERVATIONS

Mystic Marriott- Hotel and Spa
625 North Road, Groton, CT 06340
(866) 449-7390
Reservations are limited, please call A.S.A.P.

New England Society of Allergy
The New England Society of Allergy designates this continuing medical education activity for 6 credit hours in Category 1 of the Physician's Recognition Award of the American Medical Association.

The New England Society of Allergy is accredited by the Massachusetts Medical Society to sponsor continuing medical education for physicians.

RETURN TO: Please fill out and Mail to:
Doron Ber, M.D., 41 East Main Street, Mystic, CT 06355
(Phone: 860.536.0995)

NUMBER

ACTIVITIES
Saturday A.M.
Children's Aquarium Tour
Saturday P.M.
Guided Tour of Mystic Seaport

Ages of Children:

PLEASE SIGN UP ASAP SINCE PLACES ARE LIMITED
FOR EACH ACTIVITY

☐ Yes, I will be attending the 2002 Fall Meeting

Name _____
Address _____
Phone _____ Fax _____
☐ Member ☐ Non member SS# _____

The pre registration fee of $25 must be received on or before September 10, 2002

Make checks payable to the New England Allergy Society and return with this form. On-site registration will be available after September 10 for $75, payable by check or cash only.

▼ WORD-OF-MOUTH ADVERTISING

Why would Tracy Hosac print 600 or more business cards a month? As owner of an antiques business, Someplace in Time, she actually hands out that many—every month.

Word-of-mouth is Hosac's best form of advertising. Hosac opened her doors in 1993 and since then has successfully built a steady clientele and a mailing list of thousands of names. While she had to run quite a bit of print advertising in the beginning, she now coasts steadily on word-of-mouth and scattered promotions throughout the year. With each promotion, she will run an ad in a trade magazine and send a mailer out to her extensive list of names.

Still, by far, most of her business comes from word-of-mouth. Her antique shop is unique in that forty-five separate dealers or buyers work out of her one building. Those dealers are able to pass out her cards in the building and at trade shows.

How does Hosac make word-of-mouth work so well for Someplace in Time?

1. She makes it a habit to tell people about her antiques business whenever she introduces herself.

2. She teaches all her salespeople to use friendliness. "We try to say 'Hello' to everyone who walks in the door," says Hosac. "Just a 'Hi, if you need anything let me know …' because I really think friendliness sells. If you ignore people and don't let them know you're there to help them, then they're not going to be as responsive." Just talking to customers helps them to like her store and trust her service.

3. Her prices are very reasonable, which allows resellers to shop at her store. In fact, about 25 percent of her business is to resellers, and she collects a lot of cards from and gives out a lot of cards to resellers.

4. Hosac always asks people if they know anyone interested in selling antiques, if they can send her information on other friends who may be interested in selling antiques, and if they can send her information on other friends who may be interested in doing business. This is how she keeps the network growing.

5. Hosac also believes heavily in service. She keeps a "want/wish" book for items customers are looking for, and if she's able to find one of the items she calls the customers right away to let them know. Her most recent bit of service is a tearoom she just opened. It adds a homey feeling and gives her a chance to show off china sets, with food catered every weekend. So far, the tearoom has been running successfully on word-of-mouth alone.

are, in effect, mini-advertisements that usually offer a discount or introductory special (see Figure 26.3). In most circumstances, coupon books are mailed to all homes within a ZIP-code area (the shotgun approach). While not as targeted as direct mail, these coupon books can still produce impressive results.

Postcards are effective because their message is concise and their mailing costs low. They are great for saying thanks to a valued customer, announcing a sale or new service, or distilling a list of hot prospects from a large mailing (see Figure 26.4).

Outdoor Advertising

Outdoor advertising works for promoting your product in specific geographic areas. While billboards, bus benches, and transit advertising can be very effective for the small-business owner, any successful outdoor campaign begins with your own signage.

Your outdoor sign is often the first thing a prospective customer sees. Your sign should be sufficiently bright and conspicuous to attract attention (without being garish) and sufficiently informative to let prospective customers know what is sold there.

Ride around town and observe which signs catch your eye. Note which ones don't. Then think of the impression each sign gives you. Remember that you never get a second chance to make a first impression, so give this important marketing tool your best efforts.

If you're involved in a business that has a fleet of vehicles conducting deliveries or providing a service, your company's name, logo, and phone number should be clearly visible on the vehicles. It's free advertising that allows you to increase your exposure in your market.

Billboards are most effective when located close to the business advertised. Because of their high cost, they're usually used to reach a very large audience, as in political campaigns. They're likely to be too expensive for most small firms, and some communities have strict ordinances governing the placement of billboards. In Vermont, for example, they're prohibited.

Bus-bench advertising is an excellent medium because it's highly visible, like a billboard. Essentially, bus-bench advertisers have a huge audience, held captive at red lights or in slow-moving traffic. An account executive of a Los Angeles-based bus bench manufacturing company said that an advertisement on one bus bench at a busy Los Angeles intersection would be seen by 35,000 to 50,000 people per day.

Usually, the advertising consists of simple two-color artwork with your company's name, brief copy describing the product or service, address and the telephone number. Rates and terms vary depending on the city you're in.

Call your city's mass transit department or local bus company to find out who rents advertising space on their bus-stop benches. Some outdoor advertising companies also handle this type of advertising.

Transit advertising (e.g., buses and taxicabs) reaches lots of people, especially commuters. Your ad is highly visible, and market research on transit advertising shows that it's very effective.

Specialty Items

Products that feature your company's name and/or logo can offer more diverse and long-lasting results than print or electronic ads. They work best for companies that are known for their service and attention to the customer. So when a customer buys a T-shirt with your company logo

on it and wears it all over town, he or she is like a walking advertisement and endorsement for your company.

You can inscribe your company's name and/or logo on visors, T-shirts, sunglasses, matchbooks, calendars, pens, pads of paper, magnets and lots of other items. You can sell the pricey items and give the inexpensive specialties gratis to customers for patronizing your business.

Cooperative Advertising

You can spend a lot of money advertising your product/service, but those costs can be reduced by using co-op advertising. Each year, manufacturers budget millions of dollars just for cooperative advertising with their distributors and retailers. Unfortunately, much of this money is never spent.

Cooperative advertising is a cost-effective way for manufacturers, retailers, or distributors to reach their target markets. Although co-op advertising policies differ from manufacturer to manufacturer, most will pay a portion of the advertising costs and supply the retailer with photos or graphics to use in the ad (or sometimes the entire ad itself), whether for print, radio, or television. A manufacturer's contribution to a cooperative advertising campaign can range from lots of money to promotional gimmicks and point-of-purchase displays.

Using co-op advertising cuts down not only on the media cost but also on the production and creative expenses as well. A smart advertiser will factor co-op advertising, if available, into his or her budget. The major drawback to co-op advertising is that some manufacturers have more restrictive programs than others.

The most striking benefit of any affiliated advertising is the increase in foot traffic. Though the item's gross profit may not be substantial, add-on items with high markups will add to a retailer's bottom line. The best advice is to test the waters.

Another form of cooperative advertising is sponsored by shopping districts or centers, which feature an advertisement from each retailer in the shopping center. These promotions are often found in local newspapers for back-to-school specials, St. Valentine's Day, Fourth of July, Mother's Day, and Father's Day.

Be careful to coordinate the cooperative advertising within your overall marketing scheme. Only use co-op

FIGURE 26.3 Coupon

FIGURE 26.4 | **Postcard**

Who can help you grow your business and cultivate connections to New Hampshire's green industry?

New Hampshire Plant Growers' Association

*Promoting ornamental horticulture
in the Granite State since 1952*

Join the New Hampshire Plant Growers and:

- Stay informed about events, workshops, and classes
- Get invited to visit horticultural operations around the state
- Expand your network of other growers, retailers, suppliers, and horticultural researchers
- Receive our valuable magazine, *The Plantsman*
- Keep up with NH horticultural news
- Learn how to manage your business better
- Be represented on legislative issues affecting our industry

All NHPGA members also receive an NHPGA directory, banner, window sticker, and signs.

To join NHPGA, visit our Web site at
www.nhplantgrowers.org
and click on "industry professional"
and then "how to join."
Or call 603 225-0653.

NEW HAMPSHIRE
**Plant
Growers**
QUALITY GARDEN CENTERS
& GROWERS

advertising if it meets your needs. If you've chosen a different approach in your advertising campaign, don't switch in midstream just to take advantage of free advertising dollars.

THE CREATIVE CAMPAIGN

Advertising is used for three main reasons:

1. To promote awareness of your business
2. To establish your company's niche in the market
3. To generate sales

Regardless of which advertising medium you select, your advertising message must grab attention and attract prospective buyers who might otherwise not know a thing about you.

Creative messages have five characteristics. They are:

1. To the point and easily understood
2. Truthful
3. Informative
4. Sincere
5. Customer-oriented

When developing your creative campaign, plan on budgeting at least five percent of the total advertising budget. If your budget is sufficiently large, you can hire an advertising agency to put together your campaign, including its creative elements. If you aren't able to hire an advertising agency or don't feel the need for one, you can hire freelance copywriters and graphic artists to help you develop a creative campaign.

A large part of your creative campaign will be developing a theme, tag line, or memorable jingle. Ads in a campaign should tie together so that each time they're seen or heard, they remind consumers of your product. Start with a strong headline. In the body copy, stress your product or service's benefits. End the ad with a "call for action" encouraging your audience to do something—try your product, make a phone call for more information, attend a gala opening, visit a web site, and so on.

Designing the Advertisement

Most big, corporate advertisers spend millions of dollars with Madison Avenue firms to analyze their markets.

They learn what their customers' needs and concerns are by studying psychographic data (looking at a group's behavior patterns, attitudes and expectations) and using focus groups. The resulting ads are effective because they are very deliberately conceived.

Effective advertising begins with analyzing your company, the products or services you want to advertise and the type of customers you want to attract. Your ad must speak to your target market (see Figure 26.5). Here are some guidelines for creating successful ads.

- *Create a sense of immediacy.* Because people are less likely to respond to an ad as time goes by, advertising relies on urging people to act immediately. People need to be told what response you want—"act quickly," "limited-time offer," or "call now."
- *Repeat your message.* Throughout your ad, reinforce the message regarding your product or service's benefits. Repetition sells because the more times someone hears or reads something, the more believable it becomes. Repetition is particularly important in advertising because you normally don't have the full attention of your audience. A powerful case for repetition is that, according to scientists, we retain only 15 percent of what we hear.
- *Hit the hot "buttons."* Different people respond to different features of a product or service. One person may want quality, while another likes easy maintenance or the newness or design of an item. Decide what's going to appeal to your audience and then tell them why your product or service fits the bill perfectly.
- *"Sell the sizzle, not the steak."* This old advertising axiom means sell the benefits, not the features. While there's nothing wrong with talking about the features of your product or service (a four-door car with anti-lock breaks), what will appeal to your customers are benefits (easy to get in and out of, prevents skidding in snow).
- *Evaluate other ads.* Collect competitors' ads and study them. Note any trends or changes in their strategy.

In advertising layout terminology, "white space" is the blank area surrounding the headline or framing the

advertisement to separate it from other advertisement on the page. Small-business owners seldom use white space creatively in their advertising, but it can dramatically set off your advertisement from the others, especially when it includes a dramatic headline. White space adds visual impact to print ads surrounded by dense columns of type, such as in newspapers and the yellow pages.

Also, choosing an ad size that is different from standard formats will help your ad to stand out in a publication.

MEASURING ADVERTISING EFFECTIVENESS

Regularly test the effectiveness of your advertising campaign by taking these steps:

- *Advertising only one item in one ad.* Have no references to the item on the business premises. Then count the calls and requests for the advertised item.

- *Running the same ad in two different publications with a different identifying mark on each.* The reader is asked to bring in the ad to receive a special price or discount. See how many ads come in from each source.

- *Omitting a regular advertising project for intermittent periods and watching any change in sales.*

- *Tracking sales every time you place a new advertisement.*

- *Asking your advertising agency to perform a "post-analysis" on your broadcast buys.* This compares the number of rating points you bought with the number of rating points actually achieved after your schedule ran. Your ad agency can also obtain coupon redemption figures or card insert responses from your print schedules.

- *Always asking customers how they heard about your business, your product, your event, etc.*

These checks can give you an idea of how your campaign is performing. It's more difficult to measure the effectiveness of your television advertising than it is when you use the newspaper. There are no coupons to be clipped, for instance, and you may not have an immediate, dramatic response to your ad. But your advertising agency can supply you with some figures on who's seen your ad.

WORKING WITH ADVERTISING PROFESSIONALS

Professional advertising agency personnel and media representatives can help you plan your advertising efforts. Ad agencies earn a large portion of their income in commissions from advertising media placed on behalf of their clients. The ads cost the client the same whether placed through an agency or directly with the media. However, agencies bill clients for other services performed, such as consultation, copywriting and artwork.

Selecting an Advertising Agency

Before you begin the search for an ad agency, have a clear idea of what you want and which media you prefer. Some advertising agencies specialize in different industries, and some work with either local or national clients. Some will coordinate an entire marketing campaign; others will only handle advertising. Ask colleagues for referrals and whether they're happy with the relationship.

Make a list of your marketing and advertising objectives and have it handy when you start your inquiries into ad agencies. At your request, agencies will often provide samples of their work or references from their other clients.

You also need to know your advertising budget and which agencies can accommodate you. Some may work with only large accounts, while others are better suited for small businesses. And don't forget to talk about fees and payment plans.

CHAPTER 27

Sales

Every business shares one objective, regardless of the industry it's in: to generate enough sales to cover overhead and profit. Achieving this goal requires focusing on the customer before, during and after the sale. A satisfied customer will recommend your company to other prospective customers and, more important, will continue to buy from you. Keep in mind that returning customers are your most profitable ones—it costs five times as much to establish a new customer as it does to sell to an existing one.

Sales, which entails getting your product or service into customers' hands, differs from marketing, which focuses on educating customers about the benefits of your product or service. But no matter how great it is, no product or service can sell itself. To sell successfully, a business needs a sales strategy, a trained sales staff to implement that strategy and sales management.

Your sales strategy involves prospecting for new customers, deciding which product or service features you'll promote to which customers, determining where you'll sell and figuring out which techniques you'll employ in order to sell your product or service.

Sales training for your staff is an investment that pays big dividends. Not only does it increase a salesperson's knowledge—sales training will make him or her more valuable to your company, and more loyal!

PLANNING FOR SALES

Successful sales don't happen by chance. They're the product of careful strategizing and hard work. To attain your sales goals, be familiar with the selling process.

Sales Forecast

An accurate sales forecast helps you form a budget and plan. Two of the most common ways to project sales for your business are the sales force survey and the executive committee survey.

The Sales-Force Survey

Every salesperson is asked to develop individual sales projections for the upcoming year that take into account past performance, including number of customers, revenue per customer and total sales generated. Using past performance as a basis, the salesperson then projects increases, if any, in the number of customers and the average revenue generated by the total number of clients. For instance, if a salesperson had been servicing 750 customers the previous year at an average of $500 of sales per customer for a total of $375,000 and projects that his customer base will increase by 100 new customers in the coming year with average per-sale revenue pegged at $520, then the sales projection would be 850 x $520 = $442,000. That's an increase of 18 percent in sales from the previous year. If your business sells more than one product, the sales projection should take into account all revenue streams generated through sales efforts.

The Executive Committee Survey

The business owner forms a committee, usually consisting of him- or herself and those managers involved in the sales process who are responsible for analyzing the market and developing a quantitative outlook concerning the sales potential of the business. Like the sales force survey method, the executive committee survey bases the sales projection not only on conditions in the industry, the market and the economy, along with trends among competitors and customer demand, but also on past sales performance and the internal climate of the business. For instance, if you've sold 10,000 units of product A at an average price of $8 per unit, the total sales for that product would be $80,000. Based on market conditions and internal support from the business, the executive committee projects unit sales to increase by 10 percent to 11,000 at an average price per unit of $8.20 for total projected sales of $90,200 for product A. If your company sells more than one product, you'd conduct this type of sales projection for each product to arrive at a total projected sales figure.

While the executive committee method of projecting sales is a nice way to centralize the planning process, it doesn't take full advantage of the practical experience and understanding of the market that salespeople bring to the process. Since salespeople constantly deal with customers and obtain feedback from them, their input is key. Including salespeople in the planning process is also valuable from a motivational standpoint. It lets them know that you appreciate their knowledge and skills. They feel good, not only about the product but about the company as well.

By combining the survey and executive committee methods, you can build a consensus among your executive managers and salespeople as to what constitutes an accurate sales projection for the company. Have each salesperson submit an individual sales projection to you or the sales manager and then have the executive committee form its own forecast. Compare the two to develop a final projection (see Figures 27.1 and 27.2).

The Sales Plan and Budget

Once the sales projection has been finalized, develop a strategy or sales plan that will enable the company to reach its goals. The main focus of the sales plan is to determine how sales will occur and what the cost of those sales will be. Some issues you'll want to address include the flexibility a salesperson will have in pricing, how to handle returns, policies for servicing products, compensation for sales personnel, and market responsibilities for each salesperson. But perhaps the foremost consideration is whether to employ a sales force or conduct sales efforts through independent representatives.

Closely related to this aspect of the sales plan is cost. How much can you afford to spend to make the sale? Some entrepreneurs feel that they can spend whatever it takes. If the market is willing to bear an inflated price for the product, that strategy might be applicable. Most small businesses, however, operate in a very competitive environment where pricing, along with service, support, and promotion, is integral to sales. So most companies can't spend whatever it takes to make a sale. They have to work within a budget—see Figure 27.3 for a sample budget.

The costs incurred to make the sale are a large part of the sales budget. For instance, it will cost you more to employ a sale force than it will to contract with independent reps or to sell through direct marketing. However, while employing a sales force is costly, it allows you to control sales more effectively and provide better service to your customers.

To determine whether you can afford salespeople (and if so, how many), use the "cost method," in which the average amount to employ a salesperson is divided into a specific amount budgeted for sales. For instance, if projected sales for the upcoming year are $3 million and 8 percent is budgeted for sales, that would equal $240,000. If sales supervision is 30 percent of the sales budget, $72,000 would be allocated for this purpose. That would

FIGURE 27.1   Sales Projection by Sales Force Survey

Date _____   **Salesperson** _____

Approved by _____   **Title** _____

Customer	Type of Industry	Sales Calls per Year	Total Current Sales	Projected Sales Increase	Total Projected Sales	Product A	Product B	Product C	Product D
		Total							

| FIGURE 27.2 | Sales Projection by Executive Committee Survey |

Date _____ **Manager** _____

For period ending _____

Customer	Type of Industry	Revenue per Customer	Total Current Sales	Projected Customers Sold	Projected No. of Customers	Total Projected Sales
	Total					

FIGURE 27.3   Sample Budget

Date _____   **Manager** _____

For period ending _____

Item	Jan.	Feb.	Mar.	Apr.	May	Jun.	Jul.	Aug.	Sep.	Oct.	Nov.	Dec.	Total
Total													
Projected Sales													

leave $168,000 for the sales staff. If the average cost to employ a salesperson is $42,000 per person, the total number of salesperson the company can afford would be:

$$\frac{\$168,000}{\$42,000} = 4 \text{ salespersons}$$

When doing a cost analysis for sales, include base salaries and commissions for the average cost to employ a salesperson. After you've completed the cost analysis, you'll have a concrete idea of whether hiring a sales force is compatible with your marketing strategy. This is extremely important, because if your marketing strategy is to have nationwide distribution, you'd be hard pressed to do that with only four salespeople as illustrated in the preceding example. If all you had was $240,000 to spend on sales, that money might be better spent contracting with independent reps or by mounting a direct mail campaign (if your products are compatible with this type of strategy).

The four figures needed for the sales budget are:

1. Projected sales
2. Salaries and commissions
3. Advertising and special promotions
4. Sales administration

After finalizing the sales projection, include all the details regarding company sales in the sales budget and allocate these figures in months, with estimates for seasonal variations.

Defining the Sales Organization

Most firms spend, as a general rule, between 5 and 10 percent of sales on sales-force costs. Large firms often spend more. Sales-force costs are broken down into two categories: compensation and expenses. When the funds are available, most entrepreneurs prefer building an in-house sales force for their company. The main advantage is that you can train them your way and be sure that all the salespersons' efforts will be concentrated solely on your product.

When building a sales force, however, you must define the positions that will be required to develop the sales organization, the objectives and responsibilities of each position, the hierarchy that will be needed to develop effective communication channels, and the organizational format.

Defining the Sales Positions

In most cases, the sales force consists of a number of different positions. The ones you institute depend on funds you have available, your sales goals and how your product is distributed. Some positions consist only of taking orders from customers who've already decided to buy, while others involve persuading an individual to buy in a cold-call sales situation. Sales personnel can be divided into the following categories.

- *Delivery people* don't generate sales but are responsible for the prompt and safe delivery of the product.
- *Inside order takers* help make the customer's buying experience a pleasant one
- *Outside order takers* service customers throughout a specific geographic territory.
- *Public relations salespeople* are responsible for performing promotional activities and providing other services for the customer.
- *Technical salespeople* have a great deal of technical knowledge along with superior selling skills, and can discuss the product or service in depth with the customer, if necessary.

Organizing the Sales Force

Once you've decided which positions you'll include on your sales force, develop an organizational plan that defines communication channels, the flow of authority, and the criteria for organizing the sales force.

When organizing for sales, keep in mind that most businesses selling consumer services don't apply restrictions to their salespeople. They are free to sell the company's services to any account in any geographic region, since the main goal is to build volume within a given trading area.

You may want to organize your sales staff by using a combination of structures discussed below. Most small businesses are limited in their resources and rely on the expertise of their sales staff. For instance, suppose one of your salespeople has extensive knowledge of a specialized and important product you sell to a few major accounts, but the rest of your products are more consumer-oriented. A good way to organize your sales force would be to assign the salesperson with the specialized expertise to the major accounts purchasing that product while dividing the rest of the salespeople by territories to handle the remaining products. Or, if one of your salespeople is more comfortable handling large accounts while another is more effective with smaller accounts, organize your sales force to take advantage of these strengths—your sales will grow as a result.

Your organizational plan needs to address territories, product line, types of customers or size of the account, and the functional organization of sales.

Territories

The most common way of organizing a sales force is by physical territories. In this type of structure, a territorial manager supervises a number of reps, each of whom has a specific geographic territory in which to operate. The first step in instituting a territorial format is to divide your market into territories, making sure that all districts provide the sales representatives with equal sales potential and workloads. This will give each rep a fair chance to make money. Equal sales territories will also make it much easier for you to evaluate sales performance. In establishing your territories, take into account indexes, such as the buying power of the population and number of businesses in an area.

Product Line

Organizing by product line is especially attractive to companies offering a good mixture of diverse products or services, or products or services that are sold to a variety of different markets. Organizing your sales force by product line allows each of the various products or markets to receive the type of attention needed for successful sales. For instance, if your company sells computer hard drives and stereo CD players, it would be difficult for one salesperson to sell both products within a territory. A more effective strategy would be to have a different salesperson in charge of selling each product; that person could bring a higher level of expertise to the sale of the product line.

Types of Customer or Size of the Account

Organizing your sales force by size of account is beneficial when your company deals with only a few major accounts that represent a large portion of your business. This also enables salespeople to give their customers more individualized attention. For example, advertising agencies often assign each major account to an account executive, who does nothing but satisfy the concerns and needs of that one particular client.

Functional Organization

Organizing sales by function is desirable when a product or service requires a great deal of after-market maintenance. If you sell a product or service that requires lots of post-sale hand-holding, such as counting stock or constantly setting up and refilling point-of-purchase displays, these chores will take away from the time spent developing new accounts. Therefore, it may make sense to organize sales so that one salesperson is developing new accounts and another is servicing existing ones.

Considerations of Structuring Territories

After you've decided on an organizational method, the next step is to define boundaries for each territory. This can take a great deal of time and research, but the result will be the assignment of territories that allow your salespeople to produce a satisfactory income.

Current Sales and Customers

By reviewing your current sales and customers, you can discover how to structure a territory. Look carefully at size of accounts, location, customer demographics, any shifts or trends in sales or customer characteristics, number of calls needed to service an account, and number of accounts per territory. To analyze your current sales and customers, refer to internal records such as customer files, sales reports, and financial statements. This should provide you with a detailed picture of how sales are currently distributed, which customers account for those sales, and the amount of effort it takes to service those accounts.

Prospective Customers

To gauge sales prospects, do some market research. Sales potential within a specific market can usually be determined by analyzing the area's potential spending characteristics, purchasing power, present sales volume of the type of product or services you'll be offering, and the proportion of the total sales volume you can reasonably obtain. There are many helpful sources of previously compiled information, including the Census Bureau (www.census.gov), which publishes statistical information in a series of reports called Economic Censuses. These Economic Censuses cover a variety of industries and geographic regions. You can also extract a great deal of data about local business conditions from these reports.

If you determine the sales potential in an area, you can then establish the number of potential customers by matching the demographics to actual customers. This will provide you with a good framework for the territorial structure of your firm. For instance, when using geographic territories, if an area has more potential sales and customers than one salesperson can handle, you'll have to decide how the company can best deal with the situation. Based on your research, you may have to organize that geographic market differently—by account, by product, or unrestricted.

Transportation

Another important factor is transportation. How easily can a territory be serviced? Say you've structured your sales force by account and a salesperson has three clients: one in Los Angeles, one in New York, and another in Dallas. All the accounts are major customers, and this particular salesperson has a great deal of expertise with the company's product, yet the transportation costs to provide sufficient customer service are tremendous. If these costs prove too burdensome, you'll have to reorganize that particular salesperson's territory so that travel is not such an issue.

That doesn't just go for air travel. Check the highways within territories to determine ease of access within a given market. For instance, if you were organizing territories in Los Angeles County, you might choose to divide it into two regions—North and South—because the freeway system in Los Angeles is so congested that travel from the northern part of Los Angeles to the southern portion could take hours out of the salesperson's day. Keeping the salespeople concentrated in specific areas of Los Angeles County would decrease their time on the road.

MAKING THE SALE

Since every customer has unique needs, a cookie-cutter approach doesn't work for determining how your sales personnel will approach, interact, and service each customer. Sales is very much a creative process, and each salesperson needs to define how he or she will accomplish that sale, within company guidelines, of course.

Finding New Customers

If you've done your market analysis, you'll have a pretty good picture of who your current customers and prospects are. In fact, you may even have developed prospect lists for the territories—a valuable tool for your sales force.

While a list of prospects provided to the sales force is a good starting point, your salespeople have to learn to do that on their own. In their prospecting, your salespeople first define your target market according to the general demographic characteristics identified from your research. Next, they start building a list of possible customers based on those demographics.

Although possible customers may meet all the demographic requirements set forth in your research, not all of them will need your product, nor will all of them have the financial means to purchase it. The trick in good prospecting is to qualify possible customers to determine if they are prospects.

In some companies, qualifying possible customers is done by insider salespeople who determine the interest level and ordering requirements prior to setting up an appointment for the outside salesperson. In a small business working with a limited budget, prospecting can be accomplished through other avenues such as direct mail, fliers, cold calling, and so on. The idea behind qualifying is to screen the list of possible customers to avoid wasting time with individuals and organizations that really have no desire or lack the financial means to buy your product. This time can then be invested in prospects with greater potential.

You can often find good prospects through networking, by making yourself visible in local community activities as well as in industry activities. You don't necessarily want to pitch your products at the events you participate in, but do keep your eyes open to any opportunities that you may see.

Be sure to read your local newspaper each day. You may come across a good prospect in an article or an ad.

Understanding Your Customers

Once possible customers have been qualified as good prospects, start collecting as much information about them as possible, so you can develop an understanding of their needs and goals. The more you know about a prospect, the better chance you have of making a sale.

Part of the process of analyzing your customers' needs and goals is to conduct a needs analysis of each prospect. To conduct a needs analysis, try to understand the psychology of how people arrive at purchasing decisions. People are generally motivated by price, quality, service, performance, and convenience. Each of these economic factors has a different value for different people. Discovering the value that a particular prospect places on the various factors is one of the goals of a needs analysis.

Although price is not the only determinant in the purchasing decision, many salespeople make the mistake of believing it is. The reality is that prices higher than those of the competition can be justified if they offer well-defined benefits relevant to the customer.

Aside from economic factors, other things that motivate a customer to buy include individual needs based upon lifestyle, personal goals, and safety-related necessities. Many times, these needs play the largest part in the buyer's final purchasing decision. For instance, ego and lifestyle strongly influence some people when they purchase a car, home, or clothing. Someone buying a Mercedes isn't necessarily concerned about price as much as the car's safety record, engineering excellence, and the social statement made by owning such a car.

Since many factors can affect the purchasing decision, the salesperson must identify each prospect's needs and then develop a strategy that reflects those concerns. Here's where a good salesperson is adept at listening and observing. By listening, he or she can read between the lines of remarks a prospect might make over the phone or at a meeting or in response to a question. For instance, a prospect might say, "If I had a personal computer, it would improve my productivity!" Or, "My current car is much too slow!" In both statements, the prospects have identified needs.

Remember that people don't buy a product or service—they buy satisfaction for their wants and needs. We buy a particular brand of soap because we want soft skin, more lather, or deodorant protection.

An astute salesperson can learn a lot about a prospect from his or her clothes, car, and office furnishings. A prospect who is wearing a Rolex, an Armani suit, a silk tie, and Gucci shoes is not likely to be as concerned about price as he is about quality, superior design, and workmanship.

Also observe mannerisms and the way that a prospect answers questions. Body language can reveal a great deal. Is there excitement in the person's voice? Is he sitting with arms crossed, in a defensive posture?

Finally, try looking at the situation from the customer's viewpoint. Try to empathize with the needs of the buyer so you can better understand where he or she is coming from.

As you ask the prospect—and individuals close to him or her—questions, be sure to write down their responses and any of your observations in a logbook where you record the results of your sales meetings (or use a standardized sales follow-up report as shown in Figure 27.4). By logging your conversations and observations, you can go back and analyze them to determine the prospect's needs when forming a strategy to meet them. Also, prospects are impressed if you can reference details from past conversations. This shows that you're keenly interested in them and their business, and will work hard to satisfy their needs.

Handling Objections

No matter how well prepared any salesperson is, he or she will inevitably confront objections that need to be resolved before closing a sale. When handling objections, let the customer speak and listen carefully to what he or she has to say. Don't interrupt, and let the customer finish before you attempt a response.

Before responding to any objection, make sure you thoroughly understand it. Ask the prospect questions to clear up any confusion. Using a clarification question, you can turn the objection into a positive situation. For instance, if the prospect objects to the product or service because the competition has a better price, you might

FIGURE 27.4   Sales Follow-up Form

CLIENT INFORMATION

Company name	Type of business
Company address	

City	State	Zip	Telephone	Fax

Contact	Title

Proposal

SALES TRACKING SHEET

Date	Notes	Date to Follow Up	Salesperson's Initials

respond by acknowledging that the competition does have a better price and then follow up the statement with the clarification question: "So, what you're really interested in is purchasing the best product for your money?" This is a direct question that clarifies the prospect's need. Almost invariably, the prospect will say, "Yes." At that point, you can once again explain that your product comes with a one-year guarantee and a repair policy that includes loaners, while your competitors don't. Build value for your product in the prospect's eyes.

When dealing with objections, the trick is to recognize the customer's concerns, so that you can address them and take action. Some of the more common objections include:

- *"I need more time."* Probably the most common form of objection, delaying or stalling allows the prospect to postpone the purchasing decision to a later date. When dealing with the delay, determine whether the customer really needs more time or really wants to get rid of the salesperson. Knowing your customer should help you to make this call.
- *"I don't need it."* A prospect who claims not to need a product or service may be reacting to a poor presentation or may truly feel no need for the particular product. Again, be polite and positive when responding to this objection and try to redirect the discussion toward the benefits as they relate to the prospect.
- *"I don't have the money."* A prospect who really needs something will find the money to buy it. Usually, the prospect is concerned about price when making this objection. Generally, if price is the major obstacle, the prospect may be trying to determine what the best price is before making a decision. If the prospect is genuinely concerned about the cost of the product, responding with an affordable way to buy the product may overcome the objection. The main concern when facing this objection is to determine whether the prospect is negotiating for a lower price or better terms or will respond to your turning around the presentation by justifying the price with superior quality.
- *"I'm not sure about this product."* Sometimes a prospect may like a competitor's product better, or a competitor may have said bad things about your product. Whatever the reason, when responding, don't downgrade the competition. Talk about the benefits of your product. If necessary, point out warranties and guarantees, and provide a demonstration.
- *"I'm not sure I want to deal with your company."* The prospect may already be loyal to a particular company or product brand, or may have had a bad experience with your company. Usually, when dealing with this objection, you'll have to break down the barriers over time by keeping in touch with the prospect, sending him or her news releases and updated information. Eventually, you may convince the prospect that your product is superior to that of the competition or that your company is working hard to develop solutions to the problems the prospect has experienced.

The Trial Close

One of the best ways to make sure the prospect understands what you're saying and is ready to buy is to attempt a "trial close." As the name implies, a trial close checks the readiness of the prospect to actually close the sale and indicates his or her receptiveness to your product or service. You can attempt a trial close after a major selling point, after finishing the presentation, after responding to an objection, or just prior to closing the sale.

Trial closes don't ask for a decision to buy—they ask for the prospect's opinion. Based on that opinion, the salesperson can then form a strategy to close the deal if the prospect has given a positive response or proceed to address other concerns the prospect may have raised.

A trial close should be very simple and casual and is usually presented as a question. For instance: "Do you think the product fulfills your needs?" or "Based upon the benefits of the product, do you think we can do business?" A positive response indicates that the prospect is almost ready to close. If the response is negative, the salesperson may need to ask more questions to pinpoint other concerns.

You can perform a trial close several times during a sales presentation. It's a good way to check in with your prospect to see whether effective, two-way communication is occurring.

Closing Techniques

Closing a sale can sometimes take a great deal of work. It means being patient enough to determine the prospect's needs and address any concerns. It also means recognizing opportunities when they arise.

To close a sale, the timing has to be right. Trying to close the sale before the customer is ready can jeopardize it. Wait too long to close a sale and the prospect could lose enthusiasm. The right time to close a sale is when the prospect starts showing signs of being ready to buy. You have to be able to recognize these buying signals and attempt the close when you see them.

One buying signal that's very positive is when the prospect begins to ask questions about the product. That means the interest level is high, and the person may only need prompting to close the sale. A second signal is when the prospect asks an associate what he or she thinks of the product. Depending on the other person's answer, the prospect may be ready to close. A third sign is that the prospect shows a lot of enthusiasm about the product and begins to examine it closely. As the person examines the product, answer any questions and generally give him or her enough time to look over all the features of the product before asking for an opinion. A positive response means you only need to give a little push to close the sale.

Another sign to watch for is when the prospect becomes less guarded and more relaxed. Usually, when the sale is not yet definite, prospects are guarded. They watch what they say, the way they sit, and so on. Once they reach a decision about purchasing a product, they will usually try to wrap up the meeting either by announcing they don't need the product or by relaxing and becoming friendlier. If that happens, all they need is for you to pop the question.

Adapt your level of intensity to match that of the prospect. If he or she is laid-back, don't use an aggressive sales approach. Make the prospect feel comfortable so that when you attempt the close, the level of pressure does not come as a surprise.

Whatever closing technique you choose, wait quietly for an answer after asking for the order. Don't say a thing while the prospect is deliberating whether to buy. Usually, anything you say will take the pressure off the prospect to make a decision. Remaining quiet can be nerve-racking, but while the prospect is deciding what to do, be positive and think of appropriate responses to use once the prospect states a decision.

Usually, a prospect won't wait long to reply. Most will provide an answer within a minute. If the reply is positive and the sale has been closed, get the order in writing, thank the customer for the business and then leave. Keep it simple when wrapping up the sale. Don't say too much. If you're overly enthusiastic and keep talking about the sale, you may say something that will change the buyer's mind.

Finally, if you don't make a sale, ask for a referral. If you've done your job correctly and have made a professional presentation, even buyers with no use for your product may know someone else who does.

CHAPTER 28

Direct Marketing

Direct marketing of your product or service involves anything that attempts to sell it on the spot: direct mail, coupon advertising, telemarketing, direct-response TV, door-to-door sales, home shopping, and internet shopping (covered in the next chapter). This chapter focuses on two methods most useful to small businesses—direct mail and telephone marketing.

DIRECT MAIL

Direct mail can help small businesses find new customers and create new sales. The key in any direct-mail campaign is the mailing list. It must be accurate, up-to-date, and suited to reaching your immediate marketing goal. You can either generate your own list or buy one from a list broker (look under "Mailing Lists" in your Yellow Pages).

Once you've developed your own mailing list, you can create separate lists, based upon any number of classifications: frequency of purchase, amount of purchase, demographic data, and so on. Your computer software's merge-and-purge feature will help you clean up your list and avoid duplication and sending mail to people who don't want to receive it. Another benefit is that letters can be personalized, both in the salutation and in the text.

The biggest advantages of direct mail are that you can measure its results and test different variables (how the product is priced, what payment terms are offered, different expiration dates for the offer and so on).

Your direct-mail campaign can be as simple as a postcard, letter, or e-mail sent weekly or monthly. Use them to thank customers for their business, remind clients of their next appointment, or announce a sale, new product, or discount.

With any type of direct mail, appropriately timed follow-up is key. Mailings with telephone follow-ups are most effective. Don't wait too long to contact your customers after doing your mailing—after several days, call to ask if they've received your card, letter, or e-mail. If they have, now's the time to make your sales pitch. If they haven't, mail them another ASAP.

There are many books and articles on the subject of direct mail. *Successful Direct Marketing Methods* (eighth edition) by Bob Stone and Ron Jacobs, published by McGraw Hill, is a good one, with more than 200,000 copies in print. On the web, there's

Direct Mail News at www.dmnews.com, for news on direct, database, and internet marketing. And there are always direct-mail professionals available to help—check your Yellow Pages for listings.

TELEPHONE SALES

Since the 1980s, marketing by telephone has gained increasing acceptance as an effective and efficient sales tool. Not only does telephone marketing produce results—more than half of all goods and services are sold by phone. It's also cost-effective—telephone marketing costs about one-third as much as direct marketing.

Telemarketing is useful because:

- It's as easy to reach a desired market with the telephone as with a targeted mailing list.
- You can pre-qualify prospects for personal follow-up.
- The telephone allows you to talk directly with the sales prospect without having to meet in person.

The success of a telephone marketing campaign depends on the goals you set and the resources you allocate to reach them. The first step is to clearly define employee responsibilities and reporting structures. Let all employees know how many calls they need to make and what percentage of those calls should result in qualified leads.

If you have prospects calling in on a toll-free line, sales representatives who answer the calls should determine the extent of interest and whether or not a salesperson should return the call. They can do this easily by asking a series of prepared questions.

Since telemarketers face rejection throughout the day, there's often a very high turnover in the field. If your company does a lot of telemarketing, have your sales staff work no more than four-hour shifts at the telephone to increase productivity and avoid burnout.

Prospecting

Prospecting is the search for potential customers or buyers. The telephone is such an effective marketing tool, in fact, that many "traveling salespeople" have given up traveling to recruit customers over the phone.

To identify who needs your goods, start with a pre-screened list of prospects (see Figure 28.1). Callers will ask them a series of questions to further determine if they are qualified. Depending on their answers, you will either delete them from your list or keep them.

For calls to be successful, each telemarketer should have a checklist for determining a prospect's interest and should be responsible for getting responses to each of the questions on that list. Here are some of the items you should consider when putting together that list:

- What are the customer's needs?
- Is the person you're speaking with the decision-maker? If not, who is? And what are the criteria for making the decision?
- How can your company help the customer's company reach its goals?
- Do you have a media kit or other follow-up information to send to the customer after the call?
- What are the customer's concerns or objections?
- How can you respond to those concerns or objections?
- How will you follow up to ensure customer satisfaction once an agreement has been made?

Sales Techniques

A sales pitch delivered over the telephone, while different from face-to-face negotiations, isn't necessarily less effective. In fact, there are many advantages to making a sales pitch by phone. On the telephone, it's easier to remain focused on the matter at hand. Here are a few ways to get the prospect to listen and increase your chances of making a sale.

- *Create a selling mood.* Come across as knowledgeable, friendly, helpful, and trustworthy. Speak firmly and clearly and amplify your voice so you don't lose the person.
- *Know your sales pitch.* Prepare a script but memorize it—don't read it. Change any words that don't feel comfortable and speak naturally, with assurance. Practice your script by using a tape recorder so you can hear any weaknesses in your presentation.
- *Be assertive and specific.* Tell the person the advantages of dealing with you. Being vague will make your listener lose interest or suspect that you have something to hide.

FIGURE 28.1   Prospecting Sheet

CLIENT INFORMATION   Send media kit ☐

Company name				Type of business	
Company address					
City	State	Zip		Telephone	Fax
Contact			Title		
Decision maker			Title		

GOALS OF THE CALL

GOALS OF THE CUSTOMER

WAYS TO HELP CUSTOMER FULFILL GOALS

OBJECTIONS OF CUSTOMER

RESPONSE TO OBJECTIONS

WAYS TO ENSURE CUSTOMER SATISFACTION

- *Meet objections.* Really listen to what the prospect says and read between the lines. Address issues head on. Objections can often be opportunities in disguise.
- *Be courteous.* Don't chat on and on and don't try to top a story the listener tells. Saying "I see" or "Tell me more" helps show you're really interested in what the person has to say.
- *Control the pace.* Slow down when making important comments so that you can emphasize those points. This will get the listener's attention at just the right moments.
- *Don't use a lot of "ums" or "ahs."* These sounds indicate that you're not sure of what to say. Slow down or go back to studying your material if you find yourself using these "non-words."
- *Ask questions.* This way, the person won't feel talked at.
- *Don't monopolize the conversation.* If you don't let the prospect get a word in, that person will be convinced you're not listening. If that's the case, he or she may decide not to listen to you. And if the prospect isn't listening, it's unlikely a sale will take place.
- *Don't use inappropriate humor.* Jokes that fall flat or make you sound silly won't project the professional image you want. Don't crack jokes unless you know the customer well.
- *Don't rush the person.* If the prospect is a slow speaker, be patient. This will pay off, especially if the lead is a good sales prospect. Speeding the prospect along can cause anxiety or antagonism—or both.

Make sure your sales staff takes careful notes so they know what the client wants and is willing to pay. While this practice can be disturbing to a client who's sitting across from the salesperson, it can be accomplished easily over the phone without making the salesperson seem rude.

On the phone, sales negotiations are more brief than in traditional sales meetings. Much of the small talk is avoided, and business is conducted efficiently. If an impasse is reached, it's much easier to say goodbye and call back in a few hours when you have a new approach than to leave a meeting and come back at another time.

Whenever you make a call, eliminate all distractions from your work area. If you lose your concentration because you start looking at other work on the desk, you'll not be able to focus on your prospect, who may realize that you're not giving the call your undivided attention. Remember that nothing makes a client feel less important and less inclined to buy something for you than lack of attention.

Everyone knows that body language is important in face-to-face meetings, but it can also help telephone negotiations. Adopting an upright posture as opposed to slouching can help you remain alert and attentive to the caller. While this is more of a psychological boost than anything else, salespeople claim it really does work.

One of the best ways to improve communications on the phone is to take notes during the conversation. In addition to helping you remember what was said after you hang up, it also keeps you attentive during the call. When taking notes during a conversation, include a column of facts and statements as well as a column of your impressions of what was said. Be sure to maintain these notes for your records.

Repeat and verify all key facts, and take responsibility for getting the message right. Don't make it sound as if the prospect is unable to get a clear message across. Don't say something like, "What you just said, Mr. Rice, was very confusing. You didn't explain yourself well. Could you repeat that for me?" Instead, say something like this: "Before we move on, Mrs. Rice, I want to make sure that what I've understood is accurate. Are you saying…?"

However, don't confuse understanding with agreement. Agreement can only come after mutual understanding has been reached. Although speaking clearly helps understanding, experienced telemarketers agree that it's not always what you say that sells the client, but how you say it. The tone, volume, and inflection of your voice are often more important than the words you choose. When making your sales pitch, pay attention to volume, diction, and speaking rate. Speaking too loudly, too quickly, or too slowly can irritate a potential customer and distract the person from the purpose of your call.

Your choice of words is also critical in shaping your phone image. Speech experts claim that positive action words are the best choice for creating a good phone personality. Stay away from passive verb structures and negatives.

Closing Sales

Closing a sale over the phone usually costs less than one-fifth of what it would to send a salesperson to make the same sale in person. For a small company, this can mean the difference between making a profit and breaking even when you include travel and per-diem expenses.

Once you've made your sales pitch and determined your prospect's interest, you'll need to make at least one more call to close the deal. Experienced salespeople agree that careful preparation for closing can give you the edge.

Before making a call, make a list of both your company's and the prospect's viewpoints, goals, concerns, and needs. Add any concessions you'll be willing to make as well as those the other party may make. Carefully consider these aspects from both standpoints before you call the other party, and you'll be in a better position to negotiate a mutually beneficial agreement.

When making the call, remember that a repeat customer is more profitable than a one-time buyer. So be ready to make some concessions regarding price or delivery dates to ensure that the customer will come back to you.

After you make the call, follow up quickly. Calling your clients to say that it is a pleasure to do business with them is a nice touch that they always notice. Let clients know that they can reach you by phone any time they have a question or problem about your product or service. Good communication goes a long way to converting prospects into repeat customers.

OFFERING TOLL-FREE NUMBERS

Toll-free numbers became such a popular marketing tool in the early 1970s that phone companies have run out of 800 numbers and now assign 888 and other prefixes. Toll-free numbers can dramatically increase a response rate by 30 percent or more. If your customers are scattered across the country, having a toll-free number makes it easy for them to find out what you have to offer—and they don't have to pay for the call.

Toll-free numbers can also improve customer relations and track the effectiveness of your advertising. Allowing customers to call your company toll-free for information or orders lets them know that you value their business. Knowing that your company is available free of charge can keep existing customers satisfied with your service and eager to return when they need your product or service again.

A toll-free number can actually be an ad for your company. With an alpha translation—a phone number that spells out the name of your company—you can increase awareness of your business just by giving out your toll-free number. For example, a balloon shop might want to use a number like 1-800-BALLOON to make it easy for customers to call when they need balloons without having to remember a number. However, these numbers take more effort to dial. So if you decide to use a toll-free number with seven arbitrary numbers, remember that customers can always call toll-free information at 800-555-1212 if they forget or misplace your phone number.

Installation

Vendors of toll-free numbers vary, which can make it difficult to find the one offering the ideal system for you. To ensure you receive the best service for your company's needs, have the carriers do traffic studies, estimate costs, and make suggestions for your system. Make sure the carrier you choose can meet the demands of your business' calling patterns.

The installation, monthly service charges, and usage rates for a toll-free number can add up to a substantial sum. Your phone company can provide details. Before you invest in a toll-free number, make sure that the benefits outweigh the costs.

Another Toll-Free Option

Many small and medium-sized businesses can't afford the expense of a toll-free number. Another option is a toll-free answering service.

These toll-free answering services take orders for your product over the phone, 24 hours a day, seven days a week. For a per-order fee of about 25 cents to a dollar, the service's operator will take the name and address, credit card number, and whatever other information is needed from each caller.

While these fees take a cut of your profits, an inbound WATS (Wide-Area Telecommunication Service) line could cost thousands of dollars a month—a fixed expense, regardless of how many sales you make.

CHAPTER 29

Marketing on the Internet

The internet has revolutionized the way we do business, from e-mail (electronic mail), which allows us to instantly receive and send messages via our computers, to the World Wide Web, which gives us ready access to databases, discussion forums, classes, and other information all over the world. Many small business owners have already harnessed the marketing prowess of the internet, using it to promote and sell their products or services, prospect for new customers, keep up with the competition, and stay in touch with current customers.

DETERMINE IF YOU NEED A WEB SITE

Does the internet make sense for your business? It really depends on what business you're in and what you want the internet to do for you. Some products may not lend themselves to being sold via the internet—for example, expensive artwork and high-end crafts need to be seen in person. So do products that need a demonstration to sell them. But products that are sold by catalog, for instance, may benefit tremendously from being sold on line. In addition to reaching a wider market and increasing sales with an internet presence, you can also dramatically decrease overhead by not having to print catalogs.

Another question to ask yourself is: What do you want your web site to do for your company? Provide information to customers? Generate leads for sales? As with any other marketing strategy, being successful in your e-business (electronic business) venture requires setting goals and then determining a carefully thought-out strategy to achieve them.

Don't create a web site just because it's the trendy thing to do. Do it because it makes sense for your business, because your customers and prospects are online, and so is your competition.

A web site offers the following advantages over other modes of marketing:

- You can change content quickly, easily, and for a very low cost, unlike reprinting a brochure.
- You can easily provide customers with more information on your product or service.
- You can target markets all over the world.
- You can keep track of your competitors.
- You can easily track results of your marketing efforts.

- Your business can be open twenty-four hours a day, seven days a week.
- You build and enhance customer loyalty.

DOING BUSINESS ONLINE

There are a number of ways to do e-business – from starting a "store" on the web, to using e-mail to entice customers to shop.

One low-cost way to do business online is through forums—electronic bulletin boards offered by the major online services—where users are welcome to ask questions, give advice, or offer opinions. Many thousands of users visit these boards daily, thus providing creative marketers with a readily available large audience and free marketing ideas.

Visit forums regularly, and when you spot a user question that relates to your expertise, post a helpful reply. Along the way, mention your business' service or product, and, very often, you'll find users coming to your web site ready to buy.

Keep stoking that urge to buy through the clever use of e-mail. Offer to send your e-newsletter or e-mail your FAQ (frequently asked questions) list to provide additional useful information and to further stimulate interest in your product or service.

A support service called "auto responding" is one that can be helpful if a large volume of e-mail is preventing you from responding to customers within a day or two. This feature sends automatic replies that answer commonly asked questions, thanks them for e-mailing, or posts whatever other information or reply you want to include.

Use e-mail to contact customers and prospects. Build a list of customer and prospect e-mail addresses and use it to send out discount coupons, spec sheets, postcards, announcements, or anything else you'd otherwise mail or fax. Costs are low, and delivery is instantaneous.

However, because online communication is rife with opportunities for misunderstandings, you must follow "netiquette" (the rules of etiquette on the internet) and be extra careful to make sure your message gets across as you intend it to. Remember to never type your message in uppercase letters, which is the online equivalent of shouting. Check that your spelling and grammar are correct

and create a "signature file"—your name, your company's name, address, and telephone number—so you don't have to rewrite it every time. Use the "subject line" so recipients know immediately what you are writing about, and keep your messages concise.

FIND A HOST FOR YOUR WEB SITE

Give careful consideration to your web site address, making sure it's easy to remember and spell. Once you've settled on a name, register it and make sure no one else is using it. Submit your address or URL (Uniform Resource Locator) to InterNIC, the internet's Network Information Center, at www.internic.net, one of the many internet registration services, or have your internet service provider (ISP) do this for you. ISPs, such as America Online (www.aol.com), Verizon Online (www.verizon.net), EarthLink (www.earthlink.net), and many others provide services for hosting web sites. Visit www.thelist.internet.com for a list of ISPs.

Many ISPs provide some type of free space for members' web sites. But there are strings attached. Most ISPs require that advertisements for their service appear on your pages, and they prohibit selling at sites set up on free space. (Find out for sure by checking the provider's "terms of service," which should be prominently displayed on the welcome screen.)

Other drawbacks to setting up with an ISP are that you can't have your own domain name (such as www.your-companyname.com) and you generally are not furnished with reports that help you track who visited your web site. While you don't necessarily have to rule out free space for your business, you shouldn't use it exclusively; create another site that offers information about your products and services.

To sell successfully online, sign up with a web-hosting service that provides site storage and management. There are hundreds of these available, with prices ranging from a bare-bones $10 per month for storage space alone to $75 or more per month for storage space, free access to your site, and web-page authoring software.

Use your favorite search engine to find web-hosting options, then investigate each service before you sign up. Inquire about rates, years in business, security features, and the amount of backups they perform. If you're going to sell products, see if the service provider offers features to notify you of orders. Also ask about the different kinds of tracking reports they provide. Most web site hosts furnish weekly and even daily reports.

Always ask any potential web-hosting service for the e-mail addresses of current customers. Contact a dozen or so and ask for feedback: How reliable is the server? How fast is it? Does tech support promptly handle problems? If customers are unhappy with a web hosting service, cross it off your list.

Online Selling

Start by studying web sites that sell products or services similar to yours. What do you like—and dislike—about them? How easy is it to place an order? How fast does information download? Can you quickly find what you need?

Two web sites in particular will help you learn more about selling online: The Wilson Internet Service (www.wilsonweb.com) contains many useful and interesting articles about the best way to sell goods and services online, as well as how to market your site. You can also ask your local Small Business Development Center—which is usually housed at a college or university—for information about setting up a web site in your area.

What's true in advertising is also true for the web: You have one chance to make a first impression. If your site takes too long to load because of excess graphics or your site is too difficult to navigate, prospects may click off and go somewhere else. Companies selling their products or service must make sure that visitors can easily move around their web site, that pages load as quickly as possible, that there's an e-mail address or phone number for people who have questions or comments, and that it's easy to complete purchases.

Once those pieces are in place, address the issue of security at your site for customers to make purchases with their credit cards. Many potential buyers are concerned about security and are hesitant about releasing credit card information unless they know that a site is completely secure. When they send electronic order forms, buyers don't want hackers grabbing their credit card numbers and doing a little shopping of their own. To learn more about credit card transactions, security, and

other online sales information, visit the Wilson Internet Services site referred to above.

To show customers that you're concerned about their welfare, offer them choices. Have a toll-free number for them to call, let them send a check to your street address or fax you an order-form page that they printed from your site. You can also use special programs to conduct online transactions safely.

Here's a closer look a various ways to sell online:

By Phone, Fax, or Snail Mail

The simplest way to sell online is to have customers call, fax, or mail in their orders, just as they would with a paper catalog. Simply create an illustrated, online catalog with product information and prices. In a prominent place on each page of your site, include your telephone number, mailing address, and e-mail address so that customers can contact you—either to place an order or to ask a question.

Selling Electronically

A slightly more complex way to run a sales site is to have your customers send you e-mail to place an order, as well as to ask questions and make comments. Whoever sets up your web site will need to add a "mail to" command to a HyperText Markup Language (HTML) statement in each page at your site. Using HTML form tags, or commands, you can create order forms that your customers can fill in and send electronically to your e-mail address by using the "mail to" command or by clicking on a button. Online forms usually require Common Gateway Interface (CGI) programming and a knowledge of the HTML forms tags. Be sure to get permission from your web site host, and be aware that because order forms and CGI programs use extra computer and storage resources, you may have to pay more for your internet connection.

Shopping Cart Program

The most expensive method for operating a secure sales site is using a shopping cart program, also known as an electronic catalog system. As a customer shops, a shopping cart program accumulates information—a unique customer identification to prevent all the current orders from overlapping, customer address information for automatic computation of shipping charges and taxes, and a record of and availability for each piece of selected merchandise. When the computer signals that the order is complete, the program totals the order, takes credit card information, verifies the credit card, and writes the order to a file for later processing. This type of program provides many features, which may include automatic credit card checks, security options such as encryption (turning the credit card information into coded characters that cannot be read by outsiders), sophisticated searches, sales tax and shipping calculations, and online help for visitors. Most shopping cart programs cost hundreds or thousands of dollars to license. You can find shopping cart programs by searching online using your favorite search engine.

Another option is PayPal (www.paypal.com), a low-cost service that allows businesses to accept online payments. Winner of an award for "best e-commerce solution," PayPal is offered to customers in 38 countries and is the leading payment network for online auction web sites, including eBay.

Whatever system you use to sell online, the important thing is to use common sense. Make sure your order form is easy for customers to use and that you provide other ways to place an order for those who are wary about using their credit card numbers on the web.

Selling online also means being aware of and honoring certain rules. The primary one is: Don't "spam" or send "junk e-mail." (Spamming is the indiscriminate sending of messages to Usenet newsgroups; junk e-mail is the term for sending unsolicited messages to multiple e-mail boxes.) Another rule is to not post commercial messages to newsgroups that have rules against these types of messages.

Want more details on what to do and what not to do? The internet Engineering Task Force's Responsible Use of the Network Working Group is an organization of volunteers that helps set internet standards and guidelines. Its thirteen-page guide includes policy statements from several organizations that oversee the internet community. Called *Requests for Comments (RFC) #1855, Netiquette Guidelines*, it is an etiquette guide for all internet users. Visit www.dtcc.edu/cs/rfc1855.html to get your copy.

SETTING UP YOUR WEB SITE

Should you hire someone to set up your web site or do it yourself? Designing a web page used to require hours of laborious wrestling with HTML. But new web-authoring tools are easier to use—with many programs, building a web site involves little more than pointing and clicking a mouse.

Visit your local software store, ask your internet service provider or search online, and you'll find a multitude of web-authoring programs. If you're a beginner, look for a program that comes with an assortment of templates. All you have to do is tweak them a little, and you're done.

Even though setting up a web site is fairly easy, many business owners prefer getting professional help. But these days, with everybody and his uncle hanging out a shingle saying they're web designers, you've got to be careful whom you hire. Make sure your designers not only have the technical expertise, but also the marketing know-how. Ask how long they've been in business and request samples of their work. Talk to several clients to get their feedback. And ask if the designers are available to update your site when necessary.

Attracting Visitors to Your Site

The best-designed web site in the world does you no good if no one visits it. And attracting visitors gets tougher every day. Here are some ways to get prospective customers to your site:

- *Promote your web site in all your marketing materials.* Put your web site address, or URL, on your business cards, brochures, letterhead, product packaging, promotional items, in your ads, and anywhere you else you can think of. Providing content, such as electronic newsletters and magazines, to other sites is another way to create an online presence. Some regional phone companies are listing businesses' web and e-mail addresses in their telephone directories; call your local company to find out what their policy is.
- *Get listed with the major search engines.* Visit their web sites to get instructions for getting your URL listed with them. That way, when online users do a search for "tennis rackets," your sporting goods

shop's web site will come up. In addition to the big-name search engines, there are hundreds of smaller search engines on the web. Search online for companies that will do the legwork involved in getting your business listed with these engines.

- *Enroll in free link exchange programs.* These programs will display your company's banner on other sites if you make space for third-party banners on yours. Just as with search engines, there are many link exchange programs. Search online to find them and get feedback from other users.
- *Set up links to related sites.* A link allows visitors to your site to click on a web site address and instantly call up to another company's site. Send e-mail to related sites and ask if they'd be interested in putting up links to your site. For example, a florist could link to a local bridal shop's site.

Keeping Visitors at Your Site

Once you've got visitors at your site, how do you keep them there? "A lot of companies just stick their product information on the web and then wonder why people aren't buying," says Rosalind Resnick, co-author of *The Internet Business Guide: Riding the Information Superhighway to Profit* (Sams Publishing). Here's her advice on setting up a site that tempts users to stay:

- *Hit 'em hard.* Put all your company's key information, including your e-mail address or toll-free number, on the first screen. That way, potential customers won't have to wait until all your information loads to get an idea of what your company is all about.
- *Make connections.* If possible, hyperlink your e-mail address; this means visitors can simply click on it to open a message blank and send you a note.
- *Have fun.* People who surf the internet are looking for fun. You don't have to be wild and wacky (unless you want to). Just make sure you offer original content presented in an entertaining way.
- *Don't overdo the graphics.* If your graphics take too long to download, users will scoot.
- *Add value.* Offer something useful to customers to add value to your site. For example, customers can track their packages at the Federal Express site or try a recipe for a new cocktail at the Stolichnaya vodka site.
- *Keep it simple.* Don't build a site that's more than three or four levels deep. Internet users love to surf, but they get bored when they have to sift through loads of information to find what they're looking for.
- *Provide a map.* Use icons or button bars to create clear navigational paths. A well-designed site should have a button at the bottom of each sub-page that transports the visitor back to the site's home page.
- *Stage a contest.* Nothing is more compelling than giving something away for free. Have all contestants fill out a registration form so you can find out who's coming to your site.
- *Make payment a snap.* Make it easy for customers to pay you. Consider including an online order form and a toll-free ordering number or fax number.

CHAPTER 30

Selling Your Business

Suppose you want to retire. Or raise money for a new venture. What if you get an offer for your business or practice that's just too good to refuse? Or you finally realize that your business needs new talent to keep it on the growth track? You might even decide to close up shop and liquidate your assets. Whatever your circumstances or reasons, at some point all business owners need to plan for transitioning out of their business.

Before you decide to sell your business, first consider your alternatives. If health or timing is a factor, could you hire a manager to profitably run the business until you're again able to? Could you keep the business in the family by selling it to a son, daughter or other relative?

If these are not options, determine whether now is the right time to sell. If the economy is in a slump, you could wind up selling at a loss, or for an amount substantially below that which you might obtain a year or two down the road. An ideal time to sell your business is during an economic boom, when your industry is cycling upward, and your business is either keeping pace with or outperforming others in your industry.

WORKING WITH A BUSINESS BROKER

While it costs money for a broker to sell your business, think of the commission you'd pay him or her as a kind of insurance. Your broker will protect your investment in the business by placing the proper value on the business, finding the right buyer, getting you the best price possible, protecting the confidentiality of the sale, handling all negotiations, ensuring that all transactions are legal, and seeing that the transition to new ownership is as wrinkle-free as possible.

One of the key functions of a business broker is to act as a buffer between buyer and seller and negotiate the details of the deal at a time when emotions can, and do, run high. A small business is often one of the biggest assets a business owner has, one which he or she has spent considerable time and money building. An experienced broker knows how to price a business and can toot the business' horn in a way you might not be able to. The buyer can ask the broker pointed questions that might be difficult to ask you directly and get the answers he or she needs. The broker can also resolve any problems that develop during the course of the sale.

Finding the right buyer for your business can be time-consuming and daunting if you try to do it yourself. A seasoned business broker can read the market, knows who's buying what and who's got resources, and can weed the so-called "tire kickers" from serious buyers with sufficient financial resources who are well-suited to run a business like yours. He or she will also ensure that news of the sale remains confidential, that loyal customers, staff, vendors and suppliers find out when you're ready to let them know.

Then there are administrative issues. An experienced business broker knows what paperwork to file and when. He or she also coordinates efforts between lawyers, CPAs, bankers, insurance agents, and others.

Make sure there's good chemistry between you and your broker and that the two of you can communicate well with one another. You are paying your broker to look out for your interests, negotiate successfully on your behalf, and complete the transaction in a timely and professional manner.

Selecting a Business Broker

To find a business broker to help you sell your business, take these steps:

- *Check newspaper ads under "Business Opportunities."* Look in your local and regional papers, as well as in The Wall Street Journal. You'll frequently see businesses for sale under this heading, and just as the prospective buyer is invited to inquire about these businesses, prospective sellers should also check out who's facilitating these sales.

- *Look in the Yellow Pages under "Real Estate" or "Business Brokers."* Make sure to find a broker who specializes in selling businesses, not simply real estate. Don't let the broker list your business on a realtor's multiple listing service. Any broker who wants to do this is not willing to devote the time and work necessary to sell your business.

- *Ask for referrals.* Ask other business owners who've sold businesses who they worked with. Your local chamber of commerce can also provide referrals to business brokers, as can your banker, CPA, attorney, and financial planner.

Once you find a broker to work with, sign a contract that specifies what kind of advertising your broker will do and that the name of the business will not appear in any ads or other promotion.

Pricing Your Business

How much is your business worth? While price is a function of the value of a business (what someone is willing to pay for it), it involves other factors, such as how the deal is financed, over what term, whether there are tax or other liabilities, the value of the assets, the earning power of the business, its cash flow, and so on. Pricing a business is complicated and is not easily reduced to a quick formula.

To protect your future, your business, and your investment, work with a professional who's experienced in selling businesses and who can prepare a detailed valuation of your business. If you're not working with a broker and intend to price the business yourself, you have an enormous chore ahead of you. You'll need to substantiate your assumptions and appraisals, and you'll have to make an objective, rational judgment on what your business is worth. Unless this is your area of expertise, you will be wise to leave this work to a professional.

FINANCIAL CONSIDERATIONS

Offering to finance part of the sale can help the seller get the price he or she wants. If you decide to make such an offer, be absolutely sure that the risk you assume is well-secured and of short duration. The down payment, in cash, should be at least equal to the cost of inventory and supplies. Put the balance owed in the form of a note or mortgage, secured by the business in its entirety. Payments can be interest only, with a balloon payment of principal due at some point, or some other combination of principal and interest amortized, or not, over time. Your broker and banker can help you figure out terms that satisfy you. And at the same time, don't overburden the buyer with payments that suffocate his or her cash flow.

The term of the note is typically three to five years, with the balance due and payable on or before this time. If the buyer defaults, you can then re-acquire the business intact, retaining the buyer's down payment and all loan payments to date. These provisions, of course, need to be written into the contract.

The Lease

If you own the real estate involved in the sale of the business and are selling it along with the business, that's fine. However, if you lease your property, the terms of your rental agreement are important to the buyer, who needs a satisfactory long-term arrangement to protect his or her investment.

You and your broker need to talk with the lessor in advance of the sale. Explain that you're considering selling your business and think it would be advantageous to renegotiate a new lease with the new owner.

THE LOGISTICS OF A SALE

Take advantage of your business broker being the liaison between you and the buyer. Be available to answer technical questions in the presence of your broker but keep communication with the buyer at a minimum.

During negotiations, never out-and-out reject an offer, no matter how outrageous it seems. This risks burning the bridge. Instead, be prepared to counteroffer—several times, if necessary. It's all part of the dance that needs to take place between buyer and seller.

Seller Concerns

No prudent prospective buyer would consummate a deal without performing due diligence of the business for sale. This entails investigating the business' and seller's history, and reviewing all financial statements and other business documents, along with thoroughly studying all the major factors affecting the company's future.

Even though buyers thoroughly research the seller, very few sellers investigate prospective buyers with the same diligence. If a seller wants successful results, then he or she has to undertake the same thoroughness by asking these questions:

- *Does the buyer have experience owning or managing a business?* Does he or she have the interest, skills, strength, and relevant experience to run a business like yours?
- *Can the buyer satisfy the future payment in an installment deal?* In a situation where the buyer's stock represents the proceeds, will the stock hold its value in the future?

- *Will the staff's needs be adequately addressed?*
- *Will the seller's present staff and procedures mesh with those of the buyer's?*
- *What kind of policies and procedures will be put into effect after the sale is made?* This becomes especially important if the selling owner is going to stay on after the acquisition.

If you're not working with a broker and you have to qualify buyers yourself, start by reviewing the buyer's financial statements from the past five years. Verify the buyer's ability to finance the transaction; his or her balance sheet can tell you whether the buyer can handle additional debt. Ask if loans outstanding have any restrictive covenants that might prevent the buyer from incurring additional debt to finance an acquisition.

The buyer's performance should be compared to that of other companies in the same industry. This can be done by weighing the following financial ratios against industry standards:

- Profit on sales
- Profit on net worth
- Current ratio
- Inventory turnover
- Debt to worth
- Fixed assets to worth
- Sales to fixed assets
- Sales to working capital

Industry performance figures can be found in the Risk Management Association's (RMA, which was formerly known as Robert Morris Associates, www.rmahq.org) *Annual Statement Studies*. These are available in the reference section of most business libraries and through your bank. Trade publications are another resource and so is *Statistics of Income Bulletin*, published by the Internal Revenue Service (www.irs.ustreas.gov/prod/tax_stats/index).

This comparison will show the buyer's strength within his or her industry, though there may be valid reasons for variations from what is considered average. It also provides an indication of the buyer's competence as a business manager and his or her ability to sustain future growth once the sale of the business is final.

Take a look at how the buyer manages inventory, which can provide insight into his or her philosophy on sales and service. This may have an impact on any of the seller's employees who remain on board and on the business' future growth and profitability.

Another area to review is the buyer's personnel policies and benefit package. Look at the average length of service of the buyer's employees—both hourly and on salary. If there's evidence of excessive turnover, find out why.

Other ways to get more information about the buyer are to visit his or her place of business and interview key employees. Your objective is to make an informed judgment about the buyer's competence as a manager.

If possible, get the buyer's permission to talk to customers, giving assurance that you won't reveal the reason for the call. What you want to know is information on the buyer's distribution network, the impact of the company's sales and customer service policies, and the competence of the sales force. Where there's a similarity between the product line of buyer and seller, this investigation is even more important because there will probably be some consolidation of the two firms' sales or distribution networks after the sale.

Resources

Associations

American Bar Association, 321 North Clark Street, Chicago, IL 60610, (800) 285-2221, www.abanet.org

American Marketing Association, 311 South Wacker Drive, Suite 5800, Chicago, IL 60606, (800) AMA-1150, www.marketingpower.com

American Society of Inventors, P.O. Box 58426, Philadelphia, PA 19102, (215) 546-6601, www.americaninventor.org

Association of Small Business Development Centers, 8990 Burke Lake Road, Burke, VA 22015, (703) 764-9850, www.asbdc-us.org

Ewing Marion Kauffman Foundation, 4801 Rockhill Road, Kansas City, MO 64110, (816) 932-1000, www.kauffman.org

Insurance Information Institute, 110 William Street, New York, NY 10038, (212) 346-5500, www.iii.org

International Franchise Association, 1501 K Street NW, Suite 350, Washington, DC 20005, (202) 628-8000, www.franchise.org

International Licensing Industry Merchandisers' Association, 350 Fifth Avenue, Suite 1408, New York, NY 10118, (212) 244-1944, www.licensing.org

Marketing Research Association, 110 National Drive, 2nd Floor, Glastonbury, CT 06033, (860) 682-1000, www.mra-net.org

National Association for the Self-Employed, P.O. Box 612067, DFW Airport, Dallas, TX 75261-2067, (800) 232-6273, www.nase.org

National Business Incubation Association, 20 E. Circle Drive, #37198, Athens, OH 45701-3571, (740) 593-4331, www.nbia.org

National Vehicle Leasing Association, 100 North 20th Street, 4th Floor, Philadelphia, PA 19103, (800) 225-NVLA, www.nvla.org.

Directories

Bacon's Publicity Checker, Bacon's Information Inc., 332 South Michigan Avenue, Chicago, IL 60604, (800) 621-0561, www.bacons.com

Encyclopedia of Associations: International Organizations, Gale Group, 27500 Drake Road, Farmington Hills, MI 48331-3535, (800) 877-4253, www.gale.com

The Standard Rate and Data Service Directory, Standard Rate and Data Service (SRDS), 1700 W. Higgins Road, Des Plaines, IL 60018, (847) 375-5000, www.srds.com

Tradeshow Week Data Book, 5700 Wilshire Boulevard, Suite 120, Los Angeles, CA 90036-5804, www.tradeshowweek.com

Government Agencies

Department of Energy, Small Business Innovation Research, (301) 903-1414, www.er.doe.gov/sbir

Federal Trade Commission, CRC-240, Washington, DC 20580, (877) FTC-HELP, www.ftc.gov

United States Department of Commerce, Technology Administration, National Technical Information Service, Springfield, VA 22161, (703) 605-6000, www.fedworld.gov

United States Patent and Trademark Office, 600 Dulany Street, Arlington, VA 22202, (800) 786-9199, www.uspto.gov

The U.S. Small Business Administration, (800) 827-5722, www.sba.gov

Magazines and Newspapers

Advertising Age, 711 Third Avenue, New York, NY 10017-4036, (212) 210-0100, www.adage.com

Adweek, 770 Broadway, New York, NY 10003, (646) 654-5421, www.adweek.com

Best's Insurance Reports, A.M. Best Company, Ambest Road, Oldwick, NJ 08858, (908) 439-2200, www.ambest.com

Business Week, 1221 Avenue of the Americas, 43rd Floor, New York, NY 10020, (210) 512-2511, www.businessweek.com

Entrepreneur Magazine, Entrepreneur Media Inc., 2445 McCabe Way, Suite 400, Irvine, CA 92614, (949) 261-2325, www.entrepreneur.com/magazine

Fortune, 1271 Sixth Avenue, 16th Floor, New York, NY 10020, (800) 621-8000, www.timeinc.net/fortune

Inc., 375 Lexington Avenue, New York, NY 10017, (212) 389-5300, www.inc.com

Tradeshow Week, 5700 Wilshire Boulevard, Suite 120, Los Angeles, CA 90036-5804, (323) 965-5300, www.trade showweek.com

The Wall Street Journal, 200 Liberty Street, New York, NY 10281, (212) 416-2000, www.wsj.com

Glossary

Accounts payable. The amount of money owed by a business for goods or services bought on credit.

Accounts receivable. The amount of money owed to a business for goods or services sold on credit.

Accrual basis. An accounting method in which income and expenses are recorded as they are incurred, regardless of whether money has been received.

Acid-test ratio. Measures the liquidity of a business by dividing the most liquid current assets (cash, accounts receivable, and marketable securities) by current liabilities. Used by lenders to determine if a business can meet its current obligations.

Asset earning power. A ratio that determines the profitability of a business by dividing its total earnings before taxes by total assets.

Audit Bureau of Circulation (ABC). A third-party organization that verifies the circulation of print media through periodical audits.

Balance sheet. A financial statement for reporting what a business owns (its assets) minus what it owes (its liabilities) at a given point in time. The result is the business' net worth, or owner's equity.

Bonding. A guarantee by a service company to its clients that it has the necessary ability and financial backing to meet its obligations.

Break-even analysis. Determines the number of production items or services that need to be sold so that expenses are covered by income and neither a profit nor a loss is incurred.

Business plan. A written document charting a business' mission, strategies, sales projections, and plan for growth. It is used to obtain financing and provide a road map for growth.

Business Publications Audit (BPA). Similar to the Audit Bureau of Circulation, a third-party organization that verifies the circulation of print media through periodical audits.

Capitalization. The financial structure of a company, in the form of money, common stock, long-term debt, or in some combination of all three. Capital funds are invested in the business for the long term, typically in equipment, plant and other fixed assets, and are not easily liquidated unless the entire business is sold.

Cash basis. An accounting method in which income is logged when received and expenses are charged when they occur.

Chattel mortgage contract. A contract for the purchase of equipment where the purchaser receives title to the equipment on delivery but the creditor holds a mortgage claim against it.

Collateral. Assets used as security in order to obtain a loan.

Conditional sales contract. A contract for the purchase of equipment where the purchaser does not receive title to the equipment until the amount specified in the contract has been paid in full.

Cooperative advertising. Joint advertising strategy used by a manufacturer and a firm distributing its products.

Copyright. A form of legal protection to safeguard original works that are written, performed, recorded, painted, photographed, and so on.

Corporation. A form of business operation that declares the business as a separate, legal entity guided by a group of officers known as the board of directors.

Cost per thousand (CPM). Used when buying media time or space, CPM refers to the cost it takes to reach a thousand people within a target market.

Cost-of-living lease. A lease that ties yearly increases to the cost-of-living index.

Current ratio. Determines the difference between total current assets, which include the value of inventories that have not yet been sold, and total current liabilities. Not as accurate a portrayal of a company's liquidity as the "acid-test ratio."

Demographic characteristics. Attributes such as income, age, gender, lifestyle, family size, and occupation that best describe a target market.

Depreciation. The decrease in value of fixed assets for tax purposes based on either the declining-balance or straight-line method.

Disability insurance. A payroll tax required in some states that is deducted from employees' paychecks to ensure income during periods when an employee is unable to work due to an injury or illness.

Disclosure document program. A form of protection that safeguards an idea during its developmental stage.

Dollar-control systems. A system used in inventory management that reveals the cost and gross profit margin on individual inventory items.

Equipment loan. A loan for the purchase of capital equipment.

Equity. The business owner's investment in the business after liabilities are subtracted.

Equity financing. A financing method in which the business owner exchanges a portion of his or her ownership in the business to investors for new capital. Equity investment in a business usually entails the investor receiving a proportionate share of profits and having some say in how the business is managed.

Exploratory research. A method of gathering primary information for a market survey in which targeted consumers are asked general questions to elicit a lengthy answer.

Factoring. A financing method in which a business owner sells accounts receivable at a discount to raise capital.

Fair Labor Standard Act. A federal law enforcing minimum standards that employers must abide by when hiring employees.

Federal Insurance Contributions Act (FICA). A federal law requiring employers to match the amount of Social Security tax deducted from an employee's paycheck.

Fictitious name. Often referred to as a "dba" (doing business as), a fictitious name is frequently used by sole proprietors or partnerships to provide a name, other than those of the owners or partners, under which the business will operate.

First in, first out (FIFO). An accounting system used to value inventory for tax purposes. Under FIFO, inventory is valued at its most recent cost.

Fixed expenses. Expenses that must be paid each month and do not fluctuate with sales volume.

Flat lease. A lease whose cost is fixed for a specific period of time.

401(k) plan. A retirement plan for employees that allows them to deduct money from their paychecks and place it in a tax-sheltered account.

Frequency. The number of times an advertiser hopes to reach a target audience through an advertising campaign.

Income statement. Also called a profit-and-loss statement, the income statement charts the sales and operating costs of a business over a specific period of time, usually a month.

Inventory loan. A loan that is extended based on the value of a business' inventory.

Inventory turnover. A method whereby sales is divided by the capital invested in inventory, which helps evaluate how well the business owner is operating the business.

Keogh plan. A pension plan that lets business owners contribute a certain portion of their profits or a predetermined annual contribution to a tax-sheltered account, where the funds grow until retirement.

Last in, first out (LIFO). An accounting system for valuing inventory. Under LIFO, inventory is valued according to the remaining stock in inventory.

Leasehold improvements. The tax-deductible repairs and improvements made to a facility before occupation by the lessee.

Liability. Regarding insurance risks, liabilities are possible areas of exposure. While there are numerous comprehensive and special coverages for almost every known exposure a business may be liable for, insurers usually underwrite three forms of liability coverage: (1) general liability, which covers any kind of bodily injury to non-employees except that caused by automobiles and professional malpractice; (2) product liability, which covers injury to customers arising as a direct result of goods purchased from a business; (3) public liability, which covers injury to the public when they are on the business' premises.

Limited liability company (LLC). A form of business where partners are not liable for business debts since they report income on their personal tax returns. Or they may elect to be taxed as a partnership, corporation or sub-S corporation. Single member LLCs may elect to be taxed as a sole proprietorship.

Line of credit. An agreement by a bank to lend a specified amount of money over a certain amount of time, usually one year.

Manual tag system. An inventory management system that tracks inventory using tags removed at the point of purchase.

Market survey. A research method for defining the market parameters of a business.

Markup. The amount added to the cost of goods to produce the desired profit.

Measure of liquidity. The amount of available liquid assets to meet accounts payable.

Media plan. A plan that details the usage of media in an advertising campaign including a budget, time span, markets, reach, frequency, rationales, and strategies.

Modified accelerated cost recovery system (MACRS). In accounting, a defined rate and method by which a fixed asset is depreciated for tax purposes.

Net leases. A lease specifying a base rent plus an additional charge for taxes. Typically, there are net leases, double-net leases and triple-net leases. A double-net lease is a base rent plus an additional charge for taxes and insurance. A triple-net lease is base rent plus an additional charge for taxes, insurance and common-area expenses.

Net profit on sales. A profitability measure that determines the difference between net profit and operating costs.

Note. A short-term loan that will be repaid in 30, 60, or 90 days at a specified rate of interest.

Occupational Safety and Health Act (OSHA). A federal law requiring employers to provide employees with a workplace free from hazardous conditions.

Operating expenses. The normal costs of doing business.

Overhead. All non-labor expenses needed to operate a business.

Partnership. A legal form of business operation between two or more individuals who share management and profits. The federal government recognizes several types of partnerships. The two most common are general and limited partnerships.

Patent. A form of protection that provides a person or legal entity with exclusive rights by forbidding others from making, using or selling a concept or invention for the duration of the patent. Three types of patents are design, plant, and utility.

Percentage lease. A lease specifying a base rent plus an additional percentage of any profits produced by the business tenant.

Personal loan. A short-term loan that is extended based on the personal financial standing and integrity of the borrower.

Point of sale (POS) system. A computerized network operated by a mainframe computer and linked to several checkout terminals.

Profit. The excess of selling price over cost. Businesses generally consider two kinds of profits: gross profit and net profit. Gross profit is the difference between gross sales and cost of sales, while net profit is the difference between gross profit and all costs associated with operating a business.

Pro forma. A projection or estimate.

Quick ratio. The "acid-test" ratio of liquid assets to current liabilities.

Reach. The total number of people in a target market that an owner contacts through an advertising campaign.

Return on assets (ROA). A profitability measure to indicate how well the business is using its assets by dividing the net profit by total assets.

Return on investment (ROI). A profitability measure that evaluates the performance of a business by dividing net profit by net worth.

Signature loan. See Personal loans.

Sole proprietor. A legal form of operation under which only one owner can exist. Legally, the business owner and the business are the same entity, and personal assets are exposed to liabilities of the business.

Standard Rate and Data Service (SRDS). A company that produces a group of directories for different types of media listing rates, circulation, contacts, markets serviced, and so on.

Step lease. A lease outlining annual increases in the tenant's base rent based on an approximation of what the lessor thinks expenses may be.

Subchapter S corporation. A federal law allowing small corporations to pay out all income proportionately to their shareholders, who then claim the business' income and deductions on their personal income tax return.

Term loans. Loans for equipment, real estate, and working capital that are paid off like a mortgage in anywhere between one year and ten years.

Uniform Franchise Offering Circular (UFOC). A disclosure document that franchisers send to potential franchisees.

Variable expenses. Business costs that fluctuate from each payment period according to the sales volume.

Venture capital. A source of financing for either start-up or expansion capital based on providing private investors with equity positions within the business.

Worker's compensation. A state or privately managed insurance fund that reimburses employees for work-related injuries.

Working capital. Net current assets required for the company to carry on its work; the surplus of a firm's current assets over its current liabilities.

Index